THE COMMUNIST CHALLENGE TO AFRICA

THE COMMUNIST CHALLENGE TO AFRICA

An analysis of contemporary Soviet, Chinese and Cuban policies

BY

IAN GREIG

SOUTHERN AFRICAN FREEDOM FOUNDATION

First published by
the Foreign Affairs Publishing Co. Ltd.,
139 Petersham Rd, Richmond, Surrey, TW107AA, England
in 1977

This South African edition published by
the Southern African Freedom Foundation,
Sandton City, Sandton in 1977

ISBN   0 908395 19 1

Printed by Cape & Transvaal Printers (Pty.) Ltd., Parow, Cape

Contents

Chapter 1

Introduction
and Strategic Balance

Even while, in the spring of 1975, the Soviet supplied tanks of the North Vietnamese regular army swept ever nearer to Saigon, and Soviet-supplied rocketsblasted Cambodia's capital city as the Khmer Rouge prepared for their final onslaught that was to bring them their bloody victory, events were in train in Africa which were to shift the spotlight of world attention to focus on another continent many thousands of miles away, and another stage of the continuing global struggle between the Western and Communist power blocs.

Despite the illusions of the over-optimistic and the naïve that the end of the long drawn out conflict in Indo-China would usher in a new era of genuine détente and peaceful co-operation between East and West, it was in fact in March of that same year 1975, well over a month before the fall of Saigon, that reports began to come in of the arrival of the first Soviet transport aircraft in the People's Republic of the Congo (Brazzaville) which were laden with arms for the Marxist forces in Angola. Even then, Communist-backed revolutionaries were beginning the struggle for power which, in little more than a year, was to lead to a Soviet-backed Marxist minority régime gaining control of the destiny of the newly independent state of Angola.

This highly successful use of force by the Kremlin has amply demonstrated to the world that the Soviet policy of active support for "wars of liberation", far from having died with the end of the fighting in South-East Asia, is to be encouraged to an even greater degree, and this time in an area of the greatest possible strategic and economic importance to the whole of the non-Communist world. Indeed, it can be argued that if Southern Africa were to fall into anti-Western hands, the West could not survive at all.

If after events in Angola, any lingering doubts remain about the extent of the determination of Soviet Government and its allies to manipulate, and indeed even dictate, the trend of events in Africa to its own advantage, they must assuredly have been finally dispelled by the nakedly hostile manner in which the Soviet Government greeted Dr. Kissinger's plan to bring about a peaceful transition of power from White minority to Black majority in Rhodesia.

Even before the details of the plan had been disclosed various "liberation movement" leaders, known to be favoured and supported by Moscow such as Mr Oliver Tambo, President of the South African ANC and others, had described the Anglo-American attempts to bring about a peaceful solution in Southern Africa as "neo-colonialist" and "anti-African". To their voices was added that of the Soviet Foreign Minister, Mr Gromyko, who said in the United Nations General Assembly at the end of September 1976:

> "Every possible method is being brought into play, from direct subversion to violence to attempt to divert the national liberation movement away from genuine independence and freedom through political gimmickry and financial handouts."[1]

At the same time articles in *Pravda* also attacked the Western attempts at peace-making in Southern Africa and described them as being part of a "dangerous plot between imperialists and racists" and "a fraud". "Real liberation", the message from Moscow began to come through loud and clear, as the possibility of the practical application of the plan continued to hover on a razor's edge, could be brought about only by the total victory of the armed "liberation movements" and the sweeping away not only of "racist control" but also by the elimination of every vestige of Western capitalist influence in the "tottering imperialist bastion" formed by the countries of Rhodesia, and South and South West Africa.

Such sentiments soon began to be enthusiastically echoed by the official news media of Moçambique, a country in which Soviet influence had been growing steadily ever since it achieved independence from Portugal in the autumn of 1975. All the indications are that the Soviet Union will use every endeavour to ensure that events in future move towards the creation of new "Angolan situations" in which it could intervene with equal profit as far as the extension of its influence is concerned, rather than to join in any search for peaceful solutions. In short, barring a miracle, it seems that the stage is rapidly being set for a major new East-West confrontation, probably of a protracted nature, and the long-term effect of which might well prove decisive in the final struggle between the two main power blocs.

The full significance of the dramatic events of the last three years in Africa must be judged, not only by some study of the story of the policy of the Communist powers towards Africa prior to this period, but also by a general assessment of the strategic setting in the world outside Africa and the shifting global balance of power.

This study is, I hope, a contribution towards considering Soviet, Chinese and Cuban Communist regional or theatre intentions towards Africa in the light of this fast changing world situation.

The Strategic Balance

With parity in strategic nuclear missiles between the super-powers virtually achieved, the Soviet Union has continued to strengthen its conventional forces far beyond the needs of self-defence, and this despite a number of substantial Western defence cuts. "Once again," stated the International Institute for Strategic Studies' *The Military Balance* for 1975-1976, "numbers in the American armed forces have fallen by some 44 000, while those of the Soviet Union have risen by 60 000." A pattern which was repeated in the following year, 1976-1977, when the strength of the American armed forces fell by 43 000 whilst that of the Soviet Union rose by 75 000.

The manner in which the armed forces of Britain have been repeatedly cut in recent years is too well-known to need further comment here.

In Europe, there has been a noticeable recent significant increase in the offensive   strength of the Warsaw Pact forces facing the vital Northern and Central sector of NATO's front. This already stands at the formidable enough number of 31 armoured divisions and 36 infantry, mechanised and airborne divisions as against NATO's 11 armoured divisions and 18 infantry, mechanised and airborne divisions. These figures relate to peace-time conditions only. The 40 Soviet army divisions now assigned to the Warsaw Pact could probably be increased to over 80 on mobilisation. NATO's ability to achieve a speedy build-up in a crisis situation would depend largely on the speedy arrival of reinforcements from the United States.* In Southern Europe, NATO's forces have a slight peace-time numerical superiority but suffer from the disadvantage of being very dispersed.

The main Soviet striking force in Europe consists of the five armies of the Group of Soviet Forces in Germany comprising 10 armoured and 10 motorised infantry divisions. It is concentrated in East Germany and receives the highest priority for new equipment. Despite rumours to the contrary, there has been no significant transfer of Soviet forces to the Chinese frontier or elsewhere in recent years.

The full might of the Soviet position is even more obvious when weapon strengths are compared. NATO has at present some 7 000 battle tanks in operational service in Northern and Central Europe, with perhaps a further 1 750 held in reserve. The Warsaw Pact forces have available in the same area an estimated 19 000 tanks, with a further but unknown number in reserve.[2] In the sphere of artillery, the NATO forces are outnumbered by roughly three to one. During the last two years, the artillery strength of Soviet divisions has been doubled and there has been a parallel increase in numbers of multiple rocket launchers whose rôle is the carrying out of saturation bombardments. The number of tactical nuclear warheads held by Soviet forces in the area has doubled since the beginning of the 1970s and is now estimated to stand at a figure of about 7 000, roughly equal to the number held by US forces.

Stocks of conventional ammunition have also been built up and the tank strength of Soviet mechanised divisions has been increased, the latter having also recently been issued with a new type of amphibious armoured personnel carrier. Not insignificantly in view

---

*Comparison of strength of divisions can, however, be misleading in that all modern armies contain many combat units which operate outside divisional command. An estimate of total combat and direct support troops available to the two sides in peace time on the central front including such units puts Warsaw Pact strength at 910 000 and that of NATO at 635 000, according to figures from The International Institute for Strategic Studies, *The Military Balance 1976-1977*.

of the large number of rivers which the Soviet forces would have to cross during any advance into Germany, there has also been a considerable recent increase in stocks of heavy bridging equipment.[3]

The most recent additions to the strength of Soviet ground forces in East Germany include the provision of a new mobile light anti-aircraft weapons system and the arrival early in 1977 of considerable numbers of the formidable new T.72 type tanks. This is the first occasion on which these fighting vehicles have been observed to be deployed outside the Soviet Union itself. Their arrival coincides with moves apparently intended to heighten the state of readiness of East German Army units.

The offensive power of the Soviet ground forces in Europe is reinforced not only by the existence of seven Guards parachute divisions, but also by the existence of a number of highly trained specialist airborne units clearly intended for offensive operations. These include the *Reidoviki* or air commando formations whose rôle consists of long-range penetration and sabotage operations and even more specialised groups such as the *Vysotniki* or high-altitude free fall parachute troops,whose main rôle consists of sabotage and reconnaissance duties of special importance. They also include an East German parachute battalion, a Soviet reserve parachute regiment, and a Polish parachute division all of which are known to have received special training in the techniques of infiltration and subversion.[4]

As regards tactical air power, there has been an increase of about 40% in Soviet aircraft strength in Europe since the invasion of Czechoslovakia in 1968. Air force units in Eastern Europe are known to be receiving the most advanced aircraft and to be undergoing intensive training in co-operation with mobile ground forces. The Soviet long-range air force includes about 800 medium and long-range bombers capable of carrying nuclear weapons.

It was reported early in 1976 that the Soviet Union had once again stepped up its production of military aircraft sharply. Whereas in the spring of 1975 reliable estimates put the production of such aircraft at 1 700 a year, four months later authoritative Western sources were calculating that production had increased to the rate of 1 800 aircraft a year. This figure represents approximately twice the rate of United States' production. Of even greater significance was the fact that the production of defensive interceptor fighters seemed to have been stopped to allow concentration upon production of supersonic strike aircraft with an offensive rôle and of a type fully the equal of any possessed by the West.

The former British Chief of Air Staff, the late Sir Andrew Humphrey, said that the rate of production the Soviet aircraft industry had achieved was equivalent to that needed to replace the whole of the RAF's front line strength every six months. He said that this new Soviet build-up worried him deeply and that he considered that the Soviet Union was aiming at establishing a position in which it could switch from political to military actions extremely quickly.

As far as intercontinental missiles are concerned, Mr James Schlesinger, then United States Secretary of State for Defence, said in June 1975 that it was believed that the Soviet Union had made considerable progress in deploying new weapons since the beginning of the year.[5] Speaking at a news conference in Washington he gave evidence regarding recent Soviet deployment of four new missiles, the SS17, SS18 and SS19, all of which were capable of carrying multiple warheads. He expressed concern that the deployment of large numbers of such missiles could carry with it the threat of a knock-out surprise strike against the United States'own missile bases by the beginning of the 1980s.

Concern was expressed at a meeting of NATO Defence Ministers in December 1976 at the apparent imminent deployment by the Soviet Union of SS-20 mobile medium range ballistic missiles which the Secretary-General of NATO, Mr Joseph Luns, described as being capable of covering not only the whole of Western Europe but also as having sufficient range to reach targets in North Africa and the Middle East as well.

The year 1976 also brought reports of important Soviet developments in the realm of what might be called "space fiction war". These included the destruction or "blinding" of reconnaissance space satellites in orbit by means of ultra-powerful laser beams operated from earth and the experimental launching of "hunter" satellites designed to chase and destroy enemy reconnaissance or communication satellites.

Another potentially highly important development involving the use of space for military purposes by Soviet scientists was mentioned in the 1977 edition of *Jane's Weapons Systems*. The development in question was the use of "spotter satellites" for the purpose of fixing the position of hostile warships at sea in order that missiles could be launched against them from positions hundreds, or even possibly thousands, of kilometres away.

In the same month, a former Secretary of State for Defence, Mr Melvin Laird, voiced fears that the Soviet Union was cheating on the 1972 Strategic Arms Limitation (SALT) Agreement and might be developing an anti-ballistic missile system of a type which the agreement was supposed to forbid and which could give it a "significant strategic advantage" over the United States.[6]

In the winter of 1976, it was confirmed that the Soviet Union had begun equipping part of its missile force targeted on Western Europe with multiple warheads each capable of being directed upon a different target (MIRVs).[7] *The Military Balance 1976-1977*, recorded the deployment of at least 80 new intercontinental missiles during the year and there was also an increase in the number of strategic missiles carried in the Soviet nuclear submarine force.

It is, however, at sea that the Soviet Union's apparent desire to build up a position of overwhelming military power is at present most clearly to be seen. Increased Soviet naval building first began to be noticed about 1950. One of the first indications of what was afoot was the appearance of Soviet nuclear submarines. By 1957 the Soviet fleet had grown sufficiently for its Commander-in-Chief, Admiral Gorshkov, to be able to state that it was now an integral part of the country's "attack forces". The year before Mr Khruschev had begun to supplement the naval building programme by launching a huge merchant ship building programme aimed at achieving a target of 12 million tons in 1970 and 25 million tons in 1980.

The year 1957 also saw the first serious Soviet attempt to establish a naval presence in the Mediterranean. This took the form of the setting up of a submarine base at Valonia in Albania. It was doomed to a short-lived existence, however, following the development of the Sino-Soviet rift in which Albania sided with Peking and the base was abandoned in 1961. This set-back was of little consequence because, as a result of developing ties between the Soviet Union and President Nasser, Soviet engineers had begun to improve the facilities in the major Egyptian port of Alexandria in 1970. With the onset of "the Six-Day War", the chance was taken of establishing the Soviet Navy in both Alexandria and Port Said. Shortly afterwards it also obtained facilities at Sollum and Marsah

Matrouh. So began a period lasting until well after the end of the Nasser régime in which Soviet warships were able to make ample use of Egyptian ports.

Even after the recent rift between the Soviet Union and Egypt, today in the Mediterranean, ships of the Soviet fleet not only make frequent use of the Syrian ports of Latakia and Anaba, but also are quite often to be seen making use of anchorages in the Hammet Gulf off Northern Tunisia, near the Alboran Island which lies close to Gibraltar, at Hurt Bank, east of Malta, off Sollum, Cythera, south of Crete and the Cape of Trois Fourches off Morocco. A force of about 20 support ships, including repair ships, helps to make the Soviet squadron to a large extent independent of port facilities, fresh food being brought to its crews by Soviet merchant ships.

Whilst the number of Soviet warships permanently stationed in the Mediterranean is usually smaller than those of the American Sixth Fleet, they can very rapidly be reinforced both from the Black Sea and through the Straits of Gibraltar in times of tension or crisis. The speed with which the Soviet Union can now achieve a numerical superiority in naval units in the Mediterranean has been demonstrated both during the Arab-Israeli war of 1973 and during the more recent fighting in the Lebanon. In the former case, Soviet reinforcements steaming through the Bosphoros and the Straits of Gibraltar soon brought the total force available to the Soviet Commander-in-Chief in the Mediterranean up to nearly 100 warships. These included five cruisers, 22 destroyers, 25 submarines, eight landing ships, a number of frigates and missile ships and 35 support ships and AGIs (intelligence gathering vessels).

During the intense fighting in the Lebanon in the summer of 1976, the number of Soviet warships in the Mediterranean rose to 76 by the middle of June as against the 45 vessels in the US Sixth Fleet. At the end of that month, it was reported that a further 12 Soviet warships had sailed through the Bosphoros en route to the Mediterranean. These included a helicopter carrier, a cruiser, four destroyers, four corvettes and a tank-landing ship. According to Turkish sources, the latter, the 5 800 ton *Voronezhsky Komsomlets,* was carrying both marines and a number of armoured vehicles.

Soviet anxiety to be ready to take advantage of possible developments in the Eastern Mediterranean as the chaos in the Lebanon deepened was also strongly emphasised by the prolonged presence of the Soviet Chief-of-Staff, General Vikto Koulikov, on board one of the cruisers, the *Ochakov,* which was part of the Soviet naval force in the Mediterranean at that time. In late July the Soviet Union's first true aircraft carrier, the 40 000 ton *Kiev,* carrying 36 vertical take-off aircraft, of a type similar to the British Harrier (and using the title of an "anti-submarine carrier" apparently to avoid allegations that her passage through the Bosphoros constituted a breach of international regulations), sailed into the Mediterranean to make her first appearance outside home waters. She subsequently sailed through the Straits of Gibraltar and thence northwards.

The *Kiev* is reputed to be the largest ship ever built in the Soviet Union and, in addition to her aircraft and/or helicopters, carries multiple anti-aircraft and anti-submarine weapons of the most modern type. The construction of a second carrier of this type named the *Minsk* was well under way in mid-1976 and the American Navy Secretary, Mr William Midenhorf, reported in February 1976 that it was known that work had begun on the construction of a third. Although it is estimated that such ships will have an inferior general capacity to the most modern type of existing American aircraft carrier, a British authority, Captain John Moore, has written that the appearance of these vessels will be:

A powerful addition to the political impact of the Soviet fleet in peacetime. With ships capable of operating VTOL strike aircraft and trooplift helicopters, their credibility in the intervention rôle would be increased and their fleet would be much more prepared for hostilities. Such a ship's rôle could be changed merely by alteration in the number and type of aircraft embarked.[8]

Captain Moore has estimated that the Soviet Union may be aiming at building at least six such aircraft carriers in order to give increased power to the increasingly widespread operations of its navy, while a former American Chief of Naval Operations, Admiral Zumwalt, has calculated that the ultimate Soviet plan may be to build up to 20 ships of this type.[9]

The enormous concentration of Soviet naval power which has been built up over the last 20 years or so is deployed in four main fleets as follows:-

Northern Fleet	51 major surface warships and 126 submarines, some 54 of which are nuclear powered, based on Murmansk.
Baltic Fleet	47 major surface warships, 12 submarines.
Black Sea Fleet	(including Mediterranean Squadron) 59 major warships and 19 submarines.
Pacific Fleet	57 major surface warships and 74 submarines, about 30 of which are nuclear powered.[10]

The above figures refer to average peace-time strengths only and do not include strategic missile carrying submarines.

Smaller warships also included in the various fleets, but not in the above figures, include 185 submarine chasers, 280 patrol and torpedo boats, about 300 minesweepers, 100 amphibious ships and 50 intelligence gathering vessels. The navy also has its own air wing of approximately 650 combat aircraft.

Some idea of the full meaning of the above figures can perhaps be realised when it is remembered that although the threat to allied shipping from German submarines at the outbreak of the last World War was considered serious enough, the total number of submarines that Nazi Germany in fact had available for operational duty at that time was 57.

Today the Soviet Union (according to *The Military Balance 1976-1977*) has a force of no less than 231 attack and cruise missile submarines in service, 84 of which are nuclear powered. In addition, a further 78 nuclear submarines armed with strategic nuclear missiles are in commission. These latter carry between them 845 strategic missiles compared with the 656 missiles carried by the 41 submarines which form part of the United States' strategic nuclear forces.[11]

Soviet Yankee class submarines, operating off the eastern coast of the United States and engaged in similar patrols in the Pacific, now between them have any target in that country within range of their missiles.

One of the most formidable developments in the Soviet naval armoury has been the coming into operational service of Delta 11 class submarines, these vessels carrying SSN-8 missiles with a range of about 4 800 miles. In practical terms this means that Delta 11 submarines operating from positions less than 80 kilometres from their base in the Kola Peninsular will be able to hit major targets such as New York along most of the Eastern coast of the United States. The whole of Western Europe will also, of course, be well within their range. News also came at the end of 1976 of the successful testing by the Soviet Navy of its first multiple warhead missile, the SS-NX-18, fired from a submarine with a range of 7 250 kilometres.

In October 1975, Admiral Sir Terence Lewin, retiring Commander-in-Chief of the British Fleet and Commander of NATO's Channel and East Atlantic forces, said that before the American reinforcements upon which NATO ground forces would so heavily depend in the early stages of a Soviet attack could cross the Atlantic, or the main American naval striking force of 14 aircraft carriers could safely put to sea, the growth of Soviet naval strength now ensured that a "long and bloody battle" would have to be fought in the Eastern Atlantic.[12]

A practical demonstration of the potential of the new Soviet sea power had been given earlier in the year with the start early in April of "Exercise Okean", the largest Soviet naval manoeuvre since a similar exercise in 1970 which at the time was claimed to have been the largest in recent naval history. Some 200 surface warships and 100 submarines took part in the 1975 exercise. As it began, one group of Soviet ships emerged from harbours in the far northern Kola Peninsula on the edge of the Arctic Circle and sailed into the Atlantic to a position north of Iceland. It was then joined by similar groups from the Baltic.

A large force of submarines took up blockading positions in the area between Iceland and Northern Scotland. Meanwhile, a second force from the Baltic sailed down the English Channel and into the Atlantic, north-west of the Azores. At the same time, amphibious landings were carried out on the coast of Pomerania and in the Mediterranean and a Soviet squadron exercised off the coasts of Sardinia and Corsica. "Exercise Okean" also extended its bounds far outside Europe. Continuous reconnaissance missions were flown over wide areas of the South Atlantic by Soviet aircraft based in Guinea, whilst ships of the Indian Ocean squadron exercised off the East African Coast.[13]

The whole exercise was controlled by Admiral Gorshkov, Commander-in-Chief of the Soviet Navy and main architect of its expansion, from a warship in the Barents Sea which also had on board the then Soviet Defence Minister, Andrei Grechko. One of the biggest single concentrations of Soviet ships during the exercise was in the Gulf of Aden where at one time 20 Soviet vessels were reported, including a 15 450-ton cruiser and two other large warships.

Whilst most Western experts would seem to believe that the massive United States carrier force still gives the West the edge over the Soviet Union in terms of surface naval power, some at least have been voicing concern at the implications evidenced by the appearance of some of the latest Soviet surface vessels. At the end of June 1975, for instance, an article by the naval correspondent of *The Daily Telegraph*.[14] stated that the latest *Kara* class Soviet cruiser, the *Nikolayev*, was far more powerful than any major Western ship. In addition, the same article alleged that the new *Krivak* class Soviet missile destroyers, each of which is armed with four surface to surface and two surface to air missile launchers as well as four 76 mm guns, are the most powerful vessels of their type in the world.

A particularly interesting aspect of Soviet naval expansion has been the creation of an entirely new force of marines or naval infantry trained in all aspects of amphibious operations, from the capture of ports to cliff scaling. The creation of the present force began early in the 1960s and today it has an estimated strength of 18 000-20 000 men. It is divided into brigades attached to each of the four main fleets, each brigade consisting of three infantry battalions equipped with armoured personnel carriers and a light tank battalion. Its creation has obviously not only increased the offensive power of the Soviet navy in Europe, but also its ability to intervene in local wars or "revolutionary situations" in areas far from the homeland.[15]

One authority estimates that the size of the Soviet marines will increase to 20 000 men by 1980.[16]

One area in which the growing Soviet naval and military build-up is causing particular concern is Scandinavia. In a special report presented to the Swedish Government during 1975, General Sig Synmergren, Swedish Commander-in-Chief, wrote that Soviet forces had begun "an unprecedented army and naval advance along the Polar Circle". In the conclusions to his report the General found that:

The Soviet Army has stationed forces and means of

transport on the Kola Peninsula geared for an invasion of Sweden from several directions ... The operative concentrations are directed at other parts of Europe belonging to the NATO sphere of influence, but the Soviet deployment on the Kola Peninsula is so strong that it will not be deflected by Swedish neutrality.[17]

The report also stated that since the beginning of the decade, the Soviet navy had extended its zone of operations from the Barents Sea to a line running from Greenland to Iceland and the Faroe Islands. The general said that what he feared was not an outbreak of all-out nuclear war but what he described as a "Soviet advance tactic" aimed at cutting off Scandinavia from the rest of Western Europe. Similar apprehensions have been voiced by officers of NATO countries, including the former commander of NATO's northern sector, General Sir Walter Walker.

The vital importance of sea communications to Western Europe, and hence its vulnerability to any hostile moves by increasingly powerful Soviet naval forces, was convincingly demonstrated in a letter to *The Daily Telegraph* by the Editor of the authoritative *Jane's Fighting Ships* on 22 October 1975. In his letter Captain Moore said that on any one day in the year 2 800 merchant ships were in ports of the various NATO countries loading or discharging cargoes. A further 800 were in the east coast ports of North America. On the high seas voyaging between these ports at the same time were a further 3 300 merchantmen, whilst 2 750 vessels were at sea in the Mediterranean.

He also recorded that nearly 60% of the vast volume of merchant ships travelling round the Cape of Good Hope came from NATO nations and that on any one average day about 200 tankers from Western countries were at sea in the Indian Ocean travelling from or to the Persian Gulf. Such figures make easily explicable the remarks of General Francois Maurin, retiring Chief of Staff of the French Armed Forces, when he said:

> The steady build up of Soviet naval forces, especially in the Mediterranean and in the Indian Ocean, is troubling for us as for any Western nations anxious not to see its vital communications strangled by a blockade.[18]

A sobering picture of the growing strength of Soviet armed might, particularly at sea, was presented in a scenario for a NATO exercise "Hillex 75" which took place during that year. According to the scenario, the oil embargo by the Arab states had been resumed, a Communist régime had been established in Portugal and similar Communist take-overs were threatening in Italy and France. In addition, Western Europe as a whole was so near to economic collapse that its member states were unable to find the money to meet their social welfare commitments. Food riots broke out and elected governments were unable to maintain law and order.

At that stage, the scenario continued, the Soviet Union, taking advance of a promising situation from its point of view, began large-scale fleet manoeuvres on the edge of the Arctic, off the North Cape. Using these as a cover, Soviet forces took possession of a Norwegian port, accompanying this move with heavy demands on the Norwegian Government. At the same time, a huge Soviet naval force began to move down through the Dardanelles into the Mediterranean.[19] Ten years ago, and probably even five, such a scenario would have been held to portray a most improbable or even fantastic situation. Few would consider it to do so today.

The potential threat posed to Western sea communications arising from the Soviet naval build-up was also stressed by Admiral Kidd, Supreme Allied Commander, Atlantic, late in 1975 when he wrote in the December 1976 issue of *Nato Review:*

> It is undoubtedly the global aspects of sea-power that have opened up completely new horizons to the Soviet politico-military planners. We live in an increasingly interdependent world. The industrial nations depend to a large extent on the developing nations for raw materials, while similarly, the developing nations depend on the industrial nations for the capital goods which enable them to extract their raw materials and develop further. The flow of this trade, the major part of which moves by sea, is the life-blood of nations and the NATO countries are no exception ...
>
> Any interference with sources of raw materials or the flow of trade can quickly cause major dislocation—a dislocation felt more acutely in the sophisticated industrial nations with higher standards of living than in the developing countries. It is this network of trade which

today more than ever represents the soft underbelly of NATO. It offers to the Soviet Union a way around the deadlock in Europe because, if our sources of raw materials or our sea lines of trade can be dominated or even influenced by Soviet power, then, to an extent, the life-blood of the NATO nations will be in the hands of a potential enemy.

The existence of this vulnerable jugular is not new, it has been there since long before NATO was formed. However, as much of it lies well outside the NATO area, it has become exposed to an increased threat by the Soviet Union's acquisition of global seapower.

Global sea-power has given the Soviet Union the ability to interdict or pressure international trade at points well outside the NATO areas in peacetime. The Soviets can use their centrally controlled merchant fleet to undercut world freight rates thus influencing other nations to cut back on the use of their own merchant fleets and to place Alliance cargoes under Soviet control. Again, in times of peace there now exists the ability to project a Soviet national presence abroad—to 'show the flag' in ports once dominated by the Allies. In times of tension or conflict, with or without war, this maritime capability can project power overseas, to support insurrections, and to provide military support to political pressures in countries that provide vital resources to nations of the Alliance. In time of war, Soviet nuclear powered submarines could be directed against vital oil and trade routes outside the NATO area.

So far this study has been concerned with the Soviet capacity to inflict damage or exert pressure on the West through the use of armed strength. But what actual evidence have recent events given to prove that the Soviet Union is still determined to pursue the world-wide "crusade" it first embarked upon nearly 60 years ago, either through the use of arms or through the more subtle, but equally effective, weapon of subversion?

Whatever particular slogan is supposed to be governing relations between the West and the Soviet Union in the years since the end of the Second World War, "cold war", "peaceful co-existence" or now "détente", Soviet leaders have never made any secret of the fact that their long-term aims remain essentially unchanged, namely world domination. There is every indication, despite the silvery tones used at Helsinki, that they remain exactly the same today. Recent years have given enough evidence of the growing armed strength of the Soviet Union, and provide impressive confirmation of that nation's ruthless determination to work by all the means available—short of all-out nuclear war—to achieve the international goals it had set itself.

Firstly, it should never be forgotten that the collapse of South Vietnam in 1975 was due in a very considerable measure to the enormous quantities of war material which the Soviet Union continued to pour into the hands of the already well-equipped North Vietnamese Army, despite the Paris peace agreement and in absolute contradiction to solemn undertakings given at the time that agreement was signed. This blatant act of bad faith indicates only too clearly what little credence should be placed on the word of the Soviet Government whenever paper agreements stand in the way of the furtherance of its policies. Secondly, events in Portugal during 1975 revealed to an alarming degree the extent of Soviet bloc involvement in subversion and propaganda activities aimed at establishing a Communist régime in Portugal. The scale of such activities make complete nonsense of Mr Brezhnev's undertakings given at Helsinki regarding non-interference in the internal affairs of other countries. Thirdly, the trend of events in Southern Africa throughout 1976 again provided irrefutable evidence of the world-wide extent of Soviet ambitions.

In a report published by the Institute for the Study of Conflict[20] in 1975, it was stated that one important reason for the Communist Party's success in gaining great influence over the direction of the Portuguese revolution at a very early stage was that it had the assistance of a number of specially trained Czech Communists. These had been preparing for their task in Czechoslovakia where Cunhal, the Party's leader, had spent at least eight years in exile. All the Czechs had been taught to speak Portuguese fluently and within a fortnight of Cunhal's returning to Portugal in 1974, these agents—who it was thought, numbered between 250 and 300, all experts in the techniques of propaganda and subversion began to be brought into the country and put to work in the towns and villages.

An instance of extremely active Soviet interest in the Portuguese situation was the arrival in Lisbon of Mr Kallin as Soviet

Ambassador, a personality with considerable experience of working in turbulent situations and of the means of turning them to the Soviets' best advantage. Previously he had served in the Argentine and then in Chile at the time of the Allende Government. He came to his post in Lisbon from Havana.

The Soviet Union is known to have allocated very large sums of money for the use of Portuguese Communists, according to some estimates as much as £50 million in little over a year. Large sums have also been donated from East Germany for the use of the Communist dominated trade unions. By the late spring, a number of reports also spoke of the arrival of considerable quantities of Soviet and Czech arms, these apparently being intended for the use not only of the Portuguese Communist Party but also that of a variety of foreign revolutionaries who had begun to arrive in the country.

The aim of the Communists' activity in the coup of April 1975 in Lisbon was not so much to make Portugal Communist overnight, but to sever Angola, Moçambique, Guinea-Bissau and the Cape Verde Islands from Western influence.

This strategic plan was completely successful and altered dramatically the strategic situation in Southern Africa.

In August 1975 an article of considerable significance for the future direction of Soviet policy in the West appeared in the magazine *World Marxist Review*. This is no mere theoretical publication intended for academics but is the "house journal" of the pro-Moscow International Communists' Movement and directs much of its space to the practical examination of problems and tactics of the Communist movement in general and the rôle of Communist Parties in different parts of the world in particular. The article was by the magazine's editor in chief, Mr Konstantine Zarodov, who is also an alternative member of the Central Committee of the Soviet Communist Party. Mr Zarodov based his article largely on one of Lenin's books, *The Tactics of Socialist Democracy in the Democratic Revolution*.

The article appeared to be directed mainly at Western Communist parties and a central point made by the author was that Communists operating in such countries should not confine their attempts only to gaining power by operating within the system of "bourgeois democracy" and the ballot box. Instead, Mr Zarodov said they should be ready to use Lenin's tactics of revolution despite

17

"arithmetical majorities" recorded against them in multi-party elections. He emphasised that present conditions in the non-Communist world were making it increasingly possible to put Lenin's principles into practice.

A little over two months later, in late October, a notable 1 500 word article appeared in the official Soviet Communist Party daily newspaper, *Pravda,* hailing the value of the use of industrial strikes as a prelude to the mounting of revolutions. The official reason for the printing of the article was to commemorate the 70th anniversary of the Russian General Strike of 1905 which Lenin always regarded as having played a major part in the advance of the Russian revolutionary movement.

The article said that the events of 1905 had proved the value of strikes as a form of international proletarian struggle and as being

> important milestones in the liberation movement, and have the effect of stimulating the development of the revolutionary process.[21]

The article recorded that more than 100 million workers had taken part in strikes "in the main citadels of imperialism" during the year 1973-1974 and stated:

> Supporting these main actions, Marxist-Leninist parties aim politically to prepare the working class and its allies for a conscious battle for peace, democracy, and social progress.

The author also quoted Mr Brezhnev as recalling recently that Communists should be "ready for any change of circumstance, for the use of any form of struggle" and taking up the theme of the *World Marxist Review* August editorial, quoted in its support a popular slogan of Russian revolutionary days, "The path to revolution is clear—through popular uprising to popular government". The Western correspondents in Moscow considered the length of the article and its timing to mark an uncompromising stand by the Soviet leadership in support of the Communist drive for power in other countries.

A similarly uncompromising stand could be seen in the remarks of Mr Arvid Peshe, a senior member of the Soviet Politburo, speaking at a rally in the Kremlin to mark the anniversary of the Bolshevik

Revolution in November. "Our party does not recognise ideological conciliation," he told his audience, and went on to say that the Soviet Communist Party believed that class differences inevitably presuppose struggle between different world outlooks. He declared that Socialism cannot be overthrown and its victorious march cannot be stopped.[22] Speeches by party leaders at the traditional parade in Red Square to mark the anniversary of the revolution also have been noticeably harsher in tone in recent years, their main theme being the international Communist struggle and solidarity with it.

Even more disturbing than the sheer size of the Soviet military build-up during recent years have been clear indications that the Soviet High Command has been switching the emphasis in its general strategic outlook and tactical doctrines from the defensive to the offensive. Such indications appear in both the equipment and training programmes of the Soviet forces.

A report produced by The Brookings Institute in 1975, *Sizing up The Soviets,* laid much emphasis on the fact that the training of Soviet Army units in Europe was being increasingly geared to the idea of a massive offensive westwards, designed to bring them to the channel coast in possibly as little as a week.

The author of this report, Mr Geoffrey Record, stated that:

> The principle rôle assigned to ground forces under Soviet (European) theater doctrine is one of relentless attack, 'blitzkrieg' style, designed to ensure the total defeat of the enemy and occupation of vital territory ... The achievement of such unlimited goals in the case of a conflict in the European area would entail nothing short of a giant blitzkrieg across NATO's center leading to the rapid occupation of West Germany, the Low Countries and France.

There has also been an indication of increasing offensive intent at sea, as can be seen from the author of *The Soviet Navy Today,* Captain John Moore's comments on some aspects of "Exercise Okean" in 1975. Professor John Erickson, author of the Foreword, comments that, in addition to the obvious show of strength and much publicised parade of naval power, these exercises contained "unusual features", one of which was:

Convoy manoeuvres on a large scale—with "convoys" being simulated by Soviet Navy supply and hydrographic, or survey ships, or yet again by Soviet merchant ships requisitioned or under special charter for the duration of the fleet exercises. These "convoy operations" took place mainly off the Azores or in the Sea of Japan, while a Soviet hydrographic ship was deployed as a simulated "convoy" on the Eastern Atlantic. Since Soviet interest in their own convoyed shipping can only be minimal, in view of their general self-sufficiency, it can only be assumed that this phase represented a method of investigating attack procedures against Western shipping. What lends credence to this view is the pattern followed by Soviet long-range naval reconnaissance aircraft which flew tracks—IL-38s covering the Indian Ocean and the Northern Pacific, TU-95s flying out of the Somalia base and from Southern Russia as well as covering the Cuba-Conakry route—along and across the main Western shipping routes.[23]

Professor Erickson also described how during the same exercises a substantial "blockade line" was established by Soviet submarines between Iceland and the Norwegian coast, and Soviet warships were transferred on an unprecedented scale from the Baltic into the North Atlantic, thus obviously providing practice in the rapid reinforcement of Soviet naval forces committed to interdiction action against Western lines of communication between North America and Europe. He wrote further that:

In addition, the Soviet naval command was obviously interested in testing how many of their forces could break through the Baltic outlets, through the Channel and the Denmark Strait—and in what time scale. The offensive rôle of the Naval Air Force was also demonstrated by more than seventy simulated attacks using anti-ship missiles.[24]

Another contributory factor to the increasing impression current in Western circles of a growing aggressiveness in Soviet military thinking has been the steady westward shift of Soviet amphibious exercises in the Baltic. At one time almost entirely concentrated in areas near the Soviet coast, it was noted that in the sixties and early seventies their centre had moved to East German coastal waters. Since then they have moved closer and closer towards Danish territorial waters. In the summer of 1976, a sizeable Soviet naval force carried exercises almost as near the Danish coast as it was possible to do without actually infringing that country's territorial rights, whilst at the same time Soviet reconnaissance aircraft carried out patrols up to the very edge of Danish air space. The Danish Foreign Minister, Mr Anderson, professed himself to be astonished at what was happening, which he maintained was completely contrary to the spirit of the Helsinki Agreement.

REFERENCES

1. *The Times*, 29 September 1976.
2. *The Military Balance 1976-1977, op. cit.*
3. *Soviet Attack—NATO Defence Studies*, London 1975, p. 67.
4. *Ibid.*, p. 68.
5. The *Daily Telegraph*, 21 June 1975.
6. The *Daily Telegraph*, 24 June 1975.
7. *The Times*, 30 June 1976.
8. *The Soviet Navy Today*, Captain John E. Moore, Macdonald & Jane, London 1975, p. 96.
9. *Soviet Aerospace Almanack*, March 1976.
10. *The Military Balance 1975-1976*, International Institute for Strategic Studies, London 1975, p. 9.
11. *Ibid.*, p. 5 and 9.
12. The *Daily Telegraph*, 7 October 1975.
13. *Frankfurter Allgemeine*, 20 June 1975.
14. The *Daily Telegraph*, 27 June 1975.
15. *Royal United Services Institute Journal*, June 1975.
16. "General Purpose Forces: Navy and Marine Corps", Arnold Moore, *Arms, Men and Military Budgets 1976*, Crane, Russak, New York, p. 68.
17. *To The Point*, 20 June 1975.
18. *International Herald Tribune*, 4 September 1975.

19. *The Guardian,* 3 August 1975.
20. *Portugal: Revolution and Backlash,* Conflict Studies No. 61, Institute for the Study of Conflict, London 1975, p. 21.
21. *The Times,* 20 October 1975.
22. *The Guardian,* 7 November 1975.
23. Professor John Erickson, Foreword, *The Soviet Navy Today,* Macdonald & Jane, London, p. 7-8.
24. *Ibid.,* p. 80.

Chapter 2

Africa and Western Defence

In the post-imperial age, and with troubles enough at home, it is probably natural that many in Western countries prefer to regard events that occur many thousands of kilometres from their shores or frontiers as being of no particular concern of theirs and to avert their eyes from them whenever they can. Such an ostrich-like attitude is both unrealistic and potentially extremely dangerous, however understandable it may be for the inhabitants of Western European countries, and in particular Britain. All these countries are utterly dependent on vital raw materials and oil from overseas brought to them along lengthy lines of communication around Africa. Moreover, the simple facts of geography and oil production make it obvious that a pro-Communist turn of events in the Middle East or Africa could gravely affect the strategic position of the West. The Arab oil embargo may have taught some a lesson.

In the course of a lecture to the Royal Institute of International Affairs in February 1975, NATO's Southern Region Commander-in-Chief, Admiral M. Johnston, for instance, made the very clear point that should Soviet efforts to gain greater influence and increased operational facilities in states along the North African coast succeed "an entirely new dimension would be added to the (Soviet) threat which would then, in effect, surround the Southern Region".[1]

Admiral Johnston also voiced his disquiet at growing Soviet

activities in the Eastern Mediterranean and in particular in Syria and Iraq. These he saw as part of a planned Soviet drive to gain influence in areas adjacent to the source of the West's vital oil supplies. He described how in Syria the Soviet presence had been marked by the complete re-equipping of the Syrian forces with the most modern weapons since the end of the last Arab-Israeli war. Large numbers of military advisers were present there, together with Soviet technicians working on the expansion of port facilities at Tartus and Latakia. He said that owing to this presence, the Soviet Union was now in a good position to exert influence either by military pressure or by subversion on any neighbouring state. Speaking of Iraq, he said:

> In supporting the Baathist régime in Iraq with modern weapons and technology, the Soviets have gained great influence in a nation which is eminently well located to foster Soviet interests in the Persian Gulf area. As part of their largesse, the Soviets are assisting in the construction or rebuilding of a number of major airfields which will be able to handle the largest Soviet aircraft.[2]

According to the *Strategic Balance 1975-1976,* a squadron of the Soviet Air Force's TU-22 medium bombers is already based in Iraq.

Activity such as that mentioned in the Admiral's lecture has been backed by widespread Soviet intelligence activity in the area. In Iraq, the Soviet Ambassador, Mr Anatoli Barkofsky, who previously served in Egypt, Syria and Cyprus, was exposed in the press as being a member of the Soviet intelligence service, the KGB, as long ago as 1967. The Soviet military intelligence service is also known to be extremely active in the country. Many intelligence operations would seem to be based upon Kuwait where, it has been estimated, more than a third of the 45 man staff of the Soviet Embassy are intelligence officers. One of these last in 1974, Mr Viktor Eliseev, was a particularly experienced officer who had previously operated in the Sudan, Egypt and Kenya. His activities in the latter country caused him to be expelled in 1969. One TASS correspondent based in Kuwait was likewise known to be employed on KGB duties, his journalistic status enabling him to travel freely throughout the entire Gulf area.[3]

24

Soviet involvement in the People's Democratic Republic of Yemen, formerly the British colony of Aden, began almost immediately after the British withdrawal. Since then, the Soviet Union has given considerable amounts of military equipment including tanks, patrol vessels and MIG 17 and MIG 21 aircraft to the Republic's armed forces and sent aid and technicians for the enlarging of harbour facilities. Cuban pilots served in the air force and East German advisers have been responsible for setting up an efficient security service.

The harbour of Aden is now largely managed by Soviet technicians and Soviet ships, particularly naval repair ships and tankers and a Soviet-constructed naval base mainly intended for submarines has been in operation for some time along the coast of Hodeida. A naval signalling station has been established on the island of Socotra.

The People's Democratic Republic of Yemen also served as the main base for the Soviet-supported guerrillas of The People's Front for the Liberation of Oman (PFLO) who carried on a little heard of, but quite bloody, campaign against the forces of the Sultan of Oman to which a number of British contract officers are attached. Oman is, of course, a country of the utmost strategic importance for the West containing, as it does on its northern coast, the southern shore of the Straits of Hormuz through which all tankers entering or leaving the Persian Gulf have to pass. It is literally the West's jugular vein and about one tanker every 10 minutes passes through this 80 kilometre wide stretch of water. In present circumstances an attempt by guerrillas to interfere with the tanker traffic by the use of mines remains a possibility. One attempt to occupy the tip of the Ras Musandam Peninsula at the entrance of the straits was made in 1971 by PFLO forces but failed.

The vital importance of Persian Gulf oil to Western countries (and Japan) was well illustrated by figures provided in a book by experts, *The Indian Ocean and the Threat to the West*, published in 1975.[4] According to these figures, the major Western European countries at present obtain the following percentages of their total oil imports from the area:

Italy	84,5%
Britain	66,1%
West Germany	62%
France	51,1%

Even taking the development of North Sea oil into account, European imports from the Gulf are thought likely to rise by 45% during the next five years. Already Europe and Japan together take over 320 million litres of oil per day from the area.

The importance of Gulf oil to the United States is thought likely to increase rapidly in the years ahead. American imports from the area will probably increase by about 25% during the next five years. At the present time the United States is importing about seven million barrels* of oil a day, or about 40% of its present needs. According to an estimate made in the *Petroleum Review* in 1973, soaring consumption and dwindling internal production could make American demand for Middle Eastern oil grow to 18 million barrels a day by 1985, compared with the three million barrels a day of the early 1970s. The crucial and increasing importance of imported oil supplies to the United States economy is demonstrated by the fact that not only, as in Japan, has the country's rate of growth become mainly dependent upon such supplies but that the efforts now being made to find additional or alternative sources of energy are only likely to prove beneficial in the comparatively long-term. The country's shale oil deposits are, for instance, not only difficult but also extremely expensive to work and present estimates indicate that it will probably not be until the end of the century before the United States is producing sufficient nuclear energy to keep pace with its rising electricity demand.

Despite the appearance of North Sea oil, it is estimated that Western European demand for Middle Eastern oil will probably have doubled by 1985. Experts have forecast that even during the peak period of production of its North Sea oil fields, it is likely that Britain will still have to import about 25% of its crude oil supplies. These imports are particularly important as far as the manufacture of high grade fuels is concerned.

The enormous economic and strategic importance of the oil-bearing lands of the Middle East to the Western world can also be clearly seen from the figures relating to known world oil reserves. Of these 5,5% lie in the United States, 3,8% in Western Europe and 55% in the Middle East. Whereas it is thought that American reserves are only sufficient to allow production to continue for about 16 years

---

*1 t = 7,3 barrels.

and North Sea production could be past its peak by the end of the 1980s, some Middle Eastern countries have sufficient reserves to allow production to continue for at least 70 years. At the present time, the Soviet Union exports about a million barrels of oil a day, mainly to Eastern Europe. However, rising demand and backwardness in drilling techniques may lead to the USSR also becoming a major customer for Middle East oil, at least until its own reserves in Siberia can adequately be exploited.

Every day, in a never-ending stream, tankers with over a million tons of Middle East oil round the Cape of Good Hope bound for Western countries. Every year a quarter of Western Europe's food supplies also come round the Cape. It is, of course, these facts which give the African continent its prime importance as regards Western defence: an importance that has not been altered to any material degree by the re-opening of the Suez Canal.

At the time the canal was closed in 1967 about 20 000 ships used it each year. Control of ships on the 15 hour voyage was exercised through a convoy system, two convoys sailing southward and one northward. All northern convoys laden with oil had priority, the southern convoys having to stop to allow them to pass. At that time the canal was able to handle all ships up to a maximum draught of 38 ft.* In practice this meant that it was capable of providing passage for three-quarters of the vessels in the world's merchant fleets. Today, however, all but 30% have a draught of more than 38 ft. In particular the canal will not be able to handle the new giant super-tankers which carry the bulk of Middle East oil until major development plans have been carried out. These plans will include the dredging of the canal to a depth of about 21 m and their implementation, at today's prices, will certainly prove a very costly exercise.

In the immediate future, only tankers in the region of 40 000 t as compared with the 100 000 t of the giant super tankers will be able to use the canal. Plans for enlargement do not envisage ships of more than 150 000 t using the canal before 1980. Even when such enlargements have been carried out, it is doubtful whether it will attract a high percentage of tanker traffic. One tanker owner has said:

It's far more economical to go round Africa. The cost of

*11,5 m.

putting a loaded 60,000 tanker through Suez on a run from the Persian Gulf to Rotterdam would be 4.5 dollars a ton, without canal tariffs. Sailing a bigger tanker round the Cape to the same port costs 1.20 dollars a ton."[5]

Studies by experts have indicated that about one-third of the tankers for whom the Suez route is the shortest route will not use it when sailing fully laden and, that half the tanker force will still not use it even when sailing in ballast.

Another significant factor to be borne in mind when considering the importance of the Cape as against the Suez route is that between 80% and 90% of merchant ships now being built are of a weight of over 200 000 t and some exceed 400 000 t. Such ships require a draught of 18 to 27 m. The opening draught of the Suez Canal remains at 38 ft. Operations to deepen it to even 15 m would cost an estimated one billion dollars at least: an outlay that would almost inevitably be passed on to canal users in the form of higher charges, once again emphasising the economic advantages of the Cape Route.

The Soviet Navy's first major introduction to the Indian Ocean came early in 1968. In February its Commander-in-Chief visited India and the following month a squadron consisting of a *Sverdlov* class cruiser, two destroyers and accompanying tankers sailed into Madras harbour. Similar visits quickly followed to Bombay, Mogadishu, Umm Quasr, Karachi, Aden and Colombo. Between November 1968 and the autumn of 1969 a second round of visits followed. The vessels carrying them out were drawn from the Pacific, Northern and Black Sea Fleets and included two submarines. The ports visited included Aden, Hodeida, Umm Quasr, Dar es Salaam, Mombasa, Bandar Abbas, Chittagong and Port Louis. About the same time an Alligator class tank-landing ship visited the Sudan.

In 1968 the British Government announced its decision to withdraw British forces from the Persian Gulf and the Indian Ocean. It has been estimated that Soviet naval activity increased fourfold in the area between that date and early 1976.

It is, of course, the potential vulnerability of these Western lines of communication round the Cape to a hostile sea power that has occasioned much of the alarm at the appearance of growing numbers of Soviet warships in the Indian Ocean. Between 1968 and

1971 a total of 81 surface ships, submarines and auxiliaries was observed in the region. The number of Soviet warships in the Indian Ocean at any one time has varied but has averaged between 18 and 22, although sometimes a greater number has been listed. In the autumn of 1974, for instance, the number of ships in the Indian Ocean Squadron was put at between 25 and 30, including new attack submarines. In July, a further group including the helicopter carrier *Leningrad* sailed round the Cape of Good Hope into the Indian Ocean from the Atlantic. In the spring, this group returned to the Atlantic round the Cape and sailed up the west coast of Africa before returning to the Black Sea.

The re-opening of the Suez Canal has considerably facilitated such movements by cutting the sailing distance from the Black Sea to the Indian Ocean by well over 3 000 kilometres, reducing time in transit by as much as 70%. Whilst ships of Western European navies on their way to the Indian Ocean also get some benefit, it is to a much lesser extent. All Soviet naval vessels, including new aircraft carriers such as the *Kiev,* are now able to use the canal, but the largest type of American carriers such as the *Forrestal* will not be able to do so until it is widened and deepened. United States naval vessels deploying to the Indian Ocean from home bases such as Norfolk in Virginia will not gain any appreciable advantage in sailing time by using the canal.

In addition to Aden, where a new medium sized Soviet floating dock will soon be in operation, Hodeida is able to accommodate destroyers and frigates as well as submarines. Umm Quasr, the Iraqi port at the head of the Persian Gulf constructed and expanded with Soviet aid, is also available to the Soviet Indian Ocean Squadron. Amongst other ports offering facilities is Visakhapatnan, situated midway between Madras and Calcutta and constructed with Indian and Yugoslav aid. It is believed that Mr Brezhnev obtained important concessions as to the use of the port by Soviet submarines during his visit to India in 1973. Soviet minesweepers frequently make protracted stays in the harbour of Chittagong, and Soviet warships are also allowed use of the docks and harbour of Singapore.

There has been a noticeable increase in Soviet interest in Mauritius recently with more than 100 Soviet trawlers anchored in waters near its coast during the year 1974-75. In a curious incident that came to light, it was discovered that a Kuwait firm had bought port facilities from the Mauritian Government apparently as part of a plan hatched by the Soviet KGB to obtain the use of such facilities for Soviet ships by undercover means.

On the African coast, the port of Berbera in Somalia is rapidly being transformed into a major Soviet military and naval base. Soviet activity here began with the building of a fishing port for Somalia between 1963 and 1969. Since 1972, a considerable number of improvements have been made to the harbour which can now accommodate ships of up to 12 000 t. Ships of the Soviet Indian Ocean Squadron frequently visit the port which has been controlled by a Soviet harbour master for the last five years. The harbour contains a floating barrack ship with room for 200 to 300 men plus a machine shop. Facilities newly constructed with the aid of Soviet technicians include an oil storage depot whose capacity was being trebled to take over 150 000 barrels of fuel during 1974. At the same time, a housing compound south-east of the harbour reserves for Soviet use was being doubled. The year before, a powerful Soviet naval wireless station was set up, it being believed that this was intended to be the communications centre for Soviet operations in the whole area. It is now thought that there may be plans to build a second harbour to the west of Berbera.

The Soviet Union also has free use of all Somali airfields. One of these, Uanle Uen or Dafet, near Mogadishu, is known to be suitable for the use of Soviet TU-95 Bear D long-range reconnaissance aircraft. Based there, such aircraft would be able to carry out surveillance missions over a large area of the North West Indian Ocean, including the whole of the Red Sea and the Gulf of Aden. This airfield has also been extended recently.

In addition, the Soviet Navy is known to have some facilities at the Southern Somali port of Kisabu and there have been indications of possible plans to expand other ports, including that of Mogadishu, the capital.[6]

In June 1975, Mr James Schlesinger, then United States Defence Secretary, presented evidence including aerial reconnaissance photographs of the existence of a large Soviet missile store at Berbera. Indicated on the photographs were a missile handling and fuelling area, storage areas, bunkers and an assembly building. He stated that the buildings and areas shown on the photograph were clearly intended for the storage and handling of surface-to-surface and air-to-surface anti-ship missiles.

Mr Schlesinger's statement gave rise to a barrage of denials from both the Soviet Union and from Somalia that this base existed. A somewhat bizarre episode then took place in which a number of Western journalists, including a television team from the American Broadcasting Company, were brought into the country at the Somali Government's expense in order that they could examine the alleged base and see its "harmless nature" for themselves. After a three-day journey in sweltering heat from Mogadishu, the journalists were allowed to approach an obvious military installation including a large hangar very much like the one in the photographs, but they were stopped some distance away and then told "now you have seen it" and were promptly escorted away from the scene without more ado.[7]

Subsequently, Mr Roy Mason, then British Secretary of State for Defence, was stated to have been impressed with information he had received from the United States regarding the alleged missile base and to have arranged for copies to be distributed to the defence groups of the two main British political parties.[8]

In his statement, Mr Schlesinger described the base as being apparently 80% completed. Some naval experts bearing in mind that Soviet missile carrying cruisers, destroyers and submarines have no means of re-loading once they have fired while still at sea, consider that the stockpiling of missiles in such places as Somalia, Cuba, and possibly Guinea, could indicate that Soviet planners are preparing against the contingency of a long war at sea.

Farther to the south of Somalia, the ports of both Zanzibar and Dar es Salaam are in the hands of governments more favourable to Peking than to Moscow, but it would not be surprising if Soviet naval units were able to gain some facilities there in any period of tense East-West confrontation that might occur. Both ports have certainly been frequently used for the unloading of cargoes of Soviet bloc arms intended for the "liberation movements" in Southern Africa.

It is thought that Soviet emissaries began attempts aimed at receiving permission from the new Marxist Government of Moçambique for the setting up of a Soviet base in the important harbours of Maputo (formerly Lourenço Marques) and Nacala soon after Moçambique became independent in June 1975. Similar attempts were believed to have been made during the year with the object of obtaining concessions in the Comores Islands after they became independent.

Since 1969, all the countries with a coastline on the Indian Ocean between Tanzania and Bangladesh, with the exception of Saudi Arabia, Oman and the United Emirates, Quatar, Bahrain and Kuwait have received quite frequent and, on occasions, prolonged visits from Soviet warships. These visits were made by nearly every type of modern naval vessel, including submarines. Apart from the obvious "showing the flag" rôle of such visits, experts also consider that another purpose is probably a long-term study of oceanographic, environmental and operational problems in distant waters. Admiral Sergei Gorshkov is on record as describing long-distance cruises as a "school of moral-political and psychological training" for participation in modern war.

Admiral Gorshkov has also emphasised the propaganda importance of such visits as those that have been made to countries bordering the Indian Ocean in the following words:

> The visits of Soviet ships to foreign ports and the contacts between our sailors and the citizens of other countries have helped the common people to understand better the peace-loving character of Soviet foreign policy, the mission of our army and navy which are called upon to guard vigilantly the security of our Soviet motherland and the other countries of the Socialist community, and to defend the cause of world peace.[9]

There is also some indication that it has been Soviet policy to use visits by Soviet warships in the Indian Ocean, as in the case of the Mediterranean, to demonstrate practical support for régimes sympathetic to it which may be under internal or external threat, and to warn off those who may be trying to bring about the collapse of the régime concerned. An American researcher, Mr James McConnell, has, for instance, recorded that on 17 April 1970 two Soviet cruisers arrived at Mogadishu for an official visit to Somalia scheduled to last five days. However, at the end of this time the ships showed no sign of leaving.

On 27 April, 10 days after the arrival of the Soviet ships, the pro-Soviet Somali Government of General Siad Barre which had itself come to power by means of a coup the year before, announced that it had discovered a plot aimed at overthrowing it and replacing it by "a puppet government working for the interests of imperialism". To what extent the plot existed in reality or to what extent its "discovery" was merely a ruse to provide a convenient excuse by which the government could consolidate its hold on the country by use of emergency measures remains doubtful. The point of interest is, however, that the two Soviet cruisers extended their "five-day stay" into one of nearly a month, not apparently leaving until the second week of May. By that date, the government had the situation in the country firmly under control. Mr McConnell concluded that the long-term effect of such seemingly "gun-boat diplomacy" by the Soviet Navy:

> ... might be the creation of a more "progressive" Indian Ocean community than one would expect from the normal course of events. The region is highly unstable and régimes come and go, whether radical or conservative. There is no reason to believe that the natural outcome of the flux consequently favours one or the other trend, but if the Soviets throw military support to radical régimes which remain exposed to the random mercy of political fate, the cards will be stacked in favour of radicalism."[10]

The steady increase of Soviet naval strength in the Indian Ocean area during 1975 and 1976 caused increasing concern to a number of governments highly dependent on vital lines of communication in those waters. A concern that was heightened all the more because this increase of strength coincided with the closing of the Royal Navy's communication centre in Mauritius and the Royal Air Force's staging post at Gan in the Maldive Islands. These events meant the virtual completion of the British withdrawal from the area. Amongst those who voiced their concern at that turn of events were the Prime Ministers of both Australia and New Zealand. The latter said that reconnaissance flights by aircraft of the New Zealand Air Force had identified no less than 28 Soviet warships moving in or out of the Indian Ocean during the course of one month in the early part of 1976. New Zealand's unease was further increased by apprehension that Soviet attempts to negotiate facilities for "fishing trawlers" from the government of the island of Tonga might be the prelude to an extension of the tentacles of Soviet naval power into the South Pacific.

Observers also considered that British withdrawal from Gan could well increase Soviet interest in obtaining naval or air facilities in the strategically important Maldive islands spread over 700 km of the Indian Ocean just south of the Equator. In Mauritius the emergence of a Marxist party as the winner of most seats in a general election late in 1976, even though it was denied power through the formation of a coalition by other parties, seemed to offer new opportunities for the Soviet Union to gain advantage on the island.

Practical Western concern regarding the potential Soviet threat to the security of sea communications in that vital area has been shown by a considerable increase in French naval strength since 1974. By January 1975, 14 French warships or about one-tenth of the effective French Fleet were based in the Indian Ocean. By early 1976, these had been joined by another four vessels, including two submarines, France retaining base facilities both at Djibouti and on Reunion Island. The most important long-term Western reaction to date, however, has been the decision by the United States Government to transform a "communications facility" on the British owned atoll of Diego Garcia into a "maritime support base"

The atoll, U-shaped and covering only 45 km^2 is situated almost in the middle of the Indian Ocean, lying 2 000 km south of the southernmost tip of India and about 3 200 km east of the African coast. It has a good harbour and plans call for the establishment of refuelling facilities capable of catering for a carrier force and also for aircraft, including air-tankers. The present airfield runway is to be extended from 1 800 to 3 600 m, and minor ship repair facilities are also to be established. The United States Congress voted to allocate the equivalent of R13,5 million for the necessary construction during the financial year ending in April 1976 and a further R10,5 million for work during the following financial year. Britain will exercise joint control of the military installations together with the United States and any action other than that of a purely routine nature undertaken by US forces based at Diego Garcia will be a matter for joint prior discussion by the United States and British governments.

The importance of the Diego Garcia base, once completed, lies in the fact that the United States Navy is reported to have met with considerable logistic difficulties when attempting to maintain task forces for long periods in the Indian Ocean at vast distances from its existing bases.

Present bases convenient for operations by the United States Navy in the Indian Ocean area are all too scarce. A special study prepared for the National Strategy Information Center of New York, by Dr Alvin J. Cottrell and Mr Walter F. Hahn, called *Indian Ocean Naval Limitations,* stated:

> Requirements for such a facility was critically emphasised during the Vietnam war when US ships deployed from the east coast of the US to the Tonkin Gulf and denied use of South African ports either had to take advantage of a random British tanker in the Indian Ocean or be accompanied by a tanker sent from the Atlantic fleet at considerable expense.[11]

A considerable further increase in Soviet naval activity in the Indian Ocean occurred during 1975, including the arrival of four landing ships. The increasingly frequent appearance of such craft in distant waters has illustrated yet another aspect of the growth of Soviet military power. This growing long-range capacity to carry out amphibious warfare and sea-borne interventions could be of great possible relevance in the context of local wars in the future.

In the early 1960s, the Soviet capability to carry out even short range amphibious operations was almost non-existent. The Soviet marines or "naval-infantry" had been abolished shortly after the end of the 1939-45 war and such landing ships and landing craft as it possessed consisted of a motley collection of ageing ex-German, Japanese and American vessels mostly of very small tonnage. The beginning of a new offensive policy became evident, however, early in the 1960s with the re-establishment of the marines and the beginning of the construction of a series of classes of landing craft. Today the strength of the marines has grown to some 15 000 men. This force is divided into four brigades, one brigade being attached to each of the four regional Soviet fleets. Marine units have their own (amphibious) light armoured support and artillery.

A 4 000-ton tank landing ship (Alligator class) has been developed which has accommodation for an entire marine battalion below decks plus 25-30 tanks or other vehicles on deck. The Soviet Union has 12 such vessels in service at the present time together with well over 100 smaller tank landing and assault craft constructed over the last 12 years. According to a study produced by the American National Strategy Information Center,[12] the number of

Alligator landing ships in service is likely to have risen to 20 by 1980 with a corresponding increase in "follow-up" craft. In practical terms, this would mean that the Soviet Union will then have the capability for a sea-borne lift of 20 000 marines (as against 3 000 in 1965 and 17 000 today) and a lift of 62 000 t of equipment (as against 3 500 t in 1965 and 41 400 t today).

Although Western observers believe that most Soviet amphibious training to date has been concentrated upon preparation for support operations on the flanks of Soviet forces making an advance into Western Europe, there have also been indications that a capacity for long-range operations is also being developed deliberately. The presence of Soviet landing ships at times of tension in the Mediterranean has already been remarked upon. An article in the *Soviet Military Review* of August 1974 made a point of emphasising that a marine must not only be able to withstand rough seas, but also must be ready to "rush ashore after a prolonged voyage"

A report issued by NATO's Northern Atlantic Military Committee in June 1976 noted that:

> Soviet amphibious capabilities remain largely limited to relatively small operations in close-in areas. Nevertheless amphibious craft, presumably with Naval Infantry aboard, are increasingly seen out of home waters. This is probably one more development which awaits its turn. Sea lift capabilities are slowly increasing to include air cushion vehicles and roll-on roll-off container ships.[13]

A large tank-landing craft, presumably of the Alligator class and apparently carrying marines, was reported to be amongst the vessels of a Soviet naval force, which also comprised a guided missile destroyer and a tanker, sighted about 50 km off the West African coast early in January 1976 when the outcome of the Communist bid for power in Angola was still in some doubt.

On the subject of Soviet amphibious capability, Captain John Moore has commented that while some people are inclined to belittle the size of the present Soviet amphibious capability because of the comparatively few large landing vessels available to it, they would:

> ... do well to remember the vast number of ships in the Soviet merchant marine and the fact that these as

Government run vessels can be switched to naval operations with a minimum of delay.[14]

The Vietnamese war provided the Soviet Union with ample experience of the problems of large scale supply to friendly forces at the end of long sea lines of communication. The extent to which it was able to supply the colossal tonnage of arms and equipment despatched year after year for the use of the Vietcong and North Vietnam provided apt proof of the extent to which the growth of Soviet naval power had been accompanied by the growth of the size of its mercantile marine. What an effective aid to the implementation of the policy of aiding "liberation movements" this latter growth could be was widely demonstrated by those operations. Prior to the closing of the Suez Canal, the main line of supply ran through the Bosphoros and the Dardanelles from Odessa, and thence down the canal and across the Indian Ocean and South China Sea to Haiphong. The voyage of well over 11 000 km normally took just over a month using the largest and most modern ships of the Soviet merchant fleet of about 14 000 t and with a speed of 16-18 knots. An average of 47 Soviet cargo ships a month arrived in Haiphong harbour via this route. The closing of the canal presented the Soviets with very considerable difficulties in maintaining this flow of supplies to their Vietcong and North Vietnamese allies. The round trip to Haiphong and back even for the newest ships sailing at top speed then took five months. Despite this fact, a system was introduced which assured the arrival of 22-25 ships in Haiphong each month without overstraining Soviet resources.

Such a capability could be more easily applied to any country in Africa or on the shores of the Indian Ocean.

Given the scarcity of naval vessels which Western countries at present have available for service in the Indian Ocean, the vast size of this ocean, and the fact that the distance from the entrance to the Red Sea to Durban in South Africa is 5 250 km, one of the greatest problems facing Western defence chiefs in any emergency would be to locate and keep track of enemy warships.

Allied reconnaissance aircraft operating from the Persian Gulf area could cover a reasonable proportion of shipping routes as far south as the northern edge of the Moçambique Channel, between Madagascar and the East African coast. But the region southwards to the Cape and the South Atlantic area could be covered, at present, only by units based in South Africa. The importance of these waters has already been mentioned but perhaps can be seen even better from the fact that it has been estimated that a grand total of 24 000 ocean-going ships a year or 66 a day round the Cape. About 17 of these 66 are tankers carrying oil and a similar number in ballast. Over 1 000 ships call at South African ports each month, well over 50% being bound to or from Western Europe. The importance of the Cape shipping route to NATO countries alone can also be glimpsed from the fact that in the one month of February 1972 a total of 476 freighters and 112 tankers belonging to NATO countries passed the Cape.

The extent to which traffic on the Cape Route has increased during the last 20 years can be noted from the manner in which the number of ships calling at South African ports increased from 6 300 in 1957-58 to 12 701 in 1967-68 and to 16 395 in 1974-75. In the month of January 1975, a total of 651 vessels passed the Cape of Good Hope. Of these 58 tankers and 47 freighters were of British nationality, 19 tankers and 18 freighters Norwegian, 13 tankers and 42 freighters Greek, 16 tankers and 21 freighters West German, 32 tankers and 10 freighters French and five tankers and 25 freighters Dutch. The seemingly small total of three United States tankers and eight freighters was greatly augmented by the passage of 98 tankers and 47 freighters sailing under a Liberian flag of convenience, but mostly under charter to United States companies. Altogether a total of 250 tankers and 253 freighters from NATO countries rounded the Cape during this period, as did 21 freighters of Warsaw Pact origin.

These figures give added weight to the words of two American experts who have written that:

> The importance of the Cape Route issues not only from the conveyor belt of oil from the Middle East. Conservative estimates suggest that fully 70 per cent of the strategic raw materials needed by the members of the North Atlantic Treaty Organisation ply the waters round Africa. This figure encompasses not only the flow of materials from the Middle East and Asia, but also essential supplies from Africa itself. In short, in an era in which the industrialised nations of the West have discovered painfully not only their interdependence, but also their glaring vulnerability to disruptions in the economic lifeblood of energy supplies and raw materials,

the Cape Route—and the continent ringed by it—have assumed a new significance that in many ways exceeds that of their rôles in the heydays of colonial experience.[15]

Durban, the largest harbour in South Africa, handles over 20 million tons of shipping each year. Its docks include extensive repair yards and some shipbuilding yards. The port's dry dock can take vessels of up to 30 000 t and in addition there are also floating docks. Partly in order to relieve congestion in Durban and other existing ports, an enormous new harbour is now being constructed north of Durban at Richards Bay. When completed it will replace Durban as the country's largest port. It is specially intended to handle bulk ore carriers and container ships. Although primarily commercial in purpose, it is considered to have considerable potential for naval use under emergency conditions.

Major extension work is under way at the ports of Port Elizabeth and East London, and in Cape Town work on the vast Ben Schoeman Dock is being completed. When finished the dock will double the capacity of the port and will include special deep sea berths capable of accommodating the largest container ships either already built or planned. Another maritime project of importance is the plan of a consortium of European shipbuilders to build one of the world's biggest dry docks at Saldanha Bay. It is planned that this will be able to accommodate the largest vessel afloat today, and will be designed so that two very large vessels can be in dry dock at the same time. A spokesman for the consortium said that it would be the only place on "long haul" between harbours serving the Arab oilfields and Europe or the east coast of America where super-large vessels would be able to be repaired in dry dock conditions.

At the present time, super-tankers passing the Cape are serviced from the land as they cannot enter existing South African ports. A considerable amount of major repair work is sometimes affected by engineers brought out from the Cape whilst a tanker is still at sea. Major spare parts are transported by helicopter with such routine requirements as fresh food and mail. Sometimes crews are also exchanged by means of a helicopter lift.

The best known South African asset as regards the defence of allied shipping routes is undoubtedly the Simonstown naval base, about 25 miles from Cape Town. Here the size of the dockyard is at present being tripled at a cost equivalent to 45 million US dollars.

39

Machine shops in the base are also to be re-equipped with 17 million dollars worth of new machinery over the next 5 years. Berths for frigates are to be increased from eight at the present time to 24, those for submarines from seven to 13. The base is also equipped with a syncrolift, the most modern form of equipment for drydocking a submarine or vessel of similar size, and it is planned to introduce a second soon. When all the extensions have been completed the base will be able to accommodate 50 warships under emergency conditions.

The base will thus continue to be able to cater for very much more than just the needs of the South African Navy. Government spokesmen have made it known that it will still be available to ships of navies of friendly countries despite the unwise abrogation of the Simonstown Agreement by the British Government.

Ten kilometres north of Simonstown, at Silvermine, lies one of the most elaborately equipped underground naval communication centres in the world. Opened in 1973 after construction estimated at a cost of the equivalent of 30 million US dollars, the centre is linked to the British Admiralty in London and to the United States. The centre can be linked to worldwide communication units in the United States of America, Britain and all NATO headquarters.

A system of Video screens covering the entire area from the East coast of South America to Bangladesh and southwards from the bulge of the coastline of West Africa to the Antarctic enables the position of all known shipping in the area (or a section of it according to choice) to be displayed at will.

A mass of information stored in computers enables the duty officer, at the touch of a consol, to bring before him on the screen all relevant details regarding a particular ship's size and type, course, speed, nationality, cargo, or of a naval vessel's weapons, search and rescue capability, last port and destination, etc. The same type of information is available regarding all aircraft in the area. The centre has space reserved for officers of allied navies for use in wartime or emergency.

Surveillance of all shipping out to 80 km from the South African coast is undertaken as a routine duty by the South African Navy and Air Force, but the performance of long distance reconnaissance by the latter is handicapped at present owing to the difficulty of obtaining adequate aircraft from Western countries for political reasons. Information obtained by the air force's Shackletons and Albatrosses is, however, passed to the United States and Britain by means of the Silvermine communications network.

British Nimrod maritime reconnaissance aircraft are required but the British Government will not give permission for their sale to South Africa.

The South African Navy is equipped with two destroyers carrying anti-submarine helicopters, six anti-submarine frigates, 11 minesweepers, six corvettes and four patrol craft. There is also a naval reserve 10 400 strong equipped with two frigates and seven minesweepers. The Daphne class submarines were built for the navy in French shipyards after the British Government had refused to accept an order for vessels to be built in Britain. Three more submarines are reported to have been ordered from France.

The air force, which is the largest in Sub-Saharan Africa, has two maritime squadrons equipped with Shackleton and Albatross aircraft which carry out the shipping surveillance previously mentioned, one light bomber squadron equipped with Canberra aircraft and one with Buccaneers, two fighter squadrons equipped with Mirage aircraft, one reconnaissance squadron, four helicopter squadrons, four ground attack squadrons and four transport squadrons.

The army's peace-time strength of one armoured brigade, one mechanised brigade, and four motorised infantry brigades would be supplemented on mobilisation by the addition of the strength of the reserve 138 000 strong Citizen Force. There is also a 75 000 strong reserve local protection force known as the Commandos, which includes 12 air squadrons equipped with private aircraft. National service lasts for two years, while conscripts do a further period of five years reserve service which includes a few weeks annual training either in the Citizen Force or in the Commandos. Recently the armed forces have commissioned a number of non-White officers in the Coloured units.

In the police force which also receives training in counter-insurgency techniques as well as its normal duties, Black constables serve under the same conditions as White constables.

South Africa has now developed a considerable armaments industry which can meet in whole or part the demands of the services for small arms and other infantry weapons, armoured cars and military vehicles, ammunition and wireless equipment. Jet training-aircraft have been manufactured for some time and Mirage jet fighters assembled near Johannesburg.

The importance of South Africa as regards Western defence does not lie only in its strategic position on the West's vital lines of communications and its considerable military strength but also as provider of essential strategic raw materials at a time of growing world shortage.

At the present time Southern Africa is estimated to possess 95% of the non-Communist world's known reserves of the platinum group of metals, 90% of its known reserves of chrome ore, 74% of its reserves of vanadium, 70% of its reserves of gold, 73% of its reserves of manganese ore and 30% of its reserves of uranium. In terms of current production, South Africa now produces 77% of the non-Communist world's gold supply, 87% of its platinum, 32% of its antimony, 32% of its manganese, 32% of its diamonds (both gems and stones for industrial use), 48% of its chrome ore and 36% of its asbestos. Altogether about 65 different minerals are produced, including in addition to those listed above, nickel, fluorspar, vanadium, copper, and titanium. The last named is an important material for the production of high speed aircraft. In addition, Rhodesia was producing an estimated 10% of the non-Communist world's chrome ore supply in 1973 as well as 79% of its corondium and smaller quantities of some seven other metals, including copper, gold and nickel. Rhodesian reserves of chrome ore, together with those of South Africa, account for an estimated 98% of the entire non-Communist world's supplies.

South West Africa produces some 21% of the non-Communist world's diamonds and a number of important minerals, including uranium. The last is of particular consequence for Britain owing to the fact that in 1970 the British Government signed a contract with the Rossing uranium mine of South West Africa for the supply of approximately 1 500 t of uranium a year. These supplies are crucial for the development of Britain's atomic energy programme which, when the second generation of atomic reactors are in operation at the end of the present decade, will require a supply of about 2 000 t of uranium a year. Supplies from alternative sources would almost certainly prove considerably more expensive.

The London Institute for the Study of Conflict has summarised the general economic importance of South Africa in the following terms:

> South Africa produces more energy than France or Italy,
> as much crude steel as France, Sweden and East
> Germany, more corn than Canada, more wool than the

United States, more wine than Greece, more fish than Britain. As *Fortune* pointed out several years ago, the Witwatersrand industrial complex is the largest south of Turin. It towers economically over the African continent. Although it covers just four per cent of the area of the continent, and has less than six per cent of its people, it accounts for more than a quarter of the gross national product of the entire continent.[16]

South Africa's importance to Britain as a trading partner is so well known as to need no comment here. British exports to South Africa rose from R586,8 million in 1972 to R823 million in 1974. The book value of British investments in South Africa in 1971 was estimated at £651,7 million and £997,2 million in 1974. The yearly flow of British investment estimated at £53,1 million in 1970 was put at £73,2 million in 1972 and £87,4 million the following year.

British investment in South Africa was estimated to total at least R3 000 million early in 1977, and United States investment at more than R1 500 million. More than 300 major American companies had subsidiaries in South Africa.

REFERENCES

1. *RUSI Journal*, June 1975.
2. *Ibid.*
3. *Soviet Objectives in the Middle East*, Institute for the Study of Conflict. Special Report, London 1974, p. 18-19.
4. *The Indian Ocean and the Threat to the West*, Patrick Wall, MP, Anthony Harrigan, W.A.C. Adie, and the Institute for the Study of Conflict, Tom Stacey International, London 1975.
5. *To The Point*, May 1975.
6. *The Soviet Presence in Somalia*, Institute for the Study of Conflict, London 1975, p. 9-10.
7. *The Times*, 30 June 1975.
8. *The Times*, 15 July 1975.
9. "The Navy of the Soviet Union", *Soviet Military Review*, June 1975.
10. James McConnell, *Soviet Naval Development Capability and Context*, Praeger, New York, 1973, p. 398-399.
11. *Indian Ocean Naval Limitations*, Admiral H. Moorer, National Strategy Information Center Inc., New York, 1976, p. 11

12. *Arms, Men and Military Budgets, op. cit.,* p. 68.
13. North Atlantic Military Committee Press Release, 10 June 1976.
14. *The Soviet Navy Today, op. cit.,* p. 155.
15. *Soviet Shadow Over Africa,* Walter F. Hahn and Alvin J. Cottrell. Centre for Advanced International Studies, University of Miami, 1976, p. 47.
16. *Soviet Strategic Penetration of Africa,* David Rees. Institute for the Study of Conflict, London, 1976, p. 15.

Chapter 3

Target Africa

Early in December 1975, Mr Daniel Moynihan, US representative at the United Nations, made an outspoken attack upon the Soviet Union's activities in Africa, and in particular on its increasing support for the Marxist revolutionaries in Angola which was producing an ever graver crisis in that country. Addressing the General Assembly, Mr Moynihan said that the era of European colonisation of the African continent dating from the 17th century had just come to an end, but now "a new European colonising, colonial imperial nation appears on the continent of Africa, armed, aggressive, involved in the direct subversion upon the land and the people of Africa."

A European colonial power is back, a new colonial power mightier than any that ever preceded it. It has come with arms, its armies, with its technology, its ideology, and the recolonisation of Africa commences.

Mr Moynihan left his hearers in no doubt that the power he referred to was the Soviet Union. In another speech, he had said previously that even as the Soviet Union poured military supplies into Angola and in effect landed Cuban troops there, it was consolidating its military facilities on the North Eastern coast of

45

Africa—clearly a reference to the developing Soviet hold on Somalia.

Despite the growing volume of alarm voiced by Western and some African leaders, there was no sign whatever as 1975 closed that the Soviet Government intended to change its policy. On 27 December, for instance, the Soviet Government newspaper *Izvestia* in a long article stated:

> The events in Angola have shown once more that an anti-colonial revolution does not end with the achievement of independence. It has to be defended and carried forward.
>
> Hence, it is quite natural that assistance to the national liberation movement, MPLA, which has become the ruling party in the young independent state, should be continued.
>
> Some of the leading personalities in the US and other imperialist powers are trying to put at the Soviet Union's door the responsibility for the outbreak of the conflict in Angola, and accuse it of disturbing the "balance of power" in Southern Africa and pursuing a policy that is in "conflict" with the relaxation of tension.
>
> The Soviet Union and other countries of the Socialist community have been giving for many years, in accordance with UN decisions, political, moral, and material support to the armed struggle of the national liberation movements in Africa including the Popular Movement for the Liberation of Angola (MPLA) which proclaimed the People's Republic of Angola on 11 November.
>
> It can be said now that thanks to the staunchness of the MPLA fighters and assistance from the Socialist countries, the aggressors' plans to liquidate the People's Republic of Angola by blitzkrieg methods have been diverted.

Such words fitted well with reports of continuing Soviet deeds. Reports in the first week of January 1976 said that the MPLA forces had been heavily reinforced by the arrival of further contingents of Cuban troops who were then estimated to have totalled between 7 000 and 10 000. Heavy casualties were said to have been inflicted on the non-Communist forces by the Soviet-made surface-to-surface missiles which continued to reach the MPLA in large quantities.

In mid-January, a senior Cuban official was quoted in *The Guardian* as saying that his country would continue to send troops to Angola even if the Organisation of African Unity demanded an end to foreign intervention.

All these omens have added weight to the words of Mr Jonas Savimbi, leader of UNITA, one of the pro-Western Angolan groups in conflict with the MPLA, who said in December 1975:

> The face Russia is showing in Angola should be a warning to the continent. It should remind us of the Soviet intervention in Czechoslovakia and Hungary.
>
> This is a serious warning for Africa when, for the first time, Russia is not acting with caution at all. They are openly coming in, sending their arms and sending their personnel.
>
> They want to impose a government in Angola, the MPLA, so that they will have many advantages. They will be able to establish a naval base in Angola and from that they will be able to control the route round the Cape. They will force the African countries in this area which do not agree with the Soviet Union to come more and more on their side.[1]

One small indication of the increasing importance which Africa was coming to have in Soviet strategic thinking and planning, even before the collapse of Portuguese rule on the continent, was given in a Soviet publication which openly describes how Moscow plans to expand its influence.

The booklet concerned was published in 1974 by the Soviet *Novosti* news agency's publishing house and is entitled *Password "Anguimo"*. Written by three *Novosti* correspondents who had visited Moscow-backed "liberation armies", including the MPLA, in Angola, Moçambique and Portuguese Guinea.

The opening pages of the booklet state:

> Africa is a crucial area on the scene of the world national liberation movement. The post-war period has seen many African countries shaking off the fetters of colonialism and embarking on the road of independent national and social development. In 1973, the number of politi-

cally independent countries was 41. This has wrought significant changes in the political structure of the world and has upset the hitherto existing balance of forces, to the disadvantage of imperialism.

The historical process of Africa's decolonisation, however, has not ended. Angola, Moçambique, and Guinea-Bissau (formerly Portuguese Guinea) remain in Portugal's possession; the Republic of South Africa, Namibia, occupied by it, and Rhodesia, remain as much a land of white supremacy as ever ...

Openly or secretly backed by the imperialists of Western Europe and America, the ruling circles of Portugal, South Africa and Rhodesia have been bending every effort to retain these areas of colonialism and racialism. Portugal is still able to hold on to its colonies because of the assistance it receives from the NATO countries.

The imperialist powers regard the southern part of Africa as their principal bridgehead for attacking the independent African states. The military and strategic importance of this region has grown immeasurably of recent years following the closure of the Suez Canal.

The booklet then goes on to point out the importance of Southern Africa economically, saying:

South Africa, for instance, holds first place in the capitalist world's production of gold, platinum, manganese and chromites; second in the production of diamonds, and third in the uranium concentrates. Foreign investment there amounts to some 5 600 million dollars. British monopolies net something like 140 million dollars in yearly profits from South Africa, and the American monopolies, about 100 million.

In the same year, a Soviet African expert, E.A. Tarabin, wrote in a special study *The New Scramble for Africa* (Progress Publishers, Moscow, 1974, p. 149) of how important Africa was economically to the capitalist world as a source of raw materials. He predicted that this importance would be likely to increase sharply and that by 1980 deliveries of chromites from South Africa and Rhodesia to Western countries, for instance, would have risen from the 1,9 million t of

1970 to four million t; deliveries of iron ore from South Africa, Liberia and Mauritania would have increased from the 57,8 million t of 1970 to 80 million t, and supplies of bauxite from Guinea and Ghana from 2,2 million t to 15 million t.

Other Soviet comments over the last two or three years on the importance of Africa to the capitalist world have included an article in *Pravda* of 14 August 1976 in which the author, L. Valentinin, stated that:

> In US imports, the share of strategic raw materials imported from Africa amounts to 100 per cent of the industrial diamonds, 58 per cent of the uranium, 44 per cent of the manganese, which is used in the steel smelting industry, 36 per cent of the cobalt, essential for aircraft engines and high-strength alloys, 33 per cent of its oil and 23 per cent of its chromium, used in the manufacture of armour, aircraft engines and gun barrels.

It would be the greatest mistake, however, to regard Soviet interest in Africa at this time as being merely opportunist adventurism designed to fill the vacuum caused by the disappearance of Western colonial rule and the diminution of Western influence. Given all the circumstances, events in Angola, Somalia and all other areas of the continent, where the hand of the Soviet Union is plainly visible, should instead be seen as the logical consequences of policies first devised in the very early days following the Communist revolution in Russia, and pursued, notwithstanding a number of tactical shifts and turns, as part of a general plan to ensure the eventual triumph of "Socialism" throughout the world.

The importance of bringing about the collapse of Western colonialism and influence in what has come to be known as the Third World was, in fact, discussed by Lenin even some time before the revolution. In his book *Imperialism, the Highest Stage of Capitalism,* Lenin laid much stress on the value of colonial territories to the Democracies and examined the possible consequence of the collapse of the colonial system. He maintained that the governments of the industrial states of Western Europe were being more and more compelled to embark upon programmes of colonial expansion in order to create new markets in which to sell their goods and to find new sources of raw materials. Taking this view, he developed the theory that the search for these markets and raw materials and the

49

control of the inhabitants of the colonial and semi-colonial territories had become vital to the continued existence of the Democracies. From this it followed, he held, that if the colonies could be wrested out of colonial control, a mortal blow would have been struck to the whole capitalist system itself—thus easing the way for the ultimate victory of Communism.

The importance of spreading the revolutionary message amongst the peoples under colonial type rule was a theme encouraged by the Soviet revolutionaries even in the first few months after their own seizure of power in Moscow in the winter of 1917, despite their many preoccupations both at home and in Europe. For instance, on 7 December 1917, Lenin, then the first Chairman of the Council of People's Commissars, supported by Stalin who held the post of People's Commissar for Nationalities, issued an appeal to all "toiling Muslims in the East" (including those in Africa). The appeal outlined the course of the Soviet revolution and then went on to say:

> But Russia does not stand alone in this holy cause ... the workers and soldiers of the West are already flocking to the banner of Socialism and shaking the bastions of imperialism to their foundations. And far-away India, which has been enslaved for centuries by the modern robbers of Europe, has already raised the standard of revolt, in organising her Soviets, throwing off the hated chains of slavery and calling on the peoples of the East to fight for their freedom ... You are not threatened with oppression by Russia and her revolutionary Government, but by robber imperialism, which has turned your countries into impoverished and exploited colonies ... lose no time in shaking off the chains of oppression in your countries.[2]

One of Stalin's chief assistants, in those early days in his post of Commissar for Nationalities, was Sultan Galiyev. He came to be regarded as the Communists' first expert on Islam, and the relationship of Communism to the Third World. Before being dismissed from his post in 1923 and ultimately disappearing in the Stalin purges, he developed a line of propaganda which held that freedom for the colonial territories was not possible unless they adopted "Socialism" and that national and social revolution were inseparable.

In October 1918, Communists and Communist sympathisers from Asia, the Middle East and North Africa were called together to a conference in Moscow to discuss the practical problems involved in bringing about a "unification of the revolutionary forces of the East". This resulted in the formation of a League for the Emancipation of the East. However, for tactical reasons, it was decided to confine its activities for the time being to Asiatic Russia and the Middle East. Two years later, a move of considerably greater lasting significance was made in the shape of the holding of the First Congress of the Peoples of the East at Baku. Nearly 2 000 people attended this conference at which one of its main organisers, Mr Gregory Zinoviev, was said to have come near to making a call for a "holy war" against British Imperialism and to have stated:

> The real revolution will develop only when the eight hundred million inhabitants of Asia are united with us, when the African continent is united with us, when we see that hundreds of millions of people are on the move.

One of the most important tasks of the Baku conference was to find means of implementing the resolution on the national and colonial question which had been passed at the Second World Congress of the Comintern held just previously. This resolution was based upon a draft then prepared by Lenin and presented to the Congress by the Indian Communist, Mr Manabendra Nath Roy.

Lenin's thesis opined that European capitalism was mainly reliant for maintaining its strength not upon European countries but upon their colonial possessions. If it was to survive it must maintain control over these territories both as markets and fields for the exploitation of both labour and raw materials. In particular, he stated that Britain, which he described as the bulwark of imperialism, had been suffering from over-production for the last 100 years. He claimed that the loss of her colonial possessions, upon which she relied as markets for her goods and suppliers of raw materials, would mean that the capitalist system in Britain would collapse. In addition, he believed that the extra profits made by the colonial powers from their possessions were one of the main sources of the strength of the contemporary capitalist system. The destruction of the capitalist system in Europe, he claimed, would only be possible when it was no longer able to draw upon Third World resources.

However, in the 1920s, on the tactical side, the rôle of the Communists in colonial territories was laid down as entering into non-Communist nationalist organisations in order later to direct the course of their revolutions along Communist lines. Lenin made it very clear that the alliance with non-Communist elements was only to be of a temporary nature. He explained:

> The Communist International must support the bourgeois democratic national movements in colonial and backward countries only on condition that in all backward countries, the elements of future proletarian parties which are Communist not only in name, shall be grouped together and trained to appreciate their special tasks, viz, to fight the bourgeois-democratic movements within their own nations. The Communist International must enter into a temporary alliance with bourgeois democracy in colonial and backward countries, but must not merge with it and must under all circumstances preserve the independence of the proletarian movement, even if in its most rudimentary form.[3]

One of the first major steps taken towards aiding the spread of revolution in areas outside Europe was the setting up of special schools for the training of Communist supporters from them. One of the first of these was the Sun Yat-Sen University established in Moscow early in the 1920s. This was specially for members of the Chinese Communist Party. Prior to 1949, most Communist Chinese leaders and senior cadres were trained here.

Another of more direct relevance was the University of the Eastern Toilers established as early as the spring of 1921 in Tashkent. This was intended for the training of cadres from all colonial territories including Africa and Latin America. Four years later, Stalin claimed that there were about 10 different groups of students at the Eastern University who had come from colonial and semi-colonial territories. The syllabus included the history of the Communist Party and of the Soviet Union, the history of the colonial peoples, methods of revolutionary agitation and organisation to be used in developing countries, historical and dialectical materialism, and individual psychology and the psychology of

Eastern peoples.[4]

Stalin himself described the rôle of the university as being to forge its students into

> real revolutionaries, equip them with the theory of Leninism and with practical experience of Leninism and then enable them to carry out effectively the immediate tasks on their return to their own countries.[5]

He defined these tasks as being first to "win the best elements of the working class for the revolutionary movement and found independent Communist parties". Secondly, to organise a block of the workers, peasants and "revolutionary intellectuals" who would work against any form of alliance between the "national bourgeoisie" and "imperialism". Thirdly, to "establish the hegemony of the proletariat in the national revolutionary movement". He also advocated that they should strive to sever the urban and rural "petty bourgeoisie" from the influence of the "national bourgeoisie" who were the allies of "imperialism" and to bring about an alliance between the "national revolutionary movement" and the proletarian movement in the "progressive" (i.e. Communist) countries.

Stalin's views on the importance of working to fan the flames of revolution in colonial and other Third World countries in order to bring about the destruction of Western capitalism were just as clear cut as his predecessor in power, Lenin.

He stated:

> If Europe and America may be called the front, or the arena of the major battles between socialism and imperialism, the unequal nations and the colonies, with their raw materials, fuel, food and vast store of manpower, must be regarded as the rear, the reserve of imperialism. To win a war it is necessary not only to triumph at the front, but also to revolutionise the enemy's rear, his reserves. Hence the victory of the world proletarian revolution may be regarded as assured only if the proletariat is able to combine its own revolutionary struggle with the liberation movement of the labouring masses of the unequal nations and the colonies against the rôle of the imperialists and for the dictatorship of the proletariat.[6]

One aspect of the Soviet drive to destroy the Western colonial system and areas of Western influence now began to manifest itself for the first time. This was the organised effort to turn public opinion in the Western countries themselves against the whole concept of "imperialism", and the retention of colonial possessions. To this end, the Comintern employed the services of one who, from the early 1920s until the time he met a grisly, and still largely unexplained, death hanging from a tree in a French wood at the time of the German invasion in 1940, proved himself to be one of the ablest and most hard-working political organisers of the times—Willi Munzenberg.

Under Munzenberg's direction and inspiration, ever increasing numbers of Anti-Imperialist Leagues were formed throughout the Western world. At the beginning of 1927, representatives of these groups were brought together at The Congress against Colonial Oppression and Imperialism held in the Palais Egmont in Brussels. This event, skilfully stage-managed from behind the scenes by Munzenberg using funds supplied by the Comintern, succeeded, as the individual Anti-Imperialist Leagues had done, in attracting a considerable amount of non-Communist support, particularly from amongst prominent intellectuals of the day who did not realise the true nature of the directing force. Mr Fritz Schatten has recorded that the Congress:

> developed into a great protest against the colonial policy of the Western powers, while by way of contrast the anti-colonial attitude of the Soviet Union was lavishly praised.[7]

The theme of anti-colonialism was again paid great attention to at the Sixth Congress of the Comintern in Moscow in 1928. At this Congress, it was decided that the planning of activities directed towards countries with negro populations should be based upon the classification of these countries into three main groups. They comprised the colonial and semi-colonial territories in South Africa; Central Africa; and North, Central and South America. A call was made to the coloured population of the United States to pay special attention to the plight of "their brothers in Africa". A call that was to be taken up again by some American Black Power leaders 30-40 years later.

Despite the considerable attention paid to Africa, the Comintern's efforts reaped little in terms of lasting practical results. Mr George Padmore, for instance, the West Indian negro official charged with special responsibility for Africa, was able to achieve little progress apart from giving some assistance towards the establishment of the Communist Party of South Africa. One major reason for the lack of success of his efforts to extend Moscow's influence in Africa and many other areas outside Europe at that time, was the fact that very few Soviet officials had ever visited the countries which had now become the target of their endeavours or even had time or opportunity to study their affairs in any depth. It was a handicap which was to be rectified in a most marked manner at a later stage.

The late 1920s showed the highwater mark of the pre-war Soviet bid for influence in the Third World. From then until the outbreak of the Second World War, Soviet leaders became increasingly immersed in deepening troubles in Europe and for a time also their own internal difficulties. Individual Communists did, however, sometimes continue to engage in some revolts and disturbances in other non-European areas, sometimes in company with more than usually surprising allies. During the Arab rebellions of 1929 and 1936 in Palestine, their leader, Hadj Amin Al Heseni, ex-Mufti of Jerusalem, and a man of extreme right-wing and anti-Semitic views who was to spend much of the 1939-45 war years as an honoured guest in Nazi Germany, was supported in his efforts by two well-known Middle Eastern Communists, Mr Fuad Nasr and Mr Nimar Oda. Both these two acted as his advisers and performed liaison duties on his behalf.[8]

When Stalin and his ministers again had time to apply their minds to the renewal of the anti-imperialist offensive in 1947, the line of attack shifted significantly. In September of that year, Zhdanov made a major speech when addressing the Communist Information Bureau or Cominform (the short-lived successor to the Comintern which had been abolished as a gesture of goodwill to the Western wartime allies). Speaking to this body, Zhdanov presented the world with the allegedly unavoidable choice of either joining the camp of nations headed by the Soviet Union or the United States. There could, he said, be no question of "a middle way" or any possibility of adopting policies of such a type as that of "positive neutrality". This new harsh line from the Kremlin, which was to remain the hallmark of its policy throughout the Stalin era, was quickly echoed in its whole strategic approach to the anti-colonial campaign.[9]

Henceforward, the word went out that there was to be no more talk of co-operation, even of a temporary nature, with "bourgeois" nationalists. Instead, the whole emphasis must be on preparation for militant action and, wherever opportunity offered, armed revolt. It was maintained that this policy must be carried out even in former colonial territories which had already achieved their independence under "bourgeois" nationalist governments. Contempt was heaped upon non-Communist nationalist leaders. Mr Ghandi, for one, was described as a "traitor and demagogue" who had never been sincere about obtaining his country's independence. Leaders of such African nationalist movements as were then in existence were attacked as being "lickspittles" or "lackeys of colonialism".

One direct result of the new emphasis was the outbreak of armed revolts led by Communists or Communist sympathisers in the late 1940s in Indochina, Malaya, Burma, the Philippines and Indonesia. It was the eventual failure of all these revolts (save that in Indochina) plus the increasing number of colonial territories which had either obtained independence peacefully or were clearly approaching it by the mid-1950s that left the Communist Parties isolated. They were unable to play a significant part in the course of events which before very long necessitated a re-examination of their whole strategy.

Three years after the death of Stalin, at the 20th Congress of the Communist Party of the Soviet Union in 1956, Khruschev and his then Foreign Minister, Shepilov, amongst others, proposed a revision of the plans for fomenting colonial revolutions. Lengthy discussions followed on the subject of the usefulness and practicability of co-operation between Communists and non-Communists in the "national liberation movements".

It was at that Congress, too, that decisive new moves were decided upon to improve the amount of information available to the Soviet leaders and those serving under them about the countries of the Third World, particularly those in Africa. One then prominent member of the Soviet hierarchy, Anastas Mikoyan, made a blistering attack upon the existing channels of information available, saying sarcastically:

The Academy of Sciences does have an institute that

studies the problems of the East, but all that can be said of it is that although in our day the whole East has awakened, this institute is still dozing. Isn't it time for it to rise to the level of current requirements?[10]

On the policy side, the 1956 Congress was followed by a number of meetings of specialists. One of particular importance took place in Moscow in 1957 and was attended by experts from Communist China in addition to those from the Soviet Union. At its conclusion, an important declaration was issued which attempted to provide answers to some of the important questions raised at the 20th Party Congress. The statement read:

> 1. Communism recognises the objective advantage of the Afro-Asian movement for independence because, although the existence of new, independent states does not subjectively facilitate the victory of Communism, it objectively weakens imperialism.
> 2. The socialist camp, as the natural partner of the new states of Asia and Africa, desires to consolidate the independence of these new states by means of improved diplomatic, economic, and cultural relations, and thus free them from the pressure of Western imperialism and of Western capital.
> 3. The struggle of many peoples for their national independence against colonial aggression and feudal oppression makes it necessary to form an anti-imperialist and anti-feudalist united front of the workers and peasants, the urban petty-bourgeoisie and other patriotic and democratic forces.[11]

This declaration in effect marked a reversion to the pre-1947 policy under which Communists in colonial countries were instructed to concentrate, for the time being, on helping the efforts of "bourgeois nationalists" and "liberation movements" instead of initiating armed action on their own.

Meanwhile, a general overhaul of the Soviet governmental machinery for implementing policy towards Africa was proceeding. Before 1957, the Soviet Foreign Ministry had had no department devoted entirely to African affairs. The British colonies in Africa, for instance, came under the brief of the Ministry's Second European Department which also dealt with Britain itself. This department also concerned itself to some extent with African territories bordering British colonies, but the remainder of the continent came under the jurisdiction of the Near and Middle Eastern Department. In 1968, however, a special African Department was established within the Ministry. A new programme of research work on African affairs was introduced utilising some already existing state-controlled institutes. That on North Africa was carried out by institutes concerned with Oriental research whilst Black African affairs were investigated by the orthographical department of the Academy of Sciences. Soviet academics have always made it clear that the main aim of researches by such institutes was to provide material to assist in the forming and implementation of government policy. The Director of the Moscow Oriental Institute, Professor Gaforov, is, for example, on record as stating in an article that because of "the growing political and world economic importance of Africa" the task of the institute is to "publish works of importance for the educational institutions and governmental departments engaged in the practical tasks in the East".

The most important and far-reaching action taken in the overhaul of Soviet African policy making, however, was the setting up in 1957 of a separate Africa Institute dedicated to research work under the direction of the late Professor Ivan Potekhin, a veteran African expert who had been imparting instructions to members of the Communist Party of South Africa at the well-known Lenin school in Moscow as early as 1931. Mr Moses Kotane, a leading member of the South African Communist Party who became its Secretary-General, was one of his pupils. Mr Kotane later said of him:

> I came to know him well both as a man and a talented young scholar. Afterwards I met him many times in Moscow, in Africa, and at the Africa Institute where he was Director.
> We used to have long and very interesting talks and each time he revealed a deep understanding of the most complex problems of South Africa. His great scientific contribution lies in the fact that he was one of the first scientists who approached these problems from the

Marxist standpoint at a time when bourgeois science dominated in African studies. The creation of a group on African studies in Moscow and the subsequent foundation of the Africa Institute marked the appearance of the Soviet Marxist School of Africanists. Potekhin has also made a great scientific contribution to that development.[12]

Soon after its foundation, the new Africa Institute in Moscow embarked upon a comprehensive research programme. This programme had three main objects. Firstly, it was to undertake a general objective study of African problems of all types including those of a cultural, linguistic and social, as well as of a political nature with the object of transmitting to appropriate government departments reliable information on which to base decisions. Secondly, to provide a Marxist-Leninist interpretation of both past and present African problems, and so enable Communist theory about African affairs and Communist propaganda directed towards Africa to be put forward in a "scientific" manner. Thirdly, to provide Marxist-Leninist solutions which could be offered to élite African circles in a manner best calculated to ensure their acceptance.

In addition to being director of the Africa Institute, Professor Potekhin also became prominent in a number of new bodies formed specially to promote Soviet interests in Africa. He was Chairman of the Soviet Society for the Furtherance of Friendship with the Peoples of Africa and a member of the committee of the Soviet Afro-Asian Solidarity Committee. Most importantly, his influence was also strengthened by the fact that he became chief adviser to the Soviet Foreign Ministry on all African affairs.

Addressing a meeting of the Soviet Afro-Asian Solidarity Committee in 1959 he said:

I venture to appeal to all African people to unite ... remember in your sacred struggles you are not alone ... The people of my country, the Soviet Union, have always come out in favour of the right of nations to self-determination and national independence.[13]

Writing in *Izvestia* early in 1960, Potekhin said that the Africa

> deal with a wide range of problems directly connected with the struggle of the African people for independence, for emancipation from the chains of imperialism, and for the formation of sovereign independent states ... The activity of the Institute will support the extension and consolidation of friendly relations between the Soviet Union and the countries of Africa, while at the same time acquainting the Soviet people more closely with the history and culture of the African continent, which is now advancing vigorously towards complete emancipation from the yoke of the imperialist colonialists.[14]

By 1960, the results of Potekhin's Institute researches were already starting to attract increasing notice and to make a greater impact on Soviet policies. These results were condensed into a virtual blueprint for a diplomatic offensive. In the spring of that year, he produced a report under which the African countries were divided into four categories, for each of which a different approach was recommended. These categories being:

1. African countries which had already obtained independence. In those it was recommended that the Soviet approach should be concentrated upon attempts to influence foreign policy, political alignment and economic policy.
2. Countries whose independence was obviously imminent and where the possible use of violence could no longer be considered. Here it was thought that the main form of Soviet activity should be carried out through front organisations.
3. Countries whose independence was not imminent and in which outbreaks of violence were likely to succeed and should be encouraged.
4. Countries in which the struggle to change the status quo had not yet started.[15]

Mr Potekhin also developed his theories in a book *Africa Looks to the Future*. In this, he stressed that Soviet policy would have to be flexible enough to allow Marxist principles to be adapted to local conditions. However, he also made plain his belief that Marxism-Leninism could become the "guiding star" of Africa despite all difficulties.

Mr Potekhin placed great emphasis on the importance of the Soviet Union's securing a dominating influence over the economic planning of African countries as a priority task. He also advocated that attention should be paid to destroying the cultural heritage passed on to newly independent countries by their former rulers. Mr Pieter Lessing, author of *Africa's Red Harvest,* comments:

> In short, what he advocates is a sustained allegation that the colonial powers destroyed a high African civilisation which, with the help of the Soviet Union, is there for the Africans to regain.[16]

With the appearance of the first of Potekhin's reports and to a large extent the adoption of his advice by his masters, the Soviet offensive, aimed at expelling the last remnants of colonial rule from Africa, got well and truly under way. It has been an offensive in which all the many weapons and tactics of modern propaganda and political warfare, and in some cases subversive warfare, have been employed to the full. The manner in which they have been employed over the years is described to some degree in the following chapters of this study.

As far as the general direction of Soviet policy has been concerned during the last 15 years, perhaps the most striking element, particularly in view of current events in Southern Africa, has been the increasing blatancy with which Soviet authorities have stressed their whole-hearted support for the "liberation movements" and "armed struggle", despite all the talk of peaceful co-existence and détente elsewhere in the world.

Thus in October 1965, despite the turmoil caused in Africa by Rhodesia's unilateral declaration of independence, the Soviets still preferred to move cautiously and adopt a "low profile". A leading article in *Pravda* warned "the young nation states" (of Africa) that the USSR could not "take their place" in solving their national liberation tasks. It stated that any such action by the Soviet Union would carry the risk with it of "world thermonuclear war".[17] Six years later, however, a leader in the important Moscow monthly publication, *International Affairs,* which appeared just before the 24th Congress of the Communist Party of the Soviet Union at which the Soviet Union's current alleged "peace programme" was launched, made it clear that "extremely important spheres of international relations" were to be excluded from "peaceful co-existence" and these exceptions included the activities of "liberation movements", "international class struggle" and "the confrontation of ideology".[18] The Soviet Union, the article stated, would "as before, unswervingly support the people's struggle for democracy, national liberation and socialism".

An interesting illustration from a Moscow source indicative of such open pledges is that of Mr Brezhnev who stated:

> The peoples of the last colonies are waging a heroic, and often armed struggle for their liberation. Soviet Communists fully support this just struggle.[19]

These were not just idle words for in a book written by two Soviet journalists after a visit they had paid to the MPLA in Angola in 1972, they stated:

> There is in Moscow, in Kropotkin Street, a building of unpretentious proportions. In it is located the Soviet Committee for Solidarity with Asian and African countries. People don't all fully realise what an intense and rewarding amount of work in organising assistance to the peoples fighting for their liberation goes on in this building. Here they discuss the plan for the admission of new students from Africa; arrange with the various departments concerned about the despatch of clothing and medical supplies to the liberated areas of Angola; and organise seminars and conferences and exhibitions and reports about the struggle of the peoples in the colonies. And they're also occupied with dozens and hundreds of other matters integrally linked with the noble word "solidarity".
>
> The Solidarity Committee is only one small unit amongst the groups directly concerned with aid to the fighting people of Angola. Ships sail from Soviet ports to Africa carrying various cargoes, and among them are many shipments addressed to the MPLA. The partisans assail an enemy garrison with weapons in their hands sent from our country to the fighters for freedom. That is

the way the first country of socialism is fulfilling its international duty.[20]

The booklet published by the *Novosti* News Agency, *Password Anguimo,* mentioned earlier, also stressed the amount of material aid being sent from the Soviet Union to guerrilla movements in Portuguese Africa prior to the ending of the campaign against Portuguese rule. The author wrote:

> The Soviet Union's material assistance to the national revolutionary parties and their armed forces is considerable. It supplies military equipment, means of transport, hospital equipment, medical supplies, dressing materials, foodstuffs and consumer goods to the liberation forces, to the population in the liberated areas, and to refugees ...
> Soviet public organisations such as the Afro-Asian Solidarity Committee, the All-Union Central Council of Trade Unions, the Committee of Youth Organisations, and the Women's Committee have also been playing an important part in the active support of the national liberation movements. Their yearly shipments of foodstuffs, clothing, footwear, fabrics, medical supplies and medical equipment, cars, etc., to these countries are enormous.[21]

With the almost complete disappearance of colonialism from Africa and other areas of the world, increasing hints are being dropped by Soviet sources that new "liberation" struggles may well become necessary against "neo-colonialism" or "imperialist lackeys" and "feudal" or "capitalist" elements in the newly independent countries. Another *Novosti* booklet published in 1975 stated that:

> As the national liberation movement gains momentum the struggle for national liberation will grow increasingly into the struggle against the exploiter forces, both the feudal and capitalist ones, in the Third World countries. Of great importance for rebuffing imperialism, frustrating its conspiracies and preserving the gains of the national liberation movement is the alliance with the socialist countries and with the international Communist

movement.[22]

The same booklet records that

> in the opinion of Communists, one of the tangible results
> of détente for the liberation movements is that now US
> imperialism cannot interfere in the affairs of other
> countries so freely as it did not so long ago ...

The precise relationship between the threat of the use of force and
such matters as the supply of military aid to the "liberation
movements" as well as many other means of exerting political
pressure on the outside world, have been a subject of intense
discussion by Soviet experts since the early 1970s. These discussions
are of a very much more sophisticated and far-reaching nature than
those which set the pattern for Soviet policy during the 1960s. To
aid in such discussions and provide a ground for decision-making,
not only have new research institutes, such as the Institute of the
USA and the Far East Institute been established, but the work of
existing ones has been directed to the practical study of current
world political and military problems and the publication of studies
on these subjects to a greater degree than ever before.

The impressive amount of attention and research being paid to
Africa and the question of Soviet aid to movements engaged in
"armed struggle" was illustrated in 1974 by the publication of a
major work of over 440 pages entitled *The Armed Struggle of the Peoples
of Africa for Freedom and Independence.* This detailed study was compiled
by a team of writers from the Institute of Military History of the
Soviet Ministry of Defence, in collaboration with other experts from
the Africa Institute and the Institute of Social Sciences. The authors
made the attitude of the Soviet Government on the main subject of
their work perfectly clear:

> The Soviet Union battles persistently for international
> recognition of the lawfulness of armed struggle by
> colonial peoples and recognition of their right to self-
> defence and of the principle of legality and justice, of aid
> and support to peoples waging a war for national
> independence. The Soviet Union and the brotherly
> socialist countries have given and continue to give the

peoples of Africa continuous military and economic aid and political support in their sacred struggle against their oppressors. The internationalist stand of the USSR in their quest is formulated in the CPSU programme: "The CPSU and the entire Soviet people will continue to take action against all aggressive wars, including wars between capitalist states, and against local wars directed to the suppression of popular movements for liberation, and they regard it as their duty to support the sacred struggle of oppressed peoples and their just liberation wars against imperialism."[23]

The authors went on to make a careful analysis of the type of "struggles" or insurgency likely to occur in Africa. At the lowest end of their scale came revolts such as that which occurred in Madagascar in 1947 or Angola in 1961. These they consider as occurrences which had only "an amorphous military organisation" and lacked any central political leadership. Secondly, came those which were better organised but had no properly worked out political purpose. Into this category, they put such affairs as the Mau Mau revolt in Kenya in 1952.

Thirdly, there were revolts such as Lumumba's in the Congo which had an "attractive" political programme but not the political or military organisation or unity to enable them to succeed. The two highest categories consist of armed risings led by a "political front" type party such as the Algerian FLN, where it was held success depended upon satisfactory relations between the "front-party" and the armed wing of the movement, and finally:

National liberation wars headed by revolutionary democratic parties with a relatively high level of political and military leadership and firm links with the masses.

Into this highest category of "liberation movements" came—according to these Soviet experts—the PAIGC in Guinea-Bissau, the MPLA in Angola, Frelimo in Moçambique, the ANC in South Africa and ZAPU in Rhodesia.

They believe that the fighting ability of movements in this category "is determined to a significant degree by the approximation of their leaderships' views on Marxist-Leninist ideology and

65

their co-operation with Communist Parties and Marxist-Leninist groups".[25]

In addition to the research being done on the "armed struggle" and the most profitable ways of supporting it, from the Soviet Union's point of view, a critical examination has also been made of ways and means of furthering the task of increasing Soviet political and economic influence in African countries. Setbacks suffered by the Soviet Union in the early 1960s in Guinea, Ghana, Mali, etc. were followed by intense, and almost introspective, ideological discussion and argument in Soviet Party and political research circles, about how far African leaderships, parties and movements could be expected to approximate to certain Soviet political and ideological ideals. These ideals were exhaustively defined and redefined. A pronouncement in a Party publication in October 1975 would seem to summarise the position as regards the present official Soviet position on the precise nature of the régimes it hopes to see develop in Africa as a first step towards "building socialism" in that continent.

> The decisive requirements for the successful preparation of the preconditions for building a socialist society must be public ownership of the tools and means of production, the bringing of the broad popular masses into government of the society and the state, and the presence of an alert and organised vanguard in the person of a Marxist-Leninist Party. "There is not and cannot be socialism", L.I. Brezhnev had said, "without the directing rôle of a Communist Party armed with the ideals of Marxist-Leninism and proletarian internationalism."[25]

Fundamental to Soviet statements on Africa at the present time is the "two roads theory", i.e. that each newly independent African state has the choice of taking the "capitalist road" taken by such countries as Malawi, Tunisia, Liberia, the Ivory Coast, Morocco, Senegal, etc., or the "non-capitalist"—meaning "socialist"—road. According to this theory, those countries which take the "capitalist road" run the danger of submitting themselves to a "constant inflow of foreign capital" and becoming "constant suppliers of raw materials". This, it is maintained, will perpetuate their "lop-sided economic pattern", and "result in increased dependence on the capitalist world, dependence which constantly threatens to batter the young states' economies in view of the mounting crisis in the West". It is also said that their ties with capitalism will act as a bar to any attempt on their part to "radically solve their complicated social problems".

Those countries, however, which take the "non-capitalist path" which leads in the end to "socialism" are said to be acting in tune with ideas with which "millions upon millions of Africans associate their hopes for a better future" because "the historical development of independent Africa inevitably leads its people to acceptance of the socialist idea". Examples of countries which have taken the "non-capitalist road" are cited as being Algeria, Guinea, Somalia, Tanzania, the Congo (Brazzaville), Guinea-Bissau and Moçambique.

That any African country which takes the "non-capitalist" path can look for a reward in the shape of support and protection from the Soviet Union and its allies is nowadays being made increasingly clear. A typical passage from a Soviet source is found in a *Novosti* booklet, *Africa Makes a Choice*, published in the last half of 1975. The relevant passage ran:

> The adoption of a socialist orientation is conditioned by both external and internal factors. The formation of the world socialist system and its strengthening and emergence as the decisive factor in the development of human society constitutes a constant external factor facilitating the adoption of such an operation. For the newly liberated countries, the socialist community fulfils the rôle of the international proletarian vanguard—on account of its strength, the model it provides and the necessary support it offers to the people of these countries (repelling counter-revolution exported by imperialism, rendering economic and technical aid, and so on). This enables the young states to develop in the non-capitalist direction despite counteraction by imperialism.[26]

The Chinese Enigma

Contact between China and Africa existed as far back as the 14th century when the famous Chinese explorer, Cheng Ho, delighted the Emperor, Yung-Lo, by bringing back a giraffe which so charmed the latter that he received it in the "Hall of Receptions". Cheng Ho's voyages down the East African coast took him as far south as Zanzibar and during them he received valuable "tributes" from the local inhabitants, including gold, ivory and tortoise shell. Sometimes he would also bring back Africans known as "Devil Slaves" to serve in the Imperial Chinese Court. In 1411, the ruler of Egypt sent emissaries to the Chinese court complete with gifts of various kinds including mules and horses. From then on until the 1950s, however, it would appear there was little official recorded contact at government level between China and any African country. Curiously enough after this 500-year gap, Egypt was to figure prominently at the beginning of China's post-revolutionary interest in Africa, almost two decades ago.

A few African nationalist politicians had visited China even before the Communist forces had finally consolidated their victory in that country. For instance, Mr Walter Sisulu, then Secretary-General of the African National Congress of South Africa, visited Peking after the Soviet-inspired World Youth Festival of 1953. Most of the few contacts there were at that time between African and Chinese politicians took place at such festivals, rallies and conferences run by the various well-known international Communist front organisations, with their headquarters in Eastern Europe. In 1955, however, came a different occasion which was to prove a particularly important one for the forming of new links between China and Africa. That was the First Asian-African Conference held in Bandung, Indonesia, in April 1955.

Twenty-nine countries took part in that conference, of which seven were African states. These being Egypt, Ethiopia, the Gold Coast (Ghana), Liberia, Libya and the Sudan. The Egyptian delegation was led by President Nasser, whilst the Chinese delegation was led by the Prime Minister, Chou En-lai, himself. Friendly contacts between the Chinese and Egyptian delegations soon developed and these led to discussions about the possibility of developing trade between the two countries. When at the end of the conference, Chou En-lai invited any delegates who wished to do so to visit China, two members of the Egyptian delegation were the only ones from Africa to accept, and further discussion on trade took place in Peking. The Chinese delegation was also, however, able to make other useful contacts, including some with members of African nationalist movements which were already thinking about the possibility of armed revolt. One leading member of such a movement, present as an observer, was Mr Moses Kotane, of the South African ANC, who later was to become head of his organisation's office in Dar es Salaam.

As the result of the preparatory talks held at Bandung and in Peking, a Chinese trade office was opened in Cairo by the end of the year. This new commercial link came at a particularly valuable time for Egypt, as just previously the country had suffered a severe economic blow in the shape of a refusal by Western buyers to purchase—at the price asked—the cotton crop upon which Egypt was dependent for 80% of her export earnings. Both China and the Soviet Union now gave timely offers of help.

Diplomatic relations were established between China and Egypt in May 1956. The importance attached to this event by the Chinese Government was shown by the high ranks of the first Ambassador it appointed to Cairo, Chen Chia-Kang, formerly Assistant Minister for Foreign Affairs, and of his deputy, Chang Yueh, formerly deputy director of the West European and African Affairs division of the Peking Foreign Ministry. For a time, the embassy in Cairo became the main base for the expansion of Chinese influence in Africa. The work of the diplomats stationed there was supplemented by the arrival of an increasing number of Chinese delegations on visits to African countries.

During 1956 and 1957, Chinese delegations visited Ethiopia, Morocco, the Sudan, Tunisia and Ghana. A member of the Chinese Communist Party's Central Committee, Jung-Chen, the first member of that committee ever to visit Africa south of the Sahara, led a delegation to the Ghanaian independence celebrations in that country in March 1957. At the same time, a considerable traffic began from Africa to China. Visitors from Libya, Nigeria, Senegal and South Africa all went to Peking.

Only a week after the first Chinese Ambassador had taken up his post in Cairo, President Nasser nationalised the Suez canal, thus setting in train the events which were to culminate in the Anglo-French landings in Suez in the autumn of 1956. During the crisis, China sent messages of support to Egypt and in November offered a £1.8 million loan. More important, however, was the effect that the failure of the Anglo-French venture, coupled with the successful launching of the first Soviet space satellite, had on the minds of Chinese leaders. The lesson they thought they saw clearly was that the control of events was rapidly passing from the hands of the "imperialists", thus giving greatly increased opportunity for members of the "socialist camp" to advance their cause. At the Moscow celebrations to mark the 40th anniversary of the Russian Revolution in November, Mao Tse-tung made a celebrated speech in which he said:

> It is my opinion that the international situation has reached a turning-point. There are two winds in the world today, the East wind and the West wind. There is a Chinese saying "Either the East wind prevails over the West wind or the West wind prevails over the East wind". I believe it is characteristic of the situation today that the East wind prevails over the West wind.[27]

These thoughts were put into even plainer words by Prime Minister Chou En-lai addressing the National People's Congress in Peking in February 1958:

> A decisive change has taken place in the international situation that favours our socialist construction, the socialist camp, the cause of world peace, and the progress of mankind ... Everybody can now see that, compared with the imperialist camp, our socialist camp has definitely gained supremacy in population and popular support ... Even the imperialist aggressors cannot but admit that they stand before an invincible socialist camp headed by the Soviet Union, stronger and more united than ever before.[28]

The tribute to unity under the leadership of the Soviet Union now appears to be somewhat ironic, in view of the bitter quarrels which broke out between China and the Soviet Union a very few years later. There is some reason to doubt the sincerity of the remark, even at the time it was made, for the Chinese authorities were later to trace the origins of their dispute with the Soviet Union back to two years earlier, 1956. However, there would seem to be no doubt that these two speeches did usher in a new period in which Chinese leaders became so convinced of the growing military and economic superiority of the "socialist camp" that they felt it was perfectly safe for the countries within it to proceed with the work of fomenting worldwide revolution, free from any serious threat of Western interference.

The Chinese leaders had increasingly come to look on their own successful revolution as the most promising model for the development of events throughout the Third World. As far back as 1951, for instance, Lu Ting-yi, a leading propagandist for Mao Tse-tung's Government, had claimed that the Chinese revolution was a classic example of the sort of revolution that should take place in colonial and semi-colonial countries and that "Its experience is of incalculable value to the peoples of such countries".[29]

From 1958 onwards, Chinese propaganda began to adopt increasingly the line already urged by the Soviet Union many years previously. This was that revolution in one area such as Africa should not just be regarded as an end in itself, but as an act which formed part of a worldwide onslaught against "imperialism". Just after the close of the First Conference of African States in Accra in April 1958, the Chinese journal *Jen-min Jih-pao*, stated in an editorial:

> The awakened African people are concerned not only with African affairs but also with the destiny of the whole world. Events in Africa once again show that the anti-imperialist national independence movement is a force of peace. The African people have emerged in the international political arena as a new force for peace ... No matter what obstruction and interference the colonialists resort to, the torchlight of independence and freedom in the hands of the African people will illuminate their broad future. The bright future of Africa knows no bounds.[30]

At the same time, there began to develop in Peking the policy that before long was to do so much to bring the dispute with the Soviet Union into the open. This policy was based on the thesis that there could be no thought of co-existence between Communist and non-Communist countries until all the peoples "oppressed" by "imperialism" had secured their freedom and "imperialism" itself had been destroyed.

Meanwhile on the practical plane, rising Chinese interest in Africa was reflected in a very noticeable increase in the flow of delegations from and to China. Eighteen African delegations visited China in 1958, 39 in 1959 and 88 in 1960.

By 1960, the decolonisation of Africa was in full swing and the chaos that followed the granting of independence to the Belgian Congo that summer was about to provide both China and the Soviet Union with the first "promising" situation south of the Sahara in which to try and further their aims. To aid its efforts in expanding its influence in Africa, the Chinese administration now began to establish a more elaborate machinery. Mr Pieter Lessing records that new organisations set up at that time included the National Afro-Asian Solidarity Committee in April 1960. The Chairman of this, Liao Cheng-Chih, was also First Secretary of the overseas operations department of the Chinese Communist Party. In addition, there was created the Chinese-Africa People's Friendship Society in April 1960 and the Special Committee on Relations with the Peoples of Africa. A special committee to co-ordinate the work of these various committees was also apparently established.

As far as government ministries were concerned, the Ministry of Foreign Affairs had, in September 1956, transferred responsibility for African affairs from the West European and African Affairs Department to a newly created department to be known as the West Asian and African Affairs Department. Later on in 1964, this department was subdivided into separate North African and West African Departments, an African Affairs Department and a West Asian Department. Another official instrument for aiding the implementation of foreign policy towards Africa was the Commission on Cultural Relations with Foreign Countries. Until the beginning of 1964, the African affairs side of its work was handled by the Asian and African Affairs Department. It was then taken over by a newly formed African Affairs Department which was divided into three sections, one dealing with English-speaking African countries, one with French-speaking and one with Arabic-speaking African countries.

Three other bodies, the Asia-Africa Society, the Research Institute on International Relations of the Academy of Sciences, and the International Relations Institute are believed to have given some aid in research on African problems. In addition, from the early

72

1960s onwards, the Chinese Government has made considerable use of the various so-called "public bodies" under its control in its penetration of Africa. These include such organisations as the All-China Federation of Literacy and Art Circles, the All-China Athletic Association, the Political Science and Law Association of China, the China Islamic Association, and the All-Chinese Journalists' Association.

The year 1960 also saw the appearance of a new argument increasingly used by Peking propagandists to attract the support of African peoples. This being that both China and Africa shared a history of exploitation by the same imperialist powers and both had suffered the degrading insult of being regarded as inferior races by the same White people. Since China had freed herself from exploitation through revolution and had emerged as a modern socialist state, it was, therefore, in a unique position to understand the feelings and problems of Africans and lead them towards salvation and victory over their enemies. Parallel with this argument ran a second one: namely, that China, being a Third World country herself, had a much greater affinity with Africa than any other White outsider, the implication being that other outsiders included the Soviet Union as well as the Western powers.

The central message of Chinese propaganda began to emerge even more clearly as the 1960s opened, namely that 'armed struggle" or revolution was the only means of defeating "imperialism". The possibilities China then saw opening up before it in Africa were summarised in an edition of the Chinese Peoples' Liberation Army, *Kung-tso T'ung hsun,* and were quoted by the American author Bruce D. Larkin:

> Among the independent countries in Africa, if only one or two of them complete a real national revolution, solving their own problems of resisting imperialism and reaching an internal solution of a democratic national revolution, the effect will be very great. The time is ripe for action, the revolutionary wave will be able to swallow the whole African continent and the 200 million and more Africans will advance to the forefront of the world. We should take a long-range view of this problem.[31]

The same article maintained that Africa was the centre of the

73

anti-colonial struggle and also the arena in which East and West would fight for control of the "intermediate zone": the power bloc that gained control of that zone controlling the world. It was held that the "rightist" leadership of some African countries would be overthrown by revolutionary struggle. Every effort should, therefore, be made to instruct the African people in the details of the Chinese revolution "in order to reveal the true nature of both new and old colonialism".[32] Enemies of revolutionary policies who could not be attacked as White supremacists were to be labelled as equally evil "neo-colonialists".

A further impetus to Chinese efforts in Africa was the eventual triumph of the FLN forces over French rule in Algeria, an event that just preceded Chou En-lai's tour of Africa at the end of 1963 and the beginning of 1964. To the Chinese leaders and propagandists, this victory not only seemed to prove that Africa was indeed ready for revolution but also that they were correct in their proclaimed belief that "armed struggle" was the only means by which imperialism could be vanquished. These sentiments were summed up in a message to Algeria's first President, Ben Bella, from the Chinese Government in March 1962.

> Algeria's independence ... shows that the people of Algeria and those of the rest of Africa are invincible and that imperialism and colonialism, old and new, can be defeated. The brilliant example set by the heroic Algerian people is sure to help to bring about a further upsurge in the national independence struggle in Africa.[33]

Chou En-lai's tour encompassed visits to Egypt, Algeria, Morocco, Tunisia, Ghana, Mali, Sudan, Ethiopia, Somalia and Tanzania. The tour was clearly intended to set the seal of approval from the highest level on the work already done by Chinese missions and agents of various kinds, and to mark the opening of a full-scale campaign to make China the central driving force behind revolution in Africa.

One major difference between the Chinese and Soviet approach was the growing Chinese conviction that the colonial and ex-colonial territories and the Third World in general did not form just the "rear areas" or reserves of "imperialism", as Stalin had believed, but actually constituted the main front upon which the decisive battles between "imperialism" and the "socialist camp" would have to be fought. A theory was developed in which the Western "imperialist" countries came to be compared with the cities of the world, while revolutionary guerrillas operated in the Third World, which represented the countryside.

Mao Tse-tung had maintained in his writings that if guerrillas could obtain control of the countryside in a nation, the cities and towns would be isolated and denuded of vital supplies and so surrender, almost of their own accord. Similarly, so Chinese strategists now began to say, if the countries of the Third World could be won over to the "socialist camp" then the Western powers would correspondingly become isolated and bereft of vital raw materials, and so ultimately fall almost without a struggle.

During his tour of Africa, Chou En-lai made several pronouncements which seemed aimed at exhorting the African people on to the utmost efforts in the cause of armed revolution. In Mogadishu, for instance, he said:

> The African continent which has given birth to a brilliant, ancient civilisation and suffered from the most cruel colonial aggression and plunder, is now undergoing earth-shaking changes. More than 30 African countries have become independent, and African peoples still under political oppression and partition are waging heroic struggles to win independence and freedom. Revolutionary prospects are excellent throughout the African continent.[34]

Visiting Dar es Salaam in 1965, he was even more explicit and made it clear that he regarded the African revolution, although important in itself, as being also part of events of much wider scope. He explained that:

> An exceedingly favourable situation for revolution prevails today, not only in Africa, but also in Asia and Latin America. The national liberation movement in Africa converging with that in Asia and Latin America has become a mighty torrent pounding with great momentum on the foundations of the rule of imperia-

lism, colonialism, and neo-colonialism. The revolutionary storms in these areas are vividly described in Chairman Mao Tse-Tung's famous verses: "The four seas are seething, clouds pouring and waters raging, the five continents are rocked by storm and thunder."[35]

Yet, although there is little doubt about the long-term serious intent behind such fiery words and others of similar vein frequently uttered by Chinese spokesmen down the years (often scornfully dismissed as mere "incantations" by Moscow and its supporters), it would seem that Chinese policy has—particularly of late—been conducted in a considerably more cautious manner in practice.

Certainly Chinese planners are under no illusions as to the shortcomings of some of the elements claiming to be acting in furtherance of the revolutionary cause on the African continent. Even in 1961 when China was still comparatively new to African affairs and was in the early stages of the long drawn-out attempt to obtain a dominating influence in the Congo, a country which it has regarded as being the key to Africa, a secret Chinese report which fell into Western hands revealed both the thoroughness and degree of caution with which Chinese analysts were going about their work. In this report it was stated that:

> At present, the national liberation movement of the Congo is mainly led by the capitalist (bourgeois) nationalist elements. Among them wavering and compromise prevail and so they cannot undertake correct and firm leadership. The strength of the nationalist party is also scattered and there is no single force which can unite the whole country. ... The scope of activities (of political parties) is limited to one place and they are in continuous process of splitting up.[36]

Until the latter part of the 1960s, there is no doubt that China nonetheless did attempt to affect the drift of the tide of events in Africa through the use of subversion and attempts to instigate armed revolt in a fairly widespread fashion. Thereafter, however, such operations appear to have been conducted on a considerably more selective basis and more cautiously. The reason for this change of policy was probably threefold.

Firstly, Chinese attempts at subversion in the early and mid-1960s resulted in a number of extremely embarrassing situations in the relationships between various Chinese and African governments being brought about and caused the closure of a number of Chinese embassies. This was a more than usually important loss in view of the vital rôle such bases played in the whole Chinese operation in Africa. Secondly, the planning and administration of overseas operations in Peking was seriously disturbed by the tumultuous years of Cultural Revolution. Thirdly, increasing rivalry with the Soviet Union and fears of Soviet expansionism led to a considerable part of the Chinese effort (particularly as regards intelligence operations, for instance) being diverted to watching, and on occasions, trying to block Soviet moves.

Considerable quantities of Chinese arms and other military supplies have reached some "liberation movements", particularly the one led by Gizenga in the Congo and some in Southern Africa, over the last 16 years or so. China has also played a significant part in the training of guerrillas. However, the burden of the available evidence would seem to show that despite some dramatic reports early on, probably caused by the sheer novelty of the involvement of China in an area so far outside its own boundaries such as Africa, the actual volume of supplies despatched to the "liberation movements" in general is not, and never has been, equal to that supplied by the Soviet bloc. The one important exception to this rule is probably that of Frelimo in Moçambique which for a number of years received aid mainly from China. However, Soviet aid and influence later became paramount here.

General Chinese policy towards the question of support for the "liberation movements" and other revolutionary organisations in Africa at the beginning of the 1970s was summarised by Mr Bruce Larkin in the following manner. If a "liberation movement" adopted a pro-Soviet attitude, China would probably give aid to a competing one if one existed in a viable form. If a certain group was the only revolutionary organisation operating in a certain territory, China would probably give it some aid, even though it was also receiving aid from the Soviet Union.

In countries where two or more movements were operating and refused to form a united front, China would probably try and keep in contact with factions in each group.

Communist China would, however, appear to be—any way at the

77

present stage—reluctant to become involved, even by proxy, in actual military conflict between pro-Soviet and anti-Soviet "liberation movements". Chinese aid given to Mr Holden Roberto's FNLA during the 1975/76 fighting in Angola appears to have been hesitant, scanty, and quickly terminated when it became clear that the Soviet-backed MPLA was likely to emerge as the victor.

In general, Communist Chinese policy in Africa over the last two or three years has come to reflect increasingly the general Peking strategy of attempting to mobilise the countries of the Third World into a form of united front. The aim of this being first of all to put economic and other forms of pressure on the industrialised, but now medium-sized, powers of Western Europe and similar countries in other areas, with a view to persuading them together with the Third World countries to fight against, what the Peking Government alleges is, the present "dictatorship" of the two super-powers, the United States and the Soviet Union. Fundamentally, it would seem that the long-term aim of this strategy is to bring about a position in which the present two super-powers are held in check by growing world hostility and suspicion, while Communist China has time to build up its armed forces and economic strength and emerge as a new and even more formidable super-power itself. There would certainly seem to have been no abandonment of the ultimate goal of establishing the Peking brand of Communism as the dominant political force in the world.

For the present, however, the main Chinese aim would seem to be to do everything it can to counter growing Soviet military, economic and political influence, while gathering about it as many as possible of what Madame Mao has described as "black friends, small friends, and poor friends". The support of "liberation movements" will continue, but will not, it seems, be pushed too blatantly or to the point where there is a serious danger of uniting too many of China's enemies against her.

REFERENCES

1. *The Guardian,* 13 December 1976.
2. *Izvestia,* 22 November 1917.
3. *Selected Works,* Lenin, London 1947, Vol. II, p. 850.
4. *Communism in Africa,* Fritz Schatten, George Allen & Unwin

Ltd., London 1966, p. 300.

5. *Pravda*, 22 May 1925.
6. *Selected Works*, J.V. Stalin, Moscow, 1952-55, Vol. V, p. 57.
7. *Communism in Africa, op. cit.*, p. 65.
8. *Ibid.*, p. 68.
9. *Pravda*, 22 October 1947.
10. *Current Digest of the Soviet Press*, 4 April 1958, p. 100.
11. *Ibid.*, p. 100.
12. *The African Communist*, No. 62, Third Quarter, 1975, p. 98.
13. *Africa's Red Harvest*, Pieter Lessing, Michael Joseph Ltd., London, 1962, p. 28.
14. *Izvestia*, 24 January 1960.
15. *Africa's Red Harvest, op. cit.*, p. 30.
16. *Ibid.*, p. 34.
17. *Pravda*, 27 October 1965.
18. *International Affairs*, No. 4, 1971, p. 4.
19. *Password "Anguimo"*, Pyotr Yenskufov. Novosti Press Agency, 1974, p. 24.
20. *N H Xapade et Zambesi*, Ignat Yeu and P. Mikhalev, 1972, p. 6.
21. *Password "Anguimo", op. cit.*, p. 24.
22. *The Communist Movement Today*, Boris Leibzon, Novosti Press Agency Publishing House, Moscow, 1975, p. 19; (2) *ibid.*, p. 18.
23. *The Armed Struggle of the People of Africa for Freedom and Independence*, p. 337-8.
24. *Ibid.*
25. *PO Tropam Voyny*, 1972, p. 23.
26. *Africa Makes a Choice*, Gleb Starushenko, Novosti Press Agency, Moscow, 1975, p. 19.
27. *China's African Revolution, op. cit.*, p. 17.
28. *Current Background No. 492.* (A Survey of the Communist Chinese Press, published at the US Consulate-General in Hong Kong.)
29. *China's African Revolution, op. cit.*, p. 7.
30. *Survey of China Mainland Press*, US Consulate-General, Hong Kong.
31. *China and Africa 1949-70*, Bruce D. Larkin, University of California Press, Berkeley and Los Angeles, 1971, p. 167-168.
32. *Ibid.*, p. 168.
33. *Peking Review*, 6 July 1962.
34. *New China News Agency*, 3 February 1964.

35. *Ibid.*, 5 June 1965.
36. *China and Africa 1949-1970*, Bruce D. Larkin, *op. cit.*, p. 55.

Chapter 4

The Bid for Influence — Tactics and Weapons

Much has been said in certain quarters of the setbacks and difficulties which the Communist powers have frequently experienced during the course of their drive for influence on the African continent, and of the very real nature of these periodic defeats there can be no question. Yet when all has been taken into account, it cannot be denied that considering that Soviet influence was almost non-existent in Africa 25 years ago and Chinese Communist influence totally so, the achievements of the Soviet Union and to a lesser extent Communist China in attaining their present level of influence in African affairs have been remarkable. This success has, of course, been greatly facilitated by the ability of the governments in Moscow and Peking to pursue a definite strategic line, without having to account to public opinion at home for the vast outlay in financial and other resources involved.

In the course of their parallel, but competing, campaigns to gain commanding advantage in Africa, both Moscow and Peking have employed much the same tactics and weapons which can be divided into two main categories. Firstly, overt, and often entirely legal, methods such as those of diplomacy and economic aid, and secondly, covert and clandestine methods including the use of widespread espionage and subversion and the supply of arms to guerrilla groups or revolutionary movements. Half-way between the two might be said to come the massive use of propaganda, including, not infrequently, the advocation of armed revolt, the manipulation of various types of front organisations and the use of types of training courses, many of which include heavy doses of political indoctrination.

While the use of covert and clandestine methods is described in succeeding chapters, the object here is to consider the use of more overt tactics.

Diplomatic penetration

As has already been noted, the post-war Soviet drive to gain influence in Africa did not really begin until the latter 1950s, and was at first almost entirely concentrated upon North Africa. As its first ambassador to Egypt after the overthrow of King Farouk, the Soviet Government chose one of the most experienced members of its diplomatic service, Mr Daniel Senyonovitch Solod. Fluent in English, French and Arabic, he had been despatched by Stalin to the newly independent states of Syria and the Lebanon immediately after the end of the war and before long won himself the reputation of being the most able Communist representative in the Middle East. He specialised in both gaining friends for the Soviet Union and in working up a feeling of resentment amongst those with whom he came into contact against the Western powers.

Mr Solod was recalled to Moscow in 1950. However, some signs of the considerable success of his work appeared in the subsequent opening of negotiations between Syria and the Soviet Union for trade and military agreements.

Three years later, he was appointed ambassador to Cairo, and soon achieved success equal to that he had had in Damascus and Beirut. Apart from being responsible for initiating the first trade deals between Egypt and the Soviet Union, he also started the first agreement for the large scale supply of Soviet arms to Egypt. President Nasser later told an Egyptian newspaper how this had come about. The President said that Mr Solod had taken him aside at a diplomatic reception and asked him "point-blank" whether the Egyptian Government would be interested in buying arms from the Soviet Union, saying that if it should be, he would undertake to pass this information on to the right quarters. Nasser recalled that he had answered Solod

in the same tone, saying that I found his offer extremely
interesting and that I should be prepared to enter into
negotiations in that sense.[1]

The importance of Solod's post in Cairo at that time was not
confined to Egyptian affairs and forging links with other North
African countries. A number of radical insurgent movements,
including those from Kenya, Angola, Moçambique, the Congo and
Tanganyika, amongst others, had established offices in Cairo, and
so the city became an excellent "listening-post" in which to gain
information about their activities. In February 1956, Mr Solod was
recalled to Moscow to become head of the Middle East Department
of the Soviet Foreign Office. As such, he was responsible for the
direction of Soviet operations in Egypt, Syria, Iraq, the Lebanon
and Jordan as well as in the Sudan, Ethiopia, Libya, Tunisia and
Morocco.

Early in 1960 came his appointment as Soviet Ambassador in
Guinea, a country which for a variety of reasons had been selected
as the first country in which his government hoped to secure a firm
base from which to develop its influence in West Africa. The
subsequent activities of the man Western correspondents had named
"Mr Trouble-maker" long before his arrival in Conakry and their
outcome are described in Chapter 5.

The early years of the Soviet bid for influence in Africa also saw
very considerable efforts to establish a firm base in Ethiopia.
Although up to the middle of the 1950s, Soviet propaganda had
habitually attacked Emperor Haile Selassie as being a feudal and
reactionary ruler, a new appraisal by the Kremlin's African experts
took in the fact that the prestige of Ethiopia stood high in the eyes of
many members of the independence and "liberation movements"
which had recently come into being or were forming, and policy was
switched to take advantage of this situation.

In the autumn of 1959, Mr A.V. Budakov left his post as head of
the African Department of the Soviet Foreign Ministry to become
ambassador extraordinary to the Emperor's court in Addis Ababa.
The choice of Ethiopia as one of the first countries in which to try
and develop its new Africa policy is also partly explained by the fact
that it was virtually the only country on the continent which had

previous historical ties with Russia of any significance. These were explained by the fact that in the 1880s leaders of the Russian Orthodox Church became interested in forming a union with the Coptic Church of Abyssinia with which they considered their own church had many features in common.

Diplomatic relations between the two countries were established in 1902 (they were renewed by Stalin in 1943), and a number of Russians came to visit, and in some cases work, in the country. Soviet spokesmen have been quick to lay stress on these links and on the friendly relations which they claim had "always" existed between their country and Ethiopia.

With the rapid decolonisation of Africa, a pattern quickly developed in which the Soviet Union and other East European countries sought to establish diplomatic relations with each new state in turn as soon as possible after it had gained independence. The first concrete step towards this end usually took the form of the despatch of large delegations, including senior officials and sometimes even ministers, to attend each country's independence celebrations. Today Soviet embassies and usually several from other countries of the Soviet bloc exist in all major African countries with, of course, the exception of the Republic of South Africa, South West Africa and Rhodesia.

News of a further extension of Soviet influence came in October 1976 with reports that a Soviet mission was to be established in Gaborone, capital of Botswana. The mission, which was expected to be of ambassadorial level, was said to be planning to base its operation on a town house and 12 flats in the city.

By the early 1970s, the Soviet Union had more diplomats trained in African languages than in those of any other continent. Courses available for members of the Foreign Service included those in Hausa, Swahili, Amharic, Somali, Luganda, Bambara, Mandigo and many other languages and dialects.

The spread of Communist Chinese embassies throughout Africa has proceeded almost as rapidly as in the case of the Soviet Union. They have, however, as previously mentioned, been hindered to some extent by the succession of scandals caused by the flagrant manner in which their "diplomats" operating from their embassies often engaged in subversion and incitement to revolt during the early and middle 1960s; and the wave of unease that consequently spread among some African governments regarding Chinese inten-

84

tions.

Subsequent to the establishment of diplomatic relations between China and Egypt in 1956, a Chinese embassy was opened in Rabat, Morocco, late in 1958 and in Khartoum early the following year. Diplomatic relations between China and Guinea were established in December 1959, with Ghana, Mali and Somalia in 1960, and with the Congo and Tanzania in 1961. In the short space of time between December 1963 and February 1964, Chinese embassies were established in six further African countries, these being Zanzibar, Kenya, Burundi, Tunisia and the Congo (Brazzaville).

As Chinese embassies were established, they often became vital points of contact, not just between the Chinese government and the government of the country concerned, but also for establishing contacts much farther afield. Chinese ambassadors were quite often to be found in countries far from those of their appointment engaged in making approaches aimed at opening up new fields of influence and bringing about the establishment of diplomatic relations with yet more countries.

The Chinese Embassy in Ghana under its ambassador, Mr Huang-Hua, soon became an important centre for such activities as did the embassy in Dar es Salaam, which was under the charge of a senior Chinese diplomat, Mr Ho Ying, formerly director of the West Asian and African Affairs Department of the Chinese Foreign Ministry. One expedition of many he made was to the Ugandan capital of Kampala, just a week after that country gained independence in 1962, a visit which resulted in the swift establishment of diplomatic relations.

In 1964, Mr Ho Ying made a similar visit to Zambia to congratulate that country's leader President Kaunda on the attainment of independence. In Tanzania, Dar es Salaam's usefulness as a contact-making base was further enhanced during the early 1960s by the manner in which increasing numbers of "liberation movements" came to establish their headquarters in that capital.

During the early years of Chinese interest in Africa, an important part was also played by the Chinese Embassy in Somalia. Mr Alan Hutchison has recorded that a senior Somali government official of that period told him that the government was sure that the Chinese Embassy situated in a very large house protected by a high wall on the outskirts of Mogadishu, the capital, was one of China's most important transit and diplomatic training bases in the whole of

Africa. One of its principal rôles seemed to be in the training of Chinese diplomats and other officials in African languages. Both local and specially imported instructors were employed by the embassy for this purpose. The official said that by 1963 the embassy had an officially registered staff of no less than 230 persons— obviously far more than were required just to handle relations with Somalia.

In selecting sites for their embassies in Africa, the Chinese government has apparently not infrequently been motivated by a marked desire for prestige as well as for efficiency. The Chinese embassy in Burundi, an impressive building owned by the King, was reported to have been purchased for £40 000. In Lusaka, they acquired a showy mansion belonging to a South African business- man, and in Tanzania what was believed to be the most luxurious house in the country, a home belonging to the Aga Khan.

By 1970, China had established diplomatic relations with 15 African countries. Five African states which had such relations had broken them off because of the latter's disruptive policies already referred to. A rapid increase in the number of African countries having formal contact with China followed during the early 1970s. During the one year of 1972, for instance, Dahomey, Chad, Mauritius, Madagascar, Togo and Zaire all established diplomatic relations with Peking. By the end of 1974, the only members of the Organisation of African Unity which had not done so were the Ivory Coast and Gabon.

Visits and Delegation Exchanges

A very important part in the efforts of the Communist powers to cement relations with the countries of Africa has consisted of the issuing of large numbers of invitations to influential individuals from heads of states downwards and to delegations to visit the Soviet Union or Communist China, and conversely the despatch of large numbers of varied delegations (from those concerned with arrangements for the provision of military aid to cultural affairs) to visit African countries.

On occasions, invitations have been sent to heads of state or leading political figures, even before diplomatic relations have been established, as was done in the case of the Emperor of Ethiopia who was invited to visit the Soviet Union in the summer of 1959. Despite his reputation as a feudal monarch who showed little apparent concern for the social advancement of his people, he was, according to Mr Fritz Schatten, received by the Soviet leaders with "unequalled pomp" and much honour. He was presented with a magnificently equipped aircraft intended for his personal use. During his visit, the emphasis of the Soviet leaders was not upon the need for "Socialism", but the need for "co-existence" on a worldwide scale and on the "traditional friendship" between the Soviet Union and Ethiopia. That approach seemed to make a considerable impact upon the emperor.

In the two years between 1964 and 1966, official visits to China were made by an impressive number of East African political leaders including Mr Ali Shermarke, Prime Minister of Somalia, President Osman of the same country, President Abboud of the Sudan, President Nyerere of Tanzania, President Kaunda of Zambia, President Obote of Uganda, President Massemba-Debat of the Congo (Brazzaville) and the Queen of Burundi.

Visits of African politicians and others to China first became noticeable in 1958 when such visitors came from eight different African countries. In 1960, the number of countries from which they were drawn had increased to 29.

As well as heads of state, the Chinese Government also invited

heads of armies, men just under the leadership, and ministers, notably those connected with the information services, like Achieng Oneko in Kenya and the Somali Minister of Information, Ali Mohammed Hirare. Visitors of this sort would certainly have helped China to build up a picture of African conditions—social, political and military—at a time when she was anxious to increase her knowledge of the continent. Some, like Kawawa of Tanzania, or Kenyan Vice-President, Oginga Odinga, were possibly chosen because it was felt that one day they might occupy the highest office. But most of those normally regarded as 'China's friends' were of direct use to China, and were cultivated for immediate practical reasons. Ministers of Information controlled the output of news and could therefore influence attitudes towards China, either by suppressing unfavourable news about China's activities or by feeding what amounted to Chinese propaganda to their media. This happened in a number of countries where China was on good terms with Ministers of Information, notably Somalia and Tanzania—where Radio Tanzania staff had standing instructions not to carry stories damaging to China.[2]

The Communist Party of the Soviet Union sometimes issued invitations to the ruling parties of countries in which the Soviet Union was currently taking a special interest, and which showed sufficient signs of taking the "non-capitalist" path. They were invited to send delegations to Moscow. One example was Algeria, where delegations from the ruling party were guests of the CPSU Central Committee every year from 1963-1968. Guinea and Mali were two other countries which engaged in the same sort of exchanges during the 1960s.

Some of the more recent visits of African leaders to Communist countries include those of General Gowon, formerly President of Nigeria, to Peking in 1974. Lagos Radio described that visit at the time as being more important than any other visit hitherto made by the general. President Kaunda also visited Moscow in 1974. In the course of that visit, the Zambian President had talks with President Podgorny and Mr Kirill Mazorov, First Deputy Chairman of the USSR Council of Ministers. Also taking part in the talks were the Soviet Minister of Foreign Trade, and the Chairman of the Council of Ministers State Committee for Foreign Economic Relations. At the lunch during the visit, President Kaunda expressed appreciation for support given by the Soviet Union in the "struggle against colonialism" and described the talks as having been very fruitful.

Visitors to Moscow during 1975 and 1976 included President Neto of Angola, President Machel of Moçambique and Mr Joshua Nkomo of the Rhodesian ANC. His visit, according to his supporters, was "very successful". The year 1976 also saw the beginning of a fairly constant exchange of delegations at a lower level between the Soviet Union and Angola, Moçambique and Guinea-Bissau.

Economic Aid and Trade

Soviet policy regarding economic aid to, and trade with, African countries was described in some detail in the November 1975 issue of the Soviet magazine, *International Affairs*. The article concerned stated:

The Soviet Union emphasises its readiness to co-operate with all independent African states, including those following the capitalist road, on the basis of equality and mutual benefit. The USSR regards such co-operation as a manifestation of the mutual desire to promote the struggle against imperialism and facilitate the shaping of a new, independent Africa.

Then, however, the author, O. Orestov, commented:

Understandably, co-operation is particularly successful between socialist countries and socialist-orientated states of Africa.

He continued:

In collaboration with socialist countries, Africa has built more than 250 power projects, among which the Aswan hydro-power station in Egypt holds a prominent place. A steel-melting shop was constructed with Soviet assistance at the El Hadjar metallurgical plant in Algeria. The Soviet Union will also help Nigeria with the construction of its first metal works. Ethiopia's largest state-owned enterprise, the Assab oil refinery, has been built in co-operation with the USSR. The Polish People's Republic will construct an oil refinery in the People's Republic of the Congo. Czechoslovakia assisted in the construction of a major tyre works in Ethiopia. With Soviet help, Somalia has built a meat-packing factory in Kisimayu, which is now the largest enterprise of its type in tropical Africa. The USSR and the Republic of Guinea are working together on the construction of a major bauxite-mining combine in Kindia. This co-operation has special political significance, too. To the peoples of African countries, it means an absolutely novel experience in joint work with foreign states, with the entire fruit of this work remaining in the hands of these peoples. Their previous destiny was to watch how, after having built an enterprise on African soil, capitalist firms shamelessly exported the profit yielded by that enterprise. The socialist countries, on the contrary, build industrial enterprises which become the full property of the state sector in newly-independent states. Moreover, when construction is still under way, the socialist countries give every possible assistance in the training of local technical personnel who will eventually run the enterprise in question. This also contributes to the formation of new social relations and the emergence of new contingents of the working class.

Closer collaboration between African states and socialist countries inevitably affects the nature of international trade. African countries have in many cases breached the trade monopoly of the capitalist West, having rejected the services of the latter and turned to the socialist countries for industrial equipment and other goods.

At present, thousands of Soviet people are selflessly working in Africa. Doctors, geologists, teachers and many people of many other occupations are to be met in Algeria and Sierra Leone, Ethiopia and Guinea, Nigeria and the Congo, Tanzania and other countries. They are willingly sharing their vast know-how with nations that were denied friendly help for many decades.

Hence, the Soviet Union and other socialist countries are Africa's dependable allies in the struggle against the forces of imperialism, neo-colonialism and racism.[3]

Although Soviet aid to Egypt first began in 1958 and both Guinea and Ethiopia received Soviet credits in 1959, its aid programme cannot be said to have really begun until 1960 and did not get under full way until 1963. By that date, Egypt had already received credits amounting to 5 000 million US dollars, and other countries such as Mali, Guinea and Ghana had received smaller, but still substantial, sums. Three years later, in 1966, American experts estimated that more than 4 000 technicians were at work in various

African countries, *most* of them being concentrated in Guinea, Algeria and Mali (Egypt was excluded from the estimate).

Between 1959 and the end of 1973, the Soviet Union promised 1,3 billion dollars worth of economic aid to African countries excluding Egypt and had despatched to them about 400 million dollars worth of "project aid"; i.e. equipment, materials and technical services supplied by means of concessionary credits for such purposes as the construction of factories, geological surveying and agricultural development. Apart from military aid which is considered separately and "project aid", this assistance was also intended for the purposes of providing medical facilities, food supplies to countries affected by famine and the granting of trade credits to finance imports for commercial or government use.

Amongst the more ambitious and interesting projects which the Soviet Union has been associated with in Africa south of the Sahara during the years, has been the Kindia bauxite-mining complex in Guinea. This is the largest aid project the Soviet Union has been involved in on the African continent, outside North Africa. The project is of particular interest because it would seem that there are indications that it could be of considerable direct benefit to the Soviet Union itself. It was, for instance, stated in a survey of writings by Soviet experts on the aluminium industry in the USSR that shortages had occurred of high-grade ores needed for the manufacture of aluminium. The new mines at Kindia have an estimated yield of 2,5 million tons of high-grade bauxite per year for 30 years. Their products are earmarked for sale to the Soviet Union and, moreover, for at least 12 years or more after completion of the delivery of the Soviet aid involved, they will in whole or part represent repayment of the credit of 92 million dollars extended by the Soviet Union to sponsor the project in 1969. One expert, Mr John Desseks, has commented that

> therefore, through their aid efforts the Soviets have substantially assured themselves of a substantial source of good-quality bauxite.[4]

Soviet aid to Guinea in the early 1960s was implemented by inexperienced Soviet officials with disastrous ineptitude. It left vast supplies of equipment and goods, of a type totally unsuitable for use in Africa, rotting and rusting in dumps or on quay sides. The evidence would seem to be, however, that the lessons of this bizzare comedy of errors were soon well learnt, and there is no indication that they have been repeated either in Guinea or elsewhere on any significant scale. Recently the USSR has promised to assist Guinea in creating a scientific research centre. It has also given assistance in the establishment of the country's national airline and the training of its pilots.

In November 1968, agreements were signed between the Soviet Union and Nigeria pledging the former to provide credits worth 140 million dollars. This sum was intended for the construction of an iron and steel complex. Most Soviet aid to Nigeria has been intended for the development of the country's mineral and agricultural resources, but the Soviet Union has also been showing an increasing interest in the Nigerian oil industry. In 1972, it signed an agreement under which it undertook to assist Nigeria to build an "oil education centre" at Warri. This centre was to be managed by the Soviet agency Technoexport. Under the agreement, the Soviet Union was to supply training equipment and instructors for the centre, whilst Nigeria was to contribute towards the cost of its construction. The aim of the centre is to train Nigerian employees of the National Oil Corporation set up in April 1971 as part of strongly Soviet supported moves towards government nationalisation. The National Oil Corporation has been demanding an increase in its share of Western owned oil companies.

The series of setbacks for Soviet policy towards Egypt following the October 1973 war was followed by increased interest in Libya, despite the supposedly anti-Marxist although revolutionary policies of its leader, Colonel Gaddafi. Following the visit of the Soviet Premier, Mr Kosygin, to Tripoli in May 1975, the official Libyan News Agency announced early in June that the Soviet Union had agreed to provide Libya with an atomic reactor. Soviet sources said that this was being provided "for peaceful purposes" under one of several agreements aimed at "consolidating and widening co-operation between the Soviet Union and Libya".[5]

In East Africa, one of the most recent aid projects in which the Soviet Union has become involved concerns plans for the construction of a 14 000 Kw hydro-electric power station in Tanzania. A team of experts from the Leninropyeki Institute visited the country to discuss the project in 1975.

Some Western experts consider that it is possible to see in the application of Soviet aid policies towards certain countries a direct link with the obtainment of strategic goals, as well as the general spreading of political influence. One, for instance, has expressed the view that in the case of six countries these goals were particularly clearly visible. He has stated that in Ethiopia, to which Soviet aid was first committed in 1959, the United States had a large wireless communication station which was important to its forces in the Middle East. He further points out that in 1963, when the Soviet Union first committed itself to aid Algeria, France still occupied important bases in the country and that:

> The 106 million dollar lines of credit extended to both states in those years probably had, as one purpose, to increase the Soviets' leverage to persuade host govern-ments to terminate the Western bases ... The modest economic credits offered to Tunisia in 1961 and to Senegal in 1964 might also have been in part designed to improve Soviet diplomats' standing when arguing for military non-alignment and the closing of the substan-tial French bases in both countries.
> The United States retained its Ethiopian facility throughout the period under review, as did France its base in Senegal. However, the French withdrew comple-tely from Tunisia by 1964, and from almost all installa-tions in Algeria by 1968 and from the last in 1970. But Soviet economic and military aid to Algeria was consi-derable (over 121 million dollars worth of project aid was committed by the Soviet Union by 1973), and it may have been a significant factor in persuading Algerian leaders that they could afford to press the French to evacuate bases before the date (1972) provided by the Evian accords.[6]

The ability to use Algerian naval and air bases would obviously be a very considerable advantage to the Soviet Union in the furtherance of its strategic policies in the Mediterranean, particular-ly in view of the comparative proximity of the United States Polaris submarine base at Rota in Spain. As part of its aid programme, the Soviet Union has, in fact, helped the Algerians to expand and bring up to date the former French bases, in addition to supplying the great bulk of the country's military equipment.

Maybe the Soviet Union and Algeria through their front organisation Polisario have designs on the phosphate mines in what was formerly Spanish Sahara.

Two other countries in which there would seem to be a clear tie-up between the provision of economic aid and definite Soviet strategic objectives are Guinea and Somalia.

Before the Soviet Union entered into a second aid agreement with Guinea in 1960 involving the former in an outlay of 22 million dollars, the two countries concluded an agreement for expanding and modernising the airport at Conakry.

Mr John Desseks wrote:

> Guinea was then virtually without important international friends besides the Soviet Union and its allies, so that the Soviets could expect that their leverage over the recipient government might be strong enough to secure access to the field for its military aircraft, if not on a regular basis at least at times of crisis.[7]

Modernisation of the airport was completed in 1962. During the Cuban missile crisis, the Soviet Government made a request for aircraft on their way to Cuba to use this airfield as a staging post. This request was apparently denied. After an 11-year interval, during which considerable aid continued to flow into the country from the Soviet Union (168 million dollars worth had been received by 1973) permission was given by the Guinean Government for Soviet naval reconnaissance aircraft to use the airport. This was a concession of considerable value for it enabled such planes to carry out patrols monitoring the movement of shipping in a large stretch of the South Atlantic, including those using the Cape route to and from the Indian Ocean. In addition, according to a report in the magazine *West Africa* in March 1974, the Soviet Government had then begun to put pressure on the Guinean President, Mr Sekou Toure, for the establishment of a naval base on an island near Conakry. A similar request had been turned down by the President in 1971, but it was considered by no means certain that ultimately the new one would be similarly treated.

The Belgian Defence Minister, Monsieur Paul Van Den Boeynants, was quoted in the same magazine in July 1975 as saying that two Soviet warships were already stationed permanently in the area of Conakry, where they had bunkering facilities.

Soviet economic aid to Somalia, where the important military facilities obtained by the Soviet Union in this area of great strategic significance have already been described, began in 1961, less than two years after the country had obtained independence. By 1973 the project aid commitments had totalled 22,6 million dollars. Soviet interest in the country increased markedly after a military coup in 1969 led to the installation of a government dedicated, not to "non-alignment" or generally pro-Western policies as its predecessor had been, but to policies of a "positively neutral" or generally of a pro-Soviet character.

One major Soviet aid project in Somalia has been the construction of a meat cannery at Kismayu under a barter agreement. According to its terms, the Soviet Union takes 75% of its production and also bars any attempt being made to find other and perhaps more profitable markets. The Soviet Union has also constructed a fish cannery. At the end of 1974, it was reported that two Soviet ships had delivered equipment concerned with the building of a hydro-electric power station and dam near Fanala on the River Juba. During the year, 20 bulk carriers of the Soviet Black Sea Line were stated to have brought cargoes of various types of machinery, including metal-cutting tools, lorries, and agricultural and road-making equipment, to Somalia, as well as steel, cement and other goods. On their return voyage the ships carried traditional Somali exports and products of the canneries, constructed with Soviet aid.

In February 1972, Somalia was visited by the Soviet Defence Minister, Marshal A.A. Grechko. His visit was hardly over before increased consignments of arms for the Somali forces began to arrive from the Soviet Union and that country agreed to improve harbour and air transport facilities. By the time President Podgorny visited Somalia in the summer of 1974, it was estimated that there were about 3 600 Soviet advisers and technicians in Somalia. Of these, perhaps between 1 000 and 1 400 were thought to be military personnel. As a result of President Podgorny's visit, a friendship treaty was signed between Somalia and the Soviet Union under which the two countries undertook to

expand and deepen all-round co-operation and ex-change of experience in the economic and scientific-technical spheres—in industry, farming and livestock raising, irrigation and water resources, the development of natural resources, the development of power engineering, the training of national cadres, and in other corresponding spheres of the economy. The two sides will expand trade and maritime navigation between them on the basis of the principles of mutual benefit and most-favoured-nation status in accordance with the provisions of the trade and payments agreement between both countries concluded in Moscow on 2nd June 1961.[8]

The reference to the development of natural resources has particular significance in view of the fact that the geological structure of the country points to a reasonably strong possibility of oil deposits being contained within its frontiers.

The vast amounts of Soviet economic aid invested in Egypt during the days of the Nasser epoch and its immediate aftermath drew important dividends from the Soviet strategic point of view in facilities for ships of the Soviet Mediterranean fleet in Alexandria, Port Said, and Sollum and for Soviet military aircraft at a number of Egyptian airfields.

In recent years a considerable change in the Soviet attitude towards aid to the undeveloped countries seems to have taken place, with the introduction of a new emphasis on the need to try and ensure that the USSR received some material economic as well as political or strategic return from its efforts. This was a consideration that had been voiced by A. Mikoyan, then Minister of Foreign Trade, as early as 1961. The following year, a group of economists at the Institute of the Economy of the World Socialist System started work on the effectiveness of Soviet economic relations with the Third World. In 1965, they produced a report which included the somewhat revolutionary proposals that the Soviet Union should abandon its established policy of seeking self-reliance in all fields of production, and instead base its economic relations with the Third World upon the doctrine of comparative advantage.

These experts advocated that Soviet aid and trade policy towards such countries should be concentrated upon the production of such necessities as petroleum, iron ore, cotton fibres and ferrous metals. Such production should be planned and co-ordinated so as to assure the Soviet Union of a reliable and cheap supply of raw materials, fuel and some industrial products. The Third World countries which co-operated in such plans, the theory ran, would receive a greater benefit by means of this production for the foreign market and increased output of traditional products, than they would from project aid designed merely to increase production for the home market.

In 1966, the economists engaged in this research project published a book which summarised their main conclusions. It stressed that the main factor in deciding the allocation of aid should be its ability to bring substantial economic returns to the Soviet Union, not just to bring unlimited advantages to the country that received it.

There is also some reason to think that the Soviet authorities have come to regard the provision of aid as a useful adjunct to the formation of trading links with African countries. In making trading agreements with African states, the Soviet Union has tended to favour the initiation of bi-lateral barter agreements which require the country with which they are made to import a balancing quantity of Soviet goods. An obstacle to the marketing of Soviet goods in Africa, however, has been the fact that goods produced by Western countries, particularly the former colonial powers, are much more familiar to potential customers. It is thought that one aim of Soviet aid programmes could possibly be to help overcome this obstacle by introducing attractive low-priced goods to consumers. Soviet machinery and equipment provided under an aid programme naturally creates in time a demand for spares and replacements from the USSR.

The basic raw materials which the Soviet Union seems most anxious to import from African countries under trading agreements include long-staple cotton, fruit, edible oils, coffee, cocoa and raw hides.

Chinese Economic Aid

The most interesting aid project engaged in by Communist China in Africa is, of course, the Tanzania-Zambia railway, the largest aid project ever sponsored by any Communist country.

The idea of a rail link between the two countries originated in the British colonial era and in 1952 the British Colonial Office actually commissioned a survey. In 1963, the World Bank refused a request by Tanzania and Zambia for support for the project on the grounds that there would be few economic benefits and that development in both countries would be better assisted in other ways.

Communist China's offer to build the railway was put forward in principle when President Nyerere visited Peking in February 1965. The final protocol confirming China's participation in the project was not, however, signed until 1970. The first part of the work was planned in three stages; consisting of a preliminary survey, engineering survey, design and final feasibility report. The plans called for the construction of a single track line linking Dar es Salaam with the central Zambian town of Kapiri Mposhi, thus spanning a distance of 1 850 km covering some of the most rugged country in central Africa. Construction of the railway involved the building of some 2 500 bridges and viaducts and 19 tunnels.

China's financial contribution to this work took the form of a loan of the equivalent of 401 million US dollars, divided equally between Tanzania and Zambia. It covered the construction costs and provision of rolling-stock and engines. It is also known that China committed up to 280 million dollars to the project in 1967, probably to cover survey and design work. Under the agreement by which China provided these funds, Tanzania and Zambia were, however, expected to contribute to the total cost which the Chinese authorities estimated would amount to 501 million dollars.

The work-force employed on the railway consisted of about 1 500 Chinese and 36 000 Africans. Construction work was carried on by means of two eight-hour shifts in every 24 hours. One Chinese official told a journalist that he estimated that this meant that six 12,5 metre lengths of rail were laid every five minutes 20 seconds. This totalled a new two-mile stretch of line every day. The loan given by China for the construction of the railway is interest free, but it is supposed to be repaid within 30 years starting in 1981. This means that Tanzania and Zambia will both have to find $2,7 million a year in order to accomplish this. It is, however, expected that ultimately the railway will not only pay for itself but also raise a surplus to help pay for the loan. The main freight will be Zambian copper and other exports from that country. In addition, it is hoped to use the line to assist in the agricultural development of south-west Tanzania and also to develop coal and iron ore deposits in the south of the country. In 1974, China gave Tanzania a further loan amounting to £31 million to build a branch line of 240 km to assist in the development of these products.

At a ceremony late in October 1975 at Kapiri Mposhi in Zambia to mark the completion of track laying and the start of trial operations, President Kaunda took the opportunity to pay tribute to the "assistance from China under the great leader Chairman Mao". He also stated that the liberation of the "oppressed nations" in the rest of Africa was "an international duty which we fully accept". He added:

> We would not have shouldered this grave new responsibility on behalf of Africa without China's invaluable co-operation and assistance.[9]

His words recalled those of some commentators when Chinese participation in the railway scheme was first announced, that its motive might be less inspired by desire to aid the commercial prosperity of the two countries, than to provide a new line of communication that could ferry military supplies south from Dar es Salaam to "liberation movement" base camps.

China has signed an agreement with Rwanda providing for construction of a railway from that country to Tanzania. Other major Chinese aid projects in Africa include the Belet Ven-Burao highway in Somalia, the Woulda-Werfa road in Ethiopia, the Serenje-Samfya road in Zambia, and the Mongomo-Neve road in Equatorial Africa, the Bourenz dam in the Congo, the Lagdo Dam in Cameroun, and work on the Dawhenya irrigation project in Ghana.

In Tanzania, Chinese aid projects include the Friendship Textile Mill, a farm implements factory, a shoe factory and a pharmaceutical plant, the latter being an outright gift from the Chinese Government. On the island of Zanzibar, China is committed to a sugar growing scheme aimed at making the island self-sufficient in sugar. It has also been involved in a rice-production scheme and the construction of a sports stadium and several industrial enterprises.

In 1973, China signed an important assistance protocol which provided for technical and economic aid to Ethiopia on the basis of a credit made two years earlier. A regular air service between Shanghai and the Ethiopian capital had been inaugurated the previous year. China has also provided some assistance for agricultural and medical projects in Somalia.

In the 1960s, approximately 75% of all economic aid from Communist China went to Asian countries. By 1972, however, aid to Asian countries had dropped to about 20% of the total and the majority appeared to be going to African states.

Military Aid

The approaches made by Ambassador Solod of the Soviet Union in Cairo to President Nasser, already referred to, resulted in the conclusion of an arms supply agreement in September 1955 between Egypt and Czechoslovakia. This signalled the start of the present continuing flood of Soviet bloc arms into the African continent.

As a result of this deal, Egypt received MIG-15 fighters, Ilushin-28 bombers, two destroyers, tanks, heavy artillery and small arms. It also provided for the despatch of Egyptian service personnel to the Soviet bloc for training in the use of the new equipment, whilst the first Soviet and Czech technicians began to arrive in Egypt. In November of the following year, a further agreement was signed providing for more armour and aircraft from the Soviet bloc and also two destroyers and three submarines. The Soviet Union undertook to replace all the equipment that had been lost to the Egyptian forces during the Suez War of 1956. Indeed, by the autumn of 1957 Egyptian officials were claiming that their forces had been able to increase their fighting power to twice what they possessed at the onset of the Suez campaign.

Some 18 months later, the newly independent state of Guinea, having failed to obtain arms from the United States, accepted a Czech offer of military aid. A cargo consisting of a few light tanks, field, anti-aircraft and anti-tank artillery and scout cars and small arms arrived in Conakry harbour shortly afterwards. This consignment was apparently a gift intended to give promise of even better things to come. Some Czechoslovak small arms were found in Cameroun as early as 1959 and were thought to have been supplied from Guinea. In the spring of 1960 the Soviet Union granted Guinea a substantial loan (probably of at least three million dollars) to cover the provision of arms supply. Members of the small but now increasingly well-equipped Guinean army were undergoing training in the Soviet bloc by early 1961, and in March that year the Soviet Union offered to extend military assistance to Mali in addition to a large loan for civil development. Most of the initial military equipment supplied consisted of artillery, personnel carriers and small arms. A small Soviet military training mission also arrived in Mali, whilst members of that country's army were sent for training in the Soviet bloc.

In September of the same year, President Nkrumah of Ghana accepted a Soviet offer to send 100 members of his army to Soviet training camps. The signing of an arms supply agreement by the two countries was followed by the completion of a number of others during the remaining years of the President's rule. This occurred despite the pronounced opposition of some Ghanaian officers who were becoming increasingly alarmed at the President's willingness to allow the country to become so dependent upon the Soviet Union and open to its influence. By the time of his overthrow, it was estimated that about 1 000 Ghanaian army cadets were under training in the USSR.

A Soviet attempt to use the supply of military assistance to gain influence over the chaotic events following the granting of independence to the Congo (now Zaire) in 1960 failed in its main aims. In July 1960, President Lumumba sent a request for armed assistance to the Soviet Union for the purpose of allowing him to take military action against the secessionist state of Katanga. At almost the same time, he sent a request for general assistance to the United Nations. The Soviet Union reported to the UN that it had authorised the use of five Ilushyn-18 transport aircraft assigned to the Government of Ghana to fly Ghanaian troops and equipment to the Congo as part of the UN effort to restore order. It also announced that it was arranging for the despatch of a repair workshop and a number of transport vehicles to the Congo together with technicians. In the middle of August, President Lumumba announced that he had sent a further message asking for military assistance to Moscow. The UN authorities responded by closing all airports in the country except to UN aircraft—an action which for the time being blocked any effective Soviet response to this appeal. Before any adequate alternative means of delivering the requested aid could be found, President Lumumba himself had been overthrown.

Two years later, however, a new and important opportunity had opened up for the Soviet Union on the East coast of Africa. It was characteristically quick to exploit the advantage which continues even today to have great bearing on the current strategic situation on the continent. Friction between Somalia and Ethiopia—against which the former had territorial claims—led to border fighting between the two countries, and to a Somali request to the Western powers for arms with which to build up their military forces. It wanted to turn the small para-military force it then possessed into an army of 20 000 men. The Western powers, unwilling to do anything which might bring about an escalation of a clearly potentially dangerous situation in a vital strategic area, refused to provide the amount of aid requested. The Somali Government, thereupon, turned to the Soviet Union.

In 1962, an agreement was signed by the Soviet and Somali governments under which the former committed itself to provide military aid to the value of 35 million dollars, with the aim of creating a Somali army with a strength of 14 000 in the first stages, rising to a hoped for 20 000. Supplies of modern artillery, T-54 tanks, armoured personnel carriers and MIG-15 and MIG-17 aircraft began to arrive in the country forthwith. At the same time, cadres for the new Somali army departed for training in the Soviet bloc and a Soviet military mission, approximately 300 strong, arrived in Mogadishu.

Meanwhile, during the years covered, Soviet bloc arms had continued to flow into Egypt in increasing abundance whilst a new major client for their reception had been found in the shape of Algeria. The first Soviet arms supply agreement with that country was made in 1963. The first substantial shipments of arms arrived in 1964, by which time several hundred members of the Algerian forces were reported to be receiving training in the Soviet Union and Eastern Europe.

In 1965, it was reported that Algeria had begun to receive supplies of the then ultra-modern MIG-21 fighters. In December 1966 the French magazine, *National Defence,* stated that the Algerian air force had a strength of about 160 aircraft, mainly MIGs, and that the army included four or five armoured battalions equipped with T-54 tanks; also that the army's 10 artillery groups were entirely equipped with Soviet made weapons, including some rocket projectors.

As stockpiles of weapons, particularly small arms, began to build up in both Egypt and Algeria, far beyond the immediate requirements of both countries, new advantages to the Soviet Union, resulting from its arms supply policy, began to become manifest. Writing in their book, *Arms for the Third World*, Wynfred Joshua and Stephen P. Gilbert stated that:

> The Russian arms carried by the Egyptian army into Yemen served to effectuate Soviet hostility toward Saudi Arabia. The Soviet weapons Egypt and Algeria shipped to the Congolese rebels who fought the Tshombe government in 1964-65, helped to maintain Soviet prestige in militant Afro-Arab circles. This tactic of supporting "wars of liberation" by proxy partly offset Chinese charges that the Soviet Union had betrayed the war-of-liberation commitment. The re-export device also helped to protect the Russians against risks of escalating a local conflict into confrontation with the Western powers.[10]

Further details of this re-export device in action are given in Chapter 6.

Following the left-wing revolt in Zanzibar in January 1964, and the establishment of a revolutionary Sino-Cuban backed government on that island, Soviet arms and instructors for the equipment and training of the new "people's army" began to arrive in March and some of the equipment was publicly displayed at a parade soon afterwards. Considerable quantities of Chinese arms began to arrive on the island about the same time and by that winter both the Soviet Union and China had become major suppliers of arms to Tanzania.

Before long Dar es Salaam had also become the main port of entry for arms from both the Soviet Union and China intended for the "liberation movements" of Southern Africa. Tanzania thus began to take on the "re-export" rôle already engaged in by Egypt and Algeria.

As the flow of Soviet bloc arms into Africa increased, so also did the sophistication of the weapons supplied. In 1963, for instance, the first SA Guideline surface-to-air missiles arrived in Egypt. The year previously, Egypt had also received Komar class patrol boats armed with surface-to-surface Styx missiles. Larger class guided missile patrol boats were delivered in 1964 and Algeria also received both types of vessels as the result of an agreement reached with the

Soviet Union in the spring of 1965. By 1966, it was estimated that there were between 2 500 and 3 000 tanks in the possession of the countries of North Africa and the Middle East, or approximately the same number as that used by Nazi Germany to conquer France and the Low Countries in 1940. Of this number, it was calculated that over half had been supplied by the Soviet bloc.

By the time the June 1967 Arab-Israeli war broke out, the Egyptian air force had been supplied with more than 160 MIG-21 jet aircraft, some equipped with the air-to-air Atoll missile, at least 40 MIG-19s and more than 100 earlier types of MIG. Its equipment also included SU-7 fighter bombers, training aircraft, plus helicopters. In addition, the Soviet Union had provided Egypt with a complete anti-aircraft radar network linked to SA Guideline missiles and its army had been lavishly equipped with Soviet and Czech small arms, a large number of tanks, including the heavy JS-3, and surface-to-surface Snapper anti-tank missiles.

Important developments in the field of Soviet arms supply south of the Sahara also occurred in 1967. Civil war broke out in Nigeria in June and, after the Nigerian Federal Government had failed to obtain arms from the United States to prosecute its campaign against Biafra, it turned to the Soviet Union. As a result, six L-29 jet trainers equipped for bombing and straffing missions landed at Lagos in August. Subsequently, approximately 15 MIG-17s were supplied by the Soviet Union and a 50-man military mission arrived in the country to help maintain the equipment provided. In contrast to the Soviet practice of providing such equipment under loan agreements to other African countries, in the case of Nigeria all items provided (which included weapons for the army and a small number of patrol boats) were sold to the Nigerian Government on a cash basis, presumably to offset charges that the Soviet Government was openly interfering in an internal dispute in an African country. The Soviet Government at this time was still sensitive to criticism of that type and took considerable care to try and refute it.

One Soviet authority subsequently defended the Soviet Government's action in supplying arms to the Nigerian Federal Government during the Biafran war in the following terms:

> Since the imperialist countries make wide use of the provision of weapons to their satellites, the socialist countries, true to the principle of the national liberation

movement, consider it their duty to meet requests for aid by those countries and peoples which are fighting for their independence, and which are threatened by imperialist aggression or interference in their internal affairs. So long as the imperialist powers do not agree to the USSR's proposal to forbid the provision of and the trade in arms, the USSR and other socialist countries will make use of their right to give aid to countries which need it for the defence of their national independence in circumstances of intrigues and provocation by international imperialism.[11]

Almost at the same time as Soviet arms first made their appearance in Nigeria, the Soviet Union was entering into negotiations which, through the tide of events, were to result in Soviet weapons being used in an internal dispute on the opposite side of the continent. In August 1967, the Sudanese Government announced the completion of an arms supply agreement between that country and the Soviet Union and Czechoslovakia. According to British sources at the time, the deal was intended to cover the supply of tanks, an aerial defence system and older types of MIG aircraft. The Sudanese Government forces had been engaged in hostilities against insurgents in the southern half of the country since 1955, and there is considerable evidence to show that, by at least the beginning of the present decade, they were being considerably assisted in their efforts by arms and equipment provided under the agreement. A number of reports indicated that Soviet supplied helicopters had proved particularly valuable and the Institute for the Study of Conflict in its report, *Sudan: The Long War*,[12] cited evidence provided by two Swiss reporters, who visited the country in 1971, that members of the Soviet military mission (who between 1969 and the abortive pro-Communist coup of 1971 were increasingly active), had actually taken part in operations against the Anya-Nya or insurgent forces.

The two Swiss correspondents said that they had been taken by a Soviet MIG-8 heavy duty helicopter from Juba to Meridi, a flight of 240 kilometres, during which a Soviet pilot had been at the controls for at least part of the way. Although they were told that the helicopter was on a routine flight carrying officials and supplies to towns in the south, when they were off-loaded at one port of call, and picked up by the same helicopter an hour later, they noticed that the floor was littered with spent machinegun cartridge cases. They also said that the only hotel in Juba seemed to be packed with Soviet so-called "employees of Sudan Airways". In addition they reported that there were

> between 100 and 200 serving members of the Soviet Red Army stationed in Juba, and their principal rôle was to accompany Sudanese patrols into rebel-held areas and give strategic and tactical advice. There is a fully equipped Soviet training area on an island in Lake No, which is part of the *nudd*, the immense swamp which carries the Nile through the southern Sudan.[13]

In a letter to President Kaunda of Zambia, also quoted in the Institute for the Study of Conflict's report, the Anya-Nya leader, Colonel Joseph Lagu, said:

> Your Excellency may ask how we know the Russians are in Southern Sudan helping the government and their Egyptian allies. We have seen them moving about in the streets of Juba where they are based, flying their MIG-8 helicopters and firing at us the rockets and guns of these helicopters. We have heard them communicating with each other in their tanks and in their planes. We have heard the screams of the wounded Russian pilots. We have buried the bodies of Russian airmen who perished with their helicopters.

The catastrophic defeat which met the Arab armies during the June 1967 war, and the immense losses of Soviet war material suffered by Egypt, were at first hailed by not a few Western observers as events that would teach the Soviet Union a lesson, and would force it to adopt a very different attitude as regards the supply of military equipment and advice to Third World countries in the future. Events, however, extremely quickly proved these views ill-founded. Within a very short space of time after the ending of hostilities, the Soviet Government had made it abundantly clear that it not only intended to restore the shattered Egyptian armoury but even to increase the scope of its contents. On 22 June, the

Egyptian newspaper *Al Ahram* reported President Podgorny as saying on arrival in Cairo at the head of a 25-strong delegation which included Marshal Zakharov, Soviet Chief of Staff:

The imperialists and their stooges imagine we came here to exchange mutual talk of friendship between us, but together we will prove them wrong.

Two days earlier, *The Guardian* in London had reported that substantial quantities of arms to replace those so recently lost were already arriving in Egypt, transported by a shuttle service of Soviet aircraft. This and earlier allegations of the resumption of a Soviet arms supply flow appeared to be confirmed when it was reported in *The Times* on 27 June that Cairo International Airport had been closed at short notice to allow for the arrival of large numbers of Soviet transport aircraft. At the end of July, a report in the *Sunday Telegraph* stated that about half the combat aircraft lost by Egypt in the course of the campaign had already been replaced as well as about a quarter of the tanks and self-propelled guns.

In January of the following year, an Egyptian army delegation conferred in Prague with the Czechoslovak Chief of Staff concerning future military co-operation between the two countries, and further promises of military aid were made by a Soviet military delegation that visited Cairo a year later. By 1971, the Egyptian Army again possessed nearly 1 000 Soviet tanks, including some of the modern T-54s and T-55s as well as the older T-34s, and about 150 self-propelled guns. The strength of its airforce was built up to over 400 combat aircraft plus 70 helicopters and 60 transport planes. The country was also now defended by about 250 Guideline SA-2 missiles, whilst it was believed that work had been completed on 23 sites for the more effective SA-3 missiles and work was under way on another 23 sites. The gigantic scope of the Soviet arms supply effort can, however, perhaps best be glimpsed from the fact that the total strength of the army, now very largely dependent on Soviet made small arms and transport vehicles as well as Soviet tanks and artillery, had been increased from 69 000 in 1955, when Soviet arms deliveries first began, to 250 000 in 1971, despite the need to make good all the losses suffered during the June 1967 war.

The enormous Soviet investment in terms of military aid supplied to Egypt reflects more its desire to use Egypt as a pillar of its policies in the Mediterranean and Middle East rather than a reflection of Soviet ambitions in Africa as such. However, the propaganda advantages of this vivid demonstration of what the Soviet Union could do to increase the martial powers of those it favoured on the continent, can also hardly have been lost on Soviet planners.

Increasing and, as it would now seem, well founded doubts about the durability of their hold on Egypt inspired these same planners, however, to examine the possibilities open to them should all their work in Egypt crumble before their eyes. There would seem little doubt that the Friendship Treaty signed between the Soviet Union and Somalia in 1974 was in part due to this desire for an insurance cover which would provide the Soviet Union with a serviceable base in North East Africa should the worst befall them in Egypt.

Over 1 700 members of the Somali armed forces have been trained in the Soviet Union during the last few years and the equipment provided has not only increased in quantity but also very markedly in sophistication. By 1975, Somalia had received about 250 tanks including a number of the modern T-54 type equipped with 120 mm guns making them superior in firepower to most of the armoured vehicles south of the Sahara.

The Somali Army has also received about 450 armoured personnel carriers and other armoured vehicles of various types and a very considerable number of field artillery pieces of up to 122 mm in calibre, plus anti-aircraft and anti-tank tuns, all from the Soviet Union. Its full strength includes six tank battalions, nine mechanised infantry battalions, two commando battalions and other units making a grand total of 22 000 men, thus considerably exceeding the original figure of 20 000, provided for in the Soviet aid agreement in 1962.

The navy possesses six Soviet-built patrol boats, including two carrying Styx guided missiles, whilst the airforce can muster 66 combat aircraft, almost all of Soviet design and including some MIG-17s and MIG-21s. There is also a Soviet-equipped helicopter and transport squadron.

Since about 1970, the Soviet Government has also been showing increasing interest in providing arms for Libya. In June 1975, following the visit of Soviet leaders to Tripoli, it was reported that the Soviet Union had undertaken to provide large deliveries of arms to Libya. In September, the *Sunday Telegraph* stated that:

Soviet weapons and Russian personnel to handle them are flowing into Libya at such a rate that the country seems destined to become Russia's main base for operations in the Mediterranean area, according to the latest reports.

It continued:

The Russians have already clearly decided that Libya could replace Egypt where their clumsy diplomacy lost them President Sadat's goodwill.[14]

The report said that a number of surface-to-air missiles had already been delivered to Libya as well as 375 T-55 and T-62 tanks but added that Soviet instructors were experiencing considerable difficulties in training Libyans to operate sophisticated equipment.

In April 1976, Colonel Gaddafi told a mass rally in Tripoli that the Libyan people now had "thousands of tanks and millions of tons of weapons and ammunition at their disposal to defend the Libyan revolution and its achievements".

The 1976-1977 *The Military Balance* showed Libya as possessing more than 700 Soviet tanks, including 200 T-62s. Contrary to normal practice, it would seem that most of the military equipment provided to Libya has not been donated under aid agreements but sold at prices sometimes above the usual market average. This is presumably a reflection of the Soviet Government's doubts about Colonel Gaddafi's long-term reliability.

Probably the most unlikely connection forged between the Soviet Union and the ruler of any African country in the last few years is that with President Amin of Uganda, a leader who once declared his intention to build a monument to Hitler. Despite occasional squalls and threats by the President to break off diplomatic relations with his Soviet friends, the connection survives to the time of writing and the Soviet Union has shown every sign of attempting to consolidate it, through offers of military aid. In February 1975, for instance, a Soviet military delegation visited the country and President Amin, according to Uganda Radio, told its members that he attributed all his success to the encouragement of the Soviet Union. The leader of the delegation apparently replied that what he had seen in Uganda had impressed him so much that he considered General Amin to be one of the most outstanding leaders in Africa.

The Military Balance 1976-1977 recorded Uganda as being in possession of 15 T-54 and T-55 tanks, 250 Soviet made armoured personnel carriers, Sagger anti-tank guided missiles and various Soviet artillery weapons. The airforce was stated to contain two squadrons of MIG-15, 17 and 21 aircraft. Press reports have spoken of Soviet technicians constructing a training centre to give technical training to the Ugandan army at Entebbe.

Considerable disquiet was said to have been aroused amongst African governments in the area by the steady Ugandan acquisition of arms well beyond the needs of self-defence, particularly in view of the fact that its possession of Soviet weapons such as T-54 tanks, even in small numbers, gave it a decisive superiority over that of neighbouring states.

Early in the spring of 1976, it was announced in Kampala that a new military aid agreement had been signed with the Soviet Union under which the latter undertook not only to replace the MIG fighters destroyed by Israeli action during the Entebbe raid but also to provide some long distance aircraft and other unspecified "hardware".

Despite cooling relations between the two countries, the Soviet re-supply operation that had taken place in the case of military aid to Egypt following the June 1967 war was followed by a similar operation after the October 1973 war. By 1975, the Egyptian army was estimated to be in possession of about 2 000 Soviet-made tanks (including 820 T-62 medium tanks, one of the Soviet army's most recent items of equipment), 2 500 armoured personnel carriers, self-propelled guns, and about 1 300 towed artillery pieces, including weapons up to 180 mm in calibre. A wide new range of guided weapons and anti-aircraft guns had been supplied. The airforce had been built up to a force of about 500 combat aircraft, about the same number as that then possessed by Britain. A similar, although very considerably smaller catalogue of weapons, had also been supplied to Algeria, including 15 FROG-4 surface-to-surface guided missiles.

A Pentagon estimate released early in 1976 stated that over the preceding five years, the Soviet Union had provided about 2 201 million dollars worth of military equipment to African countries. Of this about 656 million dollars worth had gone to Egypt. The number of Soviet military advisers currently stationed in African countries was detailed in the same Pentagon statement as follows:

Algeria	400	Libya	300
Egypt	200	Somalia	1 000
Guinea	110	Sudan	80
Moçambique	25	Uganda	300
Mali	33		

The statement also mentioned the presence of a 310-strong Cuban military training mission in Guinea and one 50-strong in Somalia. At the same time it was calculated that about two-thirds (over 2 300) of all Third World military personnel then receiving training in the Soviet Union came from Africa.

Military aid from Communist China has both been very much lesser in scale and directed to far fewer African countries. *The Military Balance* 1976-77, for instance, records the possession of 16 T-62 Chinese-made tanks in the hands of the Sudanese army and 14 of them in the Congo (Brazzaville). The main Chinese arms supply effort has undoubtedly been concentrated upon Tanzania, the training of whose army has been largely in Chinese hands for some time.

It is estimated that Chinese spending on military aid to developing countries rose from 250 million dollars in the 12 years between 1958 and 1970 to 300 million dollars in the years 1970-74. Of this considerable increase, however, three-quarters was accounted for by equipment supplied to Pakistan. The remaining one quarter was divided between 17 different recipients, Tanzania receiving 10% of the sum involved. *The Strategic Balance* mentions the 14 600-strong Tanzanian army as being in possession of 34 Chinese made T-59 and T-62 tanks and a number of Chinese 122 mm, and 120 mm artillery pieces and anti-aircraft guns. Training is carried out with the aid of Chinese instructors stationed in the country (as also in the case of the army of Zanzibar) and through the despatch of selected cadres to training depots in China. The Navy has received six Shanghai class motor gunboats from China, whilst the airforce has a fighter squadron equipped with MIG-17s and 19s, also obtained from China. Chinese aid to the armed forces of African countries other than those mentioned above would seem to have been confined—when it has taken place at all—to fairly small quantities of small arms, mostly consisting of copies of various types of Soviet weapons, and possibly in a few cases light transport vehicles.

The Peking Government was, however, quick to try and capitalise on the deteriorating relations between the Soviet Union and President Sadat of Egypt in the early autumn of 1976 by offering to replace the Soviet Union as a supplier of spare parts for the Egyptian airforce's MIG aircraft.

Training of Students and Technicians

In an interview with Mr Nikolai Sofinsky, the Deputy Minister for Higher and Specialised Secondary Education of the USSR, in the magazine, *Soviet Military Review,* of February 1976, a correspondent of the publication asked:

> Would you kindly tell us according to what principles and in what forms the Soviet Union grants aid to the countries of Asia, Africa and Latin America in the training of their own specialists?

The Minister replied:

> That aid is granted according to the Leninist principles of proletarian internationalism. In his day, as you well remember, Lenin said that Soviet Russia must help the Mongols, Persians, Indians, and Egyptians to go over to the use of machines, learn to ease their labour and switch over to democracy and socialism. Lenin said that more than 50 years ago. Since then, assisting the formerly oppressed and dependent peoples to overcome their backwardness in the spheres of economy and culture inherited from colonialism has been one of the main lines in the foreign policy pursued by the Soviet state.

The Minister said that Soviet higher and secondary schools started to admit foreign citizens on a "mass scale" in 1956 and that the attendance of foreign students in the USSR has been increasing steadily. In 1957, he said, a total of 134 students from Asia, Africa, and Latin America were studying in the Soviet Union, but at the present time the number was about 20 000.

He pointed out that there were contingents of students from developing countries at the universities of Moscow, Leningrad, Kiev, Kharkov, Byelorussia and Tashkent; at five polytechnical institutes in Leningrad, Odessa, Kiev and Kharkov; the medical institutes in Rostov and Vologorad; the Moscow and Ukranian agricultural institute; the Moscow institute of power engineering, the Azerbaijan institute of oil and chemistry and a number of other establishments.

Referring to the Patrice Lumumba Institute in Moscow, which was founded specially for students from the Third World in 1960, he said that it had six main facilities: engineering physics, mathematics and natural science, economics and law, history and philology, medicine and agriculture. All students undergo a course of one year at a preparatory faculty, and then study for four years in most cases at one of the university's specialist faculties. Medical students continue their studies for a fifth year.

Mr Sofinsky said that the great bulk of students who study at the various centres of learning mentioned do so on the basis of inter-government agreements. Once in the USSR, they are provided with accommodation in a hostel, a stipend, free tuition and free medical services.

On the subject of Soviet aid for the training of students and technicians actually in Third World countries, he claimed that nearly 50 000 technicians had been trained in Egypt alone with Soviet aid. He also claimed that nearly 100 higher educational establishments, secondary and technical schools had been built with Soviet assistance in developing countries. Examples were the national institute of oil, gas, and chemistry in Algeria, the polytechnical institutes in Conakry and Ethiopia and the Tunisian national engineering school.

He explained that educational institutions of this type were built and established either *gratis* or on the basis of long-term credit on the easy terms of 2,5% interest a year. He also stated that more than 20 000 specialists with diplomas granted by Soviet higher educational establishments are now back working in their own countries, many of them in the field of public education.

According to a TASS report of October 1974, about 1 000 Algerians were studying at that time in the Soviet Union. Early the previous year, an agreement had been concluded between the Soviet Union and Zambia to recognise each other's educational qualifications, principally because there were so many Zambians then studying in the USSR. In the autumn of 1974, Moscow Radio said that co-operation between the USSR and the Central African Republic had led to steadily improved relations. An agreement signed by President Bokassa on his visit to Moscow had resulted in over 20 Soviet teachers working at the University of Bangui and 60 teachers working in schools in the Republic. Furthermore, 150 students from the Republic were then studying in the USSR.

Large numbers of Africans have attended special schools for trade unionists in the Soviet Union and other Eastern European countries. One of the most important of these was the World Federation of Trade Unions' school in Budapest, first established in 1959. The Frits Heckhert High School in East Berlin also runs special courses for trade unionists and was likewise established in 1959. Other institutions providing similar training include the Institute for Foreign Students in Leipzig and the Central School of the Revolutionary Trade Union Movement in Prague.

The Soviet-sponsored World Federation of Trade Unions has assisted in the setting up of special schools for trade unionists in both Mali and Guinea.

There have been a number of reports concerning the use of the Patrice Lumumba University in Moscow as a major recruiting ground for enrolling young people of student age from Third World countries in the arts of subversion and espionage.

Although the university's rector, Mr Vladimir Stanis, has emphatically denied that his university is a "school for revolutionaries", he has also admitted that its syllabus has at least a distinct Marxist gloss. Talking to a correspondent of *The Guardian* he said:

> Be a realist, I'm a Communist, my colleagues are Communists. We consider our ideas the best and we're not going to conceal that.[15]

Twenty-five per cent of the students attending courses at any one time are Russians, most of them being specially picked by Party organisations and made well aware of the fact that it is considered their duty discreetly to proselytise amongst the foreign students.

Courses on Marxism-Leninism and Soviet history and philosophy are officially optional for most of those who attend the university but participation in them is quietly encouraged by the various

114

faculty advisers. Members of the staff are said to have unofficially admitted that these "advisers" are, in fact, experienced Party agitators whose tasks include shaping the attitudes of students.

From time to time reports have appeared of African students receiving training in the Soviet Union complaining of acts of racial discrimination towards them or even of physical ill-treatment. One of the most recent of such reports appeared in November 1975 when the Ambassador of Senegal, deputy doyen of Black African Ambassadors in Moscow, was handed a document containing a number of allegations about discrimination and bad treatment by representatives of a group of Africans studying at Ldvov in the Ukraine.

Broadcast Propaganda

One of the most remarkable aspects of the use of propaganda on an international scale since the end of the Second World War has been the enormous growth in the foreign broadcasting services of the two major Communist powers, and to some extent also the Communist countries of Eastern Europe. A growth that has been in sharp contrast to the marked tendency of both Britain and the USA to cut back such services during the same period, in the cause of economy.

In 1950, broadcasts beamed from the Soviet Union to the non-Communist world totalled 535 hours per week. By early 1965, the figure was 1 417 hours per week and rose to 1 986 hours per week in 1974. This figure was supplemented by the 1 390 hours per week broadcast by the Warsaw Pact countries of Eastern Europe (386 hours in 1950). Communist China broadcast a mere 66 hours a week to foreign countries in 1950, but had increased the figure to 1 027 by 1965 and 1 317 by 1974.

Soviet broadcasting to Africa did not begin until April 1958 and then consisted only of a programme broadcast in English and French for 15 minutes each day. The first broadcast in Swahili began in 1960, by which time the USSR was broadcasting to Africa for $33\frac{1}{2}$ hours per week. Increasing Soviet interest in events in Africa at that time was reflected by the stepping up of Soviet broadcasts to the continent to about 120 hours per week by 1964. By that date, too, broadcasts included programmes in Hausa, Lingala, Malagasy,

115

Somali, Zulu, Bambara and Italian, as well as English and French.

By 1966, Soviet broadcasts to Africa were exceeding 120 hours per week, as compared to the 57 hours per week then being broadcast by Britain in five languages only. A new Soviet broadcasting station especially beamed to East Africa had come into service the previous year. Broadcasting to Africa by the other Warsaw Pact countries of Eastern Europe began in the autumn of 1959 and by the end of August 1961 totalled 58 hours a week. Five years later, it had more than doubled and by the end of 1966 was running at the rate of approximately 120 hours per week.

Soviet broadcasting to Africa had reached a level of 167 hours per week by 1975. Programmes were broadcast in the following languages respectively:

Amharic	Ndebele
Bambara	Portuguese
English	Shona
French	Somali
Hausa	Swahili
Lingala	Zulu
Malagasy	Fulani

Seven hours per week of the total Soviet output were beamed from Radio Peace and Progress, a station which, founded in 1964, is officially claimed to have an "independent" viewpoint by the Soviet Government on the grounds that it is controlled by so-called "public bodies" (i.e. trade unions, youth organisations, etc.) and not the government. As, however, all such "public bodies" are under strict Communist Party, and hence in practice government control, the claim is clearly a spurious one, and would seem to be merely a ruse which enables the Soviet Government to deny responsibility for what has been said when, as not infrequently happens, Radio Peace and Progress adopts a more outspoken, bitter, and inflammatory line than Radio Moscow and other nations lodge protests. Mr Julian Hale, in his book, *Radio Power,*[16] refers to the fact that a number of allegations have been made in Western circles that, far from possessing any genuine independence, the station is, in fact, tightly controlled by the KGB, the Soviet secret service.

In addition to the Soviet Union, the Warsaw Pact countries broadcast to Africa for 165 hours 45 minutes per week in 1975. The main languages used were English and French. Only one such country broadcast in an African language, this being East Germany which was broadcasting in Swahili for 15 hours 45 minutes of the 78 hours 45 minutes beamed to Africa each week over Radio Berlin International. Presumably it was the Soviet bloc's wish to exploit the situation arising from the collapse of Portuguese rule in Africa which led to the sudden introduction in 1975 of programmes in Portuguese in the African service of both Radio Berlin International (5 hours 15 minutes per week) and Czechoslovakia's Radio Prague (3 hours 30 minutes per week). Belgrade Radio, in Yugoslavia, broadcast to Africa in Arabic, English, French, German and Spanish for a total of 36 hours 45 minutes per week in 1975.

Broadcasts from Communist China intended for foreign audiences began in a rudimentary form with programmes beamed from Mao Tse-tung's operational base in Yunan in 1948. By 1958, the new Chinese external broadcasting service had achieved an output of 438 hours per week, rising to 690 in 1961 and 897 by early 1964.

The first broadcasts from Communist China to Africa began in 1956 and consisted of a one-hour daily service in morse. This is thought to have been mainly an experiment to test operating and transmitting techniques as the number of potential listeners on the African continent at that time who could understand the morse code must have been miniscule. In the spring of 1958, a daily service in Cantonese was started mainly directed to the Chinese minorities in South and South East Africa and Madagascar. In September 1959, a two-hour daily service in English intended for Africans was introduced. This event marked the beginning of an era of extremely rapid expansion in the field of Chinese broadcasting to Africa. By the winter of 1961, for instance, the number of hours per week beamed to Africa from China totalled 35 hours and the service now included programmes in Swahili and Portuguese. By the end of 1964, the number of hours being broadcast had risen to 77, and Hausa and French had joined the lists of languages being used. A further noticeable increase followed during the next two years and by the middle of 1966, 91 hours of programmes per week were being broadcast.

Thereafter the rate of expansion slowed somewhat, but even so the total hours per week directed to Africa from Radio Peking had increased to 119 by 1975.

The number of African languages being used was, however, considerably fewer than in the case of the Soviet Union, including only Hausa, Hakka and Swahili, other programmes being in Cantonese and standard Chinese, English, French, Italian and Portuguese.

The Communist Chinese line on Africa can also be presumed to be echoed by Albania's Radio Tirana which broadcasts to Africa for 14 hours per week in English.

In general, the programme content of broadcasting services listed in this section consists largely of news bulletins and feature programmes concerned with international events. It is presented in such a way as to give the maximum possible backing to the foreign policy of the Communist country concerned. Such items are supported by programmes giving details of life and development in the country originating the broadcast and are designed to portray the attraction and advantages of life under Marxist-Leninist régime. Much time is also devoted to the visits of delegations from African countries as well as others in the Third World to Communist capitals.

Listeners are quite often invited to write in to the editors of particular programmes for further information on particular aspects of Soviet or Communist Chinese policy. Although the broadcasting services of both countries have always highlighted support for "wars of liberation" and attacks upon the allegedly "imperialist", "colonialist", "neo-colonialist" or "racist" policies of the Western powers, the tone of Soviet broadcasts took on a progressively sharper and more aggressive note as open Soviet involvement in the affairs of Southern Africa rapidly deepened during the latter half of 1975 and early 1976. As the hold of the Marxist MPLA was being consolidated over Angola, the directors of such broadcasts began to show increasing signs of aligning their sights on other targets. On 30 March 1975, for instance, Radio Peace and Progress, in the course of an English language broadcast intended for African audiences, said:

> The forces of racism and reaction recently have suffered resounding defeats and this compels the racist régime and their imperialist teachers to hold on to the last bastions of once powerful citadels of colonialist oppression in all possible ways. These are grounds for the Rhodesian rulers to count on the support of the imperia-

lists. It was no coincidence that the Western press viewed one of the recent statements by the US Secretary of State, Henry Kissinger, containing threats against African national liberation movements and their allies, the socialist community countries, as an expression of direct support for the Smith régime.

However, as the reluctance of the Rhodesian rulers to meet the requirements of the Africans becomes ever more obvious, there is a growing armed struggle in order to return to the Zimbabwe people the right to be the rulers in their own country. The progressive forces of Africa evaluate highly the aid which the Zimbabwe patriots are receiving in this struggle from the Soviet Union and other socialist countries.

This broadcast would seem to provide an interesting example of how Radio Peace and Progress can be used to heighten and exploit tension to the Soviet Union's advantage in sensitive areas, while the somewhat more discreet Moscow Radio uses its broadcasts to calm down Western fears about Soviet actions and intentions. For, on the very same day that this Radio Peace and Progress broadcast was made, Radio Moscow was saying in the course of its regular broadcast programme to Britain that the Soviet Union was not in any way involved in the situation in Southern Africa and that stories about the "alleged Communist threat in the south of Africa" was just part of a campaign "fanned by reactionary imperialist quarters ...".

Presumably, however, to counter the possibility that such remarks might be taken too literally by listening Soviet sympathisers to mean the USSR was in fact lessening its support for the "anti-imperialist" struggle, they were, however, accompanied by the careful statement that:

We do not conceal our views. In the developing countries as everywhere else, we are on the side of the forces of progress, democracy and national independence and regard them as friends and comrades in the struggle.

The external broadcasting services of the Communist powers are far from being only used to attack "Western imperialism" and the governments of White-ruled countries in Africa, but have, on the contrary, quite frequently been used to campaign vigorously against the governments of Black African countries which in Communist eyes show symptoms of reactionary behaviour or of failing to follow the "socialist path". A not inconsiderable amount of broadcasting time in the programmes of both the Soviet Union and Communist China is also taken up with denouncing the policies and attitudes of each other. A Radio Peace and Progress broadcast of 20 March 1975 provides not only a good illustration of this aspect but also of the current Soviet line on recent Chinese activities or alleged activities in Africa. The broadcast included the following remarks:

> The Peking leadership calculated, and is calculating on using the developing states of Africa in the struggle for consolidating their leadership both in the United Nations as well as on the international arena in general. At the same time, the Maoist régime is striving to open up new markets there for its products, to find new sources of raw materials. Nevertheless, quite often now the Maoists are resorting to outright interference in the internal affairs of African states.
>
> Peking is pursuing a policy aimed against the interests of the developing countries. As a rule it is expressed in the form of actions aimed not at consolidating the progressive anti-imperialist forces, but at splitting, dividing and isolating from one another different detachments of the liberation movement. In this way, Maoism everywhere is playing the disgraceful rôle of the accomplice in the most blatant circles of imperialism and reaction, facism and racism, in the struggle against the socialist countries, the progressive régimes of the young independent states, the national liberation movement and all the peace-loving forces.

Three days later, on 23 March 1975, the same station accused Communist China of using such aid projects as the Tanzanian railway as part of a plot to "enmesh Zambia and Tanzania in a net of treaties and agreements".

The importance of broadcasting as a propaganda weapon in Africa has been greatly enhanced by the enormous increase in the number of radios in the hands of the population in recent years. These increased from 875 000 to 4 800 000 in South Africa alone during the years 1955 to 1974, and from 360 000 to 17 700 000 in the remainder of the continent.

Front Organisations

A very wide range of both pro-Moscow and pro-Peking front organisations have been active on the African continent and amongst its peoples during the last 20 or so years. These extend from the well-known international fronts such as the World Peace Council, the International Union of Students, the World Federation of Democratic Youth or the World Federation of Trade Unions and the International Union of Journalists to organisations operating purely on a local level, sometimes under the guise of political parties.

Mr Alan Hutchison[17] has stated that at the time of the late 1950s and early 1960s when many African countries had either just received, or were just about to receive, independence, the major international fronts made a considerable impact. The international flavour of their titles convinced many Africans that by becoming involved with them, they were in fact joining important bodies with a genuine independent rôle in the international community. The front organisations' secretariats based mainly in Eastern Europe took advantage of this opportunity to win new influence by flooding Africa with reports of meetings and conferences and invitations to African delegations and individuals to visit the "Socialist" countries.

As the years went by, however, their appeal has considerably lessened because, as has happened in other parts of the world, blatant Soviet direction and manipulation of their activities has become all too obvious to many, except the most naïve and credulous. Nevertheless, they remain useful propaganda tools, particularly amongst the ill-educated and young, and serve an important purpose in whipping up co-ordinated campaigns around the world against "imperialist oppression" or in support of various "liberation movements".

The most important major Communist front formed especially for the purpose of making a bid for influence within Africa has undoubtedly been the Afro-Asian People's Solidarity Organisation

(AAPSO) which owes its origins to the Conference for the Relaxation of International Tensions held in New Delhi in April 1955 as part of the preparations for the Bandung Conference of that year. Despite its title, the organisation also includes the Soviet Union as a member. Its actual participation was contrived by the special formation of a Soviet National Asian Committee in support of the USSR's claim to be an Asian as well as a European power.

The first conference of AAPSO was held in Cairo in December 1957. It was attended by 500 delegates from Asian and African countries. The chief Soviet delegate told them:

> This Afro-Asian Solidarity Conference, its spirit and ideas, are supported by all honest men throughout the world, because it is anti-imperialist, anti-colonialist and anti-militarist, and thus at the same time just, progressive and humane ...
>
> The Soviet people support this consolidation of those forces in the Afro-Asian countries that will henceforth play an important rôle by extending the zone of peace in the struggle against the rotten system and piracy of imperialism ... Brothers, comrades and friends, lift up your heads and the end of your enslavement is at hand.[18]

A very detailed account of the activities of the Afro-Asian Solidarity Organisation during the early years of Soviet and Communist Chinese expansion in Africa is given in Mr Fritz Schatten's *Communist in Africa*, together with information on the activities of a number of other front organisations, including some of the international fronts. In addition to calling for the total end of all colonialism and all forms of White rule in Africa, where, despite the inclusion of "Asian" in its name, its activities have been entirely concentrated, AAPSO has also campaigned for the end of all other forms of Western influence including economic and other aid.

Not infrequently the meetings of AAPSO and other Communist front organisations in Africa have been the settings for heated exchanges between Soviet and Chinese delegations and their followers.

Co-ordinated Activities in "Target Countries"

In African countries in which events appear to be moving in their favour, the Communist powers have on occasion shown a tendency to push home the advantage they think they see opening before them in a manner that can touch almost every aspect of national life. Such tendencies first became obvious during the Nkrumah régime in Ghana during the early 1960s. In addition to large quantities of civil and military aid of the same type as that given to many other African countries, African military advisers became deeply involved with the transformation of the Presidential Guards Regiment into a reliable instrument for backing the régime's Marxist-orientated policies. Soviet teachers were brought in to teach in the schools, 100 state farms were constructed with Soviet help, and Soviet experts advised on a scheme for the transformation of peanut small-holdings into a state-co-operative.

By 1963, a permanent Soviet economic adviser was attached to the President's Secretariat and in the University of Ghana a Soviet expert had drawn up plans for completely reorganising the university's syllabus. Under his plans, this was to include courses on Marxism-Leninism run by Soviet instructors and a secretary from Nkrumah's ruling CPP party was appointed to a post in the Vice-Chancellor's office. Representatives of the party were also to be introduced into the University Council which had power over both selection of employees and security of tenure.

Before Nkrumah was overthrown by a coup d'état, a plan had been set in motion to bring about a major reshaping of Ghana's economy. According to some observers, this had as its ultimate object the establishment of a series of state corporations to be placed under the charge of people with the "proper" ideological training.

The influence of the Soviet Union's ambassador, Mr Rodinov, grew so much that he often felt free to intervene to try to squash any move that seemed harmful to Soviet designs, such as army officers' objections to buying Soviet equipment, and to insist, for instance, that "real Socialists" should be employed as lecturers in the university.

One of the fields in which the Soviet Union came to have the greatest interest was that of the President's security service. A considerable number of KGB and East German security service advisers were drafted in to reorganise it after an abortive attempt on the President's life.

A not dissimilar, but in some ways even more extensive, degree of Soviet involvement has been building up during the last five years in Somalia, particularly since the signing of the friendship treaty in July 1974. The importance given to its signing by the Soviet authorities was signified by the number of senior ministers and officials who accompanied President Podgorny on his visit to Mogadishu. These included Mr I.V. Arkhipov, Deputy Chairman of the Soviet Council of Ministers; Mr V.V. Kuznetsov, First Deputy Foreign Minister; General S.L. Sokolov, First Deputy Defence Minister; Mr V.A. Ustinov, Head of the African Department of the Soviet Foreign Ministry and Mr V.N. Sofinsky, Head of the Foreign Ministry Press Department. The treaty was the fourth to be signed in the area of the Indian Ocean since 1970, the others being with Egypt and India in 1971 and Iraq in 1972.

A large number of Soviet advisers are attached to the office of Somalia's ruler, President Siad Barre. The President exercises control through a regional system. There are 15 regional and 60 district commissioners, most of whom have been personally chosen by the President or his close advisers. This regional system is supported by a number of organisations whose main rôle is political indoctrination. Government control of the press is exercised centrally from Mogadishu. Films and theatrical performances are also subject to the same censorship. A great deal of the material used by the press and by the radio service is of Soviet origin. Officials in the Soviet Embassy's press department channel articles they wish to see published through the Ministry of Information or the President's political office. On occasion, they have been known to approach editors directly themselves.

In a speech in July 1972, President Siad Barre specifically rejected "African Socialism" and all other brands of "Socialism" except for the Moscow brand of Marxism-Leninism. However, observers believe that he and most of his chief assistants are more motivated by an ambitious nationalism that seeks to use Marxism for their own purposes than by pure ideology. There would seem to be no doubt as to the nature of their revolutionary views. The Secretary for the Ministry of Information and National Guidance, Colonel Ismail Ali Abokor, for instance, described the proper rôle of the mass media in 1971 as being:

124

The proper utilisation of the mass media is a means to an end. It must be harnessed to the success of the socialist, revolutionary road we have taken.[19]

The most important instruments in the scheme for indoctrination of the population into a belief that this "socialist revolutionary road" is leading in a beneficial direction are the National Guidance Centres, a web of which covers the country. These are controlled by "public relations officers" mostly trained in the Soviet bloc and directly responsible to the President's office. Their duties have been explained by a Soviet-trained Somali airforce officer writing in *World Marxist Review* as being to

conduct educational work in every city block and every village. They arrange discussions and deliver lectures on the fundamentals of Marxism-Leninism.[20]

Another rôle of the National Guidance Centres is to encourage the local population to engage in "Self-help" or voluntary labour projects in their spare time. They would appear to exercise this function in a carrot-and-stick fashion. The political officer in charge of the local section of the government's youth movement, the Victory Pioneers or *Gulwadayasha*, has at his disposal a limited amount of scarce household and other consumer goods which he can allocate to those who co-operate in the scheme. On the other hand, gaol sentences are meted out to those who fail to take part in voluntary work.

The *Gulwadayasha* was established on Soviet advice and seems to be organised on very much the same lines as an auxiliary police organisation for young people in the Soviet Union itself known as the *Druzhiniki* which was formed in 1959 and now has some seven million members. In Somalia, one of the main rôles of the *Gulwadayasha* is to act as an élite political vigilante organisation reporting on dissidents and mobilising support for government programmes. Many have been trained in the Soviet Union and have both special rights and privileges and more authority than the normal police. Some observers see in the *Gulwadayasha* the seeds of the "vanguard party" which, according to the orthodox Soviet theory, the President will need in order to establish a fully-fledged Marxist state and which he at present lacks.

Beginning in July 1974, an attempt was made to extend the indoctrination programme to the nomad tribes who comprise two-thirds of the total population of Somalia. Although the idea was apparently that of the Secretary of Higher Education, there is reason to believe that it may have first come from a close friend of the Minister, Mr Lev Mironov, First Secretary at the Soviet Embassy. The plan was to conduct the operation by means of the use of selected student teachers from secondary schools. All secondary schools were ordered to close for a year whilst it was under way and hundreds of young people were despatched from the cities to try and impart news of the coming of "scientific socialism" in remote areas.

The operation, however, seems to have been far from a success. The nomads showed themselves in the main remarkably uninterested in the news and very reluctant to share their food with the young "crusaders", as it had been hoped they would do. Many of the young people engaged in the task also became ill with malaria for which they had not been provided with adequate medicines. Before long, many of them became disillusioned and began to make their way home, despite the risk of being arrested by the police and put in gaol.

The very considerable scale of Soviet military assistance to Somalia has already been mentioned. Soviet assistance has also been a significant factor in another key element of President Siad Barre's system of control. This is the Somali National Security Service (NSS), an organisation that has been in receipt of Soviet advice and assistance since 1959.

In 1972, no less a figure that Mr Yuri Andropov, head of the Soviet Committee of State Security or KGB, himself visited Somalia presumably to assure himself that the reorganisation of the NSS was proceeding in a satisfactory manner. Colonel Suleiman, the Somali head of security and intelligence, subsequently visited Moscow to study KGB operations. About a dozen KGB officers are known to be stationed in Mogadishu, where they have their headquarters in the former Somali Parliament buildings, an edifice which in the days of the Italian occupation housed the Fascist headquarters and in which nowadays revolutionary courts try political offenders. It is believed that well over 3 000 people are now undergoing detention for political reasons.

All security and intelligence reports are open to the KGB officers and as the Somali security service has established a system of informers reaching into every section of the population, its Soviet friends are thus able to keep themselves well-informed as to every trend of opinion within the country. Many workers are interrogated by security service officers once a month, not only about their own activities but also about the loyalty of friends and relatives.

Delegations from the Italian Communist Party and from East Germany have played a part in encouraging the cementing of links with the Soviet Union, and aid has also been provided by Cuba in the shape of a number of military instructors. Some of these arrived in Somalia in March 1974 on board the Cuban ship *Vietnam Heroica,* a vessel which was later to play a considerable part in transporting Cuban forces to Angola. As well as imparting military instruction, some Cubans have also been involved in giving political lectures in a camp at Merca.

The Cuban and Soviet assisted victory in Angola and the coming to power of President Samora Machel's Marxist Frelimo-based Government in Moçambique were both quickly followed by vigorous Soviet and (in the case of Angola) Cuban endeavours to consolidate the favourable situation which had opened up for the Communist cause in these two countries.

An article in *The Times* of 9 June 1976, for instance, reported that Soviet advisers already had "direct and exclusive" control of the Angolan Defence Ministry. Joint Russo-Cuban control of the Ministry of Finance and the Bank of Angola had also been established, whilst Cubans were supervising the Ministry of the Interior and the powerful Directorate of Intelligence and Security (DISA). Cuban advisers are known to predominate on the staff of President Neto. East German advisers have been brought into the country to direct its internal administration and Romanian advisers direct the Government's agricultural programme and the development of such natural resources as Angola's considerable iron ore deposits.

The terms of the friendship treaty with the Soviet Union signed by President Neto in October 1976 during a visit to Moscow, have been described by TASS as being aimed at consistently broadening Party contacts at all levels and providing for "comradely exchanges of views" on questions of mutual interest. It was to arrange for regular exchanges of delegations; for co-operation in the training of Party cadres and for the conducting of joint research into "topical problems of contemporary social development"; the cementing of contacts between Party press organs and other sections of the mass media; and the promoting of friendly relations between "public organisations" (i.e. trade unions, cultural groups, etc.) in the two countries. It was also agreed that the ruling parties of the Soviet Union and Angola should each year implement practical plans and measures of co-operation and that military co-operation should also be further developed in the interests of strengthening Angola's "defence capacity".

The signing of this agreement was followed two months later by the signing of an agreement between Angola and Cuba which provided for Cuban assistance to Angola in the form of the despatch of experts in the fields of transportation, education, agriculture, forestry and public health.

Both the Soviet Union and Cuba have selected diplomats with considerable experience of Africa to represent them as Ambassadors in Angola. The Soviet Ambassador, Mr Boris Vorobyev, served in Nigeria from 1970 to 1974 and the Cuban Ambassador, Mr Oscar Oramas, who arrived in Luanda as early as January 1976, previously served in Guinea and Mali. Mr Oramas is also believed to hold a high rank in the Cuban Directorate General of Intelligence (DGI) which is itself under the control of the Soviet KGB.

Writing in the *Sunday Telegraph* on 20 February 1977, Mr Robert Moss said that:

> Between them, the Cubans and the Russians now decide who can enter and leave Angola, what civil liberties (if any) individuals and organisations will be allowed, what the country will export and import, and how much money will be printed. On the coffee plantations Cuban advisers are said to operate a system of forced labour: workers are shifted from one place to another, or from one job to another, without notice or appeal.

He also reported that Cuban instructors were training Angolan trade union leaders at the Lazaro Pena trade union college in Mariano. The syllabus in use includes Marxist philosophy and Cuban history. Mr Moss described the recent measures introduced by the Soviet-Cuban controlled Ministry of Finance as part of its move to launch a new Angolan currency, the kwanza, as setting an example for any other government which might wish to wipe out its middle class at one stroke. He explained:

Angolan families are allowed (on a one-for-one basis) to exchange the old Portuguese escudos for kwanzas, but only up to the limit of 20 000 kwanzas. Anyone who has more than that stashed away has to accept that his savings have been turned into worthless paper.

Cubans are in charge of the Government's "political mobilisation campaign" whereby it hopes to build up popular support for its policies. At the beginning of 1977, the Cuban army contingent in Angola of about 13 000 men was split into garrisons in the major towns of six military regions into which the country had been divided. A number of these garrisons are still periodically involved in operations against scattered anti-Communist UNITA groups. Cuban officers were in command of all airfields and were playing a leading part in the formation and training of the new Angolan airforce.

In the spring of 1976, President Machel of Moçambique announced during a visit to Moscow that his intention was that his country should become "the first fully Marxist State in Africa". A number of agreements providing for co-operation between the Soviet Union and Moçambique on cultural and scientific matters were signed during his visit, adding to the ties between the two countries provided by a series of agreements covering industrial and commercial co-operation and fishing rights which had been concluded previously.

The Frelimo Government's attempts to bring the country on to a fully Marxist course have included the employment of so-called "dynamization committees" which would appear to be copies of the Bolshevik "Street Committees" of 1917, to carry out propaganda amongst the population in places of work. The People's National Security Service, whose rôle has been defined as that of carrying a fight against "reactionary" elements, has both powers of arrest and confiscation of property; it can either hand over those it arrests to the police or send them to "rehabilitation centres" where they are put to hard labour. A number of reports have appeared to the effect that prisoners held in these camps, both Black and White, are often subjected to extreme brutality and degradation.

Control of the news media by Frelimo is complete. Would-be journalists have to train at a Frelimo-controlled school of journalism and before starting work have to take a pledge to serve the party and the revolution. A complete nationalisation of land was carried out in 1975. All educational institutions have also been taken under state control and private medical practice abolished. In February 1976, President Machel announced that all privately owned buildings would be nationalised and it was proclaimed that in future no building could be sold or transferred to another owner without the approval of the state.

Despite its originally announced intention to allow freedom of worship, the Government has carried on a considerable vendetta against the Catholic Church. In June 1975, President Machel announced that because of its former support for Portuguese rule its chapels and churches would be turned into maternity homes.

An intensive system of indoctrination of youth is being carried on. President Machel has made it clear that the country's schools must be centres for the propagation of national culture and political and technical knowledge. The knowledge they impart must be aimed at aiding the "development and progress of society". Immediately following the country's independence, 1 600 teachers and students from the University of Lourenço Marques were ordered to go and work in the countryside or factories in order to rid themselves of the "élitist" ideas imparted by the old colonial system. In a speech in the Moçambique capital on 24 August 1975, the President is reported to have said that learning was only for the rich and to have complained that once university students got their degrees all they thought about was trying to obtain capitalist positions in order to exploit the people.

A two-year period of compulsory military service has been introduced for both young men and women. It was announced that any who were not called up for this service, which includes a heavy course of political indoctrination, would have to undertake other "national tasks".

In February 1977, Frelimo held its Third Party Congress, the site being the former Portuguese Officers' Club in Maputo. On its opening day, President Machel made a nine-hour speech in which he proclaimed that Frelimo would transform itself from a guerrilla movement into a "vanguard party of workers and peasants". He said that the aim of this party would be the destruction of capitalism in Moçambique.

The following day, pledges of support for Frelimo were received from representatives of the Communist Parties of the Soviet Union, East Germany, Bulgaria and Romania. The Soviet Ambassador presented President Machel with a large red flag bearing a picture of Lenin, whilst the East German representative presented him with a bust of Karl Marx.

The proceedings of the Congress were not infrequently interrupted by outbursts of song, sometimes led by President Machel himself or by his Foreign Minister, and including songs in praise of the virtues of "scientific socialism". Of the 37 foreign delegations present, 23 represented Marxist parties in Europe or the Third World. Six other delegations represented Marxist-dominated "liberation movements", including the Patriotic Front of Rhodesia led by Mr Mugabe and the banned African National Congress of South Africa. The President of the latter, Mr Oliver Tambo, said that Moçambique was the dynamising force for political, social and economic change in Southern Africa. He said further that Frelimo's example would establish the basis of a new society in South Africa.

One of the main decisions taken at the conference was to transform Frelimo into an élitist "vanguard party" on the lines of the Communist Parties of Eastern Europe and which only the most highly politically motivated cadres would be able to join. The original announcement of this move said that nobody who believed in God would be able to join the Party, but this provision appeared subsequently to have been dropped. The masses of the population will not be eligible to join the Party itself but will be enrolled instead into its various affiliated organisations. The Party will be dedicated to "scientific socialism" through which it aims to build a "new society" at home and to assist in the expansion of the "world anti-imperialist front" abroad. It is hoped to re-vitalise the country's floundering economy through raising agricultural production by a programme which will include the introduction of communal villages and co-operative farms and by a programme for industrial expansion which will ultimately and particularly aim at the development of heavy industry. In addition to its economic purpose, it is intended that this "industrialisation programme" shall "create conditions of real equality" and "raise the political consciousness of the masses".[21]

In Tanzania, the African country with which Communist China has so far cemented the firmest ties, Chinese activities are often so surrounded by secrecy as to make details hard to come by. One observer, Mr Alan Hutchison has, however, noted that Chinese aid and other officials have to a considerable extent built up a privileged position in the country. He has recorded, for instance, that Chinese official cars, jeeps and other vehicles appeared to be able to park anywhere in Dar es Salaam despite parking restrictions, without any action ever being taken against the drivers. Chinese lorry drivers, he has said, frequently jumped long queues and seemed to tend to monopolise the middle of the road forcing all other traffic to give way. When the authorities, worried about the effect of heavy loads on a newly completed stretch of road, set up a weighbridge to prevent vehicles being overloaded, Chinese drivers just simply refused to stop at it. At Dar es Salaam airport only Chinese seemed to be allowed to greet new arrivals on the tarmac without showing a security pass.

Mr Hutchison also stated that during a meat shortage in Dar es Salaam in 1972, Chinese shoppers always went straight to the head of queues, and not infrequently bought up the entire stock of the shop in front of the anxious gaze of the other would-be customers who had been queuing patiently.

On a more sinister level, one victim of the Chinese determination to preserve a large degree of secrecy concerning their activities in Tanzania, was a Nigerian student, Mr Cornelius Orgunsawo. He applied to the Tanzanian embassy in London for a visa to visit Tanzania for the purpose of carrying out research for a thesis he was doing on the subject of the Chinese in Africa. He was told his request would be referred to Dar es Salaam. He arrived in that city in December 1969 but before a month was out he was arrested and placed under illegal detention in conditions which he subsequently described as "inhuman and animalistic".

During the early years of the Chinese aid programme to Tanzania, it would seem to have been not uncommon for aid projects to be hidden from view by high fences or hedges of bush, whilst the Chinese concerned with them assumed almost police-like powers in order to arrest or eject any strangers who strayed into the area.

Communist China would seem to have been successful in

obtaining a very considerable degree of influence over the Tanzanian news media. Its influence is particularly strong amongst journalists working for such newspapers as *The Nationalist* and *The Daily News Standard*. On at least one occasion, the Chinese embassy has used its influence to have a film that it considered unfriendly to China banned from cinemas in the country. The film, The Shoes of the Fisherman, was taken off after only one showing at a charity performance, after a protest from the Chinese embassy.

REFERENCES

1. Quoted in *L'Egypte au Mouvement,* Jean and Simon Lacouture, Paris, 1956, p. 214.
2. *China's African Revolution,* Alan Hutchison, Hutchinsons Ltd., London 1975, p. 88.
3. "Independent Africa in the Making", O. Orestov, *International Affairs,* November 1975.
4. *Chinese and Soviet Aid to Africa,* John Desseks, Praeger Publishers, New York, 1975, p. 110-111.
5. *Daily Telegraph,* 3 June 1975.
6. *Chinese and Soviet Aid to Africa, op. cit.,* p. 108-109.
7. *Ibid.,* p. 158-159.
8. *The Soviet Presence in Somalia, op. cit.*
9. *The Times,* 24 October 1975.
10. *Arms for the Third World,* Wynfred Joshua and Stephen P. Gilbert, John Hopkins Press, London, 1969.
11. *Africa Vysirayetput,* V.G. Solodovnikov, 1970, p. 175.
12. *Sudan: The Long War,* Cecil Eprile, Conflict Studies No. 21, Institute for the Study of Conflict, London, 1972.
13. *Ibid.,* p. 9.
14. The *Sunday Telegraph,* 21 September 1975.
15. *The Guardian,* 28 April 1976.
16. *Radio Power,* Julian Hale, Paul Elek Ltd., London 1975, p. 17.
17. *China's African Revolution, op. cit.,* p. 36-37.
18. Minutes of the First Afro-Asian People's Conference, Cairo, 1958.
19. *The Soviet Presence in Somalia, op. cit.*
20. Colonel Ali Mattan Hashi, *World Marxist Review,* Prague, 11 November 1972.
21. *The Times,* 9 February 1977.

Chapter 5

Subversion and Espionage

In almost every area of the non-Communist world, the history of the years since the end of the Second World War has contained repeated instances of Soviet diplomats, trade officials, journalists, etc. being given abrupt notice to leave the country to which they had been appointed on account of their indulging in acts of espionage against it. This behaviour was particularly prevalent in Third World countries where Soviet agents attempted to interfere in their domestic affairs with the aim of bringing about a change in the political situation. The newly independent countries of Africa have certainly been no strangers to such occurrences.

The main weapon for carrying out espionage and subversion for the Soviet Government is, of course, the First Chief Directorate of the Committee for State Security, or KGB, certainly the largest and almost certainly, the most efficient machine for internal repression and clandestine external aggression the world has ever seen. It would, however, be a mistake to regard the KGB as the only important weapon the Soviet Union has for waging subversive and political warfare. One noted expert, Brian Crozier,[1] has stated that the main drive of the clandestine side of Soviet policy springs not so much from the KGB itself, important though that organisation is, as from the International Department of the Central Committee of the Communist Party of the Soviet Union. This he describes as being the direct linear descendant of the old Comintern. The International Department's present director is, in fact, Boris Ponomarev, a former member of the Executive Committee of the Comintern. The latter organisation was disbanded by Stalin in 1943, when he badly wanted to reassure his war-time allies.

Other organisations which play a not insignificant part in the Soviet subversive machinery include the Communist international front organisations such as the World Federation of Trade Unions, the World Peace Council, the World Federation of Democratic Youth and the International Union of Students, etc. These attract many thousands of young people from all over the world, including many from Africa, to lavishly staged rallies usually held in Eastern Europe. Aid is also given by so-called friendship associations linking non-Communist countries with countries of the Soviet bloc. Like the international front organisations, one of the chief rôles of these is to act as recruiting agencies aimed at attracting persons into Communist Party activity, including sometimes clandestine activity, in their respective countries. They are also known to have been used as a useful field of recruitment by KGB "talent spotters" from whose members they can pick particularly suitable persons for "processing", with the aim of eventually turning them into agents.

Mention should also be made of the activities of the International Department of the All-Union Central Council of Trade Unions (AUCCTU). This department includes a research section whose duty it is to study ways and means of improving Communist methods of infiltrating trade unions in non-Communist countries, compiling lists of active trade unionists in them who might be induced to help their cause, and examining means of exploiting industrial disputes.

The First Chief Directorate of the KGB is divided into 10 departments of which three seem to be concerned with the African continent. These are the 8th Department, which covers the Arab nations as well as such countries as Yugoslavia, Turkey, Greece, Iran, Afghanistan and Albania; the 9th Department, which covers English-speaking African countries; and the 10th Department, which covers French-speaking African countries. Each department has sub-sections covering a particular country or countries.

Experience has shown that the organisation of KGB activity in foreign countries runs to a standard pattern. This depends, in the first instance, on the existence of a so-called "legal" network of agents, this network being invariably presided over by a senior KGB officer known as "The Resident". "The Resident" operates under diplomatic cover, holding an official position on the staff of the Soviet embassy, although in some cases this position may be a very lowly one, such as that of a chauffeur. No matter how low his official position, it enables the Resident to exploit the diplomatic privileges normally extended to a member of the embassy staff. The network he directs will include other members of the staff, KGB officers working under the cover of positions on the staff of such Soviet trade or other mission as may exist in the country in which he operates, and locally recruited agents, i.e. native citizens of the country in which he works.

In some cases, Soviet ambassadors themselves are known to have been experienced KGB officers, but normally it would seem that the ambassador is only kept partially informed of the Resident's activities. A special section of the embassy is usually set aside for the use of the Resident and his lieutenants and entry to it is barred to all members of the embassy staff not involved in his operations. A most interesting and detailed description of how such a "Legal" KGB network operates in a Third World country was given by a former KGB officer and subsequent defector, Mr Aleksandr Kasnachev, in a book entitled *Inside a Soviet Embassy*.[2] Although published in 1963 and based on his experiences in Burma, there is little reason to think that the basic methods of operation he describes have altered in any essential detail in the years that have intervened, or differ very much in other areas, particularly in the case of Third World countries.

The percentage of KGB officers employed in "Legal" networks at Soviet embassies appears to vary considerably from country to country. It would, however, seldom seem to be below one-quarter to one-third of the total. A chart[3] published by the Institute for the Study of Conflict in 1974 gave an estimate that of 930 Soviet diplomatic and other officials known to be stationed on the African continent (exclusive of Libya, Tunisia, Algeria and Morocco) some 200 were probably agents of the KGB. The breakdown of numbers as regards major African countries was as follows:

Country	Total Officials	Suspected Agents
Egypt	116	29
Sudan	48	9
Ethiopia	64	14
Tanzania	37	11
Kenya	39	13
Zaire	23	3
Zambia	36	11
Nigeria	64	16
Ghana	39	11

One of the highest percentages of agents in the smaller African countries was reported to be in the Congo (Brazzaville) where it was said that out of 18 officials, eight were suspected agents. A high concentration of agents for the size of the country was also shown in Senegal with 14 out of 59 officials being shown as suspected agents.

Soviet interest in the oil-bearing states of the Persian Gulf, which the chart also covered, is shown by the suspected presence of 17 agents out of 45 officials in the tiny state of Kuwait and 63 agents out of 234 officials in Iran.

Another study, *Soviet Strategic Penetration of Africa,* produced by the same Institute in November 1976, showed a total of 318 suspected Soviet intelligence officers operating in Black Africa as members of diplomatic or other official missions to African countries. The increase in the number of KGB or GRU agents in certain countries was particularly marked. The number of such agents reported to be in Zambia had increased from the 1974 figure of 11 listed above to 27. The presence of no less than 40 agents was reported in Nigeria, 31 in Senegal and 22 in Ethiopia. In addition, the first indications of the formation of Soviet intelligence networks based on official representation had begun to appear in the former Portuguese territories of Angola, Moçambique and Guinea-Bissau.

The capability of the Soviet Union for disruption and espionage activity through its intelligence services cannot, however, be measured by the scope of "Legal" KGB networks alone. The repeated evidence of defectors has made it clear that it is standard KGB practice to complement the work of such networks by building a so-called "Illegal" network, working in parallel, but quite separately, from the "Legal" network controlled from the embassy in the same country.

"Illegal" networks have their own "Residents", normally Soviet citizens who have been specially trained over many years to act the part of citizens of other countries. One very successful "Illegal" who directed the activities of a network in Britain was, for instance, given the background of a Canadian businessman, in which guise he operated very successfully for a considerable time. The utmost care is taken in the creation of convincing "backgrounds" for such agents, which is sometimes based upon that of real but obscure persons who have been safely dead for some time and have no living relatives.

Typical of the care which goes into the creation of such agents to enable "Illegals" to operate under deep cover in some harmless guise was that of Mr Yuri Loginov who was arrested in South Africa in 1967. Investigations revealed that nearly eight years had been spent in preparing Loginov for operations in the United States. He had learnt both English with an American accent and expressions perfectly, circulating amongst Americans in Moscow as part of his training, and became well versed in American customs. In order that he should have various different covers available to him, he was trained in the three very varying crafts of a welder, a bookkeeper and a travel writer. He devoted himself to an intensive study of American geography and that country's system of government and business. He travelled to Cairo where he was employed on intelligence operations against both Egyptian and American interests.

During his stay in Johannesburg, he was also employed in espionage against South Africa, but it appears that he was chiefly engaged in studying the customs, geography and history of that country in order to extend still further the artificial background that was being created for him in order that he might be all the more profitably employed elsewhere.

It would seem probable that "Illegal" networks directed by such men and recruiting their own local agents have been set-up in a number of major African countries. One purpose of an "Illegal" network is to fill the gap created should a break in diplomatic relations occur between the country in which it operates and the Soviet Union and the operations of the "Legal" network based on the embassy be brought to an abrupt halt.

138

The activities of the KGB are to some extent supplemented by the Chief Intelligence Directorate of the Soviet General Staff, or GRU as it is generally known. Although its primary aims are, as might be expected, the gathering of strategic, tactical and technical military intelligence, it has become engaged in industrial espionage and the promotion of guerrilla warfare.

The GRU has its own administration and schools, and operates its own networks abroad under its own Residents based in Soviet embassies, these networks reporting directly to GRU headquarters in Moscow. The great majority of Soviet military attachés work for the GRU, as do many of the employees of the Soviet airline Aeroflot working abroad. Although operating to a considerable extent independently, the GRU and the KGB work together harmoniously when the need arises. According to one authority on the Soviet intelligence services, the GRU has in recent years tended to become more and more a subsidiary of the KGB.[1]

As in other areas of the world, KGB activity in Africa has most often come to light when governments have abruptly requested the withdrawal of Soviet diplomats, officials and journalists or, as twice in the case of the Soviet Embassy in Zaire, entire embassy staffs.

One of the earliest of such occasions took place in December 1961 in Guinea. As recounted in the previous chapter, the previous year Mr Danil Solod had arrived in Conakry as Soviet Ambassador. At the time of his arrival in Conakry, Soviet hopes were high of turning Guinea into a first and promising ally south of the Sahara as the result of the programme of rapid economic and political penetration.

The first signs of the troubles which were to lead to a sharp reversal for Soviet hopes began in 1961, when the Executive Committee of the Guinean Teachers' Union distributed a memorandum critical of government policies. Government spokesmen alleged that copies of that memorandum had been given to "Eastern embassies". A few days later three members of the teachers' union were arrested and put on trial. The three were sentenced severely and disturbances of deepening gravity broke out almost at once.

During these, it was reported that agitators appeared amongst the crowds, it was said out of unmarked cars belonging to the Soviet Embassy. These agitators told the crowds that it was impossible for any country to be neutral and aligned neither with the East bloc nor the West, and that Guinea must decide with which bloc it wanted to be aligned. Early in December, President Sekou Toure blamed the troubles on a foreign supported plot, naming in particular "Eastern embassies". Shortly afterwards, a representative of the Guinea Press Agency, described by Guinea Radio as being "the damned soul of the plot" and of engaging in "systematic economic espionage" on behalf of "Eastern embassies", was arrested.

This was followed by a speech by the President at a public rally in which he accused plotters of giving information to Eastern embassies and with giving aid to a secret Communist organisation active in the north of the country. He spoke of investigations having provided evidence of the existence of a "subversive network" with tentacles reaching out to Dakar, Paris and an "Eastern bloc embassy". He also described the troubles as being due to the work of a Marxist-Leninist group whose "Machiavellian plan was to unleash a Marxist revolution in Guinea".

The climax to these incidents came on 13 December when the Soviet Ambassador, Mr Danil Solod, arrived with the rest of his colleagues of the diplomatic corps in Conakry to take part in the official welcome for the visiting Prime Minister of Nigeria. Almost as soon as he arrived, he was informed by the Guinean Government chief of protocol that he would not be allowed to take any part in the reception. Three days later he was on an aircraft for Moscow, having been asked to leave the country for "personal reasons", and furthermore asked to leave at once rather than wait for the usual Czech airline weekly flight.

Less than two years after these events had occurred in Guinea, the Government of the Republic of the Congo (now Zaire) demanded the withdrawal of the entire staff of the Soviet Embassy in Leopoldville (Kinshasa) after links had been found between agents operating from the embassy and armed rebels. The Soviet Government was also accused of having introduced arms into the country for the use of these rebels. When the repercussions from this incident had subsided somewhat, the Government asked the Soviet Union to sign a protocol binding itself to maintain a staff of seven diplomats only in Zaire. Despite this, however, it had increased again to 42 by early 1970.

Shortly afterwards, the Congolese authorities discovered that a new KGB network had been established whose ramifications involved the recruiting of agents in the army, the Ministry of Information, the Ministry of Foreign Affairs and the National

Documentation Centre. The Government accordingly at once expelled four proven KGB officers and again demanded that the Soviet Embassy staff be reduced to a maximum of seven.

In 1963, three KGB officers were expelled from Kenya, including Mr Yuri Yukalov, the First Secretary of the Soviet Embassy in Nairobi, another First Secretary at the same embassy, Mr Vladimir Godakov, and Mr Yuri K. Kumrein, correspondent of the Soviet *Novosti* press agency. Interestingly enough, the same three officers were still serving in Africa in 1974. Mr Yukalov held the post of First Secretary in the Soviet Embassy in Dar es Salaam, Mr Godakov was the Counsellor of the Soviet Embassy in Tripoli and Mr Kumrein worked under his usual journalistic cover in Nigeria.[5]

Altogether 10 diplomats from Communist countries were expelled from Kenya in the spring of 1966. As well as the three KGB officers already noted, the expulsions also included members of the staff of the Czechoslovak, Hungarian and Chinese Communist embassies. The Kenyan Minister for Home Affairs, Mr Daniel Moi, said in a statement at the time that more than £400 000 had been employed in attempts to "subvert the Government".

This was, however, clearly not to be the end of such activities by Communist intelligence services in Kenya, for in February 1968 the Government expelled the representative of a Soviet film-export concern because of his "espionage activities". The representative of *Novosti* was also expelled at the same time. Two months later a Czechoslovakian journalist was also asked to leave, no reason being given in this case.

Mr John Barron, himself a former United States intelligence officer, gives in an appendix to his book, *KGB,* a long list of Soviet citizens known to have figured in clandestine operations in non-Communist countries between the late 1950s and the early 1970s. Mr Barron described this list as consisting of

> only those Soviet personnel positively identified by two or more responsible sources as having engaged in clandestine activities against foreign countries. Most are known to be regular staff officers of the KGB, but a few may be co-opted agents.
> Some are GRU officers ...[6]

Of the agents listed, 151 are stated to have served in one or more named African countries during the period mentioned. All of these, except three who are noted as belonging to the GRU, appear to have been in the employ of the KGB. Forty-seven are shown as having been expelled by the government of the African state in which they were operating. A figure which, when compared with the total, would seem a sure indication that in Africa, as in other areas, the amount of KGB activity brought to public notice by such expulsions is but the small tip of a very large iceberg. Expulsions of Soviet agents, either as individuals or in groups, are shown to have occurred in the following countries:

1957	Libya	1968	Kenya
1961	Guinea	1969	Kenya
1961	Congo	1970	Egypt
1963	Congo (Zaire)	1970	Congo (Zaire)
1964	Sudan	1971	Congo (Zaire)
1964	Rhodesia	1971	Dahomey
1966	Ghana	1972	Egypt
1966	Guinea	1972	Mali
1967	Ghana		

One, presumably less successful, KGB agent named Mr Yatsyna is shown as having been expelled from two separate African states two years in succession, from the Congo in 1971 and from Mali in 1972.

The list of intelligence officers operating in Africa also includes the names of 10 Soviet ambassadors to African countries who are themselves known to have been involved in clandestine activities. Amongst these appears the name of the already mentioned Mr Danil Solod, Ambassador to Guinea in 1961, and that of three other Ambassadors to Guinea. These were Mr Vasili Yakubovsky, who served in that country in 1969, his predecessor, Mr Aleksei Voronin, who served there from 1964-1968, and his successor, Mr Anatoli Ratanov, who arrived in Conakry in 1970. The other ambassadors mentioned were:

Mr Suren A. Toumasyan, Ambassador to Libya, 1965-1970
Mr Vladimir M. Vinogradov, Egypt, 1970
Mr Aleksei Shvedov, Morocco, 1963-1964

Mr Dmitri Pozhidayev,	Morocco, 1958-1962,
	Egypt 1965-1967
Mr Nikolai Smolin,	Togo, 1966-1970
Mr Petr Slyusarenko,	Togo, 1970

Mr John Barron recorded that in recent years most ambassadors involved in such activity had taken their orders from the Central Committee of the Communist Party of the Soviet Union (presumably from the International Department mentioned earlier in this chapter) rather than from the KGB.

In 1970, relations between President Numeri of the Sudan and the very active and influential Sudanese Communist Party began to deteriorate. The President was at the time pursuing a policy of friendship with the Soviet bloc and Soviet representation in the Sudan was proportionately almost as great as it was in Egypt. Several known Communists held positions in the government, though the President himself always insisted that they did so purely as individuals and not as representatives of their party. A situation arose in which it was possible for the Soviet magazine, *Za Rudezhon*, to claim that in fact the government was: "a coalition of anti-imperialist elements—democrats and Communists".[7]

The growing friction between the President and the Communist Party arose partly out of the opposition of the latter to the President's plans to take the Sudan into an Arab Federation with Egypt, Libya and Syria. Such a move, Sudanese Communist leaders thought, would destroy the influential position they had achieved and would, before long, reduce the Party to the rôle of ineffective semi-clandestine activity that had been the lot of the Communist Party in Egypt and most other Arab countries.

The rift came into the open fully in February 1971, when the President announced that it was his intention to destroy the Communist Party. He accused it of "sabotage" and "opposition to Arab unity". He also ordered the arrest of the Party's General Secretary. On 30 June, the Ministry of the Interior issued a statement saying that this official had "managed to escape" from prison. Communist sources subsequently stated that he had "gone underground" in order to carry on Party work.

A little over a fortnight later, on 19 July, the Communist Party attempted to retrieve its fortunes by means of an armed coup. A section of the army led by Communists seized power temporarily and a Communist sympathiser, Colonel Babakr-Al-Nor, was declared head of state. However, he was at the time in London, and when he attempted to return, the BOAC plane carrying him and his chief assistant, Major Farouk Hamadallah, was forced to land at Tripoli by the Libyan authorities and both were arrested.

Three days after the onset of this Communist-led attempt to seize power, pro-Government forces staged a counter-coup and the revolutionary junta in its turn was quickly overthrown. President Numeri was once again restored to full power. Fierce and swift retribution followed, with 14 leaders of the attempted take-over being executed almost at once and many others being arrested. Informed quarters in Khartoum were said to be firmly convinced that the Soviet Ambassador and some military advisers had had prior knowledge of the coup attmept. Such suspicions were reinforced by the knowledge that the ambassador had had discussions with the acting leader of the dissident forces, Major Al-Atta, on the evening of the day it took place; no other ambassador had done so.

Indications of outside interference in the internal affairs of the Sudan were also increased by a report appearing in the semi-official Egyptian newspaper, *Al Ahram,* that when the Communist Party's Secretary-General had escaped from prison the previous month, he had taken refuge in the Bulgarian Embassy. In an interview which appeared in *The Observer* of 1 August, President Numeri said that further enquiries were being made regarding the rôle played by Communist embassies during the revolt. He said he thought that they had been "the accomplices of the Sudanese Communists", and that "certain facts about the Bulgarian Embassy were a particular matter for investigation".

The following day an announcement from the Sudanese Government made it known that both the Bulgarian Ambassador and Mr Nikolai Oriov, Second Secretary at the Soviet Embassy, had been ordered to leave the country within 22 hours. Later, the Soviet Ambassador was also asked to leave the country. As moves against, and arrests of, Sudanese Communists continued, a propaganda protest campaign of unusual vigour was begun by the Soviet Union and other Eastern European countries. *Izvestia,* for instance, revealed that the Soviet Government had warned President Numeri about "the impermissibility of resorting to extreme measures" and had told him that:

The Soviet people would not remain indifferent to the fate of fighters against imperialism for democracy and for social justice.

Communist Party leaders of the Warsaw Pact nations, meeting in the Crimea, passed a resolution condemning the "reign of terror" in the Sudan. According to reports reaching the Sudanese Government, the campaign was even carried to the extent of Soviet representatives at the United Nations distributing propaganda alleging that President Numeri was "annihilating innocent people".

That the capacity of Sudanese Communists to mount armed revolts has, despite the events of 1971, been by no means entirely eclipsed, was shown plainly early in September 1975 when a new and very short-lived attempt at a coup against President Numeri was staged in Khartoum. In this case Communist elements were said to have attempted to act in unusual alliance with the traditionally right-wing Moslem Brotherhood.

In the spring of 1972, the Mali Government expelled three Soviet officials. In the middle of 1973, a known KGB official was withdrawn from Senegal at the request of the government which also refused to renew the visa of another Soviet official. In January 1974, the First Secretary and Consular Officer of the Soviet Embassy in Accra, Mr Valentin Fomenko, was arrested and accused of espionage. It was alleged that he had received a "very secret paper" from an army officer at a place near the racecourse. Mr Fomenko was ordered to leave the country within 72 hours. Soviet diplomats had previously been expelled from Ghana in 1971. Mr Valter Vinogradov left in May and Mr Petrovich Potemkin, Commercial Officer of the Soviet Trade Delegation, in July.

One type of agent of whom the KGB has been attempting to make increasing use is "the agent of influence". This tactic involves the recruitment of a citizen of a country who already holds, or seems likely soon to hold, a position of considerable influence within it. Such influence could be either of a political nature or exercised in some other field of importance. The rôle of such agents being not so much to obtain information or to involve themselves in subversive activities in the usual sense, but gradually to persuade those amongst whom they work and, also if possible their superiors, that the foreign policy proposals or policies being put forward or followed by the Soviet Union offer the best chance of peaceful progress for all, and that close ties with the Soviet Union are, therefore, in the country's own best interests. Naturally the nearer the top of the Establishment tree such agents can be recruited, the better, from the KGB's point of view.

There is evidence that the KGB is as interested in trying to recruit and use such agents in Africa as elsewhere, and that, for instance, it had considerable success in doing so in Egypt during the period of the Nasser régime.

One day in July 1971, Mr Vladimir Nikolaevich Sakharov, a promising young KGB officer working under diplomatic cover at the Soviet Embassy in Kuwait, glanced carefully as he always did into the back window of a Volkswagen parked near a traffic roundabout on his route as he drove from the embassy to his flat. Usually there would be a litter of books, toys, or other oddments visible but on that day there was a bunch of flowers. That evening Mr Sakharov returned to the embassy. Telling the guard that "something unexpected had come up", he gained admittance to the "Referentura" or section of the building reserved for KGB officers. He remained there some time, took some documents from the safe, and late in the evening left the building and, abandoning his car, walked into the desert. By the time his disappearance had given rise to alarm amongst his colleagues the next day, he was many thousands of kilometres from the Persian Gulf.

Mr Sakharov, increasingly disillusioned both with Soviet policy and KGB activity, had been secretly in touch with Western intelligence officers for some time. The bunch of flowers in the back of the Volkswagen had been a pre-arranged signal from them that his safety was in danger and that the time had come to get out. The story he had to tell when he reached freedom shed a most interesting light not only on the KGB's use of "agents of influence" but also on many other modes of operation of the Soviet intelligence services in both North Africa and the Middle East.[9]

Mr Sakharov was the son of a former courier in the Soviet Foreign Ministry. One of his closest friends was the son of a deputy KGB Chairman. He emerged with distinction from a five-year course in Arabic studies at the Moscow Institute of International Relations and, in 1967, left for the Middle East for a further period of field studies before graduating. To assist himself in these studies, he volunteered for the post of probationary Consular Officer in the

146

small but strategically important port of Hodeida in the Yemen.

He had not been in Hodeida long before he found himself recruited into the network of the local KGB "Resident" who was working under the cover of chief engineer of the State Committee for Economic Relations. Amongst the tasks allotted to him were the selecting of potential recruits from amongst the Egyptian troops then stationed in the Yemen, and picking Arab workers who might possibly be used in attempts to penetrate the oil storage areas in what then was still British-ruled Aden in attempted sabotage bids. He also had to take note of any Yemenis who seemed to be in sympathy with Communist China.

He subsequently returned to the USSR for his graduation. His days with the Institute of International Relations completed, he refused, on his father's advice, an invitation to become a regular KGB officer and found himself posted as an attaché to the Soviet Consulate in Alexandria. Despite his refusal to join the KGB when still at home, he was immediately approched on arrival in Egypt by the Vice-Consul, he, it transpired, being none other than the local KGB Resident. The Vice-Consul made it quite clear to Mr Sakharov that he was expected to work under his instructions and that he was to consider himself under the control of the KGB.

Mr Sakharov had arrived in Egypt at a time of intense KGB activity there, its plan being to try and attempt to obtain dominance over the régime by pursuing a policy of recruiting agents amongst President Nasser's personal advisers, the governing Arab Socialist Union Party, the security services, the armed forces, and the universities. A plan was also under way for the infiltration of groups friendly to the Western powers.

Mr Sakharov was assigned to various "targets" or the study of a number of people whom it was thought might be of use within the framework of this general plan. One of these was the young commander of an intelligence unit which had the rôle of watching and protecting the foreign consulates in Alexandria. The Resident explained to Mr Sakharov that, although this officer was only "a little man" at present, such "little men" sometimes grew into "big men" and were, therefore, worth cultivating. Mr Sakharov accordingly set about attempting to suborn this Egyptian officer's allegiance with the aid of gifts of whisky and caviar.

Another target to whom Mr Sakharov was directed was the intelligence major who was responsible for counter-intelligence

147

against the KGB and the GRU in the Alexandria area. Here a scheme was devised to win his friendship, partly by arranging for his brother to be granted a scholarship to go and study in the Soviet Union. Mr Sakharov was also instructed to make his own contacts which he thought might prove useful amongst Egyptian government officials and the business community. The only group of people he was instructed to avoid being known to were Egyptian Communists, presumably because of the danger of their being under observation by the security service.

In the course of his duties, Mr Sakharov came into close touch with Archbishop Anatoli Kaznovetsky, a tall bearded man holding the position of Archbishop of the Russian Orthodox Church for all Africa. He was also known to be the most colourful KGB agent employed in the Middle East. His role was mainly to act as "an agent of influence" amongst those whom his official duties chiefly took him. This task he accomplished by trying to persuade other clergy whom he met, of all the various faiths, to accept and adopt the official Soviet line on such important issues as Vietnam, the Arab-Israeli conflict, and "world peace" in general. But he was also concerned with recruiting agents for the KGB amongst the religious community, paying special attention in this regard to the Copts.

The Archbishop also exploited his official position by making visits to other parts of Africa and gaining entry to social circles where Soviet diplomats and other official representatives were not always welcome.

Mr Sakharov first became aware that the KGB had been successful in recruiting an Egyptian in top government circles as an "agent of influence" in the course of conversation with fellow KGB officers during visits to the Soviet Embassy in Cairo. The KGB Resident there named Mr Pavl Nedosekin was an experienced officer with a reputation for ruthless efficiency going back to the war years. Mr Sakharov learnt that "the agent of influence" with whom Mr Nedosekin and his assistants were in contact was none other than Mr Sami Sharif, at that time President Nasser's personal intelligence adviser.

Mr Sakharov also learnt that the recruitment of Mr Sharif had been the result of a programme of slow and cautious seduction going back as far as 1955. In that year, Mr Sharif had been a member of one of the first Egyptian Military Missions which had gone to Moscow to arrange for the supply of military aid. It was apparently then that he first attracted the attention of the KGB. Not very long afterwards the pro-Communist head of the Egyptian Cabinet of the time, Mr Al Sabri, appointed Mr Sharif as his assistant. He returned to Moscow with another Egyptian delegation in 1957 and was again paid much attention by the KGB. It is probable that his career as an agent working under KGB control started after this visit.

In 1959, Mr Sharif was appointed Director of the President's Office of Information. This was a very much more important appointment than its title might suggest, conferring on him in effect the post of head of the Egyptian Intelligence Service and principal intelligence adviser to the President. He soon made the best of his new powers and by the early 1960s was in a position in which all appointments of Egyptian officials to posts abroad had to be approved by him. He also had charge of security investigations of officials and civil servants, as well as directing any foreign intelligence operations of prime importance. Most important of all, Mr Sharif was able to decide which intelligence reports the President should see and which should be kept from him. He, therefore, played a big part in ensuring right up to the 1967 Arab-Israeli war that Nasser's view of the world was coloured by what the KGB wanted him to see.

Mr Sharif also, possibly without the President's knowledge, made a secret agreement under which arrangements were made for Soviet training of Egyptian intelligence officers and for joint KGB-Egyptian intelligence operations. He disassociated himself from known leftists such as his former chief Mr Al Sabri, and posed as a devoted nationalist anxious that Egypt should "play off" the Eastern and Western blocs to its own advantage. In fact, however, he did all he could to use his very considerable influence to strengthen ties with the East, whilst undermining relations with the West. It is believed that, although Nasser was known to be suspicious of the too pro-Soviet leanings of certain members of his cabinet, he never felt there was any reason to distrust the judgement or advice of his chief of intelligence; a fact which obviously greatly enhanced Mr Sharif's success as an agent of influence.

In the spring of 1970, Mr Sakharov was transferred to the Soviet Embassy in Kuwait. In the short time of little over a year, before his escape and defection, he was able to learn a considerable amount about the important part of the KGB establishment in this small state played in the general regional scheme of operations. Among the plans which came to his knowledge was one aimed at promoting the downfall of the Government of Saudi Arabia through the establishment of a clandestine terrorist organisation in that country. Another concerned the establishment of terrorist cells in the oil producing sheikdoms around the Persian Gulf, a third involved the masterminding of a campaign of urban guerrilla warfare in Turkish cities. One project of particular importance in which both the KGB and GRU were jointly engaged, was an attempt to obtain dominance over the Palestinian guerrilla movement with the aim of ultimately using it as a force against Arab governments unfavourable to Soviet designs.

Whilst he was still in Kuwait, news came through that was of the utmost concern to his colleagues. At the end of May 1971, Nasser's successor, President Sadat, received information that a coup was being prepared against him. There was every indication that this move had the approval of the Soviet Union which was already finding him far less co-operative to deal with than it had President Nasser, and, in addition, it was also known that the KGB was deeply involved. President Sadat at once decided to act upon the information he had received and ordered a widespread round-up of suspected Soviet agents, including Mr Sami Sharif. Years of KGB hard work was thus largely destroyed almost overnight. Mr Sharif was placed on trial and sentenced to death for treason, although the sentence was commuted to one of life imprisonment, and a highly embarrassed President Podgorny was forced to fly to Cairo in a bid to repair the harm the whole affair had done to Soviet-Egyptian relations.

The details of the foregoing story of Soviet intrigue are recounted in full by Mr John Barron in *KGB*.

Another tactic made frequent use of by the KGB is "Disinformation". This involves the planting of false or highly distorted stories in the news media and the circulating of forged documents, etc. The object is to discredit the Western Powers, anti-Communist political parties and organisations, and in some cases to smear individuals. Such tactics have been used on a considerable scale in Third World areas by the KGB as well as in Europe. Mr Aleksandr Kasnachev, for instance, who was mentioned earlier in this chapter, spent a considerable amount of time whilst in the employ of the Soviet Embassy in Rangoon engaged upon such work. Such methods have also been used on a number of occasions in Africa.

In the course of a Soviet campaign to win influence amongst African trade unionists in the early 1960s, considerable use was made of forgeries designed to discredit non-Communist trade unions. These included a document entitled *The Great Conspiracy Against Africa* which purported to be a secret annexe to a British Government Cabinet paper on Africa.

The intelligence services of the Soviet Union, whether in Africa or elsewhere, do not operate in isolation but in close co-operation with the equivalent services of the other Communist countries of Eastern Europe.

The KGB keeps a tight hold upon the activities of the subordinate services through a system of "advisers" (sometimes known in Eastern Europe as "uncles"). KGB officers acting as advisers are stationed at the headquarters of all the East European intelligence services and forward copies of all reports of any importance to Moscow. They also control the activities of Eastern European intelligence officers who have secretly been recruited as agents by the KGB and sometimes also recruit civilians from these countries for assignments abroad.

One Eastern European intelligence service which has played a part of considerable importance in Soviet bloc operations in Africa has been that of Czechoslovakia, the STB. It is known that officers from this service were used for the first tentative Soviet bloc attempts to establish links with the government of President Nasser, because it was thought that they would be less likely to meet with rebuffs than their Soviet equivalent. The STB has also been employed on at least two occasions on disinformation operations in African countries. In the first instance, during the 1964 American election campaign, the STB printed great quantities of pamphlets containing alleged but, in fact, entirely fictitious statements of Senator Barry Goldwater which had the effect of portraying him as a fanatical racialist. These pamphlets were printed to resemble authentic American political campaign literature and distributed in large numbers in Africa and also Asia.

In 1964, the STB was, in addition, responsible for leaking three forged documents to President Nyerere. These documents set out to describe a plot against the Tanzanian Government by the United States. The latter managed to refute their authenticity but not before they had come into the possession of the local press and

151

considerable harm had been done to the image of America in the eyes of African public opinion.

One defector from the STB, Mr Joseph Frolik, has described how in 1966 he was given the task in Prague of recruiting agents for work in what was then still a new field of operation for Czech intelligence—Africa. He records that:

> We were scrambling desperately to infiltrate key agents into important posts in the new countries, which had until recently been the colonies of the European powers.[10]

Mr Frolik wrote that the STB was fortunate in this task in that "The Seventeenth of November University" had been established in Prague by the Czech Government for the training of Third World students on the same lines as at the Patrice Lumumba University in Moscow. This contained 4 500 students, mostly coloured and from Africa and the Middle East. The STB devised a recruitment system under which these students were "vetted" as to their suitability for intelligence work, while still undergoing the one-year Czech language course all had to do before entering the university itself. Those who were found suitable were allowed to proceed with their course at the university, but would also be given special instruction during it to prepare them for work as infiltrators in their own country's Establishment upon their return home. Mr Frolik states that:

> The Seventeenth of November University proved a tremendous source of material for us and I don't think it would be going too far to say that half the students had contacts with Czech intelligence at one time or other.[11]

The Soviet Union is also able to rely on the assistance of the Cuban Intelligence Service *(Direccion General de Intelligencia)* or DGI. This has also been firmly under the control of KGB advisers for some years. The DGI command structure apparently includes a special section devoted to the control of operations in the Middle East and Africa. For some time the Cuban Embassy in Paris was known to be acting as a co-ordinating station between Havana and the Cuban military instructors in such Black African countries as

Mali and Guinea-Bissau, some of whom had an intelligence rôle. In the autumn of 1966, four Cuban diplomats were expelled from Ghana and the Cuban Embassy in that country closed down. An important DGI network is known to exist covering the Mediterranean and Persian Gulf. This network included Raul Fornell Delgado, the Cuban Ambassador in Algiers, an experienced DGI officer who maintained close contact with the Algerian intelligence service and "liberation movements" with bases in North Africa. It also included Jacin Vasquez de la Garza, another much travelled DGI officer, later Cuban Ambassador to the Peoples' Republic of South Yemen. From his base in Aden, he channelled Cuban aid to Marxist guerrillas in Oman.

A sophisticated Cuban intelligence operation, apparently designed to infiltrate intelligence agents into Rhodesia in the guise of Canadian mercenaries anxious to fight in the Rhodesian forces, was brought to light early in 1977 by the defection of an American who had been recruited for this purpose by a Cuban attached to the Cuban Consulate in Montreal. Five Cubans, including three diplomats, were subsequently expelled by the Canadian Government for their part in this affair.

In African countries with which the Soviet Union has established particularly friendly relations and where it considers it has a firm political base, the KGB will quite probably not only offer to train the security services of the country concerned but will also try and exploit its operations to the Soviet Union's advantage. KGB officers in Ghana in the early 1960s were, for instance, quick to take an interest in President Nkrumah's scheme to create a special clandestine organisation for the purpose of infiltrating trained guerrillas into a large number of African countries. More recently, the Soviet intelligence service is known to have been attempting to make use of Somali diplomatic missions in other African countries to collect intelligence on its behalf and to use Somali Embassy diplomatic bags and Somali civil aircraft for the purpose of carrying sealed messages and packages to and from its agents.

Communist China

Communist Chinese support for revolutionary movements in Black African countries which have attempted to overthrow the existing non-Communist governments began with that of the *Union des Populations du Camerounaise.* The leaders of this extreme left-wing Cameroun political party visited Peking and obtained Chinese approval and promises of aid in 1958.

With the coming of independence of the former Belgian Congo in 1960, Chinese efforts in the field of subversion became, for a time, largely concentrated upon that country which Chinese leaders apparently saw as the key to central and southern Africa.

The main base for these activities was the Chinese Embassy in neighbouring Brazzaville, capital of the former French Congo, where they were presided over by Colonel Kan Mai, who was considered to be one of the most brilliant Chinese agents operating abroad. According to a Chinese defector, Colonel Kan Mai had been involved in subversive operations in Nepal prior to coming to Africa, apparently bringing a large number of Chinese agents into that country in the guise of road-builders engaged in an economic aid mission, their real purpose, however, being to prepare the ground for a revolt. The Colonel was also reported to have undertaken reconnaissance trips to Tibet and to India shortly before the Chinese invasion of those countries.

Under Colonel Kan Mai's directions, a number of training camps were set up for the use of the forces of the rebel leader, Mr Pierre Mulele, who had himself received nearly two years of training in Peking. Other Chinese subversive operations in Central Africa in the early 1960s included those in Burundi, where, after the assassination of the Prime Minister, a young cultural attaché defected from the Chinese Embassy and provided information that the Chinese were planning to support a revolt across the Burundi border by the left-winger Mr Gaston Soumialot against the Democratic Republic of the Congo. The Chinese Embassy in Burundi was closed and the staff expelled as a result of his story.

One Chinese agent active in Burundi was Mr Kao Liang, a leading correspondent of the New China News Agency and its chief African correspondent. Mr Kao Liang had been expelled from India for "unjournalistic" activities before coming to Africa. He is believed to have bribed Rwandan refugees of the Tutsi tribe in Burundi in 1962 and given them money with the aim of building up a pro-Chinese faction amongst them. The Rwandan Government later claimed that the Chinese had taken part in training Tutsis who attacked their territory in 1963 and early 1964.

In 1964, an attempt was made to overthrow the Government of the Niger Republic by the Sawaba Party. This was a left-wing organisation which had had strong ties with the French Communist Party in the days of French colonial rule. The President, Mr Hamani Diori, said after the attempt that it had been "organised, financed, and led" by Communist China and that the weapons used in it had been bought with Chinese money which had been deposited in banks in Brussels, Geneva and Accra. After being re-elected the following year, the President expressed the hope that there would be an improvement in relations with some Eastern European countries but said that there could be no question of the government recognising China: "which gives ideological and military training to nations of other countries and assists them financially to create subversion".[12]

Clandestine Chinese activities in East Africa in the early years of the 1960s were under the direction of the same agent, Mr Kao Liang, who had been active in Burundi. He was first based in Dar es Salaam in 1961, having previously served as an assistant to Colonel Kan Mai in the Congo. His official position in Dar es Salaam was head of the New China News Agency but in many ways he lived like a diplomat and made frequent visits to other African countries outside Tanzania. He established a reputation for giving many lavish and "swinging" parties and became a notable figure amongst the pro-Chinese faction active in the capital. Mr Colin Legum, African correspondent of *The Observer,* described him as being a "key figure" in Chinese diplomatic activities in Dar es Salaam and as a "go-between for the diplomats and their African contacts".[13]

A fluent English-speaker since a young man, he also kept in close touch with political exiles from Southern Africa as well as local politicians. He also made many visits to Zanzibar prior to the Chinese backed revolution there in January 1964. Mr Shcik Babu, one of the leaders of this revolt who later became Foreign Minister of the amalgamated state of Tanganyika and Zanzibar, was a "stringer" of the NCNA and a close friend of his, well-known to be fanatically pro-Chinese. It is thought that Mr Kao Liang himself assisted the planning and arranged material backing for the revolt in which many thousands died and which ushered in a savage and repressive Marxist-type régime. Mr Kao Liang now holds the important position of head of Communist China's delegation to the United Nations.

155

In 1965, Chinese policy in Africa suffered a series of major setbacks, partly as a result of the rising alarm by Black African governments at somewhat crude and ill-prepared attempts to promote subversion and revolution. Serious allegations were, for instance, made that the Chinese Ambassador in Dar es Salaam had been involved in attempts to overthrow the Prime Minister of Malawi, Dr Hastings Banda. A network of Chinese agents was discovered in Kenya involved in an arms smuggling operation and four senior trade union officials were dismissed in Zambia for accepting bribes from members of the Chinese mission in that country who hoped to encourage them to promote strikes. Investigations into a small conspiracy in Egypt aimed at overthrowing President Nasser also pointed to Chinese connections.

In addition, the Chinese Embassy in Dahomey which had been an important base for subversive Chinese activities directed against Nigeria, Upper Volta and Togoland was closed down and the staff expelled. The Government of the new Central African Republic began a large-scale drive against "foreign agents" which led to the discovery of considerable quantities of arms and ammunition brought into the country by Chinese intelligence officers and those they had recruited.

Last, but by no means least, the year also saw the overthrow of President Nkrumah of Ghana and the loss of that country both to China and the USSR as a forward base in Africa, plus the expulsion of nearly 500 Chinese experts and advisers and the closing down of the Chinese Embassy. These and other such setbacks are believed to have resulted in the formulation of a new approach towards the problem of expanding Communist China's influence in Africa, in which much greater care was to be taken that clandestine activities did not undermine attempts to gain the favour of African governments.

The main cover organisation used by Communist Chinese agents in Africa as in other areas would still seem to be the New China News Agency, in particular that section of it known as "The Military Section". According to one defector from the agency, this section is officially supposed to be strongest in "party spirit" and to have the highest "political qualification". Members are said to be recruited immediately on leaving school. They are sent to the school of foreign languages run by the NCNA and are also given special training. All are Communist Party Members.

One member of this section was expelled from Ethiopia together with his wife in 1968. The member, Mr Li Yen-Tseng, had been attached to an army unit before 1949 and then was put in charge of Chinese war reporters during the Korean war. Subsequently, he became area news editor of the NCNA in Peking and was then appointed head of the agency's office in Syria before going on to Addis Ababa.

REFERENCES

1. "Africa and the Defence of the West", Brian Crozier, *Le Monde Moderne,* p. 93.
2. *Inside a Soviet Embassy,* Aleksandr Kasnachev, Robert Hale, London, 1963.
3. *The Security of the Cape Oil Route,* Institute for the Study of Conflict, London, 1974.
4. *KGB,* John Barron, Hodder & Stoughton, London, 1974, p. 345.
5. *The Security of the Cape Oil Route, op. cit.,* p. 9-10.
6. *KGB, op. cit.,* p. 379.
7. *The Guardian,* 26 July 1970.
8. *Financial Times,* 30 July 1971.
9. This is recorded in detail by John Barron in *KGB,* p. 29-62.
10. *The Frolik Defection,* Joseph Frolik, Leo Cooper, 1975, p. 113.
11. *Ibid.,* p. 114.
12. *Radio Niamey,* 11 October 1965.
13. *The Observer,* 27 September 1964.

Chapter 6

Guerrilla Training in the Communist Bloc

Mr Norman Duka was born in September 1940 in the African location of Tsolo, just outside the South African city of East London, the son of poor working-class parents. Apart from occasional visits to his grandparents in the country at Peddie, he spent all his early years in Tsolo where he was educated at local schools. His father who worked in a shoe factory, had been politically active for some years and had become a member of the African National Congress (ANC). Whilst Duka was still in his early teens, his father took him to an ANC meeting, which was being held in the district and at which for the first time he heard speakers describe the work of the organisation and attack the pass laws and other government measures.

Before long, he found himself beginning to take part in discussions when members of the ANC called round to see his father, and he soon became involved in distributing literature and similar work. About the same time, he left school and took his first job, working for Aberdaire Cables. He used to buy the ANC paper *New Age* regularly from an old man who was the ANC leader in the neighbourhood and it was he who formally recruited Duka into the ANC. In 1960, the ANC was banned and Norman Duka found himself called to a meeting at which the ANC Chairman read a set of instructions which had come down from the headquarters of the party detailing new and clandestine methods of work.

There followed a period in which many secret meetings were held and during them the question would often be debated as to whether the time had not come for more violent forms of action. His home was raided several times by the police and when a police agent was killed in the neighbourhood his father was amongst those detained for a short period. The following year, he began working with ANC women who acted as couriers for the underground movement. This group used to deliver parcels of cloth to each other's houses and then sew them together, at the same time exchanging messages and other information. Duka used to play his part by posing as the son of one of the women, taking bundles of cloth from one house to another.

One day he was visited in his home by an older member of the ANC who told him that the work of the movement was becoming increasingly difficult because so many members had been arrested. It was, however, essential that "the struggle" be continued. This meant that it was essential that members must become better trained and organised. Some young members, he was told, had already been enrolled into the party's military wing, *Umkhonto We Sizwe* (Spear of the Nation) and were receiving military training. He was asked if he would like to join them. He replied that he would. The need for strict secrecy in the work he was about to undertake was then strongly impressed upon him, because he and the "partner" who, it had been decided, would work with him were going to be trained in nothing less than the manufacture of explosives and "fire-bombs".

The next evening, as instructed, he called at a rendezvous to meet this "partner" who turned out to be a young man of about his own age. An instructor was also present who at once started to set about telling the pair, neither of whom was introduced to the other by name, how to make petrol bombs. Both were told to return the next day, and when they did so they spent an evening receiving instruction in the use, stripping and cleaning of a pistol. On the next day there followed a walk on a quiet beach where both Duka and his partner were able to practise actually firing the pistol, the noise of the shots being drowned by the roar of the waves. He continued with such training all through 1962 and into the following year, until one day in March, the ANC veteran who had recruited him into *Umkhonto We Sizwe* called on him again, and told him it had been decided that the time had come for him to go abroad for further training. After some hesitation, he decided to do so. He was told that upon his return he would be expected to pass on to his brothers, sisters, and father what he had learnt and that the movement was counting upon him.

In accordance with instructions subsequently received, Duka and some "comrades" travelled to Johannesburg where they stayed in an African location. From there they were taken by car to the border with Botswana and, having made their way over it at an illegal crossing point, went by train to Francistown

There they were received by a new contact, a man who lived in Botswana but who also spent much time in South Africa and who was a member of both the ANC and the South African Congress of Trade Unions (SACTU). Mr Norman Duka and his companions stayed for two months in Francistown before being flown on to Dar es Salaam. On arrival, they were taken to a house outside the city which was owned by the ANC and acted as a training centre and transit camp. Their days there were filled with courses in English, history and mathematics. Frequent political discussion groups were organised and the trainees were introduced to the rudiments of military discipline, each day beginning with physical exercises at 0700 followed by the start of classes at 0900.

Norman Duka remained in this ANC base for three months until one day he was told: "A number of you will leave tomorrow for military training in the Soviet Union. Pack your things and be ready."[1] The next day he and a party of 12 others, including the four original companions with whom he had left South Africa, left Dar es Salaam by air. When they landed in the Soviet Union after a seven-hour trip, it was to find the ground covered with snow. They had been warned to dress warmly but even so the bitter cold came as a shock. Recording his experiences for a sympathetic North American organisation, Duka later recalled that:

> As we left the plane and I felt the cold air strike my face I wanted to get back in. It makes me shiver just thinking about it now.[2]

The party was met by several officials, including an elderly "European" interpreter, and they were taken to a camp which the interpreter told them was "a very good school for training"; adding the information that "many of our officers came from here". Te camp turned out to be a large one and the course upon which Duka and his companions now embarked was run to a strict routine. Each morning started with "tough exercises", although some concessions were made to the African trainees who felt the cold and they were allowed to do these indoors whilst the cold weather lasted. There followed an inspection and marching drill, and then the training classes began. These were held in a large hall and conducted in English with the help of an interpreter. In other parts of the hall, groups from other parts of the world were being instructed in different languages. The classes included instruction in the use of a variety of weapons, the use of explosives and lessons in the tactics of guerrilla and mobile warfare. In addition, there was an intensive course in Russian. The trainees' stay in Russia, which lasted a year, was not without its snags. In addition to the weather Mr Duka records that:

> There were language, cultural and national differences. Even their music bored us at first. But we managed to buy a few English records. As time went on, however, we began to enjoy their music too.[3]

In between classes, Mr Duka and his group used to meet with Russian soldiers in the lecture hall for a cigarette and a chat. They were the only Africans on this particular course and for many of the Russians it was the first time they had ever had contact with Africans. At weekends there were trips to museums and historic sites. But the long-lasting cold weather not infrequently spoilt the enjoyment of these for the Africans, sometimes forcing them to cut sight-seeing short and return to the bus just in order to try and keep warm.

Half-way through the course, they received the results of their first examinations, their instructors apparently professing themselves very satisfied with their work. When summer at length came, they were often allowed to go to a beach when work was done, and here they met other African trainees undergoing other courses at camps in the area. These came from such countries as various former French African colonies, Ghana and Nigeria, Intensive training continued all through the summer until in November of 1964 the course ended and there came final examinations which lasted for

161

three days. When these were over, the trainees were called into the senior officer's office together with their instructors. Their results, "which were very good", were read to them and then the camp commander wished them good luck in their struggle, giving examples of how guerrilla tactics had been used with great success in the 1939-45 war.

The following day, a party was given for them. They drank champagne, toasted the "success of our struggle" with Soviet officers and danced. "It was late," Mr Duka comments, "when we returned to our barracks."

A week later the time came for the African group to depart. Mr Duka stated:

We had made many friends among the soldiers we lived with. When it was time to go we shook hands, embraced and said goodbye. "Who knows," I said, "maybe we'll meet again when South Africa is free."[4]

Once again back in Dar es Salaam the group returned to the ANC centre whence they had started their trip to the Soviet Union 12 months before. They found about 40 other ANC members there, some of whom had just come from South Africa and others who, like themselves, had returned from training abroad. Mr Duka himself was given a job in the ANC office, where he worked every morning, returning to the centre for classes on military tactics "taught by members trained elsewhere". "This way," he wrote "we exchanged views on various military practices and strategies from different countries." Although he did not know it in advance, he was to remain in Dar es Salaam following the same routine for more than two years, until early in 1967 he was told by the ANC chief representative: "Well, Norman, your chance has come to return to South Africa."[5]

Mr Norman Duka, who will feature again in this study, was merely one of the first of a steady stream of would-be guerrillas and "freedom fighters" from a variety of African countries (by no means all of them in the southern part of the continent) who have made much the same sort of "pilgrimage" to the Soviet Union for guerrilla warfare training in the years since the early 1960s.

According to one Rhodesian African, Mr Temba Moyo, a member of the Zimbabwe African People's Union (ZAPU), the

162

decision to send men abroad for training was taken by that organisation soon after a conference was held at Cold Comfort Farm, near Salisbury, in 1963. The aim was to prepare for "the inevitable armed struggle against the Rhodesian régime". He himself and three other ZAPU Youth Front members were instructed to go to Northern Rhodesia (now Zambia). There he was employed in the ZAPU office in Lusaka for a time, more members of the Youth Wing arriving constantly whilst he was there. Arrivals were divided into groups of 10. In June 1964, his group, of whom two came from Bulawayo and the remainder from Salisbury, were flown to the Soviet Union for military training. After 12 months of intensive training during which he has recorded they "worked hard and learnt as much as possible" because they knew they would need all the skills they could be taught upon their return to Rhodesia, they returned to Lusaka and were subsequently employed on an infiltration attempt across the Zambesi.[6]

Another ZAPU recruit described how he had been sent with 11 other members of the organisation for military training in the Soviet Union. They were taken to a camp about 50 km from Moscow. Courses there lasted for about four months and subjects taught included political science and there was also much emphasis on intelligence work. This latter embraced instruction in the photographing of documents and important installations and also the use of photography for more sophisticated purposes such as blackmail. Elementary surveying was also included on the course as was the secret opening and re-sealing of mail, the use of codes and ciphers, etc. Trainees were also given briefings on the structure and activities of the CIA and the British M15 and M16, as well as French and West German intelligence services. The course included training in the use of small arms. Those involved in taking it were also subjected to heavy doses of indoctrination of Communist theory.[7]

A number of members of Rhodesian guerrilla organisations who have been captured and placed on trial have declared that they were tricked into being sent for military training in Soviet camps and elsewhere against their will. One who turned Queen's evidence at his trial in 1966 said that he, and some of those concerned in the case with him, had been sent to the Soviet Union after officials of ZAPU had told him at the organisation's headquarters in Zambia that they were to be given educational scholarships. He said that in his case, he had understood he was to be sent to the USA to receive

163

training to fit him for a civil post in a future African nationalist administration in Rhodesia. He had only realised that he was to be sent to the Soviet Union when the Second Secretary of the Soviet Embassy in Dar es Salaam had told him that he and other members of the group were being sent to the Soviet Union for training in "intelligence and police work".

The same sort of deception also seems to have been practised by the South West African People's Organisation (SWAPO) which decided in the early 1960s that Wambo tribesmen under the age of 30 should be sent abroad for guerrilla training. It was decided to try and persuade those selected by the organisation's command into willing co-operation with regard to leaving the country by telling them that they had been awarded British or American scholarships. With SWAPO agents inside South West Africa acting as recruiting agents spreading this message, about 900 young men left the country illegally, in many cases it appears under quite false pretences. One, for instance, said later that he had believed he was leaving for training as a motor mechanic. There is evidence that some recruits were only 14 or 15 years old, and were sometimes taken from the streets without their parents being aware of the fact. The question is sometimes asked as to why such "recruits" do not make more effort to escape the clutches of the organisation which has lured them from their homeland but the truth would seem to be that they quickly become dependent upon it for food, money, shelter and travel documents, and the further they are taken from home the more dependent they become.

Recruits from South West Africa, during this period, usually went to Zambia or to Botswana. The latter often met similarly recruited men from South Africa and Botswana in Francistown, where they were divided into groups of between 10 and 30 and then taken by air to Lusaka. From there they would go to Dar es Salaam. Some would be sent on a four-month training course in Cairo and then go for further training in Tanzania, whilst selected recruits would be given a short course in English before they were flown to the Soviet Union. There they were given a six-month's course by an English-speaking Russian officer. The course included not only the use of fire-arms and explosives but special instruction in methods of sabotaging installations and railways.[8]

In 1964, selected members of Frelimo in Moçambique were first sent from training camps in Tanzania for more advanced training in Soviet camps and special schools. These included the Komsomol School in Moscow, where instruction was given in Russian through a Portuguese-Russian interpreter. Those attending this course made contacts with other trainees from countries as varied as Algeria, Guinea, Syria, Zambia, South Africa, Rhodesia, Cuba and others. Other Frelimo members went to the guerrilla warfare training schools at Simferopol in the Ukraine.

As the campaign in Moçambique progressed, Frelimo recruits who showed themselves to have a particular aptitude for guerrilla warfare were given initial training in Tanzania, and then flown to the Ukraine for courses in sabotage techniques of 10 months duration. One group alone sent for training during 1969 numbered 85 such members.

A new turn in the training of members of the South African ANC came after the failure of the 1967 and 1968 ZAPU/ANC joint raids into Rhodesia. These failures resulted in an extensive re-examination of the tactics employed and the somewhat ambitious objective they sought to obtain of infiltrating sabotage and guerrilla groups into South Africa overland. The re-examination resulted first in the sending of a number of members of the ANC to Moscow for re-training in the techniques of underground work. The main emphasis in this re-training being the use of a cell system in which the identity of members of each cell was kept secret from the members of others, and the employment of clandestine means of communication and intelligence work. Early in 1971, the ANC members who had been on this refresher course were sent to a Soviet base at Baku on the Caspian Sea where they were trained in the use of explosives, amphibious landing tactics, the use of small arms, rowing and the use of dinghies. The purpose of such training was to prepare them for possible landing operations on the coast of South Africa

In February 1972 this group returned to Africa and to a temporary base in Mogadishu, Somalia. From there it was planned that they would set sail on the motor boat *Aventura* which would take them to a chosen landing place on the South African coast near Port St. Johns. There they would go ashore complete with their equipment in special rubber containers. Having landed, they were to set up a secret base, recruit and train supporters and begin a campaign of sabotage. They actually set off on this expedition in March but the *Aventura* developed radar and other trouble and had

165

to return to port. The idea of seaborne landings seems thereafter, for the time being at least, to have been dropped, the group being employed on another attempt to infiltrate South Africa by land instead.[9]

An account which sheds some interesting light on the training of guerrillas in the Soviet Union has come from a defector from a guerrilla movement which, whilst it operated in an area outside the bounds of the African continent, did so in a part of the world which is also of vital consequence to Western supply routes in the Indian Ocean. This was the Sultanate of Oman, key to the Straits of Hormuz at the mouth of the Persian Gulf, through which one oil-laden tanker, heading mainly for the Western world, passes on average every ten minutes every day of the year. Oman was the scene of a comparatively small-scale but bitter campaign fought by the Marxist-orientated guerrillas of the Popular Front for the Liberation of Oman and the Persian Gulf (PFLOAG), who received support from both Communist China and the Soviet Union.

Mr Salim Amir was a scar-faced bitter young man, a native of Oman who worked for a time as a civilian employee in the RAF camp at Salah. Before long he was supplementing his pay by habitual pilfering from the RAF men's quarters. Early in 1968, he decided to try his luck by joining the PFLOAG guerrillas he knew to be operating in his home area of the Arzat valley. Taking a number of stolen lighters and watches and a collection of torn documents he had carefully saved up from camp office wastepaper baskets and which he hoped would prove of some interest to the guerrillas and so ensure him a good welcome, he made his way home and was quickly in contact with them. The loot he brought with him evoked the friendly response he had hoped for, and before long he had built himself a considerable reputation as a member of the group.

Like their fellow revolutionary "freedom fighters" operating thousands of kilometres to the south in Portuguese Africa and Rhodesia, PFLOAG has relied heavily on the use of intimidation, often used in the crudest and most bloody form, to bring pressure to bear on the local population in their areas of operation in an attempt to ensure support for their cause. Mr Salim Amir showed himself not in the least reluctant to take an active part in such "operations"; indeed he devised some ingenious refinements of his own for use against villagers whose enthusiasm for the revolution seemed less than satisfactory or who betrayed a reluctance to part with food for those who claimed to serve it. Such refinements included the use of a wood burning fire over which the more sensitive parts of the unco-operative were slowly roasted.

One day he was informed that he had been selected for advanced training and, together with a small party of other recent recruits, he started off on a five-day march to the main PFLOAG base at Hauf over the border in the People's Republic of South Yemen, formerly the British colony of Aden. From there, they were flown to Aden where a leading member of PFLOAG told them that they were about to receive a great honour. They had been specially chosen to go on a long training course in the Soviet Union. After a three-week stay in Aden, during which time they were accommodated in the former British army officers' mess in Little Aden camp, a Russian military aircraft flew Amir and his group to an airport north-west of the Black Sea. Their exact destination was kept secret from them but a bus took them through a green and hilly countryside to an army camp. They stayed in this camp for three months with other groups from South America, Africa, Vietnam and Cambodia.

The trainees in that camp were given green uniforms to wear, together with caps and a gold badge inscribed with the hammer and sickle.

Their stay in that camp included a week's holiday in Moscow, the visit to the Soviet capital involving a 24-hour train journey. They were shown all the usual sights, including the Lenin Mausoleum and the Red Square. In addition, they inspected such evidence of recent Soviet triumphs as a model of a big space rocket which their guide's description gave them to understand had taken Soviet astronauts to the moon, actually in advance of their American rivals!

The 12-week course at their camp in the south consisted of a heavy dose of political indoctrination. Much emphasis was placed on the practical successes, it was claimed, the Soviet Union had already achieved in the worldwide battle against "imperialism" and "capitalism". In the Third World, they were told, the vital battle for the hearts and minds of the population was already being won. In Western Europe, the Communist Parties and their sympathisers had made notable advances in undermining resistance to the Marxist faith. Details of the progress the Communists and their allies had made in West Germany, France, Italy and Britain were cited.

167

Great play was also made of extolling the rapidly increasing military might of the Soviet Union. In case of need, the trainees were told, the Soviet Army, making massive use of tanks and other armoured vehicles and assisted by atomic and bacteriological weapons, would advance through and beyond West Germany with irresistible force, and at a pace far eclipsing that of the Nazi blitzkrieg of 1940 into France and the Low Countries.

At the end of three months, Mr Amir and his group were taken by air to Odessa and a military camp in the centre of the city. They stayed there for the next six months undergoing further training. Sundays were holidays on which they were allowed to wander around in the town as they pleased. On those occasions, they could not help noticing the differences between well fed and clothed officials and the shabby impoverished looking farm workers and other manual labourers—differences which were hard to square with the degree of equality their Soviet hosts claimed had been reached in the country.

The course ended with a gruelling final passing-out week clearly designed to test the fitness of each trainee to the utmost as an expert and fully ideologically convinced guerrilla fighter. Twenty-two trainees from Oman had started the course and 21 completed it. The missing man had suddenly disappeared from their ranks some months before having had, according to the camp officers, a brain seizure from which he never recovered.[10]

Another PFLOAG member who defected in September 1974 told how with a batch of 14 others he had undergone a course of several weeks' weapon training in Odessa, mainly concentrated upon the RCL rocket launcher and the formidable SAM-7 missile. Although up to that time that particular weapon had not been used in the campaign.[11]

Both the Soviet Union and Communist China began supporting the PFLOAG in 1968 but Chinese support dwindled until by 1974 it had become insignificant and support in the form of arms and training facilities outside the area was being provided almost entirely by the Soviet Union. Not long after Soviet aid began in 1968, a recruiting cell was set up actually inside a unit of the Sultan's Trucial Oman Scouts. This was based upon two Dhofari corporals who were secret agents of PFLOAG and, unknown to their officers, collected a third of the monthly pay of the other ranks in the unit and sent it to the PFLOAG office in Kuwait. In addition, the two corporals would from time to time receive messages from the guerrilla organisation asking them to select suitable men in the unit to be sent to the Soviet Union for training. Thus selected, they would be told to ask permission from their British officers to go on leave. When this was granted, they would disappear from the ranks of the Sultan's army and be spirited away by PFLOAG on the start of journeys to Soviet training camps.[12]

The provision of Soviet bloc training for guerrillas has certainly not been limited to members of the Southern African "liberation movements". In March 1966, for instance, the Kenyan Minister of Defence stated that about 180 Kenyan students were known to be receiving military training that had not been authorised or sponsored by the government in foreign countries. Of these, 70 were under training in Bulgaria whilst the rest were in the USSR, East Germany or Egypt. He said that the Kenyan Government was asking that this training should be discontinued—a request that does not seem to have met with much response, for in 1973 it was estimated that the number of Kenyans who had received such training in Bulgaria alone at various times had reached over 200. The assassin of the Kenyan politician Mr Tom Mboya, in 1969, was found to have been granted a commission in the Bulgarian army after receiving such training. Bulgaria has also provided training for some guerrillas from Rhodesia, as also has Czechoslovakia.

The largest centre for the training of guerrillas in the Soviet Union itself appears to be at Simferopol in the Crimea. One camp there can hold over 400 trainees at the same time and the training provided includes mine-laying, ambush techniques, fire co-ordination and general instruction in revolutionary tactics. Training is also given in driving, and also radio and television techniques. Most of the trainees who have passed through this particular camp are believed to have been Africans. In addition to the already mentioned centre in Odessa, a further training centre exists in Tashkent, and a number of Africans have received training in the political and intelligence training school in Moscow and at the Lenin Institute in the same city, the latter being reserved for students from non-Communist countries.

Some recruitment for training in guerrilla warfare, underground work and intelligence duties also takes place by "creaming off" suitable students from abroad who are attending courses at various ordinary civilian colleges. This is particularly so in relation to those attending the Lumumba University in Moscow.

There is some indication that the KGB and its military equivalent have embarked upon a policy of infiltrating agents into various "liberation movements", those recruited for this task being given guerrilla training in the Soviet Union. This would certainly seem to be the case as regards some Palestinian movements, members of which have received training in such North African countries as Algeria, Egypt and currently in particular Libya. According to Mr John Barron, in the winter of 1970 the GRU (Soviet military intelligence) despatched 30 members of such movements as it had recruited to the Soviet Union with the aim of converting them into controlled agents, while at the same time having them trained in guerrilla warfare. The same author stated that the following year the KGB and GRU officials in Kuwait were instructed to recruit an annual quota of at least three such agents a year with the purpose of using them for infiltrating Palestinian guerrilla groups after training in the Soviet Union.[13]

Guerrilla Training in Communist China

Communist China seems to have begun providing training in guerrilla warfare for revolutionaries from Africa slightly earlier than the Soviet Union. For instance, in 1961 six Africans returning to the Camerouns were arrested and gave details of a 10-week course in guerrilla warfare which they said they had attended at a military engineering college near Peking.

The syllabus of this course included training in the use of explosives, grenades, fuses and detonators, practice in planning sabotage operations, the manufacture and improvisation of explosives from locally obtained materials, instructions in the use of "imperialist" weapons, and lectures on the planning of ambushes, the fortification of villages and tactics to be used against armoured vehicles and aircraft. The course also included instruction in methods of infiltrating political and other organisations, the techniques of dealing with "unsympathetic" villagers.

The second part of the course included lectures on such subjects as "The Chinese Revolutionary Struggle", "The People's War" and "The Democratic Revolution", as well as on how to establish revolutionary bases in rural areas. These six particular trainees were sent back to Africa carrying orders for the guerrillas of the Communist-backed *Union des Populations Camerounaise* which had been involved in armed revolt in the French Camerouns since 1959.

According to a report circulated by the International Press Service of West Berlin in June 1964, a number of young Africans were then being trained in guerrilla warfare at special training centres in Harbin, Nanking and other locations in North-East China. Students were said to come from Nigeria, Angola, Moçambique, Guinea, Cameroun and the Congo.

A number of members of Southern African "liberation movements" have received training in China. One member of the Rhodesian Zimbabwe African National Union (ZANU) has described how he was flown to a camp near Shanghai in late 1968 and how he received training there for about 12 months. In addition to the normal subjects such as the use of small arms, explosives and ambush techniques, he said that the training included lessons on how to approach and "politicize" the local population in the countryside.[14] In recent years, however, it would seem that training of guerrillas actually inside China has been on a considerably lesser scale than in the countries of the Soviet bloc. Intelligence investigation of the background of various Rhodesian guerrillas killed in clashes with the security forces in the years leading up to 1973, for instance, indicated that only 14 had received training in China, compared with 39 in the Soviet bloc.[15]

One of the more detailed recent accounts of guerrilla training in China comes, not from Africa itself, but once again from a defector from the rebel forces in Oman.

The long trip to China began for Mr Ahmed Deblaan, a new recruit to PFLOAG, one day in 1968 when a uniformed guerrilla arrived in his village with a message from the movement's base in Aden. With two fellow recruits, he packed up his meagre belongings and set off on the long walk into the People's Republic of South Yemen. He and his two companions were put into a group with 20 other recruits and taken to Aden. Then came a series of flights, first to Karachi by Middle East Airways, from there to Shanghai by Pakistan Airways, and finally on to Peking by an internal flight of Chinese Airways.

The party was at first put up in a comfortable hotel in Peking and during their stay they were taken on a programme of visits to schools, gardens and the former Emperor's palaces and tombs. After this pleasant introduction to the new China, they moved to a training school where they began the work that was the real object of their visit. Dressed in simple overalls with a red Mao Tse-tung on the right lapel, they met the other students in the school in which they were to spend three months. These others included Africans and North Koreans. Instructions included unarmed combat, training with the Kalashnikov AK-47 automatic rifle, the 85 mm RCL rocket-launcher and even a 71 mm field gun, and also long periods of political indoctrination. The Soviet Union, their instructors told them, were revisionists and just as evil as the Western imperialists. Some of the indoctrination sessions were aimed at destroying any religious beliefs the trainees from Oman retained. When asked by an instructor "What is the Koran and who is the Prophet, comrade?" they were required to reply:

The Koran, the Prophet and all other manifestations of Islam are inventions of the British imperialists who are running dogs and lackeys of the US.[16]

Considerable importancce was also placed in their theoretical training on the need to work with comrades of somewhat different views when they returned home and to use such people for their own ends. They were also warned not to expect a favourable response too immediately from the local population when they returned and started operations. The teachings of Mao Tse-tung took a most important place in the syllabus, as might be expected. The trainees had to chant in unison some of the more important teachings on guerrilla tactics, and the manner in which guerrillas should treat the local population. "Be fair in your dealings with people," they had to recite. "Do not bully them ... do not ill-treat prisoners."[17]

There were further sight-seeing tours in Peking in groups of three or four. Once some of them saw a group of Egyptian students in the city but, despite their request, they were not allowed to speak to them. None of the trainees in the camp were allowed out unaccompanied. As well as visits to historic buildings of various kinds, there were also visits to factories, communes and hospitals. At one political cadre school they visited, they saw students dressed in grey and blue uniforms sitting in geometrical patterns on the floor signing revolutionary songs and roaring out in response to a "cheerleader's" question "What do we do to the Black Gang and the bourgeoisie?" "Shah, shah (kill, kill)." An interpreter explained that the "Black Gang" signified the capitalist-minded intellectual clique who had dared to consider themselves superior to the workers just because they were teachers and professors. Most of such people, the explanation continued, had been dealt with during and since the Cultural Revolution.

For the last part of their course, the trainees from Oman and their companions were taken from their camp outside the Peking suburbs northwards by lorry on a long trip to another training centre beyond the Great Wall of China and surrounded by thickly wooded hills. There they had to train extremely hard practising all the skills they had been given a grounding in at their previous camp. At the end of nine months of such training, there was a passing out parade at which Mr Ahmed Deblaan and his comrades received congratulations and a two-hour speech of exhortation from the local commander of the Chinese Peoples' Liberation Army. They also received a bound copy of Mao's thoughts in Arabic; it was identical with the four other copies he had already received during his stay in China.

North Korea

North Korea has provided guerrilla training for members of a number of different revolutionary movements around the world. It would seem that on occasions it has been used as a place of convenience to which trainees can be sent whose presence in camps on Soviet territory might prove of particular embarrassment if news of it were to leak out. Africans from a number of countries are known to have received training in North Korea, these countries including Cameroun and Burundi. In 1969 a student, Mr Israel Otieno, was arrested in Kenya on charges of being in possession of plans to overthrow Kenyatta on behalf of the banned Kenya People's Union. He admitted having received guerrilla training in North Korea in 1964.

In the same year as the student's arrest, 1969, a party of Mexican students arrived in Korea for guerrilla training as part of a KGB-sponsored scheme to foment a large scale armed rising in Mexico. It would seem that in all probability the training they received was not notably different from that given to other

173

nationalities, including Africans visiting the country for the same sort of purpose, and hence is of some relevance here.

The camp to which they were taken was in a bleak and desolate area some miles to the north west of the capital, Pyonyang. It was situated in a lonely valley between two mountain ranges and consisted of wooden barracks, class rooms and mess halls, together with administrative offices and firing ranges and demolition practice areas. Training was extremely arduous, beginning each day at 0600 with an hour of physical training and lasting late into the evening. In addition to the normal weapon training, there was instruction in assassination techniques, methods of extortion, the use of disguises and clandestine methods of travel and recruitment. In the most strenuous exercises they had to undergo, the North Korean Army played the part of "the enemy". The students had to infiltrate military bases; "sabotage" guarded vehicles; practise setting ambushes, engage in unarmed combat with North Korean soldiers and attempt to evade "pursuing patrols". Little attempt was made to provide anything in the way of recreation except occasional visits to circuses or outings in the countryside. Both sex and alcohol were barred as "useless and disruptive distractions from fighting".

No attempt was made to hide the more disagreeable facts surrounding a guerrilla's life. The students were told that:

> Some comrades will die lonely deaths of wounds which cannot be attended. Some will be imprisoned with no hope of liberation until victory. Many of you will have to discharge your revolutionary duties in the night, then work all day at ordinary jobs in which you have no interest. No matter what the hour, when the order comes to move, to bomb, to kill, you must obey instantly.[18]

Cuba

Cuba has provided guerrilla training for a large number of recruits from Latin America and a very considerable number from Africa and other areas. Much of the training has been conducted in the guerrilla academy at Minas Del Frio. It has been estimated that between 100 and 200 Africans a year alone have passed through this centre.

One African "freedom fighter" who has admitted receiving training in Cuba was an Angolan of mixed blood, Mr Rui de Pinto, who joined the MPLA whilst in Paris as a student. From Paris, he was flown to Brazzaville and from there, with 90 fellow members of the MPLA, to Cuba. Mr de Pinto has recorded:

> We landed in Havana and I spent the next seven months undergoing very intensive military training in Cuba. It was interesting and I learned many things, because it was the first time I had done any military training. We had uniforms, military rules and regulations, various courses and so on.[19]

He returned to Brazzaville in June 1967 and subsequently became a Political Commissar with an MPLA column inside Angola. A very considerable number of members of the MPLA who received training abroad appeared to have done so in Cuba.

In the tally of guerrillas killed in the years prior to 1973 by the Rhodesian security forces, nearly as many guerrillas appeared to have received training in Cuba as in the Soviet bloc, 35 as against 39.

Arms Supplies from the Communist Bloc

The first Soviet bloc arms supply operation to insurgent forces on the African continent began during the campaign of the Algerian FLN against French rule in the mid-1950s. Much of this arms supply was despatched to Algeria via Egypt, Libya and Tunisia. In addition, however, considerable quantities of supplies were sent direct in Soviet and other East European ships sailing to Moroccan or Tunisian ports. Czechoslovakian arms specialists working under the cover of posts as commercial attachés in the Czechoslovakian legation in the Moroccan capital of Rabat played an important part in arranging for the reception of such supplies.

The volume of Soviet bloc arms supplies to the FLN eventually became so great that in the last stages of the campaign French officers were estimating that 70% of the FLN's armoury was of Communist (mainly Soviet) bloc manufacture and that an equivalent proportion of its ammunition supply originated from the same source. The products of the Czechoslovakian Skoda arms works played a major part in this flow of munitions.

Supplies of arms from the same source first started to reach Africa south of the Sahara almost 20 years ago, supplies of Czechoslovakian-made arms being received by the guerrillas of the *Union des Population Camerounaise* as early as 1959. Mr Pieter Lessing has recorded that a year later, early in 1960, he personally examined crates of new rifles which had been intercepted by the authorities in the then newly independent Congo, and which were apparently destined for Lumumba's *Movement National Congolaise* and Gizenga's *Parti Solidaire Africain.*

Throughout the years of turmoil in the Congo which quickly followed, Soviet bloc arms continued to flow to such groups. Considerable quantities were despatched from stockpiles already accumulated in Algeria and Egypt, as will be related.

Communist bloc arms began to percolate through to Rhodesian guerrillas about 1962 (although only in small quantities to start with), and by about the same date were also reaching several· of the various movements that had taken up arms against Portuguese rule in Africa. The success of the extreme left-wing revolution in Zanzibar in January 1964 was followed by a marked increase in the flow of such supplies, arms being landed not only in Zanzibar harbour but also at Dar es Salaam which became the main port of entry for these cargoes. Throughout the remainder of 1964, reports appeared of Soviet bloc, and also Chinese, ships unloading such supplies there.

That period saw the beginning of an era in which Soviet bloc supplies flowed into Africa in an ever-increasing stream for the use of guerrilla movements operating against Rhodesia, Angola, Moçambique, Portuguese Guinea and South Africa. Nor have such "liberation movements" engaged in action against "imperialist rule" in the southern half of the continent been by any means the only insurgent forces to receive aid. Considerable quantities of Soviet bloc arms have found their way to movements in revolt against Black African governments, such as those of Ethiopia and the Sudan; and to guerrilla groups engaged in armed prosecution of disputes between African states such as the Algerian-backed Polisario.

One of the weapons most generally to be found in the hands of Communist-supported guerrilla groups in Africa, as elsewhere, originating from the Soviet bloc is the formidable Kalashnikov 7,62 mm automatic assault rifle. The AK-47, as it is generally known, has been produced in vast quantities in the Soviet Union and other Communist bloc countries, particularly Czechoslovakia. The original model was inspired by a German war-time design and it is the standard assault rifle of both the Soviet and all the other Warsaw Pact countries. The rifle carries a 30-round magazine and is capable of a very rapid rate of fire. It has an effective range of 400 m. By 1973, it was estimated that total production figures for this rifle had exceeded 35 million. Models produced in the Soviet bloc outside the USSR sometimes include a number of modifications. The latest Soviet model incorporates an ingenious device by which its short bayonet can be used in conjunction with the scabbard as a wire-cutter. Another weapon quite frequently found in use by guerrilla groups, including those in Rhodesia, is the older Simonov assault rifle.

Amongst the heavier weapons supplied to the PAIGC by the end of the campaign in Portuguese Guinea was the 12,7 mm Degtyarev heavy machine gun, often used as an anti-aircraft weapon, and a standard item of Soviet Army equipment for many years. One PAIGC officer who defected not long before hostilities in the country ended, stated that Soviet supplies at the time included 20 armoured vehicles but this report remained unconfirmed.

Both PAIGC and Frelimo, and later also the MPLA, have received considerable supplies of Soviet-made rocket launchers. These included the 122 mm rocket launcher with a range of 17 km, slightly more than that of the average field-gun of 1939-45 war vintage. Easily portable and capable of being operated by a three-man team, it is in many ways an ideal weapon for guerrilla forces, giving them greatly increased fire power and enabling a small party of guerrillas to inflict heavy damage on a target at considerable distance and then vanish into the forest or bush before any effective action can be taken against them. While it is not very accurate, such weapons *en masse* were used with deadly effect by the Communist forces during the campaigns in both Vietnam and Cambodia, in particular during the last stages of the bloody battle for the Cambodian capital, Phnom Penh. According to Portuguese sources, they were also frequently used by Frelimo for the bombardment of inhabited areas in Moçambique as part of attempts to intimidate the local population. In the latter stages of the MPLA's campaign against the non-Communist forces in Angola, multiple rocket launchers of this type carried on lorries and other vehicles were used by the MPLA and its Cuban allies with devastating effect. (See cover photograph.)

The Soviet-made weapon whose introduction into the final stages of the campaigns in Portuguese Africa probably made the greatest single impact, however, was probably the SAM-7 (or "Strella" rocket). Comparatively light and convenient to carry, it provides guerrillas with an extremely valuable weapon with which to off-set enemy air-power. Capable of being operated by one man and fired from the shoulder, the SAM-7 missile can "home-in" on an aircraft, guided to its target by the heat of the plane's engine from a distance of two to three kilometres. It was a SAM-7 that destroyed the jet aircraft carrying the general commanding the Portuguese Airforce in Guinea early in 1973. The general died in the crash.

Another type of weapon which guerrillas commonly make great use of are mines of all types, and here again the Soviet Union has notably added to the armoury of the African "liberation movements". A variety of both anti-tank and anti-personnel mines have been supplied to the various movements operating in the former Portuguese territory and Rhodesia. The RP, BC 200 pressure-operated anti-personnel mine contained in a wooden case (making it more difficult to detect) is one of those supplied in considerable quantities.

The extent of Soviet aid to the PAIGC was openly admitted by the movement's founder, Mr Amilcar Cabral, when he said in 1970:

> Our principal support comes from the socialist countries, mainly the Soviet Union, which gives us almost all the war materials, the arms and ammunition we use in our struggle.[20]

Soviet arms shipments to the MPLA in Angola were resumed on an ever-increasing scale shortly after the Angolan transitional government assumed power in April 1975. Subsequently, this arms supply operation became one of the biggest of its type ever mounted by the Soviet Union, as is described in Chapter 8.

The year 1976 saw a big increase in the supply of arms by the Soviet Union to Rhodesian guerrilla movements and to some extent also to those of the South West African People's Union. A number of Cubans were said to be assisting with the unloading of heavy equipment destined for the use of Rhodesian guerrillas at the port of Beira. Some of this equipment was apparently ferried to Moçambique ports by Tanzanian ships from Dar es Salaam. A Pentagon report in November 1976, for instance, said that one such vessel had recently brought a cargo consisting of Soviet 122 mm multiple rocket launchers, of the type used with effect in Angola, to Moçambique.

Reports have sometimes appeared of some of the large number of Soviet trawlers which have appeared off various parts of the African coast in recent years being used on gun-running missions to supply some guerrilla groups. Early in 1976, one such report said that a Soviet trawler suspected of landing arms on the deserted coast of the western Sahara for the use of the Algerian backed left-wing Polisario movement which had been carrying on a campaign against Moroccan and Mauritanian forces, had been intercepted by Moroccan patrol boats and escorted into Agadir harbour.

Arms Supply from Communist China

Chinese arms were first found in the hands of insurgents in Africa in the late 1950s in Cameroun. Subsequently, a mission from the Algerian FLN visited China early in 1959 and apparently was successful in securing a credit valued at about 10 000 000 US dollars for the purchase of arms and other equipment. However, it is doubtful how much of this credit was taken up before the campaign ended.

Chinese arms in very considerable quantities were supplied to Maoist Simba rebels in the Congo at the beginning of the 1960s. The Peking Government's African expert, Mr Peng Chi-tang, was believed to be the sponsor of the plan to aid this group. Amongst the supplies the Simbas received from China were 81 mm mortars, recoilless rifles, 12,7 mm machine-guns and anti-tank and anti-personnel mines. Most of these arms arrived in the Congo through the Sudan.

Many of the weapons supplied to African guerrillas by Communist China are, in fact, Chinese copies of Soviet-designed carbines, machine-guns, sub-machine-guns, recoilless rifles, rocket launchers and land mines. Numbers of these started reaching Rhodesian guerrillas in the early 1960s and ZANU in particular was largely dependent on Chinese supplies for a time. COREMO of Moçambique, the PAC of South Africa and SWANU of South West Africa are examples of movements which have looked to China, rather than the Soviet bloc, for material support, as also prior to the early 1970s did Frelimo in Moçambique.

The Chinese supply of arms to the guerrillas of the Eritrean Liberation Front began about 1968. Early in 1970, the Nairobi *Daily Nation* reported that such aid was being stepped up. The newspaper quoted Mr Osman Sabi, Secretary General of ELF, as saying while on a visit to Damascus that two shiploads of Communist Chinese weapons had arrived for the use of the movement. One of the more important items supplied by China to the ELF have been anti-personnel mines made of non-metallic materials and so particularly hard to detect when laid. Such mines were a favourite weapon of the Viet Cong. The following year, in 1971, this Chinese aid began to dwindle, however, probably because of China's growing policy of re-assessment of its attitude towards established non-Communist governments such as that of Ethiopia.

Communist Arms Supply through "Middle-men"

The arms supply operations of the Communist powers in Africa, in particular those of the Soviet bloc, have been greatly aided by the existence of a number of left-leaning independent states which have been ready to stockpile very large quantities of arms on their territory greatly in excess of their own requirements. These are then despatched for the use of insurgent forces in other African countries at the request or suggestion of the Communist Government which provided them. This arrangement, besides being convenient on geographical grounds, also enables the Soviet or Chinese Governments to disavow responsibility for arms supply operations involving particularly delicate questions in regard to their relation with African Governments or even major external powers.

A typical operation involving the use of "middle-men" states, in this case Algeria and Egypt, was the Soviet inspired arms supply operation to Marxist guerrillas in the Congo during the early 1960s. It was estimated that more than 300 tons of arms and supplies were flown from depots at Boufarik, south of Algiers, to Khartoum during December 1964 and January 1965 by a fleet of 12 Soviet *Antonov* airliners. At Khartoum, these cargoes were transferred to light aircraft and flown to Juba in the Southern Sudan. From there, lorry convoys carried them to points on the Congo border. Quite elaborate efforts were made to disguise Soviet participation in this operation. Red Star emblems on the aircraft and other identifying marks were painted out and replaced by Algerian markings. In addition, the aircraft were flown by Soviet crews but had Algerian co-pilots.

In the case of arms stock-piled in Egypt, these were transported south to the Sudan by boat down the Nile and taken from special unloading points to points on the Congo-Sudanese border by lorry. A report in the *Daily Telegraph* of 11 May 1965 stated that the main supply route to the Congo insurgents was being switched to a sea-borne one. It was said that five cargoes of arms had been unloaded at Pointe Noire during the early part of the year. War material included in that flow was reportedly carried on Soviet, Algerian, Chinese and Egyptian vessels.

The same sort of use of Soviet-made arms stored in Algeria also seems to have been made to assist in meeting the needs of the PAIGC in Portuguese Guinea. It is believed that an agreement was reached between Algeria and the Soviet Union under which stocks of arms supplied to PAIGC by the former would be replaced by fresh supplies from the USSR.[21] Despite Colonel Gaddafi's declared aversion to Marxism, Libya has in recent years shown every sign of becoming another important "middle-man" for the distribution of Soviet arms, and not only to "freedom fighters" in Africa.

Libya was, for instance, heavily involved in an arms running operation into the Lebanon through Syria in 1973, the object being to bring about the overthrow of the then Lebanese Government. Members of the Palestinian guerrilla group, Al Fatah, were involved in smuggling a consignment of arms supplied by Libya which included 1 500 Kalashnikov rifles, rocket launchers, machineguns and plastic mines into the Lebanon. The whole of this operation apparently had the express approval of Colonel Gaddafi himself, the arms being intended for the use of the Progressive Socialist Party (PSP) and the Moslem Najada Party.[22] With the outbreak of fighting between Christian and Moslem forces in the Lebanon in 1975, reports once again began to appear of the arrival of consignments of arms from Libya for the use of the latter.

One of the Libyan gun-running operations which has so far attracted the greatest attention in the eyes of the world has undoubtedly been the attempt to supply arms to the Provisional

181

IRA in Ireland. On 28 March 1973, a patrol vessel of the Irish Navy intercepted and arrested a small freighter, *The Claudia,* inside Irish territorial waters. The vessel was found to be carrying five tons of Soviet-made arms and ammunition, investigations indicating that her cargo had been loaded in the Libyan port of Tripoli. Although this particular cargo failed to reach its destination, there is good reason to believe that a number of RPG-7 Soviet-made anti-tank rocket launchers used in attacks by the Provisionals in Northern Ireland have found their way into such hands via Libyan depots. Colonel Gaddafi has himself never made any secret of his support for the IRA.

In April 1975, a 16-strong Irish Parliamentary delegation visited Libya but apparently failed to receive any assurance from the Libyan Government that no more attempts to aid the IRA would be made. According to a report in *The Times* of 21 April 1975, one reason for this failure was the demand by Libyan leaders that any such assurance by Libya must be preceded by a declaration of support by the Irish Government for the participation of the Palestine Liberation Organisation in the then forthcoming Euro-Arab Conference.

In Africa itself, Libya has during the last two or three years started to play a major part in the supply of arms to the Eritrean Popular Liberation Forces, the armed and Marxist-inclined wing of the Eritrean Liberation Front (ELF). In May 1973, Mr Osman Saleh Sabbe, the Secretary-General of the Popular Liberation Front forces, held a meeting with Colonel Gaddafi. At that meeting, the Libyan leader assured Mr Sabba of continued Libyan support. Arrangements were apparently made for the supply of no less than 150 tons of arms and ammunition, together with supplies of explosives, to the Popular forces. These supplies were scheduled to reach the PLF by the end of August. In addition, it was agreed to despatch a smaller consignment of six tons of supplies early in June.

Soviet arms from Libyan stocks also started to reach ELF forces operating in the area known as the Ogaden in south-east Ethiopia, near the border with Somalia, during 1973. These arms followed a somewhat round-about route, being shipped from Libyan ports to the Egyptian port of Harghada on the entrance to the Gulf of Suez, and thence transported to Jeddah. Here the arms were loaded onto dhows sailing to the Somali coast and unloaded at Berbera. For the final stage in their journey, they were then taken overland to Hargeisa, the main ELF base for operations in the Ogaden.

Early in September 1976, the Libyan Prime Minister, Mr Jaloud, revealed details concerning the provision of training facilities and the supply of arms by his country to the "liberation movements" of Southern Africa. Admitting that "freedom fighters" from Portuguese Guinea and Moçambique had received training in Libya, he went on to say:

> If freedom fighters in Zimbabwe and South Africa ask for training facilities here we should agree to their request.
> But after the liberation of Moçambique, Guinea-Bissau and Angola, they have other bases where they can be trained. We can support them with arms and money. In the past our support was limited because the Africans in Zimbabwe believed in seeking a peaceful solution through negotiations.[23]

Another "middle-man" of increasing importance is the People's Democratic Republic of South Yemen, in which large supplies of Soviet arms have been stockpiled. In addition to providing a base for the Marxist guerrillas operating in Oman and Dhofar, a base which includes a school for the training of child guerrillas, this state also provides considerable support for guerrilla movements south of the Gulf of Aden.

One former member of the guerrillas operating in Oman, who laid down his arms in 1976, was sent on a mission to Egypt in 1968. He later recorded that on his return he was flown to Aden and then boarded a motorised sailing boat which took him to Port Sudan and then on to the PFLOAG base at Hauf.

At Port Sudan, the boat tied up at a quay on which was a warehouse containing many crates of arms. He noticed that a number of small crates were marked for delivery to the Eritrean guerrillas of ELF, whilst the destination of a number of larger ones appeared to be Frelimo bases. Others were addressed to known guerrilla-warfare training camps in Zanzibar, whilst yet others carried labels describing their contents as "farm equipment" and consigned to harmless sounding addresses, but in fact clandestine bases in Zambia.

Guerrilla Training Camps in Africa

The French withdrawal from Algeria raised the prestige of the guerrillas of the FLN to an extremely high pinnacle in the eyes of all other actual and potential "freedom fighters" in Africa, and even farther afield. It was not long, for instance, before Mr Yasir Arafat, leader of the Palestinian Al Fatah terrorist organisation, arrived in Algiers to open an office for his organisation. He received a warm welcome and offers for the provision of training facilities and other support from the new government.

Soon, requests were being received for support from the various movements which had began armed action in Portuguese Africa, in particular from the Angolan MPLA. Many members of the latter who had shown themselves particularly adept at guerrilla fighting were withdrawn from operations for a spell and sent on a refresher course to the large Algerian training centre at Tlemcen. This had been the main training base of the FLN itself in the campaign against the French.

MPLA members would spend up to nine months at Tlemcen receiving instruction in military and civil organisation, tactics, wireless communications, map reading and the use of a compass, weapon training, booby-trap and ambush techniques, and some lessons in political theory. As well as Algerians, the instructors included East Germans, Cubans, Communist Chinese and experienced veterans of a number of successful "liberation struggles". After their course at Tlemcen, the MPLA trainees would often be attached to a specialist unit of the Algerian regular army, such as a signals company, for a further few months.

Similar training was also received by some members of PAIGC from Portuguese Guinea. At one stage, Communist China is known to have offered to pay the expenses of Rhodesian guerrillas who went for training in the Tlemcen camp. That a not inconsiderable number of members of such movements did in fact receive training in Algeria, would seem to be shown by the fact that, according to Rhodesian records, 22 of the guerrillas killed by the security forces up until 1973 had received training in that country.

Algeria has also sent instructors to other African countries to help train guerrillas. For instance, during the campaign in Portuguese Guinea, the presence of Algerian instructors amongst others was noted at the PAIGC base in Kindia, near Conakry.

During the campaign against the Portuguese two important

MPLA camps at which preliminary training was given to recruits for the movement operated at Pointe Noire in the Congo-Brazzaville and Kinkouza in Congo-Kinshasa, now called Zaire.

One MPLA member who had received advance training in Cuba and who in 1968 was a Political Commissar with an MPLA unit in a base camp near Brazzaville has described the importance placed there of the Marxist practice of holding frequent sessions of self-criticism in bringing recruits to a proper understanding of the cause and the tactics to be employed in the struggle. This member, Mr Rui de Pinto, wrote:

> Most of the criticisms, of course, were about our practical work—if someone felt he was not doing his job well, he would criticise himself and ask for criticism from the other comrades. This usually happened in the smaller units about three times a week; not on a regular basis, on fixed days, but as it became necessary. If a problem came up in a small unit, it would be discussed first at the level with the *Chefe de Grup*. Then, if it was an important matter, it would be brought up by the political commissar and discussed in the larger group at a meeting. As I was a political commissar in a section of the Bomoko column, I conducted many meetings like this. I would start by talking about the importance of our work, the importance of what we were trying to do, and what we had done over the past week or so. Then I would ask the comrades if they really thought they had done their best in our work; you know, in their military training, their studies, duties around the camps, compartment and so on."

Mr de Pinto further explained that after such sessions had been engaged in for some time:

> ... it sometimes happened that a comrade returned a bit late. But no one would go up to him and say: "You are late. Why?" No, it was not necessary. The comrade would come forward himself and say, "I am late", and explain his reasons. If it was necessary to have a criticism, they didn't have to wait for the *Chefe* or political commissar. Any of the comrades could criticise

him. And, of course, when you criticise someone else's bad practice, it becomes difficult for you to make the same mistake. So I think this method of criticism and self-criticism was, and is, very important for developing the right kind of discipline.[24]

Egypt has in the past provided training in guerrilla warfare and terrorist techniques for a number of Palestinian movements and for some members of African groups. In the early 1960s, for instance, a number of members of the South West African People's Organisation (SWAPO) were air-lifted from a camp near Dar es Salaam to a camp not far from Cairo where they were trained by Arab instructors in the use of explosives during a three-week course.[25]

Some members of Rhodesian groups also seem to have received training in Egypt at one stage.

Both the Soviet bloc and Communist China were heavily involved in the practical side of Nkrumah's attempt to turn Ghana into a major base for the subversion of a number of West African countries. A central part of such preparations was the setting up of facilities for the training of guerrillas on a considerable scale. Russians, Chinese, East Germans, Poles, Czechs, Cubans and North Koreans all played their part in these plans.

The Soviet Union's part in the affair was under the control of a KGB officer, as reported in a previous chapter. The training of guerrillas progressed efficiently and by 1965 about 350 recruits from a number of African countries had received a full course.

In the later stages of the operation, the main training camp was taken over from the Soviet instructors by Chinese equivalents. The Chinese instructors were attached to the Bureau of African Affairs, the main co-ordinating body for Nkrumah's subversive attempts. Their leader, Colonel Yen Leng, recommended that the camp be moved from its location at Half-Assini, which he thought was too near the Ivory Coast border, to Obernamasi.

Instruction included the tactics and strategy of guerrilla warfare, weapon training, the use of explosives, communications work and first aid. When some students complained that they had not been included in lessons on explosives, they were told that such training was only for those with scientific backgrounds and that "the illiterate and the unintelligent could receive only training in weapon handling".[26] Instruction in "correct" political thinking which it was held was an essential part of the make-up of a successful guerrilla fighter was also included, this being almost entirely based upon the teachings of Mao Tse-tung.

One Rhodesian "freedom fighter" who was trained in a camp near Kumasi in company with 36 other Rhodesians, under Chinese instructors, said afterwards that he had been particularly impressed with the very good grasp the instructors had of the geography of his country, despite their lack of any practical knowledge of it. Another Rhodesian, a member of ZANU, has said of his six-month training course in a Ghanaian camp under Chinese control:

> In lectures we were taught the principles of war and guerrilla tactics according to Mao Tse-tung, given lectures on the People's Army of China and shown films on how they fought the Japanese. We also had lessons on how and from where to begin the Zimbabwe revolution.[27]

The main bases of PAIGC during its campaign against Portuguese rule in Portuguese Guinea were located in the Republic of Guinea, one of the main bases being at Kindia, near the capital, Conakry. In the early stages of the campaign, training instruction was given by Soviet officers, subsequently by Algerians and later still by Cubans. Another base at Kolda was also reported to have Cuban instructors. One journalist, Mr Al Venter, reported the presence of Soviet frogmen in Conakry, these specialists being allegedly engaged in training members of PAIGC in this particular form of attack. The same correspondent reported personally seeing a Soviet team operating a radio system at Koundara in 1965, apparently providing the Eastern war zone with communications.

In 1973, under Libyan prodding, the Government of the Republic of Guinea agreed to provide a training site in the country at which Black Africans could be given training in guerrilla and terrorist techniques by Palestinians. These facilities were paid for by a grant of financial aid from Libya. The aim of the operation apparently was to enable Palestinian movements to be able to train African agents for use in areas in which it would not be easy for Arabs to move about freely. In the spring of that year, a dozen or so Palestinians were reported to have arrived in Conakry from Algiers for the purpose of choosing a suitable site for the training camp and completing final arrangements for the scheme. The Algerian Embassy in the capital was also apparently involved in the plan, being responsible for providing logistic and general support for visiting Palestinians involved in it.[28]

The main effort of Libya, as far as providing facilities for guerrilla training was concerned, goes into support for various Palestinian groups. Since late 1971 an Al Fatah training camp has been in existence at a location 75 km east of Benghazi. A second camp of greater importance is, however, reported to be in operation at Ras Hilal, some 80 km from the town of Al Bayda, which lies near the border with Egypt. A provision of 10 million United States dollars has been made for this camp, which among other things operates as a training centre for Al Fatah frogmen.

A number of Libyan army officers act as instructors at the camp, whilst others also undergo training courses there. It was reported somewhat surprisingly in 1973 that instructors at this camp included nine British mercenaries, three of them being former British servicemen with experience in Palestine and Malaya who were said to be engaged in training Palestinians in underwater sabotage techniques.[29]

Another training camp known to be in existence in Libya is at Tarhuna, about 150 km south-east of Tripoli. This camp was established in 1972 with the special purpose of providing training for the Marxist National Front for the Liberation of Morocco (NFLM). At the end of 1973, about 300 Moroccan guerrillas were undergoing training in this camp which was under the management of the Libyan armed forces.[30]

An indication of other possible ambitions in the field of guerrilla training by the Libyan Government came in the spring of 1973 when the Sudanese security authorities arrested 200 men who were trying to cross the Sudanese/Libyan border illegally. Although the group stated that they were on their way to Libya in search of food, the security authorities believed that in fact the purpose of their journey was to receive guerrilla training in Libya with the aim of starting an armed revolt against the rule of the Sudanese President **Numeri**.

For the past 10 years or so, Tanzania has provided facilities for a whole complex of guerrilla training and operational bases in support of such movements as Frelimo of Moçambique, the ANC of South Africa, and ZANU and ZAPU of Rhodesia. Mr Anthony Wilkinson, author of *Insurgency in Rhodesia*, published by the International Institute for Strategic Studies in 1973, identified eight separate camps. These included a large training camp at Kongwa, west of Dar es Salaam, which he stated was used mainly by the South African ANC, SWAPO and Rhodesian guerrillas. The main Frelimo training camp was located at Mbeya, this having Cuban and Chinese instructors. The South African ANC command and administrative HQ was at Morogoro. There was a camp at Nanchinguera at which Frelimo officers are known to have trained with the Tanzanian Army. A large refugee training camp existed at Lindi which was used by Frelimo for obtaining recruits from amongst refugees from Moçambique and finally there was a staging base at Bugandyo which was used by the Organisation of African Unity for making arms allocations to the various "liberation movements".

Mr Wilkinson also mentioned the presence of staging camps used as bases by guerrillas engaged in hit-and-run raids into northern Moçambique at Nbamba Bay, Songea, and Nwala. The presence of other Frelimo camps at such places as Nashingwea and Tunduru was reported subsequently. The Nashingwea training centre was said to have been presented to Frelimo by President Nyerere himself.

In addition, the presence of two guerrilla training camps has been reported on the island of Zanzibar, these having a staff of between 150 and 200 Chinese instructors and specialists.

It would also seem that Tanzanian territory was used as a staging base by MPLA units in transit for attacks in Angola, via Zambia. Mr Rui de Pinto, for instance, records that in April 1968 he and the majority of the MPLA column to which he was attached were flown to Dar es Salaam where they stayed for two weeks and were then taken by truck through Zambia to the border of the eastern region of Angola.

In July 1975 a delegation from the African National Council of Rhodesia under its then President, Bishop Muzorewa, visited the Morogoro area of Tanzania where they toured a large training centre for Rhodesian guerrillas. Earlier in the year, President Nyerere had made a promise to hand over the extensive Frelimo training facilities in Tanzania to Rhodesian movements in view of the successful end of the campaign in Moçambique. Tanzanian sources claimed at the time that the training camps used by Frelimo were capable of turning out 3 000 guerrillas every three months.

The Zambian Government has adopted a somewhat ambivalent attitude towards admitting that guerrilla training centres or bases exist on its territory. Completely contradictory statements sometimes come from the same Government officials. For example, one senior Zambian Government official announced in New York at the end of March 1968 that "Zambia is supporting guerrilla warfare in Rhodesia". Yet only four months later, the same official could be found stating that suggestions that guerrilla training camps existed in Zambia were "cheap propaganda by minority governments".[31] However, evidence of both the Rhodesian security forces and independent observers points inescapably to the presence of a number of bases and training camps in the country.

Mr Wilkinson reported the existence of the following camps in his survey: Nkomo Camp, 25 km west of Lusaka, the main transit camp for South African PAC and Rhodesian ZAPU; Dube's Farm Camp, used by members of both the South African PAC and ZANU of Rhodesia as a staging base; Balawale Refugee Camp, near Kalabo, which he described as being used as a guerrilla recruiting centre and transit post; and Shikongo Camp, an important arms dump and supply and distribution centre for the MPLA. He also stated that use was being made of the Mkumbi International College, which acts as both a school for refugees and as a recruiting centre.

The ending of Portuguese rule in Moçambique resulted in many of the camps in Tanzania formerly used for training purposes by Frelimo being transformed into training centres for members of the Rhodesian guerrilla groups. A network of new training camps and operational bases for the use of Rhodesian guerrillas was also rapidly established in Moçambique itself. During 1976 these camps came to be staffed by an increasing number of Cuban instructors. Early in 1977, it was estimated that between 200 and 500 Cubans were engaged in training both members of the Zimbabwe People's Army (ZIPA), as the main Rhodesian guerrilla force now styled itself, and the new Moçambique Army which was being formed from Frelimo.

The Cubans were said to be keeping well away from front line bases in the frontier areas at that time and to be mainly stationed in five camps in the Gaza and Manica-Sofala provinces.

About the same time, news was received of the establishment in the extreme south of Moçambique of at least three camps intended for the training of guerrillas whose rôle would be that of carrying out raids over the near-by frontier with South Africa. South African sources said that the camps had been established by the African National Congress assisted by London-based officials of the South African Communist Party on the urging of the Soviet Union. Pressure for the setting-up of the camps was said to have been exerted by the Soviet Government after leading members of the South African Communist Party had visited Moscow. The camps were reported to contain several hundred guerrillas under training.

REFERENCES

1. *From Shantytown to Forest,* Norman Duka, Liberation Support Movement Information Centre, Richmond B.C., Canada, 1974, p. 67.
2. *Ibid.,* p. 68.
3. *Ibid.*
4. *Ibid.*
5. *Ibid.,* p. 70.
6. *The Organiser,* Temba Moyo, Liberation Support Movement Information Centre, Richmond B.C., Canada, 1974, p. 75-76.
7. *The Fight for Zimbabwe,* Rees Maxey, Rex Collins, London, 1975, p. 100.
8. *Armed Conflict in Southern Africa,* Michael Morris, Jeremy Spence, Cape Town, 1974, p. 3.
9. *Ibid.,* p. 284-285.
10. *Where Soldiers Fear to Tread, op. cit.,* p. 37-41.
11. *Oman, Insurgency and Development,* D.L. Price, Institute for the Study of Conflict, Conflict Studies No. 53, London, 1975, p. 70.
12. *Where Soldiers Fear to Tread, op. cit.,* p. 35-36.
13. *KGB, op. cit.,* p. 57.
14. *The Fight for Zimbabwe, op. cit.,* p. 80.
15. *Insurgency in Rhodesia,* R. Wilkinson, International Institute for Strategic Studies, London, 1973, p. 47.
16. *Where Soldiers Fear to Tread, op. cit.,* p. 31-35.
17. *Ibid.*
18. *KGB, op. cit.,* 243-244.
19. *The Making of a Middle Cadre,* Rui de Pinto, LSM Information Centre, Richmond B.C., Canada, 1973, p. 74.
20. *Southern Africa: End of Empire,* Peter Janke, Institute for the Study of Conflict, London, December 1964, p. 8.
21. *Armed Conflict in Southern Africa, op. cit.,* p. 173-174.
22. *Libya's Foreign Adventures,* Brian Crozier, Institute for the Study of Conflict, London, December 1973, p. 11.

23. *The Daily Telegraph,* 6 September 1976.
24. *The Making of a Middle Cadre, op. cit.,* p. 84.
25. *Armed Conflict in Southern Africa, op. cit.*
26. *China's African Revolution, op. cit.,* p. 124.
27. *Ibid.,* p. 157.
28. *Libya's Foreign Adventures, op. cit.,* p. 7.
29. *Ibid.,* p. 16.
30. *Ibid.,* p. 4.
31. *Armed Conflict in Southern Africa, op. cit.,* p. 241-244.
32. *Ibid.*

Chapter 7

Glimpses of some "Liberation Movements" in Action

In a general study such as this, it would be an impossible task to trace the development and history of all the various "liberation movements" that have resorted to "armed struggle" on the African continent during the last 20 years or so. It is intended merely to outline the origins and activities of those in which Marxist influences have become most strongly developed and which consequently have attracted the greatest degree of support from the Communist powers. Only those have been selected whose subsequent activities have had a considerable influence in, shaping the course of events which have led to the present situation.

Ex-Portuguese Africa

Angola	*Movimento Popular a Libertacao de Angola* (MPLA)
Moçambique	*Frente de Libertacao de Moçambique* (Frelimo)
Guinea-Bissau	*Partido Africano da Independencia da Guide e Cabo Verde* (PAIGC)

According to Dr Agostinho Neto, its present leader, the MPLA was founded at a secret meeting held in Luanda in December 1956. Dr Neto explained how this meeting came about as follows:

At the beginning, in view of the police repression, we formed several political groups that pursued a common objective. Most of them operated in Luanda, the capital, the most important being the Movement for the National Independence of Angola (MINA), and the Party for the United Struggle of the Angolan Africans (PLUA). From the unification of these and other organisations the People's Movement for the Liberation of Angola was born."[1]

It is known that among important representatives of the "other organisations" mentioned by Neto as being present at that meeting were those of the Angolan Communist Party (PCA), an off-shoot of the illegal Portuguese Communist Party. One authority has stated that the organisers of the Angolan Communist Party were for the most part of European civil servants who were secretly members of the Portuguese Party. The Angolan Communist Party had built up a certain following among disaffected intellectuals in the Luanda area and had merged with other small groups to form the Party for the United Struggle of Angolan Africans which now in its turn submerged its identity in the MPLA.[2]

For the first two years of its existence, the MPLA concentrated upon attempting to set up a network of cells upon which it could build an organisation in Luanda. During this attempt, many of its members were arrested. Dr Neto became a member of its Steering Committee in 1968. The following year he was arrested and violence resulted in the form of riots in Catete during which Portuguese troops opened fire and a number of people were killed and injured. The MPLA's first President, Mr Illidio Machado, a post office employee, had been arrested previously and for a time the movement was forced to operate mainly from offices outside the country. Originally it had established a headquarters in Conakry but in 1960 this was moved to Brazzaville.

In February 1962 the MPLA attempted its first major armed operation. Its aim was to free all MPLA members then being held by the Portuguese authorities in Luanda. Attacks took place upon the military detention centre, the civil prison, and the city police station. These raids were all repulsed with some casualties. The Portuguese security forces claimed at the time to have seized some Czech-made weapons used by the attackers.

Operating from its various external offices, its leaders now began to make arrangements for its members to receive foreign military training. Most of the members selected for this were ordered to make their own way to the Congo (now Zaire), from where they would be sent to the country chosen for their training. Some went to Algeria and Morocco, others to Zambia or Tanzania. Dr Neto, who had been removed to Portugal and placed under house arrest there, managed to escape and make his way to Leopoldville (now Kinshasa) in Zaire, via Rabat. By the end of 1962 he had been appointed President of the MPLA. Serious Soviet interest in the MPLA seems to date from about that time. Neto's return to Africa was soon followed by the arrival of East German advisers and equipment to assist the movement.[3]

In Moçambique, a number of young intellectuals and students, including amongst their number Dr Eduardo Mondlane, had, as early as 1948, formed a group with the title NESAM *Nucleo des Estudentres Africanos Securdarias de Moçambique*). Although this group ostensibly concentrated upon arousing interest in Moçambique's culture amongst young people, its main driving force was nationalism and anti-colonialism. By the end of the 1950s, it claimed to have established a considerable influence and to have succeeded in the spreading of nationalist ideas. More importantly, it claimed to have established a country-wide network of members which it was hinted could be used as the foundation of a resistance network.

In October 1960 a number of Moçambicans opposed to Portuguese rule and living in exile in Rhodesia founded the *Union Democratic National de Moçambique*. A few months afterwards, another group of Moçambicans living in Tanzania formed MANU (Moçambique African National Union). This group, according to Dr Mondlanc, got "involved with the Zanzibar progressive forces under Babu, Kalum, and others". These Zanzibaris, with Chinese and Cuban encouragement, were later to be responsible for the revolution which overthrew the constitutional government on the island of Zanzibar in 1964. Yet a third movement was formed about the same time by some other Moçambicans living in Nyasaland, now Malawi.

On 25 June 1962 the three Moçambican movements merged to form Frelimo with its headquarters in Dar es Salaam. Dr Mondlane, who was elected its first president, has recorded that as soon as the movement was established:

A programme was drawn up which was discussed and

195

approved by the First Congress in September 1962."

At the same time much study was undertaken of other campaigns against "fascism". In this regard, Dr Mondlane said "Cuba was very relevant to us".[4]

One tactic described by Dr Mondlane as being used by Frelimo in those early days was the utilisation as a cover of such bodies as agricultural co-operatives. He claims that:

> We made use of these. We linked ourselves to them even under the noses of the Portuguese. Sometimes programmes appeared as if they were good for the Portuguese, and would benefit them economically. But underlying them, there was a political force working. Sometimes we had the co-operation of the paramount chiefs; sometimes we didn't. At that stage before the beginning of the war, it was necessary not to antagonise the chiefs, not to challenge them directly, but to organise a structure which at the proper time could function with or without the chiefs. This is the principal part of the work we did.[5]

At the same time, Frelimo set about finding means of obtaining military training for its members. These efforts were aided by the fact that the same year that saw the foundation of Frelimo also saw the establishment of Algeria as an independent state. Dr Mondlane has described how he and his colleagues of Frelimo at the time saw Algeria as being "the one country in Africa that was able to carry out a revolutionary war and win". He contacted Mr Ben Bella who had already agreed to provide training for Angolans and members of armed movements from other countries and requested such assistance in the training of members of Frelimo. Mr Ben Bella agreed to this request and said that he would set up a special training programme. The first group of Frelimo members was sent to Algerian camps at the end of 1962. Dr Mondlane stated:

> Each few months we increased the number, until we had a structured group, a body that returned at the end of 1963 and began training others in East Africa, and by June 1964 we had enough—at least a couple of hundred—well trained, fairly well equipped people to begin the fight."

In addition to these preparations, a major effort was mounted by Frelimo in the field of propaganda with the aim of influencing world opinion and bringing about the diplomatic isolation of Portugal. Offices were opened in Cairo and Algiers. Contacts were made in the Soviet Union and also with sympathetic circles in Western Europe, the United States and Asia. Students from Moçambique studying abroad were enrolled to represent the cause in the countries of their temporary residence and special emphasis was placed upon sending representatives to all possible conferences dealing with international affairs.

In 1954 in Portuguese Guinea, the first clandestine nationalist movement to be formed was the *Movimento para a Independencia Nacional da Guiné Portugesa* (MING), a somewhat ineffectual organisation. In 1965, however, Mr Amilcar Cabral (whose mother came from Guinea and father from the Cape Verde Islands) and who, at that time, lived in Angola where he had already taken part in the founding of the MPLA, paid a visit to Bissau, capital of Portuguese-Guinea. During his stay, he turned his efforts to sponsoring the formation of a new organisation, the *Partido Africano da Independencia da Guine e Cabo Verde* (PAIGC), using the largely inactive MING as a basis upon which to build.

PAIGC concentrated its early efforts on attempting to create an underground organisation based upon the urban working class. Mr Cabral later admitted that this had been a mistake and that he had not been familiar with the works of Mao Tse-tung and his advocacy of rural guerrilla warfare tactics until some years later. He has recorded:

> The lack of experience made us think that we could fight in the cities with strikes and other things, but we were wrong and the reality of the moment showed us that it was not possible.[7]

PAIGC's attempt to foment strikes at this time led to an ugly incident at Pidiguiti docks in Bissau in August 1959, when Portuguese troops opened fire and up to 50 Africans were killed. Almost immediately the Portuguese security forces began large scale operations to break up the PAIGC urban network and many of its leading cadres were arrested or forced into exile. Mr Cabral returned to Bissau secretly from Angola and organised an emergency meeting of the remaining PAIGC leaders. At that meeting it

197

was decided that the main weight of the movement's operations should be switched from the towns to the countryside with the object of using the "peasant masses" as its main force. Meanwhile, neighbouring Guinea had become independent and PAIGC set about establishing its main operational base in that country's capital, Conakry. Mr Cabral explains that among the advantages that this brought was the ability to

> **create** a political school to prepare political activitists. This was decisive for our struggle. In 1960, we created a political school in Conakry, under very poor conditions. Militants from the cities—Party members—were the first to come to receive political instructions and to be trained in how to mobilise our people for the fight.
>
> First some comrades from the city came to the school, then came peasants, youths (some even bringing their entire families) who were mobilised by Party members. Ten, 20, 25 people would come for a period of one or two months. During that time, they went through an intense formative programme and we spoke with them, and night would come and we couldn't speak any more because we were completely hoarse. Some of the cadres of the Party would explain the entire situation to them but we went further.
>
> We performed in that school as in a theatre, imagining the mobilisation of the people of a *tabanka*, but taking into account social characteristics, traditions, religion—the customs of our peasant population.[8]

Some PAIGC recruits then also began to be sent much further afield to obtain military training, including before long to Communist countries.

Meanwhile, the work of mobilising support in the countryside proceeded through the use of large numbers of PAIGC-trained agents. Their approach was concentrated upon the *Homem grandes,* or village elders, in each area. The aim being to impress upon them the PAIGC party line in the hope that they would then in turn use their local prestige to impress it on the ordinary villagers. By 1963, the mobilisation had progressed far enough for PAIGC leaders to consider that the time was ripe for the beginning of serious armed struggle.

Organisation

During the years of campaigning against the Portuguese forces in Angola, the MPLA developed a command structure which controlled not only the activities of its armed guerrillas, but also those of propaganda, political education and other departments. According to Mr Paulo Jorge, Director of the movement's Department of Information and Propaganda, speaking at the end of December 1972 (little more than two years before the end of the campaign against Portuguese rule), the MPLA command structure then consisted of the *Comité Director* or Steering Committee, whose members were elected by a National Congress, and of a subordinate Politico-Military Co-ordinating Committee (CCMP), which had the rôle of implementing the day-to-day decisions of the *Comité Director*.

Dr Agostinho Neto, who had now led the MPLA for 14 years, is an Angolan of mixed blood and was born in 1922. He was educated at primary and secondary schools in Luanda and in 1947 was sent to the University of Coimbra in Portugal on a scholarship provided by the Methodist Church. There he studied medicine and became the first Negro to graduate from the University of Lisbon. Whilst in Lisbon, he seemed to have joined the Movement for Democratic Unity of Youth (MUDJ). This was regarded by the authorities as being a front organisation for the Portuguese Communist Party and in 1955 he was arrested and sentenced to 14 months imprisonment. Subsequently, he returned to Angola and worked in the Luanda Hospital.

After being elected President of the MPLA at the end of his second period of detention late in 1962, he visited Moscow in early 1964 and it is alleged that he then began to receive some financial aid from the Soviet bloc. Two years later, he visited Cuba and in 1967 was made a member of the Soviet-controlled World Peace Council (WPC) Presidential Committee.

During the celebrations of the centenary of the birth of Lenin in Moscow at which he was present, he said:

> The Popular Movement for the Liberation of Angola also expresses its sympathy and solidarity with all the democratic parties and liberation movements represented here, which are fighting, often in formidable conditions, for the freedom of their nations from foreign domination of national oligarchies.[19]

Dr Neto, in addition to his political activities, has established a considerable reputation as a poet. He has a Portuguese wife who is the sister of the wife of Admiral Rosa, the so-called "Red Admiral" who played an important part in the Portuguese Revolution.

Whereas the history of the MPLA has been much affected for many years by the existence of rival nationalist organisations, that of Frelimo in Moçambique was almost equally complicated by the numerous different tribes existing in that territory of 784 961 km^2. Of the 19 tribes in the country, Frelimo, despite all its efforts, succeeded in obtaining support in any strength from only one major and two less important tribes, most of its recruits coming from a section of the Makondes, the Nyanjas and the Yaos. Even within this comparatively small recruiting base, there were seeds of disunity other than tribal ones. Nyanjas, for instance, were Christians, whereas the Yaos were Muslims. Consequently, great efforts were made to forge a new spirit of co-operation through the medium of "revolutionary unity". The movement's first President, Dr Eduardo Mondlane, explained:

> All military officers of Frelimo, all actual militants who have to fight with any kind of weapons, including just simply a hand grenade, have had to have as a goal a period of a minimum of three months of political education. In fact, all of us in Frelimo, including the members of the Central Committee, regardless of age or sex, have to be educated politically. We have an organised political education programme for giving the people a clear picture of Africa. It consists of a series of definitions of our purposes, of our goals, of our techniques of work.[10]

Much of this political education was undertaken by special Centres for Political and Military Training (CRPMGs) whose work is described later.

Frelimo's campaign was directed throughout by a Central Committee which first consisted of about 20, and then about 40, members. In 1968 steps were taken to improve its command structure by the creation of a Political-Military Committee which had the task of implementing decisions of the Central Committee and an Executive Committee which directed the day-to-day handling of problems and tasks. There was also a system of secretaries who were supposed to co-ordinate Frelimo activities in each province. The full-time mobile regular units of Frelimo guerrillas were supported by a part-time local militia.

Frelimo also possessed an armed women's wing established in 1967, and known as The Women's Detachments.

These detachments not infrequently claimed important successes and were proud of their alleged skill in "killing Portuguese". Frelimo journals sometimes carried articles by their members on such themes as "we women have the right to fight". This fighting image, however, suffered something of a setback when the leader of the women's detachments, Mrs Veronica Namiua, defected to the Portuguese during the early 1970s.

Dr Mondlane, who was elected President of the Movement at its first congress in 1962, had an academic record of considerable brilliance. He attended a secondary school in South Africa and also attended university there during the late 1940s, when he came into contact with various leaders of the African National Congress, such as Nelson Mandela, and according to his own account became involved with that movement.[11]

It was at that time too that he became convinced of the need to rally young people to the cause of nationalism. Subsequently, he went on to attend university in Lisbon and there met figures such as Dr Agostinho Neto and Mr Amilcar Cabral, who were before long to become so prominent in the offensive against Portuguese rule in Africa. After further university study in the United States, during which he obtained a Ph.D. in Sociology, he was employed on research work at Harvard and later by the United Nations Organisation. He married a White American citizen who held a Master's Degree in African studies from Boston University, and who later played a considerable part in Frelimo's work.

Other leading personalities in the movement included Mr Uria Simango, formerly a Protestant pastor who later was amongst those who received training in Peking, Mr Marcelino dos Santos, a Marxist who had studied at Lisbon University, and Mr Samora Machel, now President of Moçambique who, after receiving training in Algeria, became leader of Frelimo's military wing. In February 1969, Dr Mondlane was killed by the explosion of a book bomb in a seaside bungalow in Tanzania where he was working.

After considerable discussion and dissension, the leadership then passed to Mr Samora Machel, the pro-Soviet Mr dos Santos being appointed his deputy. Mr Machel was born in the Limpopo Valley in 1933 and began his education at a Catholic school. Refusing to attend a seminary, he continued his education by means of night classes and trained as a medical assistant. He met Dr Mondlane during the early 1960s and soon became deeply involved in the activities of Frelimo. In 1963 he went to Dar es Salaam and from there to Algeria for military training. Despite his past reputation for being more pro-Peking than pro-Moscow, he openly acknowledged the debt that Frelimo owed to the Soviet Union for aid received during the campaign against the Portuguese. When addressing the 24th Congress of the Communist Party of the Soviet Union in Moscow, he said, for example:

> We want to express our gratitude for the help which the Soviet people, under the leadership of the Party founded by Lenin, are rendering to our struggle. This help largely contributes to the development of our struggle on an even wider scale.[12]

In Portuguese-Guinea, PAIGC was fortunate in being able to recruit many of its members from the Balante tribe, the same tribe which provided many of the Portuguese Army's African units with its best soldiers. Early in 1964 PAIGC decided formally to establish a military wing which was given the name *Forcas Armadas Revolucionárias do Povo*—FARP. This was to consist of guerrilla units, a militia and a "popular army".

At the same time, it was decided that the PAIGC headquarters would be in Conakry. Mr Cabral, the Secretary-General, was placed in charge of a Political Secretariat of about 20 members. There was also to be a much larger Central Committee with about 65 members which would be in charge of various commissions dealing with such matters as security, national reconstruction, internal party affairs and foreign relations, and a Commission of Control, whose main task was to ensure the co-operation of the other commissions.

Separate military commanders were appointed for each of the three main fighting zones. The British Member of Parliament, Mr John Biggs-Davison, who visited Guinea on a number of occasions as an observer with the Portuguese forces, said after a visit to Guinea in 1969 that the main rôle of the People's Army (EP) was to provide mobile groups which could operate anywhere under the direct orders of a regional committee in aid of local guerrilla forces (GP).

He described the basic EP unit as being 21-strong and consisting of a Commander, a Political Commissar, a two-man rocket weapon crew, a two-man light machine-gun crew, six riflemen and seven snipers. Each such group contained five sub-groups with its leader and five men. The EP also operated in larger units known as Bi-Grupos which had additional fire power, including three rocket weapons, three light machine-guns and usually two mortars and two heavy machine-guns.

He said that the rôle of the militia which mainly consisted of young people in their teens, was intelligence work and foraging. It was organised in regions, zones, sections and groups. Each group included a Commander, a Political Commissar and 15 militia members of both sexes.[13]

PAIGC and FARP exercised local control of operations through district committees of various kinds, each being led by a chairman, political commissar, two vice-chairmen, one a woman, and a secretary. PAIGC also attempted to draw in the aid of the people of any villages it controlled through special village committees (a tactic also much favoured by the Viet Cong). One of the most important tasks they undertook was to try to organise the inhabitants into growing food to support the revolutionary forces. These committees also had charge of the local militia and political education. Villagers who seemed likely to become efficient cadres were sent to the Party school in Conakry.

Many of the leading members of PAIGC were in fact not natives of Guinea but the Cape Verde Islands. Mr Cabral himself was the son of a mulatto from these islands. He was born in Bafata, and, after an early education there and in Cape Verde, he was awarded a scholarship to the *Instituto Superior de Agronomia* in Lisbon. He qualified as an agronomist in 1950 and was employed by the Portuguese Government in Guinea for some time, working on an agricultural census. By 1953, he had become involved in nationalist agitation and moved to Angola to work in the sugar industry. There he met Dr Agostinho Neto and, as related, assisted in the formation of the MPLA.

As the campaign in Guinea progressed, he made no secret of the extent to which PAIGC relied upon Soviet support and aid.

Speaking at the grand rally at the Kremlin during the celebrations to mark the 50th anniversary of the Soviet Union in December 1972, he acknowledged the value of such aid to the "liberation movements" in terms that were nothing if not generous:

True to the Leninist principles and goals of the October Revolution, the CPSU has turned the USSR into the greatest power ever created by man in the service of the cause of peace, liberation and progress of the peoples, and of the well-being and creative development of the individual. Carrying high the banner of proletarian internationalism, the CPSU is acting as the most consistent and true ally of all the anti-imperialist forces, and particularly of the national liberation movement. At the present time, when the 50th anniversary of the USSR is being celebrated, a holiday which expresses the friendship and unity of the Soviet peoples, we wish to demonstrate our profound respect for the CPSU and the Central Committee.

Once more we confirm the solidarity of our fighting party with the Soviet people and express our fraternal wishes for fresh success in carrying out the great tasks charted by the 24th CPSU Congress both on a national and international plane, and in following an effective policy of peace and friendship.[14]

During 1972 and 1973 there was much bitter quarrelling by different factions within PAIGC. On 20 January 1973 Mr Amilcar Cabral was shot dead whilst returning in his car from a dinner at the Polish Embassy in Conakry. His assassin was an old associate, Mr Innocente Camil, who had helped him form PAIGC. Mr Camil held the post of Commander of PAIGC's Naval Arm and had been on a naval training course in the Soviet Union and other courses in China, Cuba and East Germany. Despite the fact that it was known that there had been a number of other plots against Mr Cabral previously by a member of PAIGC, stories were at once circulated (as in the case of Dr Mondlane) that Portuguese agents were responsible for his death. These stories were, however, quickly squashed by a somewhat unexpected source. This being President Sekou Toure of Guinea who organised an enquiry which reported that 50 PAIGC members from the mainland had admitted complicity in the assassination, their motivation apparently being that:

They were discontented because the Cape Verde Islanders had all the privileges, they lived a gilded life in Conakry instead of serving at the fronts, they were the

only people to drive around in cars and among the
wounded very few came from the islands.[15]

Mr Cabral was succeeded by his deputy, Mr Aristedes Pereira,
also of Cape Verde origin.

Propaganda and Psychological Warfare

All three movements described made great use of propaganda
and psychological warfare during their campaigns, both those
directed at obtaining support within the territory in which they
were operating and those aimed at influencing world opinion in
their support. A member of the MPLA, Mr Rui de Pinto, who had
received military training in Cuba and then became a Political
Commissar, has related how in 1968 he was told that he had been
transferred to the DIP, the movement's Department for Propaganda
and Information. Posted to the "third region", or Eastern Angola, he
was sent into an area of the country in which the MPLA had set up
a number of camps with two Italian photographers and an escort
composed of a detachment of guerrillas. The photographers took a
lot of photographs in the camps and then returned to the border.
Mr de Pinto, however, remained in one of the camps:

> Really beginning to learn and do work for the DIP—-
> from early July until the end of October 1968. Besides
> writing and illustrating some pamphlets, and other small
> publications, we also produced a small internal paper for
> our zone ... We typed it in the two main local lan-
> guages—Chokwe and Lauvale—as well as in Portuguese.
> Though very few people in this area were literate, there
> was usually someone in every Kinbo or village who was
> able to read the paper out loud to the others.
> I also started collecting information for the DIP to use
> outside, wrote a few articles, prepared some things for
> our radio broadcasts and made a few trips to the border
> to deliver these things to the DIP comrades there.[16]

Later he was transferred to the DIP centre in Lusaka, where he
was brought into contact with more foreign groups and visitors. He

stated that one very important task the DIP had to perform was to inform the MPLA forces of this foreign support so that they should be encouraged by the fact that

> everywhere in the world there are progressive people helping us—from America and Europe to the socialist countries. These people are doing their best for the success of our revolution and worldwide struggle against colonialism and imperialism.[17]

Mr de Pinto was sent on several more trips into Angola with foreign journalists, on one occasion with the British author, Mr Basil Davidson, Dr Agostinho Neto himself accompanied the party.

Similar organisations existed within the framework of Frelimo, in that case known as CPRMGs, Centres for Political and Military Training. Great importance was attached to these by Mr Samora Machel in particular. In February 1972, for instance, he spoke to a "joint meeting of instructors and other cadres" at one centre and told them that the essential task of Frelimo was to produce soldiers who would fight for a new society. He said that the work of the CPRMGs should not just be aimed at producing "killers" but to "train pure revolutionary fighters, authentic Frelimo soldiers". He interpreted the word "fighter" as meaning a "conscious and active agent in the transformation of society".

"Our watchword," he proclaimed, "is production, study and combat. This watchword synthesises the political line. Our fighter combines these three factors: production supplies the material needs of the war, political study gives us our identity, whilst scientific study enables us to develop production and improve our combat techniques."[18]

Mr Machel defined the rôle of the CPRMG as being the "laboratory" where the movement "created this agent of change, the **New Man**". He maintained that

> as important as the physical battle was the fight against the enemy in our own minds—the capitalist ideology imposed by colonialism and the feudal ideology inherited from tradition.[19]

Victory in this battle, he said, would consolidate the movement's physical victory, lay the foundation for the new society and "make our progress irreversible". As first steps towards this psychological victory, emphasis was to be laid upon the importance of instilling "national consciousness" and wiping out tribalism. Class consciousness must then be made more acute and deeply felt and the creation of unity between "workers and peasants to win power" must also be a priority objective. He stressed that closely related to the "battle for unity" was the need to "wipe out the spirit of individualism and foster a collective spirit". Summing up this part of his address, Machel stated that:

> The struggle against tribalism, racism, false religious and family loyalty, and so on, is essential if the barrel of our gun is always to be trained on the correct target.[20]

In order that the CPRMGs should be successful in producing "agents of change" in the shape of the "New Man" that he had referred to, Mr Machel said that it was essential that, in addition to their main task of training recruits to "wipe out the enemy physically", they should also organise a programme of "constant political education" at every level of the movement, including its ordinary rank and file, the women's detachment, cadres, instructors and leading cadres, etc.

Mr Machel admitted:

> our whole upbringing, our tradition, our whole life until the time we joined Frelimo made us see and cultivate as virtues what our new society rejects as defects.
> The CPRMG, in its way of life, demands a radical change in values, attitudes and behaviour. Newly arrived comrades are introduced to a life which they have certainly never conceived of, which they never thought possible, it is quite a shock.[21]

Speaking at the Second Conference of the Department of Education and Culture in 1972, Mr Machel made it quite clear that all such educational activities must be closely keyed to the movement's general political line. He explained that:

> To us education does not mean teaching how to read and write, creating an élite group of graduates, with no direct relationship to our objectives; in other words, just

as one can wage an armed struggle without carrying out a revolution, one can also learn without educating oneself in a revolutionary way ... Each of us must assume his revolutionary responsibilities in education, regarding books, study, as tools at the exclusive service of the masses. Studying must be seen as a revolutionary task to be combined with the revolutionary tasks of production and fighting. He who studies should be like a spark lighting the flame which is the people.

The principal task of education, in our teaching, text-books and programmes, is to instil in each of us the advanced, scientific, objective and collective ideology which enables us to progress in the revolutionary process.[22]

Mr Machel also laid down that through constant meetings and self-criticism, the movement's teachers and educational cadres must "eliminate old ideas and tastes" in order that they should "acquire the new mentality" and thus be able to pass it on to the next generation. He added:

We must show maximum severity towards anyone among the teachers and educational cadres who displays subjectivism, individualism, tribalism, arrogance, super-stition or ignorance.[23]

Mr Machel's views on the need for radical indoctrination of Frelimo supporters and potential supporters did not extend only to the use of propaganda and education. It extended also to the treatment given to those who attended the movement's hospitals. Speaking to a party of "health cadres" about to embark upon a course in November 1971, he said that the movement's medical staff, besides having their specific tasks, should also consider themselves as "instructors, teachers, political commissars". He continued: "The activity of our revolutionary medical staff not only cures the body but also frees and forms the mind". He emphasised the importance of political education amongst Frelimo medical staff and students so as to develop their "anti-colonialist and anti-imperialist spirit", to increase their understanding of "oppression" and make class consciousness and feeling "more deep-rooted".

As far as the patients were concerned he felt:

A strong bond of trust and hope is established between the patient and the nurse or doctor who is treating him. The patient associates the alleviation of pain and the curing of disease with the work of the nurse or doctor. This confidence of the patient and of his family and friends is an extraordinary political asset which we must use to advance the revolution. On the basis of the confidence that is established, we must help the patient to take the road of national unity, to increase his class consciousness and to learn more about hygiene, science, and culture, in short, treatment of the body should be accompanied by corresponding treatment of the mind, in order that the new mentality may triumph.[24]

Mr Machel described Frelimo's hospitals as being "centres of the revolution". They existed because of the revolution and were "closely connected with it". He thought that a patient's stay in hospital should serve to heighten his awareness of national unity, his determination to fight and his hatred of the enemy. He also maintained that "the medical's staff's professional consciousness must be based on heightened political consciousness", and that "in training our medical personnel, priority must be given to political education, to political consciousness".

In the case of PAIGC, the indoctrination of recruits and cadres was largely undertaken at the Party school in Conakry. A PAIGC Political Commissar attached to a PAIGC unit explained to a French author who visited Portuguese Guinea that great importance was paid to the political education of its members. It was explained to them that their struggle was directed neither against the Portuguese people nor against "White skin" but that:

there are Portuguese who are for us and Africans who serve the Portuguese, and that our weapons don't come from Africa but from countries where the people don't have black skin.[25]

Another PAIGC organiser said that the reason the movement had been able to make the progress it had was due to the fact that Mr Amilcar Cabral had paid such great attention to techniques of political education. He said that Mr Cabral would make cadres engaged in this task:

play a game. One by one we had to pretend, in front of him, that we were going into a village to talk to the *Homem Grande*. Everybody else could watch. If it wasn't right, if there was something wrong about it, Cabral would make us start all over again until we found exactly the right openings and the right arguments. We would start over and over again until it came out right.[26]

Like the other movements mentioned, PAIGC attempted to exercise authority over village communities through a series of committees. One political commissar, however, told the French author, M. Gerard Chaliand, that although these seemed to work well when Party officials were in evidence, they often soon collapsed when they were not. The important part played by political commissars in the fighting units of PAIGC's armed wing, FARP, was outlined by one young guerrilla who said:

The political commissar of our group accompanies us when we go into combat. Before the start of the attack he explains the reason for our battle. The military commander often tells us to respect the political commissar as the most important individual in the group.[27]

PAIGC also claimed some of its propaganda work at the Portuguese forces. One Party directive, for instance, read:

Reinforce political work and propaganda within the enemy's armed forces. Write posters, pamphlets, letters. Draw slogans on the roads. Establish cautious links with enemy personnel who want to make contact with us. Act audaciously and with great initiative in this way ... Do everything possible to help enemy soldiers to desert. Assure them of security so as to encourage their desertion. Carry out political work among Africans who are still in enemy service, whether civilian or military. Persuade these brothers to change direction so as to serve the Party within enemy ranks or desert with arms and ammunition to our units.[28]

One principal external object of the propaganda offensive of all three movements discussed was to convince the outside world of the existence of "liberated areas" within the territories in which they operated. These were allegedly large districts which were not only entirely controlled militarily by the movement concerned but also in which they had set up an entire alternative revolutionary administration complete with health and medical services, etc.

Despite extravagant claims to that effect, however, the balance of the evidence suggests that often either such "liberated areas" never existed at all or that in other cases they only included small areas of territory and usually stayed in existence only for a short time. Sometimes the truth of the liberation movement's claims about such areas was strongly disputed by defectors from the movements themselves. Dr Miguel Maropa, a former member of Frelimo's Central Committee and a subsequent defector, said, for instance:

> The liberated areas, of course, are a deliberate and calculated lie. Up until 1970, Frelimo maintained a form of control along the Tanzanian border to a depth of about 20 miles into Moçambique, because there were very few Portuguese troops available in that region, with camps, battalions of armed troops and so on. This was easy for Frelimo because the presence of the white man was light in the north and there was no government infrastructure. Then "Gordian Knot" (a major Portuguese anti-guerrilla operation) swept Frelimo out of its bases in 1970. This time though, the civilian administrators came with the troops and organised the people in the towns. Many of Frelimo's old bases became Portuguese army camps, like Tartibo, for example. The Portuguese supplanted Frelimo military and political presence with their own. But, of course, Frelimo cannot say "Well, there are no liberated areas any more" to the outside world. The existence of liberated areas, or rather the impression that these areas exist, means money to Frelimo. It increases their money-raising power by making Frelimo seem legitimate.[29]

Asked how he explained that some foreign visitors claimed to have been taken on trips through "liberated areas" by Frelimo, he replied:

> If you walk for several hours through unfamiliar jungle, how do you know where you are unless your guide tells

211

you? And Frelimo provides the guides. How many foreign visitors to "liberated Moçambique" can speak Portuguese, let alone the bush dialects that would enable them to pinpoint their location? How many visitors can distinguish different tribes on one side of a border or another? I do not deny that Frelimo can smuggle people into Moçambique to a Frelimo camp or base, but it is very dangerous.[29]

In Portuguese-Guinea, PAIGC did have some bases deep in the jungle but, despite claims about the existence of large "liberated areas", it was forced for the main part to operate on a hit and run basis from safe bases across the frontier in Guinea, sometimes with the assistance of Soviet-made medium artillery weapons firing from the safety of neutral territory. The guns concerned having been first supplied by the USSR to the Nigerian Government during the Biafran war and then passed on to PAIGC.

The very real doubts about the existence of "liberated areas" on any scale also raised doubts as to whether the health and educational services, of which the various movements made much boast, ever operated to any great extent, except, once again, in the base areas behind the safety of friendly frontiers.

Side by side with all the claims about the existence of "liberated areas", complete with welfare services, went other claims usually voiced in flamboyantly-worded military communiqués concerning "victories" scored by the movements over the Portuguese forces. Often these communiqués would claim the infliction of casualties on the Portuguese that almost grotesquely inflated their actual figure and not infrequently the "battles" they depicted never took place at all. The desired picture of an almost ceaseless guerrilla offensive was also added to by announcements of the creation of new "fronts" by the movements concerned in their countries of operation; although in fact guerrilla activity on these "fronts" was often minimal. The exaggeration that lay behind the military claims of all three movements was not infrequently revealed by correspondents and other observers.

There would seem no doubt, however, that the use of grossly exaggerated claims did "pay off" to a considerable extent in the shape of influencing considerable sections of world opinion, which had little chance (and quite often little desire) to check the real facts. It was deceived into believing that not only were the guerrilla

212

movements going from one triumph to another, and, therefore, their total victory could only be a matter of time, but also that they had very considerably more popular support than in fact they had. The fostering of this belief was designed to help bring about the isolation of Portugal.

An important weapon in the propaganda armoury of the various movements were several specially produced publications. PAIGC, for instance, produced a "national newspaper" with the title *Libertacao*. It was claimed that this was produced every day. Among the magazines and bulletins produced was a special bulletin for children. Entitled *Bluto*, it was published by the movement's youth wing, the Young Pioneers. According to a Soviet journalist who visited PAIGC, it carried:

> Stories about the heroic feats of the patriots, about history and about other countries in the world and their attitude to PAIGC.[30]

The Information and Propaganda section of the PAIGC Central Committee published a regular illustrated bulletin with the title *PAIGC Actualities.*

All three movements made considerable use of posters, some of these being supplied by sympathetic foreign organisations such as the Cuban OSPAL. Frelimo posters sometimes made a considerable point of illustrating the activities of the Women's Detachments. One, for instance, showed a smiling member of the detachment carrying a baby in one arm and a Kalashnikov rifle in the other. The caption above read:

> The antidote to cure colonialism is armed revolution. That is the only way to win total independence.[31]

Considerable use was made of radio propaganda programmes, sometimes beamed from special stations in countries bordering the area of operations.

The Use of Terrorism

Under international law as it stood until June 1977, all belligerents at a time of hostilities who wished to claim protected status (i.e. to be given the rights and privileges of prisoner of war status when captured, etc.) had to, as a prerequisite to achieving this status, at all times be able to show that they were acting under the orders of a person responsible for his subordinates, cairy their arms openly, wear a distinctive uniform or carry a fixed distinctive sign recognisable at a distance and conduct their operations in accordance with the laws and customs of war.

All available reports would indicate that there were few occasions upon which members of the fighting arms of the "liberation movements" reviewed in this chapter complied with all these four conditions. Technically it would seem, therefore, that members of these groups, as those of others operating in Africa in similar circumstances, can be described correctly as terrorists and not guerrillas. It is felt, however, that there is a need for a new definition of what can in a more practical sense be held to constitute terrorism as distinct from normal guerrilla activity. For this purpose, it is useful to consider the judgement of an American expert on the subject. Writing in *The Viet Cong Strategy of Terror* published by the United States Mission in Vietnam, Mr Douglas Pike wrote:

> It is more difficult than might first appear to distinguish between terror and violence or between terror and war. Terror is, of course, a **pejorative** word, one which each side uses to deprecate the activities of the other. Without being too far afield, it would seem fair ... to define terror as illegal violence, assuming that warfare although immoral in ethical terms, is legal in the context of international law, but that even in warfare certain acts are illegal and may properly be named terror. This latter point rests on the belief that in all things there are limits, and a limit in warfare is reached at the systematic use of death, pain, fear, and anxiety among the population (either civilian or military) for the deliberate purpose of coercing, manipulating, intimidating, punishing or simply frightening into helpless submission. Certain acts even in war are beyond the pale and can only be labelled as terror.[32]

There would seem no doubt that action falling under the above definition has been an inseparable part of the activities of most Southern African "liberation movements", the main target being "unco-operative" sections of the Black African population. To be more precise, there would seem to be two main situations in which it is used. Firstly, on a selective basis against individuals (often village headmen or tribal chiefs) whose influence the revolutionary movement concerned is likely to wish to eradicate in its efforts to seize power. Secondly, and much more indiscriminately, terrorism is used in efforts to intimidate the entire population of a village or even a whole area which has been found "guilty" of showing less than the required degree of enthusiasm for the revolutionary cause.

Usually the use of such tactics tends to grow sharply whenever the movement concerned finds itself confronted with substantial checks and set-backs. During the spring of 1972, for instance, when Frelimo had still far from recovered from the mauling it had received from "Operation **Gordian** Knot" and subsequent Portuguese operations, and its general prospects seemed much less than bright, there was a sharp shift from attacks on military targets to attacks on civilian targets. These were clearly intended to restore waning support by demonstrating that the movement still had the power to strike back draconically at those that displeased it amongst the civilian population. Of 40 Frelimo attacks in one 10-day period at that time, not one was upon a military target, the attacks including intimidation raids upon 17 different villages.

During the previous year, "exemplary action" had been taken against local tribal chiefs in the area along the Zambian border where the population had made it clear that the presence of Frelimo was unwelcome. It was reported that 32 of such chiefs had been murdered during the first half of 1971.

According to Portuguese sources, by the middle of 1973 the number of "unco-operative" members of the Makonde tribe alone killed by Frelimo since the start of the campaign had reached 450, while the numbers of maimed or kidnapped ran into several thousand. In 1971 the offensive by Frelimo in the Tete Province was accompanied by the murder of 55 traditional chiefs during the year.

The falling fortunes of Frelimo during the early 1970s also tempted the movement into a new tactic of intimidation designed to encourage support. This was the use of large quantities of anti-personnel mines supplied to them by Communist sources. Frelimo units started to plant these weapons in allotments or farms known as *machambas* situated near villages. This tactic caused great fear and panic amongst the tribesmen who relied to a great extent for their staple diet upon the crops grown on these allotments and who now began to find them too dangerous to approach.

215

At the beginning of 1973 a carefully documented report compiled by the Moçambique Services for the Centralisation and Co-ordination of Information showed that since the war began in 1969, 689 deliberate assassinations of civilians by Frelimo had taken place, and it had also been responsible for kidnapping at least 6 500 people for use as porters and labourers. At the end of the year a senior Frelimo officer, Mr Jorinas de Lazaro, who commanded a unit in the Tete area, gave himself up to the Portuguese forces saying that his defection was due to receiving orders to kill, maim or kidnap members of the local population.

Mr John Eppstein, author of *Does God Say Kill?*, has quoted figures provided for him by the Portuguese command in Angola showing that the percentage of terrorist attacks upon the (mainly Black) civilian population had risen from 13,3% of the total number of incidents in 1965 to 31,6% in the first six months of 1971. He also stated that by 1971

> the principal methods of the MPLA to secure recruits, apart from the kidnapping of isolated fishermen or hunters, is to summon the people to an undefended village, demanding some of the men or boys, or supplies of food. At any sign of reluctance the head man and a few others are shot to encourage the remainder, or, more recently, men are mutilated by cutting off or slitting their ears and left as a warning to others.[33]

One tactic used by all three revolutionary movements mentioned, as heavier and heavier Soviet weapons came into their hands, was the firing of salvoes of 122 mm rockets or heavy mortar bombs into the middle of an "unsatisfactory" undefended village from the safe distance of a number of kilometres. A highly effective form of vengeance or insurance against non-co-operation that could be made with the minimum use of manpower and in almost complete security.

External Contacts

Details of arms supplied by Communist countries, together with training and base facilities provided by sympathetic African countries, have been detailed in Chapter 4.

As already mentioned, all three anti-Portuguese movements placed great importance in their propaganda activities upon attempts to influence world opinion and, to this end, set up offices in a number of foreign capitals. The activities of some of these are examined in Chapter 9.

The three movements were visited by a number of Soviet bloc, as well as other foreign journalists, during the course of the campaign and the visits of the former were well exploited both on the return to their homeland in the shape of articles and pamphlets sympathetic to the "liberation movements" and produced by them and on the spot in Africa, as further evidence of the sympathy of the Soviet Union in the anti-imperialist campaign. One of the authors of the *Novosti* Press Agency booklet, *Password "Anguimo"*, Mr Anatoli Nikanorov, recorded a picture of one Frelimo conference he attended in the Tete Province during a visit to Moçambique in 1971. The conference was attended by both the movement's President, Mr Samora Machel, and Mr Sebastian Mabote, Commander of its armed wing, as well as members of the Central Committee.

According to Mr Kikanorov, it took place in a Frelimo base consisting of 15-20 straw huts on the slope of a thickly wooded mountain, the dense foliage hiding the base from Portuguese spotter 'planes. The base had a flag-pole in the centre and a spacious, roofed canteen, with tables and benches where the press conference, he and other Soviet journalists and cameramen had come to attend, was held. The following day, they also attended a meeting held in the base for local villagers. Mr Kikanorov reported that Mr Machel pointed the Soviet visitors out to the villagers and then said:

> Do you know where they've come from? From Russia, from the Soviet Union. I was there not long ago, attending the 24th Congress of the Soviet Communist Party. You may ask me: Why did you go there? Why have they come here? They are our true friends. They represent the first people in the world to do away with oppression in their country. And now they are helping all the other peoples of the world to throw off oppression.[34]

Mr Nikanorov also recorded that when setting out on his expedition into Moçambique he had been taken to the starting place before crossing the border as a passenger on board a 20-ton Soviet-made truck. The driver, who spoke "rather good Russian", had received training in the Soviet Union and was now in command of the Frelimo transport service. His main task was to carry personnel and equipment through Tanzania and Zambia to the Moçambique border.

Soviet camera crews and producers also made at least three special films during the course of the campaigns in Portuguese Africa. These were entitled, "The March of Freedom", "The Partisan Paths of Angola" and "Vivat Frelimo". It was claimed that these were shown many times in many different countries.

Contact with Cuba, in addition to the two major Communist powers, was established early in the respective active histories of the MPLA, Frelimo and PAIGC. All three sent delegations to the First Conference of Solidarity of the Peoples of Africa, Asia and Latin America in January 1966. In an address to the conference, Mr Amilcar Cabral, President of PAIGC, stated on their behalf:

> I bring special greetings to the Central Committee of the Cuban Communist Party, the Revolutionary Government, its exemplary leader, Commandant Fidel Castro, to whom I wish to express our wishes for continuous success and long life in the service of this country, for the progress and happiness of his people, in the service of humanity.
>
> If on arrival in Cuba, one or some of us had any doubts about the firmness, strength, maturity, and vitality of the Cuban Revolution, these doubts were banished by what we have already had occasion to see. An absolute certainty, completely unshakeable, warms our hearts and stimulates us in this difficult but glorious fight against the common enemy; no power on earth will be capable of destroying the Cuban Revolution which, in the countryside and in the cities, is creating not only a new life, but what is more important, a new man, fully conscious of his national, continental, rights and duties.[35]

One of the fullest and warmest expressions of thanks to the governments of the "socialist countries" for aid given to Frelimo has

218

come from Mr Jorge Rebelo, a member of the Executive Committee of Frelimo and now Minister of Information in the new People's Republic of Moçambique. Writing in *World Marxist Review* of June 1976, Mr Rebelo said:

> Worthy of special note is the rôle of socialist countries. They were Frelimo's main source of military supplies, and we also had their unqualified moral and diplomatic support. The socialist countries are our natural allies. Their aid to the national liberation struggle also makes for strengthening their own position. Why? Because our gains and victories weaken imperialism and thereby add to the strength of the socialist world. Support from the revolutionary forces of the globe contributed to the victory of the national liberation movements in the Portuguese colonies and this, in turn, created new possibilities in Africa for the triumph of socialist ideals.
>
> We need that support as much as in the past, for our country is virtually ruined ... We must reorientate our economy from the capitalist to the socialist world. Capitalism in developing countries wants nothing but profit. By contrast, the socialist countries help disinterestedly to consolidate revolutionary régimes. They realise that if our countries are strong, the basis of the anti-imperialist struggle will broaden. Moçambique develops relations with many socialist countries, specially with the Soviet Union, in such fields as the economy, education, public health and information.
> The socialist countries' policy of détente has contributed to gains in the national liberation struggle. This is the right way to develop international relations ...
> We realise that it is in the interests of socialism to develop relations between countries with different social and political systems. Imperialism is becoming weaker as it suffers reverse after reverse, while socialism is growing stronger. The victory of the peoples of Indochina and the liberation of Portugal's colonies confirms that détente creates opportunities to strengthen socialism and change the alignment of forces still more in favour of socialism, to the detriment of capitalism and imperialism.

219

Although the Marxist-orientated revolutionary aims of the Zimbabwe African People's Union (ZAPU) and the Zimbabwe African National Union (ZANU) have great similarity, their history has been one of bitter rivalry, not infrequently involving considerable bloodshed and loss of life. These rivalries were often deepened by tribal and personal differences, as well as those of a political or tactical nature. They have only periodically and temporarily been stilled by attmepts to form a "united front".

The Zimbabwe African People's Union was formed in December 1961 by the Rhodesian African Nationalist leader, Mr Joshua Nkomo, following the banning of two other organisations which he had led: the African National Congress and the National Democratic Party. The Southern Rhodesian Government had suppressed them on the grounds that they were involved in activities leading to the use of violence. Less than a year later, at a time of increasing unrest and agitation against the establishment of the Rhodesian Federation, ZAPU was also banned. The move had, however, been foreseen by its leaders, who had made a prior decision in the event of its being banned that the organisation at home would go underground while they themselves would operate from bases in exile. The Rev Ndabaningi Sithole, Chairman of ZAPU, established an office for the movement in Dar es Salaam with the assistance of the Tanzanian Government. Before long, however, he was referring to the section of the movement that that office controlled as the Zimbabwe African National Union (ZANU), thus in effect announcing the birth of the separate and rival nationalist movement. He also started openly to advocate the use of violence.

Meanwhile, Mr Joshua Nkomo had returned to Rhodesia where he was promptly arrested and placed under restriction. After a few months, however, these restrictions were lifted and he was able to resume political activity. A series of fierce disputes at once broke out within the ranks of ZAPU. Mr Nkomo, stung by increasing criticism of his leadership, suspended Mr Sithole and the faction based on the Dar es Salaam office who responded by returning to Rhodesia and announcing the formal establishment of ZANU as a separate force.

Friction between the two groups increased rapidly and before long disputes between the two had passed the stage of mere argument and resulted in an increasing number of violent clashes and murders. The first violence directed against the Government of Southern Rhodesia began to take place in 1963 and a steadily growing number of incidents of various types occurred during 1964, many of these involving the murder or savage intimidation of Black Rhodesians by members of opposing nationalist factions.

Mr Clifford Dupont, Minister of Justice, alleged that Mr James Chikerema, who was then known as one of Mr Nkomo's chief assistants, had recently returned to Rhodesia from Peking with a considerable amount of money which was being used to pay the "thugs and hooligans" of the People's Caretaker Council (PCC), a ZAPU front organisation. Cases of attempts to smuggle arms into the country were also discovered. In August 1964 both the PCC and ZANU were banned. In the same year, Mr Petrus Oberholzer became the first White farmer to be a victim of terrorist violence, being killed by members of the ZANU "Crocodile Group". Meanwhile, members of both ZAPU and ZANU had been going abroad for training in the techniques of guerrilla warfare in growing numbers.

In 1965, the year of the Unilateral Declaration of Independence, three members of ZAPU were found guilty by a court in Salisbury of receiving military training in China and of bringing large quantities of weapons into the country. A member of ZANU found guilty of dynamiting a railway engine was also found to have received training in China.

The actual declaration of Rhodesia's independence in November by Mr Smith's Government was followed by a series of pronouncements on the forthcoming escalation in the campaign of violence by leaders of ZAPU and ZANU, many of whom had now based themselves in Zambia. These pronouncements, however, received somewhat less than whole-hearted support from the head of state of that country, President Kaunda, who said regarding those who made them:

> I have got tired of talking to these gentlemen who are so fond of chicken-in-the-basket. It is stupid for these nationalist representatives of Nkomo's ZAPU and Sithole's ZANU to shout from the comfort of Zambia: "We are going to kill all whites". Not all whites are guilty. Africans are making whites feel that if black majority rule came about they would be killed anyway. These nationalists are betraying the human race as much

221

as Mr Smith. The only thing that stops me chasing them out of Zambia is that they are representatives of people with whom we have no quarrel.[36]

Nevertheless, 1965 saw the beginning of a period lasting until the early 1970s in which Zambia, even if partly unwillingly, was to become the main forward base for guerrilla operations against Rhodesia. These operations for the most part consisted of a long drawn-out series of small-scale raids across the Zambesi valley which had as their primary objective the setting up of guerrilla bases inside Rhodesia and the incitement of the Black population of Rhodesia to join forces with the guerrillas operating from outside its frontiers. For the most part these operations appear to have been singularly unsuccessful.

An account of one expedition which would seem in its futility to have been typical of not a few during the mid-1960s was given by a guerrilla who took part in it and was taken prisoner by the Rhodesian security forces. This particular group crossed into Rhodesia in May 1967. Its principal rôle was supposed to be to sabotage railway lines and blow up government buildings and banks. However, they found the thick bush country almost impossible to traverse and, after only nine kilometres from their starting point, abandoned their arms and equipment.

At his trial, a member of the group said that he had been surprised at the hostile attitude of local villagers whom the group had come across before being rounded up. Instead of welcoming their appearance, they had seemed to support the government and its counter-guerrilla operations. Another member of the same group claimed that he had been tricked into joining the guerrillas and had tried to desert from a training camp in Tanzania. He had only agreed to join the group involved in the operation after being put in prison there.

By the end of 1966 the Rhodesian security forces could claim to have inflicted 100 fatal casualties on the guerrilla forces, whilst any tangible results achieved by the latter had been extremely small. The campaign was, however, about to take a new and potentially more serious turn.

At the end of July 1967 the first elements of a large body of guerrillas crossed the Zambesi on the western side of the Victoria Falls. This force was a combined group consisting of both members of ZAPU and the African National Congress of South Africa. The

222

intention apparently was for this group totalling about 80 guerrillas to split into small parties and to avoid contact with the security forces. They were to make their way into central Rhodesia and there set up guerrilla bases.

The group turned out to be exceptionally well equipped and armed, not only with the usual small arms but also with rocket projectors, bazookas and land-mines. They were also in possession of field radios and a plentiful supply of maps. A series of engagements developed between parties from this group and the security forces which resulted in the death or capture of most of its members whilst the remainder retired over the border. However, the fiercest fighting so far seen also resulted in the death of seven members of the security forces.

Early in 1968 another combined ZAPU-ANC force crossed the Zambesi carrying with it, in addition to its own equipment, arms it hoped to issue to guerrilla recruits inside Rhodesia. Their main objective was to establish a chain of camps extending southwards into the country which would be used as recruiting bases. The camps they constructed were well concealed and their operations remained undetected for three months. Their eventual discovery arose from the fact that the curiosity of a game warden was aroused by the unusual movements of game in his area. Whilst investigating the cause, he came across tracks which it was clear to him had been caused by the passage of a considerable number of people from outside the locality.

His investigations led to the uncovering of the group's activities and in subsequent operations by the security forces it was split into small sections most of which were again destroyed, although not without considerable fighting. The self-confidence with which the group had started out on its mission was shown by the fact that amongst the items captured during its destruction were a number of bronze medals apparently intended to be worn at victory parades. Whilst the fighting was still in progress, ZAPU announced that the ultimate aim of the group had been to penetrate through Rhodesia into South Africa. The members of this group included Mr Norman Duka, whose experiences whilst undergoing guerrilla training in the Soviet Union have been related in some detail earlier in his study.

According to his own account, he and his comrades were divided into four groups before crossing the Rhodesian border from Zambia and told that each one was to go via Rhodesia to a different area of South Africa and there to mobilise the local population to take part in a guerrilla campaign. Mr Duka himself survived the destruction of the force and, with others who did so, sought sanctuary beyond the Botswana border, only to find himself there sentenced to a term of seven years imprisonment.

Early in 1968 a smaller group of guerrillas also crossed the Zambian border into Rhodesia, some of whom had received training in Communist China. Before long, they too were rounded up and were found to have in their possession, in addition to copies of the *Thoughts of Mao Tse-tung* and various propaganda leaflets, two flags bearing the following slogans:

> All Whites must be killed, we are to free Zimbabwe from bloodshed ...
> Zimbabwe for Black and Not for White. Kill Smith and his running dogs.[37]

A number of isolated attacks upon White farmers and other civilians, sometimes resulting in deaths, had already occurred by that date. Early in 1968 the *Rhodesia Herald* recorded that during the course of his trial one prisoner from a guerrilla group had said that the general policy was not to attempt to kill all Whites but only members of selected groups. Asked if such target groups included women and children, he replied:

> A war is a war. You cannot select women and leave them out of it. Even if I were to see a child at a vantage point I would kill it there. European adults were once children.[38]

Despite the general lack of success of the guerrilla offensive at that stage, evidence continued to accumulate that many of those engaged in it were receiving increasingly sophisticated training. A Rhodesian security officer, for instance, said that the sites of six guerrilla camps discovered close to the Botswana border had obviously been chosen by those with expert knowledge of guerrilla tactics. The camps included stores of small arms, plastic explosives, booby-traps, books on guerrilla warfate and propaganda literature. They were skilfully camouflaged.

The defeat of the joint ZAPU-ANC operations on top of other failures had a devastating effect on guerrilla morale as a whole and both ZAPU and ZANU went in for a prolonged period of re-appraisal. Disputes within the movements and internal criticisms of their leadership which had been partially concealed now began to come out into the open. Mr James Chikerena, a prominent member of ZAPU, speaking on its military wing, the Zimbabwe Liberation Army, deplored

> ... the depth, and height of decay, corruption, nepotism, tribalism, selfishness, and gross irresponsibility on the part of the military administration from top to bottom ... It has no commander. It has no administration. It has no team spirit. It is corrupt.[39]

Equally serious for the guerrillas was the fact that the disorderly, and sometimes violent, behaviour of many of their members stationed at base camps in Zambia was getting them into increasing disrepute with the Zambian authorities. The ever-present friction between members of ZAPU and ZANU was increasing sharply. In early 1970 these internal difficulties started to come to a climax. In April, a major clash occurred on the outskirts of Lusaka between members of different tribal factions with ZAPU. The clash resulted in a number of people being injured and others listed as "missing". It caused President Kaunda to give a severe warning that unless such events ceased, ZAPU would be expelled from Zambia.

The situation was further worsened by the arrival of orders from Mr Joshua Nkomo, then under restriction in Rhodesia, that ZANU and ZAPU must amalgamate. The effect of this order was to increase dramatically the seriousness of the splits within ZAPU and the increasing bitterness led to more violence culminating in a grenade attack on ZAPU headquarters in November. By early 1971 the two movements, far from having joined forces as ordered to by Mr Nkomo, were in a state of almost open war. In March ZANU elements mounted a raid on ZAPU headquarters in Lusaka and kidnapped 21 members of the latter organisation.

Further violent incidents resulted in all members of ZAPU being rounded up by the Zambian authorities and confined to remote camps. The Zambian Government then issued an ultimatum to the two movements that they must either amalgamate or leave the country. The patience of the Zambian authorities with Rhodesian guerrillas was being additionally strained at that time by growing indications that, in addition to their habit of forcibly inducting

Rhodesian Africans living in Zambia into their ranks, they had also started to use the same sort of practices towards Zambian nationals.

Finally in the spring of 1971, ZAPU and ZANU leaders announced at a press conference held in Lusaka that they had agreed to unite their two organisations under the banner of the Front for the Liberation of Zimbabwe (FROLIZI) led by Mr Shelton Siwela, one of ZAPU's military commanders. The latter took the title of head of the Revolutionary Command Council.

Article one of its political programme, published some months after its formation, stated that its aims were

> to organise and unite the people of Zimbabwe into a revolutionary combat force aware of its interests, win the broad masses of the people to the armed struggle and to the side of the progressive world outlook, wage a protracted people's war of national liberation until victory is won, achieve total political and economic control of our motherland, establish and consolidate a people's revolutionary army which would protect and defend the people's revolutionary gains, establish a democratic and socialist state, and overthrow all vestiges of colonialism and cut off links with imperialism.[40]

The second article announced the Front's intention to

> establish and develop an independent socialist economy based upon the policy of national planning and owner-ship and control of land, capital and all means of production and distribution by the people, and actively work to abolish the distinction between town and country.[40]

Another article proclaimed the intention to

> establish and develop solidarity with revolutionary movements, organisations and governments in Africa, Asia, South America and elsewhere.[40]

The constitution of FROLIZI provided for the establishment of a branch and district system and for a women's section and a youth league.

Meanwhile, the continued failure, and often heavy casualties, of such operations against Rhodesia had made the development of a new strategy all the more necessary. In 1969 Mr James Chikerema, then Vice-President of ZAPU, explained to Mr Gus Macdonald of Granada Television the direction in which, as a result of past failures, his movement's military thinking was going: "We will go to our own areas and infiltrate ourselves in the population," and "organise our masses," he said.[41]

Infiltration parties sent across the border were to be told not to fight, unless they had no option, and to move as fast as possible towards villages and, once there, change into civilian clothes and start attempting to recruit and train the population.

Only a short space of time passed after the formation of FROLIZI before it became clear that all was far from well within its ranks. The news emerged that no members of ZANU's executive, and only two of ZAPU's, had, in fact, joined the new body. In effect, the two former organisations were continuing to operate independently as before, with FROLIZI existing merely as a sort of isolated splinter group. A ZANU spokesman broadcasting over Radio Lusaka, in fact, described it as being "an organisation of money-mongers, disgruntled men, anti-revolutionary position seekers, and tribalists".

In the spring of 1972, after months of growing criticism and acrimony, its Chairman, Mr Sehlton Siwela, was replaced during its inaugural conference by a veteran guerrilla fighter, Mr James Chikerema. This was followed by a new announcement of ZAPU-ZANU "solidarity" and the creation of a Joint Military Command (JMC) which was supposed to co-ordinate recruitment and training, operations, logistics and the gathering of military intelligence. In point of fact, however, ZAPU and ZANU continued to plan and execute their operations independently as before, whilst their intelligence gathering operations tended to be stifled by the fear that each had that the other was "riddled" by spies of the Rhodesian security forces.

In the meantime, despite the continuing internal chaos of the Rhodesian guerrilla movement, events had transpired to present it with new opportunities of which it was not slow to take advantage. These events were the growing extent to which Frelimo forces had managed to establish themselves in areas of Moçambique close to the north-eastern border of Rhodesia and Frelimo's readiness to allow such areas to be used as bases for operations against Rhodesia. From about the middle of June 1972 an infiltration of guerrillas started over the border from Moçambique into the deep bush country of north-eastern Rhodesia and into the Matusudna mountains.

In this wild and extensive area which the security forces found difficulty in patrolling adequately, the guerrillas succeeded in establishing some bases and arms caches which remained undetected for a considerable period. They also succeeded in building up some support amongst the local population, by methods which included both intimidation and enrolling the help of some local spirit mediums. Some of these people were forcibly abducted to guerrilla bases in Moçambique to undergo "political education" whilst others were "educated" or intimidated into helping the guerrillas on the spot. One form of **assistance of particular value,** performed by the spirit mediums or by witchdoctors who had been won over by the guerrillas, lay in the form of persuading the local population **not to disclose** the presence of the latter to any passing patrols of the security forces. The guerrillas also succeeded in enlisting the services of some local tribesmen as porters and intelligence agents and even recruits for their fighting units.

The existence of this new guerrilla front became apparent early in December 1972, when a series of attacks on isolated White-owned farms in the Centenary District of Rhodesia, near Moçambique border, began. In the weeks that followed, a series of incidents involving **the use of land-mines** by the guerrillas took place, which inflicted some casualties on the security forces. These attacks marked the start of an entirely new phase of the campaign and were to continue spasmodically over the next two years until the arrival of the independence of Moçambique transformed the whole of the Rhodesian/Moçambique border into a potentially active area of operations with consequences which still have to be unfolded fully.

Two further aspects of Rhodesian guerrilla tactics during the early 1970s deserve special mention. The first was the considerable effort made by the guerrilla operations to disrupt the attempts being made by the British and Rhodesian governments at that time to arrive at a negotiated settlement of their dispute regarding the constitutional future of the country. In July 1971, for instance, while Lord Goodman, the British Government's representative, was actually in Salisbury, nine cases of arms and explosives were found hidden in the warehouse of a van hire firm. It transpired that they had been smuggled into the country from Zambia. Another attempt to create serious internal disorder whilst the outcome of the negotiations was still pending involved the despatch of three members of ZANLA* who had received special training from Chinese instructors at the ZANU guerrilla training camp at Itombi in Tanzania to Salisbury. Their orders were apparently to shoot down as many White citizens as they could, thereby creating the maximum possible tension at the time of the visit of the Pearce Commission. Arrested before they could put the plan into operation, they were found to be carrying automatic weapons, grenades and explosives and a very large quantity of ammunition.

About the same time as these events, evidence began to reach the Rhodesian security forces of the adoption by the guerrillas of a new form of recruitment that was to become of progressively greater importance. This took the form of persuading a number of African teenage school children to cross the Zambian (and later Moçambique) border and undergo training in guerrilla camps.

One Rhodesian guerrilla leader, writing a few months before the Portuguese revolution radically changed the entire strategic outlook in Southern Africa, said that the main aim of the guerrilla forces at the time, November 1973, was to

> attenuate the enemy forces by causing their deployment over the entire country. The subsequent mobilisation of a large number of civilians from industry, business and agriculture would cause serious economic problems. This would have a psychologically devastating effect on the morale of the whites, most of whom had come to Zimbabwe lured by the easy privileged life promised by the régime.[42]

Shortly before this statement was made, Mr Herbert Chitepo, National Chairman of ZAPU, speaking at a conference of the movement, admitted that in the past it had placed too much emphasis on the military aspects of its activities and not enough on the political education of those whom it wished to recruit. He said:

> We have tried to correct this tragic error by politicising and mobilising the people before mounting any attacks

---

*Zimbabwe African National Liberation Army, i.e. the armed or guerrilla wing of ZANU.

against the enemy. After politicising our people, it became easier for them to co-operate with us and to identify with our programme and objective.[43]

The ZANU build-up in Moçambique continued during 1972 and 1973, as did the operations of the organisation across the border into the Centenary area of Rhodesia. The main objective of these at that time was apparently the preparation of the local population for participation in a "protracted war". In December 1974 it seemed for a short time that the long-standing feud between ZANU and ZAPU might be about to be brought to an end when the two organisations announced that they were to merge their identities under the joint command of the African National Council led by Bishop Muzorewa as its President and the Deputy Secretary-General of which was to be Mr Joshua Nkomo.

But almost simultaneously events occurred which made the likelihood of further strife almost certain. This was a revolt in a ZANU training camp, a revolt which was partially tribal in origin and partly caused by the fact that a growing number of the rank and file of the movement was becoming increasingly frustrated at what appeared to be the general inclination of ZANU leaders to neglect their operational duties in favour of power-seeking intrigues. The repercussions of this revolt were to rumble on for over a year and were to lead to much violent animosity between members of the Karanga and Manikya tribes within ZANU and to clashes in which it has been estimated that over 400 people were subsequently killed.

In August 1974 talks took place between the ANC and Mr Ian Smith, Mr Vorster and President Kaunda. One result of the failure of these talks to arrive at any firm agreement for the constitutional future of Rhodesia was the rapid appearance of cracks and strains due to tribal, political and personal differences within the various African movements. Before long the ANC had split into two factions, the one led by Bishop Muzorewa and the other by Mr Joshua Nkomo.

Despite the "cease-fire" arranged during the summer of 1975 in an attempt to provide a calm background to the talks between Mr Smith and Mr Nkomo, which were held in a further attempt to provide a negotiated settlement, sporadic guerrilla attacks continued to occur. The occasion of the eventual breakdown of the talks early in 1976 was the signal for the immediate escalation of the campaign aimed at ending White rule in Rhodesia and installing a revolutionary Marxist régime as soon as possible.

A study produced by the Institute for the Study of Conflict[44] had revealed that practical preparations for this new campaign were, in fact, well under way before the Smith-Nkomo talks broke down in March. By the middle of January, 400 trained guerrillas were reported to have been transported by means of an air-lift from Tanzania to the Tete Province of Moçambique where they joined others already in camps there. About 600 members of this force proceeded to infiltrate across the Rhodesian border in two main groups, one on the north of the border territory and the other through the Chimanimani and the Inyanga mountains. These were not routes that had been used before and these advance parties of the guerrilla force met with considerable success in establishing themselves in well-placed base areas.

Whilst the aircraft that had brought the guerrilla reinforcements carried recruits from Moçambique back to Tanzania for training, a further guerrilla force arrived, about 750 strong, at the Moçambique port of Beira. By the end of April it was estimated that a total of 1 500 guerrillas had been committed to this new front, whilst it was thought that a further 2 000 were in training in Tanzania.

With actions occurring between the security forces and guerrillas almost every day in the important Chipinga farming area about 30 km from the Moçambique border and 300 km south-east of Salisbury, further indications came of the possible implications of President Machel's repeated promises to give every possible aid to the "liberators" of Rhodesia. Early in April it was reported that the Rhodesian police post at Villa Salazar in the remote south-east of Rhodesia had been fired on for the 23rd day running by forces from across the Moçambique border. This would have seemed to be the first of a steadily escalating series of incidents in which regular Frelimo troops engaged Rhodesian forces directly.

At the same time as these signs that the guerrilla offensive was gaining momentum appeared, however, also came news showing clearly that the spectre of savage "in-fighting" between factions which had haunted the Rhodesian guerrilla movement since its very earliest days was very far from being dispelled. In late March Mr Herbert Chitepo, Chairman of ZANU, was killed when a bomb planted under the driving seat of his car exploded outside his home in Lusaka. Investigations later showed that the bomb had been planted on the orders of "General" Josiah Tongogara, the head of the movement's military wing.

231

Meanwhile in Moçambique, on the advice of the so-called "frontline" African states, Angola, Tanzania, Moçambique, Zambia and Botswana, a new guerrilla command to be known as "the Third Force" had been established.

By June 1976 the existence of this Third Force was becoming the focus for yet more disputes. The Publicity Secretary of the External Wing of Bishop Muzorewa's section of the ANC said in Port Louis, Mauritius (at the time of the holding of the meeting of the Organisation of African Unity in that capital), that fighting had broken out in the Third Force. This had contained members of both factions of the ANC. Earlier Bishop Muzorewa had accused the Presidents of the "front-line nations" of creating the Third Force over the heads of existing organisations and alleged that

cadres and recruits which are openly loyal to the ANC leadership are being tortured and liquidated.[45]

Together with these reminders of continuing dissension within the guerrilla ranks came further information on the radical and revolutionary nature of the movement's aims. ZANU pamphlets and literature found in Rhodesia early in the year contained such statements as to the movement's intentions, once the war in Rhodesia had been won and the country was in its control, as

a truly socialist, self-supporting economy will be established and organised on broad principles enunciated by Marxism-Leninism.

Another stated:

ZANU is guided by the principles of Marxism-Leninism. It aims at achieving a socialist revolution.[46]

In June, Mr Austin Chakandra, ZANU's representative in London, said in the course of a speech:

We are fighting not only for majority rule—the guerrillas are fighting for more—for a new kind of society in Zimbabwe. The far aim is to establish a socialist society. Of course, we realise that this cannot be achieved overnight. It will mean a protracted struggle. If Nkomo

232

and Muzorewa come to power such a chance would not be available.

I think the society we envisage is what the people of Rhodesia want, though they will have to be politicised ... they may not know what we mean by a socialist society.

If independence is achieved through the barrel of a gun, the country will be ruled not by civilian politicians but by political soldiers, the freedom fighters.

In the new Zimbabwe, there will be no parliamentary democracy, no voting and no canvassing.[47]

One of the more important events of the latter half of 1975 was the attempt to convert "The Third Force" into a new unified guerrilla command to be known as the Zimbabwe People's Army, or ZIPA. A pamphlet published by the Liberation Support Movement in Canada in September described the new organisation as having been formed as the result of a merger between:

the military wing of the former ZANU (ZANLA) and the military wing of the former ZAPU (ZIPRA). It was formed for the purpose of rescuing the Zimbabwe liberation struggle from the chaotic situation that had been created by the ANC leadership. It is an armed body of men, which was formed for the purpose of resuming the armed struggle, intensifying this armed struggle and carrying it to its logical conclusion and finally establishing a just and popular socio-political order serving the interests of the people of Zimbabwe.

The pamphlet also stated that moves were well under way to transform the guerrilla organisation into a revolutionary vanguard. A special department was reported to be operating within the ZIPA command structure charged with: "shouldering the political tasks that are normally shouldered by a revolutionary political organisation". The main task of this department was to give "political direction" to the guerrillas fighting inside Rhodesia. Within a few weeks, however, disputes had broken out once again with the emergence of what one Western diplomat described as "ZIPA-ZANU and ZIPA-ZAPU" factions.

The announcement of the Rhodesian Government's acceptance of Kissinger negotiation proposals was the signal not only for increased rivalry within the guerrilla movements but also for fierce pronouncements from a number of its leaders that nothing but the complete capitulation of the latter Government to guerrilla demands would lead them to abandon their declared aim of establishing their rule by means of "armed struggle" and ultimate military victory.

Shortly before the opening of the Geneva Conference to discuss the Kissinger plan in October it was announced that Mr Robert Mugabe, leader of ZANU, and Mr Nkomo had come together to form yet another organisation, this time to be known as the Patriotic Liberation Front. Shortly afterwards, Mr Mugabe was reported in the *Daily Telegraph* of 18 October as saying that a majority-ruled Rhodesia would be governed on the "socialist" lines of Tanzania and Moçambique and that "the white exploiters will not be able to keep one acre of their land". As the Geneva talks opened, ZIPA condemned them as "irrelevant". As the talks wound their somewhat tortuous way through the succeeding weeks, the fighting in Rhodesia, far from coming to an end as had been hoped, tended to escalate considerably. By the end of October the Rhodesian security forces were reported to be bracing themselves to meet a major offensive and it was estimated that more than 2 000 guerrillas were already operating inside the country whilst as many as 3 000 others were thought to be preparing in Moçambique camps to cross the frontier in coming months.

Early November saw the occurrence of large scale "hot-pursuit" raids by Rhodesian forces across the border into Moçambique during which a number of camps in which ZIPA forces were mustering were said to have been destroyed and considerable casualties inflicted on the guerrillas. Towards the end of the month, the largest single action of the campaign occurred in a clash in which 33 guerrillas were killed by Rhodesian security forces in a 14-hour battle. At the same time the Rhodesian forces claimed that a total of 173 guerrillas had been killed during the month, a higher figure than the total fatal casualties inflicted in the whole of 1975. It was said that altogether 1 356 guerrillas had been killed during the year as against 103 members of the security forces.

As the year neared its close renewed reports began to appear not only of the possibility of Cuban intervention in Rhodesia but also of returning frictions within the guerrilla movement. Clashes involving a considerable number of deaths and injuries amongst rival factions of guerrillas in three camps in the Tete Province of Moçambique

234

were amongst the incidents reported. A report in the *Sunday Times* of 9 December also spoke of mounting anger amongst the population of some areas of Moçambique concerning the behaviour of the guerrillas quartered in various camps in the country. The report said that the guerrillas

> take what they want—at gunpoint if necessary—from nearby villages, where the tribesmen, mostly Tongas, Nhunhues and Angones, are forced to provide fresh meat, chickens, bread, maize meal and sugar. From Russian and Cuban military supplies the guerrillas get butter, cheese, beer, and canned food which are largely unavailable throughout the rest of the country.

The same report said that the total number of guerrilla camps in the Moçambique provinces of Tete, Manica and Gaza had grown to over a hundred and that the guerrillas of ZIPA virtually controlled these three provinces.

Previously the five African "front line presidents" were said to have warned Rhodesian guerrilla leaders, including in particular Mr Robert Mugabe, to keep criminal elements within their ranks out of Zambia where the authorities were said to be nervous that such elements could become an increasingly serious threat to internal law and order in that country.

Use of Terrorism and Psychological Warfare

Of all the campaigns of revolutionary-inspired guerrilla warfare so far fought in Southern Africa, there would seem no doubt that it is Rhodesia that has seen the most widespread use of terrorism by the guerrilla forces as a means of attempting to obtain support from the local population. The details of the continually growing list of incidents frequently involving the use of brutality of a most barbarous type have been supplied not only by Rhodesian Government sources but by independent observers, some of these being by no means unfavourably disposed towards the guerrillas' cause.

In addition to deliberate murders, there have been a number of cases of mutilation of "sell-outs", i.e. Africans who refuse, or who are reluctant, to support the guerrillas. These have included the cutting off of the lips or ears of both men and women who refuse to co-operate and, according to Rhodesian police reports in at least one case, a man who lost his ears in this way was then ordered to eat them. Africans have also been bayoneted, beaten with rifle butts and thrown in the flames of burning buildings. In one case in 1975, a woman was soaked in paraffin and then burnt to death.

Another incident of particular savagery, also reported in 1975, gave grim evidence of the deliberate use of terrorism in an effort to discourage the habit of many African workers from Malawi of finding employment in Rhodesia. The incident occurred when a number of African labourers were having a beer-drinking party on a tribal trust land in the Centenary area, near the border with Moçambique. A party of guerrillas suddenly appeared and, on learning that one of the labourers came from Malawi, seized him and forced him to lie naked on the ground. After he had been beaten with rifle butts, his colleagues were forced to hold him down and a log was placed under his ankles. His feet were then hacked off with an axe, following which he was bayoneted and his friends ordered to bury him. Miraculously, however, the guerrillas departed before this could be done and he survived to reach hospital.

According to official Rhodesian figures, a total of 247 civilians died in the country between December 1972 and June 1975 as a result of terrorist action. Of these only 16 were White and the great majority of the African deaths were caused by terrorist action. A considerable number of Africans have died or been injured when buses have hit landmines laid by the guerrilla forces in a deliberate effort to disrupt communications upon which the economic and community life of rural areas is dependent. In one single incident of this type, 24 Africans were injured, 15 of them seriously, the casualties including three young children aged four or five.

African trading posts and schools have frequently been targets for terrorist attack and a number of African teachers have died as a result. One primary guerrilla aim has been to intimidate African labour from working on isolated European-owned farms so as to compel their abandonment. Consequently, in the course of attacks on such farms, particular attention has often been shown to attempts to destroy the living quarters of the African work force.

Neither ZAPU nor ZANU seems to have been as prolific in the production of propaganda material for actual distribution inside Rhodesia as were the guerrilla movements opposed to Portuguese rule in their respective territories. Considerable use, however, has been made of propaganda broadcasts over Radio Zambia from

236

Lusaka. To this was added during 1976 a new voice beamed from Maputo, the capital of Moçambique. The voice is that of a broadcaster known as "Lord MacDuff", or sometimes "Lord Haw-Haw".

In fact, he is a Mr Ian Christie, a former member of the Scottish Communist Party which he is alleged to have left because he believed that it was too moderate. Previously he worked for the Frelimo authorities as editor of a magazine known as *Moçambique Revolution*. His first contact with the Frelimo leader, Mr Samora Machel, occurred when he was working as a journalist in Dar es Salaam. His broadcasts were reported as going on the air every evening at 2000 for 15 minutes. Claiming that victory was certain for the guerrilla forces and appealing for the utmost support for their efforts, he emphasised that:

> The only way to end oppression, humiliation and the privileged life of a handful of white racist settlers is through armed struggle.[48]

Other broadcasts from Moçambique in African languages also repeatedly called for support for the *Chimuranga* or guerrilla war. These were said to be having some effect amongst some younger sections of the population near the border areas, and, in particular, amongst secondary school children, several hundred of whom were believed to have obeyed calls to make their way to guerrilla training camps in Moçambique.

South and South West Africa

The African National Congress (ANC) first came into being in 1912 as an organisation dedicated to promoting the interests of the Black population in South Africa. After the Second World War it developed close ties with the small, but militant, South African Communist Party and when the Nationalist Government came to power also with other left-wing groups opposed to this Government. In 1952 it took part in the organisation of a "defiance campaign" and called for the introduction of a "freedom charter" which would establish "democratic rights".

Later some of its more militant elements split from it to form the Pan-African Congress (PAC) which, unlike the ANC, disapproved of any idea of working for reform with other groups composed of Whites and Coloureds and demanded a programme of radical action.

A programme of marches, demonstrations and other "protest actions" in which both organisations took part during the early 1960s culminated in the tragic and traumatic events at Sharpeville and Langa and the banning of both movements in April 1960.

The ANC, however, had partly expected this move and, helped by the Communist Party, had set up a skeleton underground organisation in advance of the event. Many of the ANC leaders also then began to prepare themselves and their followers for the idea of undertaking an "armed struggle" against the Government, with the ultimate aim of its total overthrow and replacement by a "Socialist democratic state".

A military wing of the ANC was established with the title *Umkhonto We Sizwe,* or Spear of the Nation. The rival PAC also established a military wing, in its case with the title *Poqo* ("only", i.e. "only for Blacks"). The latter began a programme of violent action during 1962, which included a number of cases of murder, arson and attacks on property. According to the report of a judicial Commission of Enquiry set up to investigate its action in the Transvaal, it relied for rescruitment to a very high degree on intimidation. The Commission stated:

> Bantu recruits, who are mostly illiterate, are simply told that the whites and other nationalities *(inter alia,* especially Indians against whom strong resentment apparently exists) must be driven out of the country by terrorism and murder. Bantu are warned that the same treatment will be meted out to those who do not co-operate.

The report continued:

> The expounders of the movement's policy do not take great pains to explain the details of the constitution to illiterate Bantu. Their method is to recruit members by making an appeal to the patriotism of the Bantu, and by intimidating those who are unwilling with threats of

violent murder and mutilation, as well as the use of sorcery ... Members are also given to understand that they will be protected by means of scorcery, especially where they are instructed to take part in crimes.[49]

Meanwhile, the "High Command" of the ANC's Spear of the Nation had been drawing up plans for a very much more sophisticated and far-reaching revolutionary campaign.

Operating from a secret headquarters at Lillisleaf farm, near Rivonia in the Transvaal, it devised a scheme known as Operation Mayibuye (Operation for the Return of Africa). The preamble to the plans drawn up stated:

> It can now truly be said that very little, if any, scope exists for the smashing of white supremacy other than by means of mass revolutionary action, the main content of which is armed resistance leading to victory by military means ... we are confident that the masses will respond in overwhelming numbers to a lead which holds out a real possibility of successful armed struggle.[50]

The plans called for the training of an internal force which would be reinforced by means of the arrival of an "external force". The internal force was to operate in the Eastern Cape district, North Western Cape, Natal-Zululand and the North Western Transkei. Recruits were to be sent abroad secretly to receive military training. During the long drawn-out guerrilla war that was foreseen, it was hoped that the "mass of the population" could be drawn in on the revolutionaries' side and armed.

In the event, the South African Police became alerted as to unusual comings and goings at the Rivonia farm house and virtually the whole of the "High Command" were arrested before the operation had got beyond the planning and very early preparatory stage. There can, however, be little doubt of the serious intent behind the plan. A prominent South African radical, Mr Ben Turok, has, for instance, said that by the time the arrests at Rivonia occurred in July 1963, many leaders and hundreds of the best cadres (of the ANC) had been sent out of the country for training in preparation for the impending revolt.

The arrests at Rivonia struck the ANC a crushing blow. The difficulties it found in recovering were increased by the fact that many of its most experienced members who had gone abroad for training in preparation for Operation Mayibuye were now in effect stranded in exile and unable to do anything to help repair its rapidly collapsing network at home. In addition, its most notable African member, Mr Nelson Mandela, had been arrested sometime earlier.

Members of the South African Communist Party had been deeply implicated in the planning for Operation Mayibuye and some were amongst those arrested while a considerable number of others had sought sanctuary abroad, but it continued to operate underground. A new disaster struck it in November 1965, however, when its leader, the late Mr Braam Fischer, whose duties had, amongst other things, included keeping in touch with the Party's London-based Overseas Committee through a series of coded communications, was tracked down and arrested. He was subsequently sentenced to life imprisonment on a number of charges, including those of presiding over meetings of the command of Spear of the Nation at Rivonia and planning acts of sabotage and violent revolution.

After these successive disasters suffered by the revolutionary movement, little was heard of moves towards the development of "armed struggle" in South Africa during the remainder of the 1960s, although in 1968 a number of people were accused of being members of a *Poqo* group which had planned to kill police in Victoria West. In the following year, others were sentenced to terms of imprisonment accused of having plotted violent revolution in the country in collusion with foreign organisations under Communist leadership. The evidence against some of the latter of those charged indicated that their activities had included making a reconnaissance of selected places on the coast to test their suitability for secret landings from submarines.

Periodically also ANC leaflets appeared in scattered locations, quite often carrying diagrams of how to make petrol bombs and simple, but quite deadly, hand-grenades. It appears that at least one member of the ANC did succeed in making his way south through Rhodesia after taking part in guerrilla operations in that country. He was Mr Edward April, who had received guerrilla training in the Soviet Union and who was arrested early in 1971 in Natal.

In 1972 an ambitious scheme involving members of the ANC was uncovered, some of the details of which have already been referred to. This concerned a plan to land a party of ANC members who had received training in the Soviet Union on the South African coast

240

from a ship sailing from Mogadishu. The plan came to nothing when the ship developed a radar fault early in the voyage.

Information also came into the possession of the security forces about this time that the failure of the ANC's plan to infiltrate large bodies of guerrilla fighters through Rhodesia into South Africa had led to a considerable re-assessment of future operational plans. A number of ANC members were sent to the Soviet Union for special "refresher courses". During these, they received instruction in the mechanics of running an underground organisation, in communications and intelligence duties. The main emphasis was on methods of constructing a network based on a cell system in which members were deliberately kept uninformed of the identity of members of cells other than their own. According to Mr Michael Morris, a plan was devised whereby this network was to operate under the general instructions of ANC supporters based in London who would also be responsible for arranging all joint operations or contact between cells.[51]

ANC supporters have repeatedly emphasised that the movement aims not merely at ending the present system of White rule through a successful revolution but is also fundamentally anti-capitalist and will be content with nothing less than the establishment of a thorough-going "socialist" state. Mr Ben Turok, for instance, has written:

> Given the favourable circumstances, there is good reason to predict that a black liberation struggle will produce a progressive government. Support for this view is to be found in the character of the leadership of the ANC, in the importance given to continuing collaboration with the S.A. Communist Party, and, above all, in the generally progressive positions taken by the ANC on international questions.[52]

In an interview in *World Marxist Review* of December 1975, Mr Oliver Tambo, President of the South African ANC, declared:

> It is important that world opinion should understand the true nature of the people's movement in our country. Some people are still inclined to think that the struggle of the black population is a struggle for civil rights. But this obscures the national liberation character of our

movement.

Perhaps this is partly due to the over-emphasis at certain times on the struggle against apartheid, instead of the struggle against the entire system of national and class oppression ...

The ANC declares that our movement is a national liberation movement, that it is fighting not simply for civil rights, but for the overthrow of the colonial régime and that it is committed to struggle for the seizure of power by the mass of the people.

Agitators from the ANC were reported to be active during the riots in Soweto and other African townships during the winter and spring of 1976 but the most potentially serious activity, thought to involve members of this movement, would have seemed to take the form of a small scale guerrilla raid across the frontier from Moçambique into the Eastern Transvaal early in December. Although involving only four men, the raid was the first of its type and was presumably a consequence of the establishment of guerrilla training and base camps in the southern part of Moçambique with the aid of the South African Communist Party, as described in Chapter 5. Two South African policemen were seriously injured when one of the four guerrillas threw a Soviet-type hand-grenade into their patrol vehicle. After the four had been arrested, a number of magazines for Soviet-made AK-47 rifles, as well as further supplies of grenades, were found in iron trunks which they had been carrying.

The origins of the South West African People's Organisation (SWAPO) can be traced back to the Ovamboland People's Organisation (OPO) and the Caprivi African National Union (CANU). OPO was formed in 1957 by some members of the Wambo tribe assisted by a number of White radicals, including members of the South African Communist Party. The organisation was blamed, by a judicial inquiry in 1960, for having been responsible in company with the South West African National Union for inciting riots in the native township at Windhoek in which a number of persons were killed and injured.

During the early 1960s SWAPO became firmly committed to a highly militant programme aimed at bringing about the end of South African control of South West Africa. By 1966 it had begun to recruit large numbers of Wambo tribesmen for guerrilla training abroad. The same year, the movement produced a plan of campaign under which the country was divided into various regions and which called for the beginning of attacks on such targets as police stations, strategic bridges, railway lines and White-owned farms and White officials. Wambo chiefs who were unsympathetic to SWAPO were also to be murdered. Small groups of armed SWAPO guerrillas then began to move into South West Africa, mainly via Angola, in order to begin setting about accomplishing this plan. By the spring of 1966, it was estimated that there were a further 250 SWAPO guerrillas in reserve in training and base camps in Zambia and Tanzania. Serious armed action in South West Africa began with an attack by a SWAPO group on a settlement controlled by the Department of Bantu Affairs at Oshikango. Spasmodic attacks and incidents continued to occur during the remainder of 1966, 1967 and 1968, whilst the police inflicted a number of casualties on the SWAPO groups responsible and captured a quantity of arms, most of which proved to be of Communist Chinese or Soviet bloc origin. The number of SWAPO attacks, never large, fell to an ever lower average during 1969 and 1970, and SWAPO morale was reported to be showing considerable signs of decline.

In May 1971, a new SWAPO "offensive" was heralded by the killing of two policemen and the wounding of seven more when a mine planted by SWAPO guerrillas exploded under their patrol vehicle. The use of this type of weapon increased. During the next two years, the number of attacks on the security forces again started to rise, whilst the close relationship that had been established between SWAPO and the MPLA in Angola clearly foreshadowed the possibility of the former being able to extend the number of safe bases at its disposal from which to extend its operations.

In 1975 and early 1976, incidents included attacks on tribal chiefs and tribal policemen. In April 1976 four members of the South African Army were killed and seven wounded in an attack by a 42-strong party of SWAPO guerrillas. The MPLA victory in Angola brought with it inevitable fears that the sizeable Cuban field force in that country would now be employed in active support of SWAPO's operations but up to the end of the year there was no apparent evidence of this threat materialising.

One possible contributory factor towards Cuban caution in this regard is that SWAPO has increasingly come to suffer from the same sort of internal disputes that have plagued the Rhodesian

243

guerrilla movement. Not only is the movement divided into an internal and external wing (the former being reputed to be more moderate) but there has also been considerable criticism within its ranks of its leader, Mr Nujoma, who, unlike some of its other leading personalities, is a known Marxist.

REFERENCES

1. *Portuguese Colonies: Victory or Death*, Agostinho Neto, Tricontinental, p. 17.
2. *Armed Conflict in Southern Africa*, *op. cit.*, p. 111.
3. *Ibid*, p. 123.
4. *Portuguese Colonies: Victory or Death*, *op. cit.*, p. 223.
5. *Ibid.*
6. *Ibid.*
7. *Ibid.*, p. 142.
8. *Ibid.*, p. 144.
9. *Password "Anguimo"*, *op. cit.*, p. 22.
10. *Portuguese Colonies: Victory or Death*, *op. cit.*, p. 257.
11. *Portuguese Colonies: Victory or Death*, *op. cit.*, p. 257.
12. *Password "Anguimo"*, *op. cit.*, p. 25.
13. *Nailing a Lie*, John Biggs-Davison M.P., Congo African Publications, p. 21-23.
14. *Password "Anguimo"*, *op. cit.*, p. 25-26.
15. *Armed Struggle in Southern Africa*, *op. cit.*, p. 181.
16. *The Making of a Middle Cadre*, *op. cit.*, 1973, p. 89.
17. *Ibid.*, p. 102.
18. *Moçambique: Sowing the Seeds of Revolution*, Samora Machel. Committee for Freedom in Moçambique, Angola and Guinea, 1974, p. 14-20.
19. *Ibid.*
20. *Ibid.*
21. *Ibid.*, p. 37-45.
22. *Moçambique: Sowing the Seeds of Revolution*, *op. cit.*, p. 37-45.
23. *Ibid.*
24. *Ibid.*
25. *Armed Struggle in Africa*, Gerard Chaliand. Monthly Review Press, New York and London, 1969.

26. *Ibid.,* p. 74.
27. *Ibid.,* p. 54.
28. *Guinea-Bissau: Towards Final Victory,* Liberation Support Movement Center, Richmond, B.C., 1974, p. 35.
29. *The Zambezi Salient,* Al J. Venter. Robert Hale & Co., London, 1975. Appendix 5, p. 336-341.
30. *Password "Anguimo", op. cit.,* p. 59-60.
31. *Armed Conflict in Southern Africa, op. cit.,* p. 86.
32. *The Viet Cong Strategy of Terror.* United States Mission in Vietnam.
33. *Does God Say Kill?,* John Eppstein, Tom Stacey, London, 1972, p. 80.
34. *Password "Anguimo", op. cit.,* o. 131.
35. *Portuguese Colonies, Victory or Death, op. cit.,* p. 104.
36. *Armed Conflict in Southern Africa, op. cit.,* p. 33-34.
37. *Rhodesia Herald,* 8 March 1968.
38. *Rhodesia Herald,* 8 March 1968.
39. *Reply to Observations on Our Struggle,* James Chikerema. Monograph, 17 March 1970.
40. *The Zambesi Salient, op. cit.,* p. 342-350.
41. *The Zambesi Salient, op. cit.,* p. 348.
42. *The Fight for Zimbabwe, op. cit.,* p. 163.
43. *Zimbabwe News* No. 7, 9 September 1973.
44. *Southern Africa: New Horizons,* Peter Janke. Conflict Studies No. 73, Institute for the Study of Conflict, London, 1976.
45. The *Daily Telegraph,* 29 June 1976.
46. *Rhodesian Report,* May 1976.
47. *The Star,* 10 June 1976.
48. *The Sunday Times,* 11 April 1976.
49. *The Paarl Commission,* paragraphs 10-11.
50. *Strategic Problems in South Africa's Liberation Struggle,* Ben Turok. Liberation Support Movement Information Center, Richmond, B.C., Canada, 1974, p. 48.
51. *Armed Conflict in Southern Africa, op. cit.,* p. 25.
52. *Strategic Problems in South Africa's Liberation Struggle, op. cit.*

Chapter 8

Angola 1975-1976: A Case Study of Intervention

As for the Soviet Union, like all genuine friends of the oppressed people, it will not remain indifferent to the destiny of Angola.

The above words were uttered not, as might be expected, by some Soviet spokesman during the last traumatic two years of Angola's history; they appeared in an official Soviet Government policy statement as long ago as 1961.

As such, they would seem to belie amply (even if nothing else did) the pretentions of Mr Kosygin during his visit to Britain 15 years later that, to the leaders in the Kremlin, the countries of Southern Africa were just names on a map.

That the words of the 1961 statement were not just simply words has been shown already by the summary of the very considerable assistance given to the Marxist-dominated MPLA in Angola throughout the course of its campaign against Portuguese rule. Soviet concern for the "destiny of Angola" has, during the last two years, presented the world with a picture of the massive and unrelenting use of military assistance in Southern Africa by outside Communist powers.

This action by the Soviet Union and its ally, Cuba, in an area many thousands of kilometres from their own borders, has posed the most serious questions for the future peace, not only of Africa, but of the whole world. On 28 January 1976, President Kenneth Kaunda of Zambia said regarding Soviet and Cuba intervention in Angola: "A plundering tiger with its deadly cubs is coming in through the back door."

The reasons for the Soviet wish to help shape the destiny of Angola, other than the alleged concern for "oppressed people", are indeed substantial enough. In addition to its strategic importance, both as regards providing bases for a possible guerrilla attack upon South West Africa and for surveillance of Western communications in the South Atlantic, its economic potential was not long ago considered to be one of the most promising of any country on the African continent.

Known Angolan mineral resources include deposits of copper, gold, nickel, diamonds, uranium and phosphates. Much of the country has not been properly prospected, but experts consider that its geological fomation gives promise of still more valuable minerals to be found. An American agricultural expert in a study published in 1964, *The Geography of Modern Africa*, stated that the possibilities for developing agriculture in the country were "enormous". Its main agricultural products are timber, sisal, tobacco and rice but it also possesses a large fishing industry. During the 1950s a large influx of foreign investment began coming into the country. One consequence of this was the rapid development of light industry in the urban areas.

To the north of the country, the province of Cabinda contains oil deposits whose development by a subsidiary of the American Gulf Oil Company has made the country the third largest producer of oil in Africa south of the Sahara (the two largest being Nigeria and Gabon).

A large refinery complex exists at Malongo which is fed by 100 offshore oil wells. In 1974 these wells were producing 180 000 barrels of oil a day. Nearly 50% of this production went to the USA, other consumers being Portugal, Canada, Japan and West Germany. In the same year these oil resources earned the Angolan exchequer no less than 500 million dollars in royalties, capital participation and other types of oil taxation.

Diamond production, also extremely important to the Angolan economy, has been in the hands of Diamang, a subsidiary of De Beers. The West German firm of Krupp has been heavily involved with various other Western concerns, including General Electric, the

Export and Import Bank and Portuguese companies, in the development of mineral ores for export to West Germany and Japan. The Krupp contract provides for the development of an estimated 250 million tons of minerals in various parts of the country. Other foreign concerns have been involved in developing deposits of phosphates and sulphur.

Angola, secured as a firm Marxist base, could, therefore, clearly be seen as a most valuable asset towards the development of both Soviet military and political strategy on the African continent.

The events that were to lead to months of internecine warfare, the deaths of many thousands of Angolan citizens, the destitution of many more, the collapse of the once bouyant Angolan economy and ultimately to a total victory for the MPLA, were set in train in April 1974 when the coup in Lisbon toppled the Portuguese government of President Caetano.

On 15 January 1975 an agreement providing for the granting of independence to Angola was signed between the new Portuguese Government and representatives of the three "liberation movements" which had been campaigning against its rule in Angola. These movements were the *Movimento Popular de Libertaçao de Angola* (MPLA), the *Uniao Nacional para a Independencia Total de Angola* (UNITA) and the *Frente Nacional para a Libertacao de Angola* (FNLA).

The agreement was signed in the Portuguese town of Alvor and not unnaturally became known as "the Alvor Agreement". It provided for an immediate formal cease-fire between the Portuguese and guerrilla forces and for the granting of independence to Angola on 10 November 1975.

The agreement also set out the measures by which the country was to be administered until the day of independence arrived. This was to be through a transitional government acting in conjunction with a Portuguese High Commissioner. The transitional government was to be directed by a Presidential Council of three members, one from each of the "liberation movements". The post of Chairman was to be held by rotation. There was also to be a 12-man ministerial cabinet composed of representatives of the FNLA, MPLA and UNITA in equal proportion and representatives appointed by the President of Portugal.Public order and security was to be ensured by the establishment of a unified military force, consisting of 24 000 Portuguese troops and a further 24 000 drawn in equal proportion from each of the three "liberation movements".

The transitional government began its working life on 31 January 1975. A major part of its work was supposed to be concerned with organising elections for a Constituent Assembly which was to have been held within nine months of its inauguration. Candidates for this assembly were to come exclusively from members of the three "liberation movements". Under the Alvor Agreement, the Portuguese President was given the right to designate the transitional government's Minister of Economy, Public Works, Housing and Urbanisation, Transport and Communications. Other governmental posts were allotted as follows:

FNLA: Ministers of the Interior, Health and Moral Matters, and Agriculture.
MPLA: Ministers of Information, Planning and Finance, and Justice.
UNITA: Ministers of Labour and Social Security, Education and Culture, and Natural Resources.

There was also to have been a six-man National Defence Council. Ultimate control of defence and security, however, was vested in the hands of the Portuguese High Commissioner who had the assistance of a "Unified General Staff" consisting of the commanders of the three Portuguese fighting services in the country and representatives of the three "liberation movements". Portuguese troops were not to be withdrawn finally from Angola until February 1976.

The three movements which were now supposed to control the country had a history of antagonism, which had sometimes led to bloodshed, dating back to the early years of their campaign against Portuguese rule. This antagonism was based not only on political differences but also to a considerable degree stemmed from the basis of their tribal support. The FNLA, for instance, derived from the Angola People's Union (UPA) founded by Dr Holden Roberto in 1954. Originally, the UPA was mainly concerned with attracting support from the Bakongo people whose territory lies in Northern Angola and this area remained an FNLA stronghold. Despite the fact that it received some Chinese assistance, its political affiliations were very much more directed towards the West. The FNLA had particularly close relations with Zaire, the President of that country being Dr Roberto's brother-in-law.

UNITA drew its support from the South, mainly from the

Ovimbundu, the largest single tribe in the country. Although UNITA's leader, Dr Jonas Savimbi, who founded the party in 1966, was originally somewhat attracted towards China and Cuba, he later became orientated towards Western values. He tried to attract foreign investment into the country with the aim of bringing about its rapid development in the framework of a mixed economy. UNITA had strong connections with Zambia where its main bases were located during the early part of its campaign against Portuguese rule.

The Marxist-dominated MPLA under Dr Aghostino Neto, whose career has already been outlined, was led mainly by men who like Neto himself came from the Mbundu tribe situated in Central Angola, although drawing most of its rank-and-file support from urban workers of all races in Luanda and the other large towns. At the time the transitional government was established, it was numerically the weakest of all three movements.

The practical feasibility of these somewhat complicated transitional arrangements, as far as assuring a smooth transfer of power was concerned, was further weakened by the fact that little provision had been made for any means of enforcing them. Within a very few weeks, the functioning of the transitional government was under serious strain with the rivalries between the three "liberation movements" becoming ever more manifest. The MPLA began to emerge in an increasingly strong position despite its comparative lack of support in the country as a whole, partly as a result of its superior organisation and partly because of the fact that its representatives held control of the capital Luanda and the vital Ministries of Finance and Information, and also such posts as Secretary of State in the Departments of the Interior, Industry and Energy and Labour and Social Security.

The power and prestige of the MPLA also began to increase for another and quite different reason that was in the end to prove decisive. In March 1975 reports were received of the landing of 25-30 Soviet aircraft in the Congo (Brazzaville) carrying arms destined for the MPLA. These were then conveyed overland to the Luanda area. Soon afterwards, heavy fighting broke out between MPLA and FNLA forces near Luanda. Both sides blamed the other for the outbreak. In further fighting, the FNLA headquarters in Luanda were destroyed and MPLA units occupied the docks area, so opening the way for the direct unloading of Soviet arms supplies by ship that was to come later.

FNLA forces were forced to withdraw to the north-east of the capital and by May fighting had spread to the Caxito area, 65 km to the north. The first seaborne Soviet supplies intended for the MPLA then began to be landed directly in Angola. A Soviet freighter docked at Luanda in May carrying an estimated 150 t of arms for the MPLA. This was soon followed by the arrival of a Yugoslav vessel, the *Postyna,* carrying trucks intended for the same destination. This direct supply of arms was supplemented by the ferrying of Soviet supplied arms previously stockpiled in Tanzania. Two vessels left Dar es Salaam early in May bound for Pointe Noire in the Congo which was to become a major place for the trans-shipment of arms intended for the use of the MPLA.

Arms were also flown from Dar es Salaam to points such as Serpa Pinto, in the south of Angola and at that time occupied by the MPLA. During May five Soviet ships and one East German vessel arrived at Pointe Noire. By that time, the MPLA had acquired two landing craft which were employed for the purpose of transporting East German-supplied armoured personnel carriers from Pointe Noire to Angolan waters. It is probable that these were unloaded on the coast north of Luanda. In that area at least one Soviet vessel is known to have unloaded arms intended for the MPLA into fishing boats which then put them ashore at isolated spots.[1]

This increasing flow of arms was accompanied by a mounting propaganda barrage on the part of the Soviet news media. A typical broadcast from *Radio Moscow* in March 1975, for instance, proclaimed that the "true independence" of Angola could only be secured if the political line of the MPLA was followed "unswervingly". The announcer explained that it was only the MPLA that represented the aspirations of the Angolan people. The tone of Soviet press comment at this stage was well illustrated by an article in *Izvestiya* which appeared on 21 May, claiming that the struggle for "the liberation of Angola" was "the cause of all progressive mankind".

The military forces of the MPLA's two rivals FNLA and UNITA were subsequently both expelled from their last strongholds in and around Luanda. UNITA re-grouped in the south and FNLA in the north. By early August Luanda had been completely occupied by the MPLA. The government ministries which had been placed under FNLA and UNITA control were taken over by civil servants selected by the MPLA and they were appointed as "director-generals".

Jubilant MPLA officials, convinced that the tide of war had changed in their favour, began handing out lapel badges, posters, white and yellow T-shirts bearing the slogan *MPLA—a Victoria e Certa* (Victory is certain). Journalists in Luanda were taken on guided tours of wrecked FNLA offices, the walls of which had been holed by the projectiles from recoilless rifles and pockmarked by small arms fire. Deaths resulting from the fighting in the city of Luanda itself since the early months of the year were estimated to have reached a figure in excess of 500 by that date. Municipal administration was rapidly collapsing into a state of complete chaos with increasing shortages of fuel and food supplies.

The rapidly worsening situation led to a swift increase in the number of Angolans of Portuguese descent seeking to leave the country. This swelling of the flood of refugees included many doctors and technical experts, thus increasing the administrative breakdown that now began to grip the whole country. Under an evacuation plan hastily announced by the Portuguese Government in response to increasingly urgent demands from the White population, it was planned to fly out 80 000 to 90 000 refugees a month during August, September and October. Long columns of both Black and White refugees also began to make their way southwards towards the border of South West Africa.

In the middle of August, some 4 000 refugees arrived at the South West African town of Oshakati in one single convoy. This enormous exodus of refugees not only caused local government to collapse but also brought agricultural production largely to a standstill. Crops of sisal and cotton stood in the fields unpicked whilst mining operations came to a complete halt.

A statement on 16 August by the acting Portuguese High Commissioner that in view of the deteriorating situation he was resuming "Executive Powers" was promptly answered by a counter-statement from the MPLA that the movement would not abdicate its government function or its responsibility to the "Angolan people". Throughout the mid-winter months, the flow of Soviet arms into Angola for the use of the MPLA continued. This flow was sometimes aided by sympathetic elements in the Portuguese army who were on occasion seen conveying cargoes of arms from the Luanda docks to MPLA headquarters. One observer mentioned in the *Economist's* Foreign Report asserted that two boatloads of Soviet arms a week arrived for the use of the MPLA during May, June and July. At the same time, the airlift of arms to airfields in the Congo was stepped up. Most of these arms were transported by Soviet long-range Antonov 22 heavy transport aircraft. These are four-engined aircraft with titanium reinforced floors which can carry up to 200 000 lbs of cargo over great distances at a speed of over 650 kph.

The increasing successes of the MPLA were also aided by the fact that a number of Portuguese Communists and other supporters of the extreme left ruling Armed Forces Movement in Portugal had been appointed to important official posts in Angola. There were allegations that on occasions units of Portuguese forces actually aided the MPLA in the conduct of military operations. On 13 July, for instance, the FNLA's headquarters issued a statement from Kinshasa, the capital of Zaire, claiming that

> Portuguese troops, supported by armoured units directly under the command of the Armed Forces Movement in Angola, have intervened on the side of the People's Movement for the Liberation of Angola, which has concentrated its forces in an all-out assault against the Front's installations in Luanda.[2]

On 22 August, UNITA made a formal declaration of war on the MPLA. Mr Marques Kakumba, UNITA's Deputy Minister of Foreign Affairs, said that his movement would refuse to negotiate with the MPLA any further but would fight its troops wherever they were to be found. The statement attacked the MPLA leader, Dr Aghostino Neto, for dreaming of "dominating Angola with Soviet missiles".[3] The missiles he referred to were undoubtedly the Soviet 122 mm surface-to-surface rockets. They were used in quantity by the MPLA forces and were effective enough when used as single weapons but, with the arrival of Cuban forces that soon followed, they were fired in salvoes from multiple launchers either carried on jeeps or on specially built lorries. Though not very accurate, even the noise made by salvoes of these weapons as they travelled through the air had a considerable demoralising effect on the largely untrained troops of UNITA and FNLA.

Meanwhile, Soviet propaganda support for the MPLA continued unabated. A somewhat new note, however, became noticeable. This was that the MPLA was saving the "Angolan people" from having their freedom crushed by reactionary foreign intervention. On 31 July, for instance, *Moscow Radio* stated of the MPLA:

> Supported by the population, Luanda is preparing to give a rebuff to the forces of external and internal reaction.

On 13 August, the same station triumphantly reported that:

> The army formations of the MPLA have taken complete control of the capital Luanda. One of the contributing factors for this success came undoubtedly from the support of the people. The people are supporting the Liberation Movement.

By the end of August weapons available to the MPLA as the result of the Soviet arms supply effort were reported to include Czech-made armoured cars. At the same time the MPLA was also said to have armed some 7 000 civilians in the course of forming the "popular power movement" that became one of the main instruments for implementing its policies.

Early in September the Portuguese Government, recognising the facts of the situation, announced that it regarded the Alvor Agreement as "suspended". This was followed by an announcement on 19 September that all Portuguese troops were to be withdrawn from the country by 11 November.

A correspondent of the British Communist Party's newspaper *Morning Star,* who visited the country about that time, presented an interesting picture in his report of the degree of political indoctrination even then being carried out by the MPLA in the areas in which it had only recently won control. He recorded that:

> Political work goes on among returning refugees ... The MPLA's message is clear—the flag of independence is not enough, the struggle must continue until all exploitation is ended. It is a message which makes no compromise with tribalism, racism, or fake nationalism—but is gaining ground steadily.
> After basic political explanation, village action Commit-

tees are elected at general meetings, these split into groups caring for health, education, etc.

Among the people who fought the liberation war, popular organisation is strong, and political consciousness very high. **Village** activists will discuss the struggle in Latin America and Asia, and not just local problems. Particularly impressive is FAPLA (the MPLA armed forces) which knows exactly why it is fighting.

The **commonist** greeting from peasants is the MPLA 'V' for victory sign, incorporated into a handshake ... FAPLA maintains constant vigilance and we saw the very effective way it deals with FNLA provocations, its light mobile tactics being completely superior to the more conventional methods of FNLA."[4]

Despite the *Morning Star's* correspondent's remarks about the superiority of the MPLA's tactics, it would seem likely that its continuing successes over its two rivals FNLA and UNITA were due just as much to the superiority of Soviet-supplied fire power. During a visit to a UNITA training camp at the end of September, a correspondent of *The Times* stated that he noted a great contrast in the equipment of the MPLA troops with their Soviet AK-47 rifles and rocket weapons.

The Times correspondent said that of the 700 men and women in the camp he visited hardly a third had arms of any kind. Although four ex-Portuguese armoured vehicles were parked in the middle of the camp, none of them was in working order. Such small arms as the UNITA members in the camp possessed seemed to consist entirely of weapons captured either from the Portuguese or the MPLA. The so-called camp hospital contained nothing but a few bandages and half-empty medicine bottles.

Within a very short space of time, the odds in the continuing fighting were to be even more heavily weighed in favour of the MPLA. In October the first definite reports began to appear of the arrival of troops of the Cuban Expeditionary Force in Angola. From prisoners' statements and other evidence, however, it would seem likely that, in fact, the first advance parties began to arrive at least two months earlier. During September a Cuban vessel, the *Vietnam Heroica,* had been seen in the harbour at Pointe Noire, together with another vessel from the same country. These ships off-loaded trucks, armoured vehicles and a large number of crates into an Angolan ship. This same ship also took on board a group of mainly Black Cubans wearing military uniforms. Between 500 and 600 of these were said to have told people in the harbour area that they were on their way to Angola.

On 12 October another Cuban ship, *La Playa de Habana*, arrived at Pointe Noire and again about 500 Cubans in full battle kit disembarked. Trucks, crates and some tanks were also unloaded. The unloading of the Cuban vessels on both occasions was reported to have taken place in a special area of the docks where Soviet supplies for the MPLA had previously been landed.

Pointe Noire was not, however, the only place used for the disembarkation of the rapidly increasing Cuban Expeditionary Force. On 9 October, American State Department sources released a report which stated that four ships loaded with approximately 10 000 tons of Soviet arms had arrived at a small port south of Luanda. The report also alleged that the vessels concerned had aboard between 200 and 400 Cubans.

October was also the month which saw the introduction of South African forces into the situation on a limited scale in a bid to redress the balance now tilting so sharply in favour of a Communist victory. In February 1976 a report appeared in the South African newspaper, *Rapport*, which purported to give details of how this involvement had come about. It was based on an interview between the newspaper's Washington correspondent and an assistant of Senator John Tunney, Mr Bill Coughlin, who had had talks with South African, UNITA and FNLA leaders the previous month.

The report was subsequently summarised in *The Times* with the comment that most of the facts contained in it were probably correct. The report stated that at the end of September it had become all too clear to the UNITA leader, Dr Savimbi, that his movement was soon going to be in urgent need of help in view of the increasing flow of Soviet supplies to the MPLA. His first request for aid was to President Mobutu of Zaire, who responded by sending UNITA 11 armoured cars. Early in October, he received a message from President Mobutu which said that "an American friend" wanted to help.

The "American friend" said that the USA would not be willing to send troops to Angola but that arms would be provided. Arms from United States sources were duly despatched and received but they consisted of small arms only and not the type of weapons which could match the heavy equipment the MPLA was by then receiving. Accordingly, Dr Savimbi asked President Kaunda of Zambia and the President of the Ivory Coast Repblic to try and arrange South African assistance, with the result that South African forces, acting on request of not only Dr Savimbi but also the heads of the African states mentioned, crossed the border in a strength estimated at between 1 200 and 1 500 men and began a rapid advance northwards along the Angolan coast. There would seem to be no doubt that this move was also prompted by the urgings—and even assurances of support—of an increasingly anxious United States Government.

Later in the autumn of 1976, Mr Harry Schwarz, a leader of the South African Progressive-Reform Party, was to say in the House of Assembly in Cape Town that the South African forces could have captured Luanda but were pulled back as the result of representations from the United States Government, presumably as a result of Congress's failure to support any form of intervention against the MPLA. Mr Schwarz explained that he had visited South African troops in Angola with Mr Piet Botha, the South African Minister of Defence, who had told him that the force could have advanced as far as Luanda. When Mr Schwarz asked why it had not, Mr Botha replied that the United States had pleaded that it should not do so.[5]

As 11 November, the date set for the departure of the remaining Portuguese troops and the Portuguese High Commissioner approached, brief hopes of a cease-fire between the rival movements and an orderly transfer of power were finally dashed by the MPLA. On the 4th of that month, they issued a statement formally denying that there was any possibility of a cease-fire in advance of the Portuguese departure. The Soviet Union had already stated that it would be ready to recognise the MPLA as being the legal government of the country, once the day of independence arrived.

On 11 November the Portuguese flag duly came fluttering down the mast above the old fortress of San Miguel in Luanda. The High Commissioner, after making a formal statement recognising Angolan independence, together with the 2 000 men who represented all that was left of Portuguese military power in the country, boarded the ships that were waiting for them in the harbour and sailed away. By the following day, the MPLA government which now claimed to be the only legal authority in the country, could claim to have received recognition from a number of countries, including North

Vietnam, Romania, East Germany and Guinea-Bissau. As part of their independence celebrations, enthusiastic MPLA supporters put up such a joyous barrage of automatic and light anti-aircraft fire that a Red Cross aircraft approaching Luanda airport was hit by two bullets and had to return to Lisbon without landing. Representatives of 13 Communist, but only three Western, countries attended the independence celebrations.

The MPLA's claim to have the legal right of government over the country, despite the rival claims of UNITA and FNLA, was to a large extent based on the fact that even two months before the date of independence the MPLA had by a combination of a "guile and strong-arm tactics" (as an article in *The Times* described it) and thanks to its superiority in armaments, managed to capture no less than 12 out of 16 provincial capitals. Accordingly, it was able to claim that its forces exercised legitimate control in the greater part of the country.

Within a few days of the proclamation of independence, the first reports began to appear of the arrival of Soviet officials and technicians in Luanda. The giant Antonov transport aircraft began to land directly at Luanda airport for the first time. At least four were seen there by 15 November. These reports were followed by others concerning the arrival of a consignment of T-54 tanks as well as armoured cars for service with the MPLA. These were apparently shipped to Conakry in Guinea and then loaded up again for transit by sea to the Luanda area.

An article in the Johannesburg *Star* of 18 November quoted reports from Luanda that all the signs were that the MPLA was about to launch a determined offensive against its rivals. Daily flights of Soviet cargo planes brought further supplies of 122 mm rockets, anti-aircraft guns, artillery, mortars and small arms.

An announcement from the official MPLA spokesman in Luanda, Commander Ju-Ju, then said that the movement was now ready to roll back what he called "foreign aggressors and Angolan hirelings". The same spokesman, however, admitted that the situation south of the capital where the MPLA forces were being heavily pressed by UNITA columns was "very bad".

Meanwhile, increasing signs began to appear of the sort of régime which the MPLA had it in mind to impose on the war-torn country.

The Guardian, for instance, stated in a leading article on 18 November:

The Stalinists are Stalinists the world over, for which the latest evidence is in the inaugural acts of the new régime in Luanda. The régime, called the MPLA (the Popular Movement for the Liberation of Angola) and armed by the Russians, controls a fairly small slice of Angola but that slice includes the capital and the principal port. Thus, when the Portuguese got out a week ago, the MPLA were the only people to take over. This is how Mr Dioganes Soavida has become Minister of Justice. He has lost no time announcing the principles of jurisprudence for which the people have suffered all these years.

First, people's tribunals will be formed, initially in Luanda and later throughout the country. Second, labour camps will be set up. And third, verdicts will take account of the will and decisions of the popular masses who will attend each trial. In other words, the first thought that crosses the mind of the Minister of Justice is not how this opportunity shall be seized to promote justice and mercy, but what will be a good way to punish people. The next thing is to find people to punish.

And lest the people's tribunals and the labour camps should lead to unpleasant misunderstandings, the MPLA has decided to expel Reuter's two correspondents. Not a bad week's work by the standards the MPLA has set itself.[6]

Further information from Angola during the month spoke of the many members of the population whose jobs had come to an end as the result of the fighting in areas controlled by the MPLA, being conscripted for service in the MPLA forces or for labouring work in a "produce to resist campaign". An acute food shortage became apparent in Luanda and villages administered by the MPLA, and so hundreds of "Dig for Victory" type posters appeared on walls and buildings. One of the principal journals *Dario de Luanda* appeared with a centre page full of colour pictures showing aspects of Soviet resistance to Fascism and "Imperialism."

Children as young as eight years old began to be conscripted into the MPLA's youth movement, the People's Revolutionary Pioneers. A correspondent of the *Daily Telegraph*, describing a propaganda photograph of such children issued under the caption "The Future of the Revolution", wrote:

> One boy of about nine holds his wooden Thompson-style weapon broadside to his chin, eyes staring resolutely from beneath his tilted army beret. In front of him stands another boy, earflaps of his helmet down, attentive in camouflaged battledress. A third looks towards the camera, cradling his wooden gun. Perhaps he is seven years old. These boys were being taught how to defend themselves. How to attack and kill at special training camps.[7]

The diamond mining town of Henrique de Carvelho now became an important reception centre for the continuing flow of air-lifted Soviet military supplies. Situated to the south of Luanda and reputed to have the finest all-weather airfield in the country, it was said to be the scene of the arrival of "massive" quantities of new supplies and to be defended by a force of about 4 000 Katangese mercenaries who had originally been trained by Colonel Mike Hoare in the Congo before serving for a time with the Portuguese Army and then being "bought over" by the MPLA.

Whilst the UNITA columns advancing from the south with South African support met increasingly heavy opposition, those of the FNLA to the north of the capital became the object of a fierce MPLA counter-attack and before long were in acute difficulties. In an attempt to restore the position, the FNLA committed about half its total available strength in the north to a counter-attack near the village of Ouifangando, situated between the FNLA headquarters in the town of Ambirz and Luanda. The attack was stopped by four MPLA armoured cars and the FNLA forces then came under a furious barrage from 122 mm rockets. These were fired from projectors mounted on lorries, 10 to a vehicle. An FNLA officer afterwards described the crews of these lorries as being White and said that their tactics consisted of appearing briefly in front of the hill which was the FNLA objective, firing a salvo, and then rapidly retreating behind the cover of the hill to reload.

The FNLA force, the officer said, was subjected to a barrage of perhaps 1 000 rounds from these weapons before withdrawing. Later the same day, they tried to resume the attack only to be subjected to another paralysing rocket barrage which lasted for two hours and forced a retreat. A bitter doctor at the FNLA hospital in Ambirz trying to cope with the wounded from this engagement, said:

> We don't even have asprin in our hospitals. A load of medicine the Chinese sent us had the labels in Chinese and we had to throw them away. Why won't America help us the way the Russians are helping the MPLA? Must we fight alone?[8]

The situation of the FNLA was indeed now fast becoming desperate. A few days after the battle at Ouifangando, its garrison at Ambriz had to suffer the humiliation of watching helplessly a convoy of 12 Soviet-bloc ships, some said to have anti-aircraft machine-guns mounted on them, sail down the coast bound for Luanda harbour carrying yet more supplies for the MPLA. Two days later MPLA units made a landing on the beach south of Ambriz supported by 122 mm rocket fire, this time directed from projectors mounted in small craft off-shore.

As estimates of the numbers of Cubans operating with the MPLA forces steadily rose, a statement from UNITA also alleged increasing direct involvement of Soviet personnel in the situation. The statement accused the Tass correspondent in Luanda, Mr Igor Ivanovitch Uvarev, of being a leading member of the Soviet military intelligence service, GRU, and of directing the MPLA's military operations. The statement claimed that there had been a steady flow of Soviet and East European advisers into Angola and what were described as "MPLA bases in Congo-Brazzaville". It said that Mr Uvarev had previously been involved in directing clandestine military operations on behalf of the Soviet Union in the Yemen where:

> As recently in Angola the Russians provided the faction they backed with tanks, aircraft, heavy artillery, rockets, assault rifles and other modern weapons ... Uvarev's standard operating procedure as practised in Yemen is more clearly in evidence in Angola, and with much the same result. Uvarev is believed to be an expert on colonial warfare ... he directs MPLA military operations from his suite at the Hotel Tivoli, Luanda.[9]

This UNITA statement also alleged that other Soviet-bloc agents in Angola included an East German, Mr Werner Voight, and Czech and Romanian intelligence officers.

Early in December it was said that 13 Soviet ships carrying military supplies had been unloaded in Luanda harbour in the course of a single week and that MPLA ammunition supplies were now sufficient to sustain the use of barrages involving the firing of 1 000 rockets or shells an hour. In order to check the UNITA advance towards the capital, MPLA gunners and rocket crews were reported to be selecting important targets and then saturating them with an extremely heavy weight of concentrated fire. These tactics had the effect of considerably slowing UNITA's progress. The accuracy of such firing convincing observers that it came from weapons fired for the most part by Cuban or Soviet personnel rather than members of the MPLA itself. 122 mm rockets were now being fired not only in salvoes of 10 from jeep-mounted projectors but also in salvoes of 24 from Soviet-made lorries.

By now the alarm first voiced in Western circles some weeks earlier regarding the escalating Soviet involvement in Angola was becoming noticeably greater. However, despite increasing expressions of concern by Western statesmen (three by Dr Kissinger in one week at the end of November), there was no sign whatever of any change of heart or intention by the Soviet Union. An article in *Pravda* on 20 December set the tone of much Soviet news media comment that time. The article opened by stating:

> The wind of positive change is now sweeping the African continent with increasing vigour. The hour of the complete eradication of colonial oppression and racism is approaching. The last racist strongholds—Rhodesia and the Republic of South Africa are making efforts to hold out against the strengthening national liberation movements and to preserve their rule. Supported by their Western patrons, they stop neither at economic blackmail of independent African states nor at open armed interference in the affairs of neighbouring sovereign countries.
>
> This can be seen clearly in the events now taking place in the young independent African state, the People's Republic of Angola. Regular South African military

units and units of white mercenaries, flouting the will of peoples, are staging an open aggression in Angola. A front of the forces of reaction, racialism and the most reactionary circles of imperialism has been created to stifle the young republic; to impose there by force of arms a régime alien to the Angolan people.

Fearing the anger of the peoples, the forces of world reaction no longer dare to stage an open armed interference in the affairs of African states in the way they used to in former colonial times. They are, therefore, using their neocolonialist agents and the armed intervention is under the flag of the splitters movements.

The author of this article said in conclusion:

The Soviet public, together with all peaceful and progressive forces of the world, expresses confidence that neocolonialists, racialists and their supporters will inevitably be defeated in Angola and that the Angolan people who have firmly taken the road of free and independent development will win.[10]

A Western journalist who visited a camp in which members of the MPLA's armed wing, FAPLA, were undergoing training, said that instruction was under the control of Cubans and that it included both political and military training, at least four hours a day being devoted to political instruction. Recruits under training at this camp included both male and female members of the Young Pioneers.

In the far north, MPLA units had, meanwhile, been having little difficulty in defeating the efforts of the small and ill-organised Front for the Liberation of the Enclave of Cabinda (FLEC) to establish a separate Cabindan state and were well on their way to establishing control of the territory.

The increasing success of the MPLA now led Admiral Hugo Bierman, Chief of Staff of the South African Defence Force, to forecast that its forces would prove invincible unless the FNLA and UNITA received large-scale supplies of arms from the West very quickly. At the same time, Mr Vorster, in an important speech, said that the "blatant" Soviet Cuban intervention was part of a strategic plan to create a string of Marxist states right across the southern tip of Africa, from Angola to Dar es Salaam". He said that the fulfilment of this plan would have serious consequences not only for South Africa but also for Zambia, Zaire and in addition, the whole of the Western world. If the Soviet Union could establish a permanent presence in Angola as well as Moçambique, it would be astride the sea route round the Cape.

These grave statements by leading South African personalities were followed by a warning from Dr Kissinger to the foreign ministers of the NATO countries, meeting in Brussels, that developments in Angola could upset the balance of power between East and West. Yet despite these warnings, the only effective counter-measure now open to the West, namely the large-scale supply of arms to UNITA and FNLA, remained blocked because of the refusal of the US Congress to grasp the realities of the situation and the paranoic fear of involvement in "foreign adventures" which had gripped America since the end of the war in Vietnam.

In contrast to the almost total Western inaction, the flow of Cuban reinforcements and Soviet war material continued. Shortly before the end of 1975 it was revealed that aircraft flying Cuban reinforcements to Angola had refuelled in the Azores. A local newspaper, *A Uniao,* claimed that a number of Soviet jet transport aircraft bound for Guinea-Bissau had been landing at the international airport of Santa Maria in conditions of some secrecy with no obvious indication of passengers or cargo. The newspaper, however, alleged that there was good reason to believe that the aircraft were, in fact, transporting Cuban troops bound for Angola. At the same time, a spokesman of the Government of Guyana announced that his government had been approached by representatives of the MPLA with a request that aircraft carrying Cuban reinforcements to Angola should be allowed to refuel in Georgetown. This request was made after both Barbados and Trinidad had refused to provide further refuelling activities. Just previously, the Government of Barbados had sent a strong protest to the Cuban Government after discovering that aircraft from Havana refuelling on the island were carrying Cuban troops dressed in civilian clothes on their way to join the Cuban Expeditionary Force with the MPLA.

US intelligence sources believed that some 5 000 Cuban troops had passed through Barbados before the Government closed the route.

264

Within the first week of the New Year of 1976, the MPLA appeared to be advancing on all fronts. Dr Jonas Savimbi, leader of UNITA, claimed on 5 January that a new MPLA offensive which had just begun was being spearheaded by at least 50 T-54 tanks. He said that more tanks had been in action against FNLA forces on the northern front and said that UNITA would run out of military supplies within two months unless logistics were forthcoming from the USA.

At a press conference held by UNITA in the town of Silva Porto, several Cuban soldiers captured by UNITA forces in recent fighting were produced. One of them, a 17-year old infantryman, related how he had been flown to Angola the previous August in an aircraft with 32 others. Another prisoner, who was asked if he would like to send a message to his family, replied:

> I would like to tell them I am all right and for all Cubans to keep their hands off Angola. I don't really know what is going on in Angola.[11]

A new element now appeared in the situation with the appearance of a Soviet guided missile destroyer steaming down the West African coast north of Angola. A Soviet tank landing ship was known to have been stationed at a spot about 500 km from the northern coast of Angola for some time, and this new indication of possible Soviet naval involvement in the area was, according to a White House spokesman, viewed by President Ford "with dismay". Although both ships subsequently moved away from the Angolan coast, a front page leading article in *Izvestia* early in January showed that, despite the repeated Western protests, there was to be no change in the Soviet attitude towards the Angolan situation.

The article, in fact, maintained that Soviet and Cuban intervention in Angola was actually aiding the development of détente, saying:

> Imperialist intervention ... in the People's Republic of Angola has been accompanied by noisy propaganda about a Soviet threat and contradictions between support rendered to the Government of the Republic and the Popular Movement and the policy of détente and lessening tension.

As far as détente is concerned, is it not true that the struggle against racism and apartheid and protection and respect for the sovereignty of the young independent countries is in reality an investment in détente?[12]

Two days later, the message was pushed home even further, and more bluntly, by the political editor of *Pravda* who wrote that:

The policy of peaceful co-existence, of relaxation of tension in relations between states with different social systems cannot be interpreted as prohibiting the peoples' national liberation struggle against colonialist oppression or the class war.[13]

Before January was out, the continued use of the Azores by aircraft carrying Cuban troops to Angola was the subject of a sharp protest to the authorities in Havana by the Portuguese Government which had lodged a previous protest. It was becoming increasingly embarrassed by the frequency with which refuelling stops were being made there by such aircraft.

Speaking to Western journalists in the southern regional town of Quibala, a commander of the advancing MPLA forces said:

The Cubans? They fight. Of course. Why not? They fight as infantry, with artillery, or on sentry duty. Whatever they are asked to do, they do it.[14]

The correspondent who reported this conversation said that although Cuban soldiers were in considerable evidence in the area they were noticeably wary of being photographed. Instructions to avoid photographers were apparently given to them before leaving Havana. Pentagon sources estimated in late January that about 10% of the Cuban army's total strength had now been committed to the operation in Angola. The same sources said that Soviet transport aircraft had been bringing fresh Cuban troops into the country at the rate of about 200 a day for over a fortnight and that the strength of the Cuban expeditionary force now stood at considerably over 10 500 men.

In addition, other Western intelligence sources, said to be "entirely unconnected" with the MPLA's opponents, revealed to a correspondent in Lusaka a formidable inventory of Soviet weapons believed to have been brought into Angola for the use of the MPLA and its Cuban allies.

These weapons included more than 100 122 mm rocket projector lorries, or "Stalin Organs" as they are sometimes known, each capable of firing salvoes of 40 rockets at one time, 12 000 single barrelled 122 mm rocket projectors, about 30 000 rifles, over 400 60 mm mortars, nearly 3 000 heavy machine-guns, about 1 400 grenade and anti-tank grenade launchers, a large number of 82 mm and 76 mm recoilless rifles, approximately 1 000 82 mm mortars and large quantities of anti-tank and anti-personnel mines.

Heavy weapons and equipment on the list included more than 500 lorries, some 160 armoured personnel carriers, about 300 anti-aircraft guns mounted on armoured vehicles, T-34 (see cover picture) and T-55 tanks, armoured cars and scout cars and five landing craft. Other equipment provided included field radio sets and uniforms.

This massive catalogue had hardly appeared in the Western press before, in late January, an official MPLA military spokesman admitted that the movement had used Soviet tanks to turn the tide of battle on both the Northern and Southern fronts. This was the first official admission by the MPLA of the use of heavy Soviet equipment during the course of the campaign—previously such allegations had always been firmly denied.

This MPLA admission of the use of Soviet armour was almost immediately followed by an announcement from the movement that the Soviet Union had been supplying MIG fighters, which it was intended would form the nucleus of an airforce that would be able to match that of South Africa "and other aggressors". Radio Luanda announced proudly that a MIG had broken the sound barrier over Luanda for the first time. Western intelligence sources believed that the landing of dismantled MIGs had begun in December and that they had been hidden at a storage depot not far from the military airfield at Luanda. It was thought that about 20 aircraft had been landed and had been or were now being assembled. The Luanda newspaper *Journal do Angola* appeared with a photograph of three MIGs flying over the military airfield and with others beneath parked on the tarmac.

UNITA forces were now falling back towards Huambo, the administrative headquarters of the areas of the country still under their control, and Silva Porto, headquarters of the UNITA command. Huambo rapidly became the MPLA's prime objective.

Whilst tank-led Cuban forces advanced on the town, a stream of instruction to MPLA supporters inside it were issued over Luanda Radio. Such elements were told: "We are almost there, intensify your guerrilla activity." Others were of a coded variety such as: "The ravens are in the boabab trees as 2.30 every day." Huambo, Angola's second largest city, had 18 000 White citizens before the civil war broke out but only 300 of these were left by November 1975 and almost all commercial life had ceased in the city.

As the MPLA southward advance continued and Huambo was abandoned by UNITA forces, the refugee problem became even more acute. South African forces had already set up refugee camps at two towns a few kilometres inside Angola but fears grew of a panic stricken flood of refugees pouring over the border into South West Africa.

On the northern front, the MPLA successes against Cabindan separatists continued and MPLA units began to direct their advance to the important oil town of Santo Antonio do Zaire.

By early February even Western observers were forecasting that a total MPLA victory throughout Angola could not be long delayed, short of a total change of attitude on the part of the Western powers. Presumably encouraged by the extremely promising situation, the Soviet President, Mr Brezhnev, sent a message to an "extraordinary international solidarity conference meeting" then being held in Luanda. The British newspaper *The Morning Star,* described the message as reaffirming:

> The Soviet Union's solidarity with the MPLA in Angola and all fighters for the African people's independence.

The message welcomed:

> The birth of a new Angola, whose people have gained independence after a courageous and long struggle under the leadership of their vanguard, the MPLA.[15]

At the same time, *Pravda* sharply attacked President Ford for "distorting the Angolan situation" and Soviet and Cuban policy in an attempt to justify American support for "rebels" against the "legitimate government".

Headlines in the Soviet press in the first week of February

proclaimed the holding of a "day of solidarity with the people of Angola". Marshal Grechko, then Soviet Defence Minister, also sent a public message to the MPLA leaders hailing the "people's armed forces of liberation for having conducted a courageous struggle against foreign aggression and internal reaction".[16]

Hard on the heels of the publication of this message came an admission from Mr William Schaufele, United States Assistant Secretary of State for Africa, speaking before the African Affairs Sub-Committee of the Senate, that the level of Soviet and Cuban aid received by the MPLA was so great that its forces would "have to prevail".

In Angola itself, the MPLA was losing no time in consolidating its rapidly developing victory through stepping up its programme of political indoctrination. The main instrument it used for this purpose was its Department for the Organisation of the Masses (DOM). One of the main areas of its activity, at that time, was the slum areas of Luanda, the museques, where much support for the MPLA had first originated. DOM organised almost daily political meetings in such locations. One DOM official explained:

We are moving from a colonial to an anti-colonial phase. We must transform the structure of our society, and the minds of our people through political instruction.[17]

Huambo had fallen to MPLA forces by the middle of January. The American State Department blamed the collapse of the defence of UNITA's capital directly upon the failure of Congress to allow the despatch of sufficient arms to the non-Communist forces in Angola.

By now, reliable reports indicated that by far the greater part of the fighting was being done by units of the Cuban Expeditionary Force, with members of the MPLA accompanying them as little more than guides. A great part of the MPLA forces themselves were said to be pinned down trying to police the vast areas the Cuban forces had overrun during the previous few weeks. Estimates by Western intelligence services now put the total number of Cubans in Angola as high as 12 000.

On 19 February, UNITA's leaders recognised the fast approaching end of their capacity to offer any further tangible kind of conventional defence. They then set about attempting to lay plans for a three-year guerrilla campaign, which it was hoped would make the MPLA and Cuban position untenable. In the north, resistance by FNLA forces collapsed entirely and the FNLA leader, Dr Holden Roberto, was said to have accepted defeat and to have left his headquarters in Kinshasa for Tunis, where he and his family intended to take up residence. The strong scent of an approaching MPLA victory now spread rapidly to other African states, resulting in a sudden upward surge in the number of countries recognising the MPLA régime diplomatically. An event which, not unnaturally, brought delighted comments from its Soviet backers:

> The success of the courageous Angolan people and their militant vanguard the MPLA, has resulted in the growth of the prestige of the People's Republic of Angola on the international arena. Within one day, 18 February, the PRA (People's Government of Angola) was recognised by 12 more states, among them a number of Western countries. Thus, the Government of the PRA is now already recognised by 74 countries, among them 40 member-countries of the OAU.[18]

The announcer then turned his attention to some of the critics of the events which he had extolled, describing them as:

> Apologists of colonialism who are seeking at any cost to keep their hold on the African continent, regarding it as a strategic *place d'armes* and a source of rich natural resources. Among them, British M.P., Conservative Winston Churchill, the grandson of the famous Winston Churchill, who directly participated in the expansion of Britain's colonial possessions in Africa, is unwilling to forget the past. In an article published by the *Daily Telegraph* today, he pours invective in impotent fury on everyone, on socialist countries for their disinterested assistance to the PRA, which he describes as 'intervention', and on Western countries, particularly on the United States, for insufficient interference in the affairs of the young Republic.
> Right-wing organs of the French press, *Le Figaro* and *L'Aurore,* write in the same vein as the British Conservative. They, too, try to slander the policy of the USSR in Africa and urge the Western powers to toughen their

stand. *Le Figaro* laments Pretoria's military superiority being threatened.

But no matter how bellicose apologists of colonialism exert themselves, the game is up. The overwhelming majority of African states have recognised the Government of the PRA as the only true representative of the interests of the Angolan people. And Western countries, even those that recently **gave** backing to the splitters in Angola, have to take this into consideration.[19]

Early in March the last South African troops (preceeded by the last pitiful wave of refugees) withdrew over the border into South West Africa. As the jubilant MPLA forces moved close up to the border, they bore with them not only their leader, Dr Aghostino Neto, but also an omen of continuing probable strife in Southern Africa.

Two weeks later, President Neto was in Conakry conferring with the Cuban leader, Dr Fidel Castro, in the company of President Sekou Toure of Guinea.

Whilst much concerning the ultimate effects of the Communist victory in Angola remained obscure, there could be no doubt of the aptness of the words of one returning British journalist, Mr Max Hastings, as to the effects in the immediate future:

In any internal power struggle in Africa, the personal risks for those involved of execution or exile have always been high. So when entering such a struggle, everybody likes to be sure that their side has at least a remote chance of winning. The message of Angola is that it pays to be on the side the Russians are on. They win. Whatever amiable mutterings the American Ambassador whispers into receptive ears, when he comes to the crunch he cannot deliver the cash, votes, or guns from Washington to back them.[20]

The fact that the present government is a minority régime, does not worry Moscow. The Soviets are not interested in mathematical percentages of votes or popularity by the people of a country but in *power*—and power is what they have actually attained in Angola.

271

Postscript

Early in 1977, additional information regarding the Angolan campaign became available from both Cuban and South African sources. That concerning the participation of Cuban forces appeared in the shape of an 8 000-word article in the Mexican magazine *Processo*. The author was Señor Garcia-Marquez, a known unofficial spokesman of the Cuban Government who is believed to keep in constant touch with Fidel Castro himself. Large extracts from the articles were subsequently relayed by the Cuban News Agency, *Prensa Latina*.

Señor Garcia-Marquez wrote that the Cuban plan for military intervention had been given the name "Operation Carbora", after a negro woman slave who had headed a revolt in Cuba in 1848. It was stated that the first Cuban contingent of 600 men had reached Angola by air by way of Barbados, Guinea-Bissau and the Congo. This force had orders to hold out until the arrival of reinforcements brought by sea transport. It was said that these first reinforcements duly arrived in the form of a Cuban artillery regiment and a battalion of motorised infantry who were landed on the Angolan Coast from two cargo ships at the end of November 1975. It is probable, however, that the actual date of their arrival was somewhat earlier, as there is every indication that in Havana accounts of the campaign and the dates of the start of Cuban involvement have consistently been brought forward in order to square with the official government story that it only took place to counter "imperialist" interference in Angolan affairs.

According to the article, the large concentration of Cuban ships bringing further reinforcements and supplies to Luanda harbour caused the MPLA leader, Dr Neto, to remark: "It's not fair, the Cubans will ruin themselves." Changes had to be made in the route of the airlift bringing similar aid after American pressure had resulted in the Government of Barbados refusing refuelling facilities. The new route involved flights by way of the Cape Verde Islands. Altogether up to 100 flights carrying troops or supplies were made from Cuba up to the end of the military operations.

A considerable cloak of secrecy was thrown over the despatch of volunteers from the Cuban Army to serve in Angola. Foreign journalists were not told of the operation at all for over two months. Families who saw the men off were instructed to keep the matter to themselves. In some cases relatives were not even told that the men were in Angola, their activities being put down to participation in manouevres.

It appears that the Cuban leader, Dr Castro, kept in constant touch with the progress of the operation, which ultimately came to involve a force of just over 15 000 men. Whenever the situation seemed critical, he is said to have taken charge himself; sometimes working for 14 hours a day in army headquarters in Havana in order to ensure the success of the venture.

The article also confirmed that the first contingents of Cuban troops sent to Angola by air had travelled in civilian clothes with civilian passports with machine-pistols concealed in their brief-cases. Light artillery ammunition, mortars and other equipment were carried in the baggage compartment of the aircraft concerned.

An official South African Government statement on that country's involvement in the Angolan fighting, released shortly after the appearance of the above article, said that the principal South African objective had been to assist the UNITA and FNLA forces to re-establish themselves in the area in which they had most popular support. The plan was to enable these forces to secure control of the whole of southern Angola and the important ports of Benguela and Lobito.

Active South African involvement began early in October when a small number of instructors and advisers, bringing with them a few machine-guns and anti-tank weapons, joined the UNITA forces defending Nova Lisboa. The MPLA attack was halted and the clearing of MPLA forces from southern Angola thereafter proceeded apace.

The South African part in these operations continued to be limited to instructors and advisers, plus a few armoured cars and mortar detachments. On 5 November, however, a flying column of UNITA/FNLA troops, whose command was assisted by a senior South African officer and which, with the support of a small number of South African specialists and by dint of using commandeered civilian vehicles as transport, made remarkably swift progress in the northwards advance. It then ran into stiff Cuban/MPLA resistance around the port of Benguela. It was here that the first wounded Cubans were captured. After being pinned down by heavy mortar and rocket fire for 24 hours, this column which had been given the code name "Zulu", finally succeeded in clearing this important coastal city and port. The weight of enemy fire encoun-

273

tered, however, led the senior UNITA/FNLA commanders to ask that South African artillery support be provided in future to counter the effects of the Cuban operated 122 mm rocket launchers which far outranged "Zulu's" own mortars. Accordingly, some South African artillery detachments with 120 mm and later 140 mm guns were brought into action.

A force of much the same composition as "Zulu", known as "Foxbat", also operated with effect in central Angola, and it was this force that became involved in the battle at "Bridge 14" in the Catofe area on 9 December 1975. This action, which lasted for three days, as mentioned previously, constituted the biggest clash directly involving South African and Cuban forces which occurred during the campaign. The South African units involved consisted of an infantry company, an armoured car squadron, a mortar platoon and artillery and engineer support. Also involved were three UNITA/FNLA infantry companies. The rôle of this "Foxbat" force was to deny access to the main UNITA/FNLA held area to an advancing MPLA/Cuban force which consisted of a Cuban infantry battalion and a "mixed" supporting battalion equipped with 122 mm rocket launchers. Further fire support was given by artillery and mortars.

"Foxbat" succeeded in stemming the enemy advance and it was claimed in the process killed 200 Cubans and about the same number of members of the MPLA. In addition, 10 76 mm guns, 22 122 mm mortars and five 122 mm rocket launchers were destroyed or captured. Four South Africans were said to have been killed during the engagement.

This official statement put the total strength of the South African force involved in the campaign at just under 2 000 men. The statement said that:

The Allied FNLA/UNITA forces supported by South African forces could have conquered the whole of Angola, but Dr Savimbi insisted that he was only interested in controlling his traditional area because he was determined to reach a settlement with the MPLA to the advantage of Angola.

274

Further testimony that the Cuban involvement in Angola began considerably before official Cuban statements would indicate, was provided in a study by Mr. Colin Legum and Mr. Tony Hodges, *After Angola, The War Over Southern Africa*, published late in 1976.[21] In this, Mr. Legum records that according to FNLA sources, 50 Cubans arrived in Brazzaville on 25 July 1975 to assist in handling Soviet arms deliveries and that Cubans had actually been observed to be taking part in the fighting by UNITA commanders by the middle of August.

He concluded that "there is little doubt" that Cubans were first brought into Brazzaville before July that year and that Cuban combat troops were thereafter drafted in batches into Angola. In view of the ultimate size of the Cuban operation, he believed that planning and logistic preparation for it were likely to have begun at least as early as May 1975.

REFERENCES

1. *Angola After Independence.* Institute for the Study of Conflict, Conflict Studies No. 64, London, 1975, p. 14.
2. *The Times,* 14 July 1975.
3. *The Times,* 22 August 1975.
4. *The Morning Star,* 26 September 1975.
5. *The Times,* 7 May 1976.
6. *The Guardian,* 18 November 1975.
7. The *Daily Telegraph,* 24 September 1975.
8. *Los Angeles Times,* 26 November 1976.
9. *The Guardian,* 30 November 1975.
10. *Pravda,* 20 December 1975.
11. *The Times,* 8 January 1976.
12. *Isvestia,* 8 January 1976.
13. *Pravda,* 10 January 1976.
14. The *Daily Telegraph,* 21 January 1976.
15. *The Morning Star,* 3 February 1976.
16. *The Guardian,* 5 February 1976.
17. *The Guardian,* 6 February 1976.
18. *Moscow Radio,* 19 February 1976.
19. *Ibid.*
20. *Evening Standard,* 10 February 1976.
21. *After Angola, The War Over Southern Africa,* Colin Legum and Tony Hodges, Rex Collins, London, 1976.

Chapter 9

Some Western Voices of "Liberation"

At the end of June 1973 a meeting was held in London organised by the overseas departments of Frelimo and the African National Congress of South Africa. The principal speakers were Mr Oliver Tambo, President of the ANC, and Mr Marcelino dos Santos, Vice-President of Frelimo. The theme of the meeting was the mobilisation of support for the "liberation" of Southern Africa.

A correspondent of *The Guardian* who was present said that both Mr Tambo and Mr dos Santos were almost obsessed with the Vietnam parallel and quoted Mr Tambo as saying: "The support of the word radical progressive movement must continue from Vietnam to us." He was also said to have declared:

> Although there is a general disposition of world opinion against the rôle of NATO in Southern Africa, we have not yet sufficiently gone below the level of governments and started to mobilise the people of the NATO countries on our behalf. We must make determined efforts to dictate policies to NATO countries and this means making the people understand NATO's rôle in supporting colonialism and racism in Southern Africa. Britain must be faced with the real alternatives, and it might be pointed out that she stands to lose more by

supporting the white régimes. Our cause is just, we want our independence, and our freedom and history must be on our side. But the Third World does have some weapons, look at America's need for Arab oil and the question of supporting Israel. But more than that, the kind of opposition against Vietnam which was organised in the US can be organised against South Africa in Britain. That is why we are here ... We must be active everywhere, keep the fire burning everywhere.[1]

Mention has already been made of the degree to which the leaders of the various "liberation movements" of Africa have relied upon isolating their opponents in the eyes of world opinion. This policy is designed to cut them off from popular support, a task in which they rely heavily upon assistance from a wide range of radical forces in Western countries as well as their own efforts. The object of this chapter is to examine briefly the past and present activities of some of these forces.

The forces upon which the "liberation movements" of Southern Africa chiefly rely in Western countries for propaganda, and sometimes certain other kinds of support, can basically be divided into three main groups. Firstly, the overseas offices of the various movements themselves. These can be found in many Western capitals, as well as in the Third World. Secondly, Communist Parties and other extreme left-wing revolutionary groups. Thirdly, an assortment of radical movements, ranging from those which share many of the general aims of the former to at least some degree, including some religious bodies most of whose members certainly do not desire a Marxist triumph in Africa, but whose dislike of the present White governments is so intense that they are prepared to support even the most extreme of their opponents almost regardless of the ultimate consequences.

It is proposed to consider each group in sequence.

The Liberation Movements' Overseas Offices

All the major movements concerned have realised the importance of establishing offices of their own in countries outside Africa to make their cause known, and, in several cases, have devoted considerable resources to that end.

The former leader of Frelimo, Dr Eduardo Mondlane, stated that even before active operations began in Moçambique the movement opened offices in Cairo, Algiers and Dar es Salaam, while arrangements were first made for student members of Frelimo to make the work of the movement known in countries farther afield. Other members were sent on missions to make contacts in the Soviet Union, in Asian countries, in Western Europe and also in the United States.[2]

In the case of the South African National Congress, a number of leading members were sent abroad to rally international support as early as 1960. These included figures such as Mr Oliver Tambo, who later became the leader of what was as first known as the movement's "Political Mission" and subsequently "External Mission". The External Mission set up a number of offices in different countries presided over by "Chief Representatives". The work of these offices was co-ordinated from Morogoro in Tanzania, where the headquarters of the External Mission were located.

African "liberation movements" with offices in London include the African National Congress of South Africa. That movement produces a 64-page quarterly journal in English, *Sechaba*, which is actually printed in East Germany.

The Zimbabwe African National Union (ZANU), has as its representative organisation in Britain is the Zimbabwe Solidarity Committee. This Committee publishes a bulletin, *Free Zimbabwe*. Another publication is *The Zimbabwe Review*, described as the "international organ of the Rhodesian ANC". It is printed in East Germany, with a "circulation department" located in East Berlin. Local offices exist in London, Lusaka, Cairo and Algeria.

The South West African People's Organisation (SWAPO), which now operates through the Namibia Support Committee, was set up in the autumn of 1975 to take charge of a new propaganda drive SWAPO was mounting in Britain directed at certain sections of public opinion, such as trade unionists, the Labour Party and students.

In addition, a considerable number of members of the South African Communist Party have taken up residence in Britain and the party's quarterly journal, *The African Communist*, is now published in London, although printed in East Germany. The story of that magazine is not without some interest, for, although at first its circulation was confined almost entirely to Britain and South Africa, a change of policy came about quite early in its existence. This was signified by a note which it began to contain after its first few editions stating that it was

> published quarterly in the interests of African solidarity and as a forum for Marxist-Leninist thought throughout our continent, by the South African Communist Party.

It would appear that its rôle is not merely that of a theoretical journal or a channel of contact between Western and African Communist sympathisers but also that of an active participant in the work of building Communist Parties in Africa. One article in an edition soon after it had been decided to widen the magazine's coverage, urged readers to form groups to "discuss the contents of every issue, and other Marxist-Leninist literature", adding:

> Such study groups can be very important. They should study the conditions in their own country, in the light of Communist theory. They should take part, as loyal members, in the national liberation struggle. They should work for the brotherly unity of all Communists in each country, preparing the way for the eventual formation of a Communist Party to advance the cause of the workers and help in building a united front of national liberation, comprising all parties and classes, and people of all patriotic views. An important task which can and should be undertaken by an African Communist study group is to prepare articles for this journal based upon a study and analysis of conditions in their own country, and the solution proposed for its problems.[3]

Not surprisingly, recent issues of *The African Communist* have followed events in Angola with great interest and its issue of the first quarter of 1976 carried a report of the enthusiastic message of congratulation and support sent by the National Chairman of the South African Communist Party, Dr Yusef Dadoo, to the MPLA leader, Dr Aghostino Neto:

> The Central Committee of the South African Commun-

ist Party greets with unbounded joy Angola's independence under the banner of the MPLA born in the fire of
struggle, first against Portuguese colonialism and now
against imperialism and local reaction. A true people's
Angola is feared by imperialism and especially by its
main bastion on our continent, racist South Africa. This
is why imperialism continues its attempts to destroy your
revolutionary gains. We have the utmost confidence in
your final victory and we pledge full solidarity in the
struggle ahead. Your victory is our victory and the
victory of all Africa.

Death to imperialism and all its henchmen. Long live
People's Angola under the leadership of the MPLA.
Heartiest congratulations and warmest fraternal greet-
ings.[4]

Some other "liberation movements" concerned with areas of
Africa other than the South also have offices or representation in
London and other European capitals, including the Eritrean
Liberation Front (ELF).

The overseas offices and representatives of the "liberation movements" have not infrequently been involved in the organisation of
international conferences concerned with various aspects of the
"liberation struggle". Such conferences are held periodically in a
number of areas, varying from Eastern Europe to Scandinavia and
other parts of West Europe, the United States, or sometimes Africa
itself or other areas of the Third World.

Typical of some conferences of this type were those held in Italy in
March 1973 and in East Germany in the early part of the same year.
The Conference in Italy was held in Reggio Emilia and was entitled
"The First National Solidarity Conference for the Freedom and
Independence of Moçambique, Angola, and Guinea-Bissau". It was
held in collaboration with "Italian Democratic Forces" and one of
the main speakers was the future president of Moçambique, Mr
Samora Machel. In the course of his speech, he said:

This magnificent celebration is taking place in the region
of Emilia Romagna, where at every turn we come across
concrete expressions of hatred for fascism and exploitation, examples of the people's determination to defend

their rights ... Today Emilia Romagna is one of the Italian regions where people's democratic power has been established, thereby defending the gains of the Italian resistance.

Correctly interpreting the interests of the people and keeping alive the deep feelings of the Italian resistance, the people of Emilia Romagna have turned their region into a front of Italian solidarity with the struggles of other peoples. Here in Reggio Emilia there is the Santa Maria Nuova Hospital, which is linked to the Zambesia Hospital by a friendship pact. In the Emilia Romagna too, there is the municipality of Bologna, also linked by a pact of friendship to our Education Centre in Tunduru.[5]

Later in his speech, Mr Machel turned to the importance of mobilising support in Western Europe in aid of the "liberation movements" when fighting Portuguese rule in Africa. He explained:

We believe that a united solidarity movement must be developed, so as to reach the numerous sectors which are not yet involved.

Popularising the solidarity movement means organising and mobilising the various sectors in factories, schools, universities, offices, hospitals, and churches. It means publicising the horrors of colonialism and the nature and success of our struggle.

Mobilising and organising also means defining the tasks of the solidarity movement, mapping out lines of action. There are two main types of tasks today: political tasks and material support.

Politically, our main concern is to isolate Portuguese colonialism from its sources of moral, political, diplomatic, economic and military support; and at the same time to make the international community recognise the political realities of our country, i.e. that the Moçambican people are regaining their sovereignty and exercising it through Frelimo, which leads and represents them.

This twofold concern gives rise to different lines of action; political parties, trade unions and other mass organisations are called upon for action involving vigilance, denunciation and pressure. Vigilance in detecting the activities of government and financial consortiums on behalf of Portuguese colonialism; denunciation of such activities; and pressure to put an end to them and make governmental institutions recognise Moçambican political realities.

Obviously this type of action must be developed at all levels; in the press, in Parliament, in petitions and popular demonstrations.[6]

The conference in East Germany followed a decision made by the Executive Committee of the Afro-Asian People's Solidarity Organisation (AAPSO) at a meeting held in Aden in February 1973. The conference was organised by AAPSO, acting in conjunction with the Africa Solidarity Committee of East Germany. It took place in the industrial city of Eisenhuttenstadt. Delegates from Africa included those of PAIGC from Portuguese-Guinea, ZAPU from Rhodesia and the South African ANC. Other delegates came from North Vietnam, the South Vietnamese "Liberation Front" (Viet Cong), Somalia, Guinea, most of the "socialist" countries, Cyprus, Ceylon, Bangladesh and Zaire.

The theme of the conference was the "forms and methods of the neo-colonialist policy of imperialism" and means of fighting against these.

In October 1975 a seminar was held in Brussels on the subject of "South African Militarism". The seminar was organised by the long-established international Communist front organisation, the World Peace Council. The principal organisations taking part included the ANC of South Africa, the MPLA of Angola, SWAPO, the Rhodesian African National Congress and anti-apartheid and "solidarity" organisations from various West European countries. It was also attended by representatives of the Soviet Peace Committee, the African Solidarity Committee of East Germany and by representatives of a number of "international democratic bodies".

Speakers attacked West German collaboration with South Africa, particularly in the form of the construction of a uranium enrichment plant and nuclear reactor in the latter country. Any idea of increased NATO co-operation with South Africa also came under fire. Mr Sean McBride, United Nations Commissioner for South West Africa, condemned what he described as South Africa's invasion of Angola. He complained that the Namibian (South West African) office at the United Nations, when it had sent a delegation to NATO headquarters to enquire about NATO collaboration in the "invasion", had been "fobbed off" with a blanket denial. He said that collaboration between NATO and South Africa composed a "threat to democratic government". He continued by stating that all democracies must demand more truthful information on this subject.

The seminar went on to express full solidarity with the MPLA and to give a warning against any attempts to "internationalise" the situation in Angola.

Such conferences proved a successful means of mobilising support and co-ordinating worldwide activity against American policy during the years of the Vietnam war and can be expected to occur with increasing frequency as the situation in Southern Africa develops.

Activities by the "liberation movement's" external representatives during late 1975 and early 1976 included those of the prominent MPLA member, Mr Paulo Jorge, who was formerly head of the movement's propaganda department (DOM). He visited Britain as its representative in October 1975. During his stay, he had discussions on the situation then prevailing in Angola with Mr Jack Woddis, head of the International Department of the Communist Party of Great Britain. *The Morning Star* reported Mr Woddis as saying of these talks:

> Our Party has always backed the MPLA as the true and only voice of the Angolan people.
> We fully support the MPLA and the people in their present struggle to defeat foreign imperialist intervention and its puppets, the FNLA and UNITA.[7]

Two members of the External Administration of the Rhodesian African National Congress, Mr Jason Moyo, the Chairman, and Mr George Silundika, were the authors of a short article which appeared in *World Marxist Review* of June 1976. In this article they stated:

> The situation today is more favourable to our people. After all, the Zimbabwe problem is not an isolated one.

It is part of the problem of the south of the continent, of all countries of the area, of all peoples fighting for liberation, whether in Indo-china or the Middle East, part of the common struggle of progressive forces against the forces of reaction. These problems have been solved in Indochina, Moçambique and Angola. As to the south of our continent, a solution has yet to come. However, the victories achieved in Moçambique and Angola mean that the enemy has become more vulnerable ...

We are deeply grateful to the socialist countries, first of all to the Soviet Union and to the CPSU, for their assistance and their policy based on proletarian internationalism. The peoples of South Africa greeted with enthusiasm L.I. Brezhnev's statement at the 25th CPSU Congress. The African National Council, for its part, does its best to contribute to the solidarity of fighters against imperialism. In days that were crucial for Angola, we shared with the MPLA the little we have.

Communist Parties and Revolutionary Groups

Support by Western Communist Parties for "anti-imperialist" uprisings in the former colonial areas dates right back to the period immediately succeeding the Baku Conference of 1920, when the victorious Bolshevik leaders first conferred with the leaders of Asian revolutionary and nationalist movements.

The importance of supporting "anti-imperialist" activities in the colonies was drummed home in somewhat dramatic language by Mr Palmiro Togliatti, a prominent Italian Communist who subsequently became leader of the Italian Communist Party. Speaking at the Sixth World Congress of the Communist International in 1928, he declared that a Communist Party, which did not

> systematically and practically support the revolutionary activity in the colonies, is not a revolutionary party but a party of idlers and traitors.[8]

Since the end of the Second World War, the Communist Parties of the West have given vigorous support to a succession of anti-colonial and "liberation movements" which have engaged in "armed struggle" for the purpose of removing direct or indirect Western influence from various areas of the Third World, not a few of which have operated in Africa.

The French Communist Party campaigned strongly against the prosecution of the war in Algeria, despite the fact that for a number of years it had been in favour of Algerian integration with France. The party still maintains close links with various parties and groups in the former French colonies in Africa. Its leading expert on African affairs, M Raymond Gyont, said that whilst decolonisation was still far from complete, it was extremely important for the party to establish contact, "especially personal contact", with the people of Africa. He added that it was the party's duty to help the Marxist groups springing up in Africa with their educational work and, when conditions seemed ripe, to help them form Communist Parties.

Members of the Belgian Communist Party were active in the Congo prior to that country's independence and, according to one report, the party acted as an intermediary between the Soviet Embassy in Brussels and Mr Patrice Lumumba when the latter was in the Belgian capital for independence celebrations. It was alleged that it was largely through its efforts at that time, that Mr Lumumba and several of his future ministers formed an affiliation with the Soviet Union.

Despite the fact that it was operating under conditions of illegality throughout the entire period, the Portuguese Communist Party carried on a continuous campaign in support of the "liberation movements" in Portuguese Africa. That campaign was not limited entirely to propaganda activities but, according to one of its leading officials, in the early 1960s also included

> organising resistance, collective desertions and mutinies in the army against the war in Angola and Guinea, and giving every possible assistance to the liberation movement in the Portuguese colonies.[9]

The British Communist Party has consistently given much propaganda support to "liberation movements" in Africa and has formed particularly firm links with the South African Communist Party. It would seem that it has also sometimes assisted African students to travel from London to Moscow for the completion of their studies. The part played by Western Communist Parties in educating African students, who come to their respective countries with Marxist theories, was praised by Professor Potekhin as long ago as 1960:

> The Communist Parties of the metropolitan territories, especially those of Britain and France, have made a valuable contribution to the cause of spreading Leninist ideas in Africa. Many thousands of Africans coming to the metropolitan territories learn many new things about the Communist movement, read Marxist literature and return home enriched with progressive ideas.[10]

One method British and other Communists have much used to pursue their policy of support for "liberation movements" and "anti-imperialism" is activity in various "progressive" organisations which have been formed by radical, but non-Communist, elements to voice opposition to White rule and sometimes other forms of government in Africa or elsewhere. The Annual Report of the British Anti-Apartheid Movement for 1974-1975, for instance, recorded that in addition to support from some sections of the Labour and Liberal parties

> the movement has received the support and participation of the Communist Party and the Young Communist League in all its various campaigns. They were particularly active in the campaign to end military collaboration with apartheid in South Africa.

The party has also given considerable aid in publicising the movement's activities, as evidenced by another paragraph in the same report which stated:

> Of the national daily and weekly newspapers covering South African issues in depth, special mention must be made of *The Morning Star,* which also unfailingly reported AAM activities.

British Communists have also been active in support of the activities of the movement now known as "Liberation" and formerly as the Movement for Colonial Freedom. Members of this movement have included the Communist Party's present international secretary, Mr Jack Woddis, and its meetings and rallies are often covered in considerable detail in *The Morning Star*. A considerable part of the movement's activities has been directed towards African affairs.

During the fighting in Angola between the MPLA and the two other nationalist "liberation movements" during 1975 and 1976, the British Communist Party called continuously for all-out support for the MPLA. Typical of this call was an editorial in *The Morning Star* of 22 December 1975 which read:

> It should be clearly understood that there are not three liberation movements in Angola; only one—the MPLA.
>
> The MPLA has led the struggle for national liberation against Portuguese colonialism for years, and now with Portugal's withdrawal, it has established the People's Republic of Angola.
>
> UNITA and the FNLA are puppet bodies backed by South Africa, and through Zaire, by the US.
>
> The so-called Democratic Republic set up by UNITA and FNLA is a fake and has not been recognised by any African state.
>
> The British Government should immediately recognise the People's Republic as the sole legitimate representative of the Angolan people.
>
> That would help to spike the guns of those in the United States and elsewhere who are trying to whip up hysteria over a phoney Soviet threat in Southern Africa in an effort to reverse the US Senate's decision.

The Senate's decision referred to was that of not to supply arms to UNITA or FNLA.

Writing in the same newspaper on 11 March 1976, Mr Jack Woddis, in an article entitled "Angola's body-blow to imperialism", hailed the MPLA's victory. He urged that it should be used as the starting point for an all-out drive to complete the elimination of White rule from Southern Africa. He maintained that:

> It is urgently necessary that the British Government be compelled by the weight of public opinion to end all support, direct or indirect, to Smith and Vorster.

The situation in Rhodesia is very critical. While guerrilla warfare is increasing, British Government ministers are failing to act decisively against Smith and his government and in support of the African majority and their liberation struggle.

The Government should intensify economic sanctions against the régime. It should call on the United Nations to introduce mandatory sanctions against the South African Government for its refusal to implement the UN sanctions against Rhodesia.

Smith and his repressive settler régime could not carry on without support from the Vorster Government. Vorster must be told in no uncertain terms "fall in line with the UN and impose sanctions on Rhodesia—or face the consequences of sanctions against yourself".

An early end to white minority domination in Rhodesia and Namibia are the immediate and most urgent problems. Victory for the liberation movements in these two territories is vital.

It would leave South Africa as the last outpost of racism and apartheid in Southern Africa, with the tide of liberation lapping its northern frontiers.

In conclusion, the head of the British Communist Party's International Department likened "imperialism" to a wounded beast, dangerous because of its fears of political changes in Europe and "the knowledge that serious threats are now nearing some of its main citadels of power and wealth—both in Western Europe and in Southern Africa". Mr Woddis demanded that

the British Labour and progressive movement throw its weight decisively on the side of national liberation, democracy, peace and socialism.

The close alliance between the British and South African Communist Parties was once again emphasised in September 1976 when Dr Yasuf Dadoo, Chairman of the latter, addressed the Executive of the British Communist Party. He said that South African Communists and members of the "liberation movement" would never forget the part played over the years by their British

288

comrades in developing forms of solidarity action of different kinds.

In the same month the British Communist Party's Executive issued an appeal to the "labour and democratic movement" claiming that in Southern Africa "the resistance of the oppressed majority is rising to unprecedented heights", and continued:

> In this moment of grave crisis it is urgent that the British labour and democratic movement exert the utmost pressure to compel the British Government to end its shameful collaboration with the hated racist régimes in Southern Africa.[11]

The appeal went on to demand the end of all British investment in South Africa, all loans by British banks and a complete ban on the export of capital goods, the end of all "direct" and "indirect" military aid to the White ruled countries of Southern Africa, including a ban on the recruitment of mercenaries, and support by the British Government for an introduction of international moves aimed at the enforcement of sanctions against South Africa.

It was further suggested that:

> Financial support for the national liberation movements in Southern Africa should be organised in Britain by the labour and progressive movements.
>
> Industrial action, too, against military and economic backing from Britain for the racist régimes would be a significant act of solidarity for the national liberation movements.
>
> The big monopolies and international firms which are the basis of the racist régimes, are the main enemies of the British working people.
>
> In aiding the national liberation movements in Southern Africa, the British people are helping their own struggle for social liberation and democratic advance.
>
> We pledge to increase still further our party's activity in support of the struggle in Southern Africa so as to hasten the day of liberation from all forms of racism, discrimination and repression.[11]

.   It is of some considerable interest that within two days of this appeal being published the International Committee of the Labour Party had passed a resolution asking the British Government to "disengage from Britain's unhealthy involvement with apartheid". The resolution declared:

> British capitalism has played, and continues to play, a vital rôle in maintaining and profiting from the apartheid régime. We believe that a special responsibility lies upon the British labour movement to help end exploitation in South Africa.[12]

It then proceeded to demand a number of steps to be taken by the British Government aimed at ending British investment in, and aid to, Southern Africa of a type almost identical to those demanded in the Communist Party appeal, and including a call for British aid to "African liberation movements".

Across the Atlantic, the Communist Party of the United States and other extreme left groups also stepped up their championship of the MPLA as 1976 began. Here again the central message was that the coming battle for Southern Africa could provide the opportunity to inflict a decisive defeat on the entire Western world.

"Momentous changes are taking place as history proceeds rapidly," wrote one revolutionary-minded contributor to an American journal at the end of January. "If the watershed of history was Vietnam," he concluded, "the fatal blow to imperialism and Western capital at home itself, could very well be in South Africa."[13]

As part of a plan to increase co-operation between Communist Parties engaged in attempts to bring about the isolation of South Africa in the non-Communist world, a delegation from the South African Party visited France in April 1975 at the invitation of the French Communist Party. According to *The African Communist:*

> During this visit, the delegation was able to visit the Federation of Hauts-de-Seine and to acquaint itself with the Party's activity at local level and in factories. It met the Party group in the Thomson factory at Gennevilliers. A fruitful exchange of views took place between the South African Communists and the Communist militants at the factory which, together with the whole of the Thomson group, does a large part of its business with South Africa.[14]

The delegation was also received at the offices of the Party's two papers, *L'Humanité* and *France Nouvelle,* where discussions took place on means of bringing about fuller coverage of "the realities in South Africa and the various aspects (political, economic, military, sporting) of collaboration between the French Government and the racist régime of South Africa".

Further discussions also took place at the French Party's Central Committee offices, and these apparently led to

> a broad and fraternal exchange of views on the development of the struggle in our respective countries and on the international situation. Particular attention was paid to the solidarity which unites the working class and the population of our country with the liberation movement of the South African people, as well as to the conditions under which it can be further reinforced.[15]

The joint communiqué issued by the two Parties at the end of the South African visit said that their discussions would lead to the "strengthening of anti-apartheid protest in France and to the French Party stepping up its campaign to end collaboration between France and South Africa".

The various other ultra-left groups in the West, Trotskyist, Revolutionary Socialist, Maoist, and Anarchist have also given consistent and enthusiastic support to the "liberation movements" of Africa, although frequently in the case of the Maoist, and, not infrequently in the case of the remainder, they voice some cynical doubts about the true purpose of Soviet aid to such movements.

Early in 1976 a new magazine *Africa in Struggle* made its appearance in Britain, apparently produced by the International Marxist Group, the British affiliate of the Brussels-based Trotskyist Fourth International. It carried a note stating that it had been produced by "revolutionary Marxist militants in order to create a debate on the African revolution". Its second edition carried articles strongly hostile to the idea of **détente** or any kind of peaceful settlement in Southern Africa. One **explained**:

> The aim of the colonial revolution, which in order to be successful must be carried through to a socialist revolution, is the absolute victory of the proletariat and

peasants. The total displacement of the bourgeoisie and the bourgeois state. These basic requirements for the building of Socialism cannot be attained, given the present objective situation in Southern Africa, without the employment of violence and terror.[16]

The Fourth International has affiliates in most West European countries and links with Trotskyist bodies in a number of other areas, including North and South America. It played a considerable part in mobilising support for the propaganda campaign in support of the Communist forces in Vietnam and is clearly willing to make the same kind of widespread effort in support of the African "liberation movements". In February 1976, for instance, its International Executive Committee passed a long resolution on the situation in Angola which contained the following clause:

> The Fourth International must take an active part in a campaign of solidarity with the People's Republic of Angola organised on a world scale. This campaign should demand the immediate and unconditional withdrawal of all imperialist and neocolonialist forces; it should call for political and material aid from the worker states and the international workers' movements, the halt of all shipments of arms and material to the FNLA-UNITA bloc, and the recognition of the MPLA and the People's Republic of Angola.[17]

One revolutionary-minded organisation giving active support on a considerable scale to African "liberation movements" is the Liberation Support Movement of Richmond, Canada. This organisation (extracts from some of whose publications have been quoted in this study), takes its stand from the viewpoint popular with some Chinese thinkers during the 1960s, i.e. that the world situation could be compared to that in a country in which guerrillas operating according to Mao Tse-tung's tactics were carrying on an intensive campaign. In this scenario, as mentioned earlier, the Third World represented the countryside in which the guerrillas were carrying out their offensive aimed at isolating and eventually subjugating the towns, meaning the industrialised countries of the West.

The Liberation Support Movement describes itself as a

> relatively small, openly Marxist-Leninist organisation which devotes a considerable portion of its energies towards advancing revolutionary developments and struggles in the "Third World".[18]

Although the movement believes that

> certain actions—legal and illegal, peaceful and violent—can be carried out in the metropolitan centres which weaken (however slightly in the present stage) the power of the corporate ruling class and its military apparatus,

it regards its main task, in the present situation, as being to

> accelerate, through various concrete forms of material support, political education and ideological struggle, that revolutionary process whereby vanguard subjugated classes and peoples in the countryside are fighting their way out of the imperialist system and contributing significantly to the emergence of post-capitalist socialist internationalism.

The movement also aims to

> work towards the formation of revolutionary internationalist structures and forms of effective collaboration across national lines ...

In a report on its activities between January 1971 and April 1972 the Liberation Support Movement claimed that three shipments of supplies had been sent to the aid of the MPLA under its auspices. These comprised six tons of clothing, uniforms and technical books and 10 000 dollars worth of medicine. The supplies were despatched to Dar es Salaam and then transported by trucks driven by MPLA members to the Zambian-Angolan border.

Early in 1971 the movement printed a first-aid manual for the use of the MPLA medical services. Consignments of this manual were sent to Lusaka for use in the MPLA medical service's training courses. According to the report, "major financial contributions" to the project came from the Angola Medical Committee in Holland, the United Church of Canada, and the Fraser Group of Vancouver. Also early in 1971, this Canadian group began a campaign aimed at "exposing the rôle of Portugal's NATO allies in assisting her in her colonial wars". It also concentrated some of its attention upon carrying on propaganda against "the rôle of multi-national companies in colonies and neo-colonies where national liberation struggles were taking place". Its production of literature dealing with aspects of the various campaigns being carried on by the "liberation movements" was also stepped up.

The LSM, in addition, was said to be working out "concrete collaborative relationships" with, amongst other groups, the Communist Working Circle (KAF/KUF) in Denmark.

In January 1972 the report records:

> We began cadre-training classes within the information centre in Vancouver. Eight members are gaining language and technical skills for work in the "countryside" with the aim of gathering up-to-date photographs, interviews and other materials dealing with the liberation struggles, and also of becoming more effective in mobilising broader support within the metropolis.[19]

Other forms of practical aid to "liberation movements" undertaken by the movement included the launching of a "food for guerrillas campaign" which resulted in the despatch of a ton of "concentrated multi-purpose food" to Frelimo and the reprinting for distribution in North America of *Angola in Arms*, the official journal of the MPLA, Frelimo's *Moçambique Revolution* and PAIGC's *Actualities*. PAIGC apparently asked the Liberation Support Movement to supply extra copies of this English edition of *Actualities* for distribution at European conferences, etc.

By 1975 the Liberation Support Movement had began to achieve a not insignificant influence amongst some section of African "liberation movements". This is indicated by some outspoken comments in the editorial notes of *The African Communist*, No. 65 for the second quarter of that year. The orthodox Moscow line behind the latter publication was to be seen clearly when it apparently began to have the gravest doubts about the loyalty of the LSM to the true Marxist faith as seen from the Kremlin, and were worried that the views of such "heretics" might begin to gain more ground amongst African "freedom-fighters". Under the title "These allies are not our friends", the magazine stated:

> *The African Communist* had received through the post a copy of *LSM News,* Volume 1, Issue 3, dated December 1974, described as the quarterly organ of the Liberation Support Movement whose headquarters are in Richmond, British Columbia, Canada. Normally we would not have paid attention to the contents of a journal of this type, but because a number of liberation movements in Africa have allowed themselves, or their leaders, to be promoted under LSM auspices, we think it as well that they should know the motives of those they may accept, albeit unknowingly, as their disinterested allies, but who in fact are vigorously pursuing political aims of their own which often conflict with those of the liberation movements themselves.

After attacking LSM leaders for echoing Communist Chinese criticism of Soviet "revisionism" and "social imperialism", *The African Communist* accused the movement of

> **seeking** to drive a wedge between the liberation movements of the entire Third World and the international Communist movement

and of

> objectively serving the interests of **imperialism.**

All "liberation movements" were warned against having "any sort of relationship" with the LSM. This warning that was considered necessary because of evidence that the LSM's "dangerous policies" had to some extent succeeded in "penetrating the ranks of many liberation movements in Africa".

Radical Protest Groups

The Anti-Apartheid Movement was formed in 1960 and for most of its existence has maintained a headquarters in Holborn, London. Although primarily concentrating on events in South and South West Africa, it has by no means entirely concerned itself with events in those two countries, but has also given vigorous propaganda support to "liberation movements" in Portuguese Africa and Rhodesia.

The movement has also established a network of important overseas connections. For instance, its Annual Report for October 1974-September 1975 records that in November 1974, its Hon. Secretary, Mr Abdul Minty, was invited to Germany by the newly formed German Anti-Apartheid Movement to work out plans for future activity, including "a campaign against the establishment of a major nuclear enrichment plant in South Africa by Steag of Essen". Later in the same month, Mr Minty and another representative of the movement were invited to attend a seminar by Dutch anti-apartheid groups. Early in 1975 the movement also sent representatives to attend a "Tribunal against colonialism and apartheid in Southern Africa" held in the Town Hall in Bonn.

Representatives of "liberation movements", anti-apartheid groups and "other organisations including the World Council of Churches" took part in this meeting in which the main emphasis was apparently on "the central rôle of South Africa in relationship to Zimbabwe (Rhodesia) and Namibia (South West Africa)".

For a week in February 1975 the British Anti-Apartheid Movement's Secretary and another member of the movement were in the Soviet Union having discussions with various organisations there which "showed considerable interest in the work of the AAM". The visit, it seems, also helped the Anti-Apartheid Movement to get "a better impression of the solidarity work done in the Soviet Union in support of the liberation struggle in Southern Africa".

At the beginning of April the Secretary was again on his travels, this time to Dar es Salaam to attend the special extraordinary session of the Organisation of African Unity called to discuss South Africa. This conference, it is recorded, "presented a useful opportunity for meeting leaders from African states and the liberation movements".

At the end of April both Mr Minty and the movement's

Chairman, Mr John Ennals, attended a seminar organised by the UN Special Committee Against Apartheid. Mr Minty was asked to open the discussion on plans for an arms embargo against South Africa on the first day. The seminar was attended by representatives of anti-apartheid movements and committees from a considerable number of different countries. On 29 April Mr Minty left for the Commonwealth Conference in Kingston, Jamaica. In June he returned to New York to address the Security Council during a debate on South West Africa. During his address, he stated that he

> provided evidence about Western military collaboration with the Pretoria régime which helped to perpetrate its illegal occupation of Namibia. He also presented documentary evidence that the NATO codification system for equipment and spares had been made available to the South African régime.

Also in June, Mr John Ennals acted as the AAM representative at the independence celebrations in Moçambique.

In Britain, the Anti-Apartheid Movement operates through 38 local groups. Its 1974-75 annual report stated:

> The movement depends considerably on well-organised local groups for its nationwide campaigns.
>
> The range of activities of local groups is wide, and includes public meetings and conferences, letter-writing, pickets and demonstrations, bookstalls, selling *AA News,* and leafleting, and constant contact with the local press and local organisations. Frequently, they make an impact nationally, as in the case of the work of the Birmingham Group on Zimbabwean political prisoners, or the Surrey Group on the loopholes in the Race Relations Act which allow advertisements for jobs in South Africa to appear in the British press.
>
> Local group support for the movement's national campaigns is crucial, and was particularly evident in the campaign to end military collaboration with South Africa and in the sponsored walks to publicise the plight of political prisoners in South Africa ...
>
> Many local groups initiate actions quite independently

297

of the London office, and publicising such action through *AA News* means that it is picked up elsewhere and repeated, or the idea is translated into another local context.

The movement also makes considerable efforts through its London office to exercise a direct influence on Constituency Labour Parties. A number of mailings are sent out each year to Constituency Labour Parties and special events are organised aimed at attracting their support. In June 1974 a special conference on "The Southern African Struggle and the Labour Party" was organised by the movement and literature despatched to constituency parties included a pamphlet protesting against British and South African joint naval exercises.

Two regional conferences intended for Labour Party members were held during the same year, one in Wales and one in Scotland. A considerable amount of the movement's activity in connection with building up support in the Labour Party is directed towards persuading members to move resolutions in accordance with the movement's policy at the Labour Party Annual Conference.

Similar activity is also directed towards the Liberal Party and the annual report already mentioned stated:

> The Liberal Party at national level, the Parliamentary Party and the Young Liberals have been regularly circulated with information on AAM campaigns and on issues relating to Southern Africa. Although it was not possible to arrange a meeting in the 1975 Liberal Assembly, a literature stall was organised and manned by AAM supporters in the party and by Young Liberals. The latter have continued to be active on Southern African issues and their Southern Africa Commission has been revived. They have been particularly active on the sports boycott as well as other aspects of solidarity work.

The movement does not, however, only attract support from political parties with representatives in Parliament, but, in addition to support from the Communist Party which has already been mentioned, also from groups which believe that the rights of British, no less than African, workers can be assured only through revolution and not reform. The annual report mentioned records:

The International Socialists, the International Marxist Group, and other political organisations participated in the 23rd March Mobilising Committee which organised the march and rally against military collaboration with apartheid. These organisations have committed themselves to support the campaign to expel South Africa from the International Lawn Tennis Federation, initiated by the South African Non-Racial Open Committee.

The report added that the International Socialists' journal, *Socialist Worker*, and the International Marxist Group's *Red Weekly*, in addition to *The Morning Star*, had given "excellent coverage to Southern African issues and anti-apartheid activities".

Two fields in which the movement has been particularly active have been those of the trade unions and universities and colleges.

Such activities include, for instance, the holding of special conferences for trade unionists. One of these was held in Coventry in January 1975 under the title of "The Worker and Apartheid". The proceedings were opened by Mrs Audrey Wise, a Labour M.P., Mr Eddie McCluskey from the Executive Committee of the Transport and General Workers' Union, Mr Don Groves, from the ASTMS and Mr Tony Ayland, from the National Association of Local Government Officers. The conference recommended that the Government should withhold financial assistance from companies operating in South Africa and in particular from British Leyland.

The conference also called for an intensification of the campaign against emigration to South Africa and for the release of political prisoners in that country. Unions were also urged to withdraw any funds invested in companies operating in South Africa and also to monitor the investments of pension funds to which their members contributed.

It is claimed that students in over 1 000 different universities and colleges receive the National Union of Students' Anti-Apartheid Movement "network mailings" on Southern Africa. It would seem that:

Regular meetings of the network each term, and frequent mailings of the network newsletter, have become part of the regular pattern, and the result has been nationally co-ordinated campaigns which provide an impetus for the local student groups and enable effective dissemination of information on Southern Africa.

The network also provides a forum for debate, nationally, on the nature of the situation in Southern Africa, and the response needed from British students.[20]

At the third special summer conference of the "network" held at Keele University in July 1974 it was decided that there should be two major priorities for activities in the year ahead. One of these should be concerned with the mobilisation of material aid and support for the "liberation movements" and the other with the organisation of a campaign to bring pressure to bear upon university and college authorities to disinvest themselves of shares and holdings in companies operating in South Africa. It was also decided to begin a boycott of Barclays Bank.

The conference set a target of £10 000 for the fund-raising effort in aid of the "liberation movements", and it was stated that a "substantial part" of this sum was reached. This disinvestment campaign led to the disruption of meetings of the Council of Manchester University and its supporters claimed a success when Lancaster University's Council decided to rid themselves of any investments in companies connected with South Africa. At the Fourth Conference of the Anti-Apartheid Movement/National Union of Students "network" in July 1975 it was decided to concentrate activities for the 12 months ahead on a "two-pronged attack". This was to include a campaign to end British Collaboration with South Africa and further fund raising in support of the "national liberation movements" and for the release of political prisoners.

As the crisis in Southern Africa deepened and the guerrilla campaign in Rhodesia was stepped up in the autumn of 1976, the Anti-Apartheid Movement began to devote increased attention to events in that country. It regarded the victory of the "liberation forces" as being an essential stepping-stone on the path to the "liberation" of the whole of Southern Africa. An editorial in its journal *Anti-Apartheid News* in April 1976 read:

The Zimbabwe people have called for international assistance in their liberation struggle. The British people have a particular responsibility in providing every possible support and aid.

The situation in Southern Africa is now developing rapidly ... the crisis for white power requires an even greater intensification of campaigns to isolate the white minority régimes as positive solidarity with all those struggling for freedom in Southern Africa.

The same edition of *Anti-Apartheid News* announced that:

The Anti-Apartheid Movement has launched a campaign to win over greater support for the Zimbabwe people and to counter the "kith and kin" argument.

A special leaflet, *Crisis in Rhodesia,* which provides factual information as well as dealing with the issues at stake, has been produced for mass circulation. All local anti-apartheid groups have been urged to organise mass distributions on 3 April.

In May the movement organised a special meeting on the subject of "Crisis in Rhodesia", speakers at which included the former Labour Government cabinet minister, Mrs Judith Hart, M.P.

The Anti-Apartheid Movement also plays an active part in the ELTSA campaign. This (End Loans to South Africa) campaign is described as being part of an international movement which aims to exert pressure on those banks in Europe and the USA involved in making "secret" loans to South Africa. A particular target of the campaign has been the Midland Bank with which the Methodist Church, one of the prime movers in the campaign, has had a considerable connection.

Another British radical protest movement very active in propaganda work in support of "the national liberation movement" in Southern Africa has been Liberation, formerly known as the Movement for Colonial Freedom. Formed in 1954, the Movement for Colonial Freedom has campaigned persistently on a large number of issues, including many which could not be considered to be of a colonial nature. They have touched on very much wider aspects of foreign and defence policy. These have included such matters as nuclear disarmament, Vietnam and membership of Western defence alliances.

Its founder, Chairman and present President, Lord Brockway, recorded in his book *Outside the Right* that, at the height of its activity during the 1950s and 1960s when great changes and developments were taking place in the colonial and former colonial territories, the movement operated extremely effectively from four small attic rooms at the top of an old building near Kings Cross Station. He said that from this meagre accommodation letters and directives poured out and that a "splendid organisation" was created which was capable of mobilising as many as 20 000 people to attend a demonstration in Trafalgar Square on any urgent issue. He also said that continuous contact was maintained with the "national movement" in Africa and elsewhere, and that when leaders of African and other nationalist movements came to London they began to turn more and more to the movement for support.

A high proportion of support for the Movement for Colonial Freedom (like that for Liberation today) came from the left-wing of the Labour Party. Some well-known Communist sympathisers, such as the previously mentioned Mr Jack Woddis and members of revolutionary groups, also came to be amongst its activists. Lord Brockway has admitted that twice the headquarters of the Labour Party in Transport House threatened to place the Movement for Colonial Freedom on its proscribed list because of what was alleged to be the presence of "fellow-travellers" amongst it ranks. However, Lord Brockway replied that the proscription of the movement by the Labour Party would have alienated African opinion.

The Movement for Colonial Freedom changed its name to Liberation early in the 1970s in recognition of the fact of the virtual end of the colonial era. Its new name, it was felt, was more in keeping with the increasingly wide scope of its activities. It continued, however, to draw much of its support from the far left of the political spectrum and to take a very active interest in African affairs. Early in 1976 Liberation was asked to send a representative to Luanda to take part in the 15th anniversary celebrations of the founding of the MPLA as "an expression of solidarity". Although the movement's Chairman, Mr Stan Newers, Labour M.P., was anxious to go, he was unable to do so and his place was taken by the movement's acting Secretary, Mr Tony Gilbert. He subsequently recorded his impressions in the movement's journal *Liberation* for April/May 1976:

By the time *Liberation* goes to press, the last South

African soldier will have left Angola.

At the end of February 1976, when delegates from over 60 countries attended an emergency conference in Luanda, the situation was very different: South African troops were deep inside Angolan territory ...

Many African, Asian, Middle Eastern and Socialist Governments saw the importance of this conference and sent official delegates. There were three delegates from Britain. Mr Bob Hughs, M.P., represented Anti-Apartheid, Jill Shepherd the Anglican Solidarity Committee and I represented Liberation.

After the delegates had received what Mr Gilbert described as a "loving welcome" from the "confident citizens of Luanda" and a speech from President Neto, the conference began:

> The delegates saw the battle in Angola as a confrontation between national liberation and world imperialism. They knew that defeat would hinder and hold back liberation struggles everywhere. Defeat would bring with it the slaughter of the heroic daughters and sons of Angola in a similar tragedy to that which befell the people of Spain in 1938. It could now as then so hearten world reaction that we could once again be at the threshold of world war.
>
> Victory, as the delegates realised, would help to weaken and isolate the racist régimes of South Africa and Zimbabwe. It would bring tremendous encouragement and aid to the people of Namibia in their struggle for freedom against illegal rule by South Africa. Now that the last invading soldier has left Angola, the world's peace and progressive forces are tremendously stronger. The people of Angola, supported by international solidarity, have opened new paths for human progress ... Our solidarity with the freedom fighters of South Africa must continue and grow to the point where the racist régimes find their rule no longer tenable.

Mr Tony Gilbert was also given the task of chairing a commission which drew up an appeal from the delegates for worldwide solidarity with the MPLA.

World Council of Churches

Of the various Church-controlled bodies which have taken up the cause of active support for the "liberation movements", probably the most important is the World Council of Churches.

This organisation owes its origins to a meeting of a provisional steering committee set up to discuss the question of the formation of a World Council in 1938 under the Chairmanship of the late Archbishop William Temple. The Archbishop clearly had few illusions regarding possible dangers that might arise in connection with such a project, for he was to make it very clear in his writings that he regarded it as essential that those concerned in it did not give the impression that the Church was becoming an agency for giving support to "left-wing politics which are often based on presupposition entirely un-Christian".

It was not until 1948 that the active life of the Council actually began, its general aims being defined to "study, witness and advance the common unity".

Its active involvement in the affairs of Southern Africa would seem to date from the "Cottesloe Consultation" held at Johannesburg in 1960 when the WCC began an investigation of the policies of the South African Government. Very soon after this "investigation" began, the three Protestant Afrikaner Churches of South Africa withdrew from the Council and the stage was set for the beginning of the campaign against the status quo in Southern Africa which has been one of the hallmarks of the Council's policy ever since.

The growth of tendencies within the organisation which Archbishop Temple had accurately foreseen and feared was accelerated the following year at the WCC Third General Assembly meeting held in New Delhi. The occasion was marked by the attendance for the first time of clergymen from the official State-supervised Churches of the Soviet Union, Romania, Bulgaria and Poland. These now came to apply for membership, despite the fact that up to then the Council had been described in Soviet bloc propaganda as a "façade for Western imperialism".

Their application had the approval of Dr Eugene Carson Blake, a leading figure in the WCC hierarchy. As early as 1954 Dr Blake had been active in arranging for delegations of East European churchmen to attend the Council's proceedings as observers or to visit

Western countries. The representatives of the Soviet bloc Churches now proceeded to claim what most Western observers considered to be a grossly inflated membership of 70 million. Consequently, when their application to join the World Council was accepted, they assured themselves of an unduly high proportion of seats in the assembly. The virtual veto over the discussion of any issue not to their liking that this granted them was met with stringent comments by some other delegates, one of whom complained:

> Until now we've boasted that the world dictates the agenda. Now the dictating is being done by the Russians.[21]

An expert on Soviet affairs at the University of Kansas, Dr William Fletcher, has stated that Soviet participation in WCC activities was undoubtedly intended to influence the organisation in such a way that its decisions and proposals would conform, or at least not conflict, with Soviet foreign policy.

The extent to which Soviet Church leaders were ready to lend their voice in support of Soviet foreign policy had already been demonstrated long before they became members of the Council. During the Korean War, for instance, Metropolitan Nikolai, then the second highest ranking functionary in the Moscow-controlled Russian Orthodox Church, had delivered a violent attack on the American forces in Korea in the course of a speech in East Berlin, accusing them of, amongst other things, "executions without trial", "dreadful tortures", the "cutting off of ears, noses and breasts", the "putting out of eyes", the "crucifixion of patriots" and the "burying alive of women and children".

It would appear that the WCC's new members did not take long to begin asserting the considerable influence their numbers gave them. For with the outbreak of the Cuban missile crisis in the autumn of 1962 and the subsequent US blockade of the island, a statement was quickly issued by officers of the Council announcing their "grave concern and regret" regarding what they termed the "unilateral action of the United States".

The Council also took a severely critical view of American policy during the Vietnam War, and its opposition to American participation in the war led it to raise the sum of 210 000 dollars for the support of American draft dodgers and deserters who had taken refuge in Sweden and Canada. Whilst the Council itself denied any intention of encouraging disaffection in the American armed forces, a somewhat different line was taken by its youth organisation through the pages of its publication *Risk*, which addressed such messages to US servicemen as "You must go beyond the question of conscientious objection, the just men desert".

Another such message, in the same publication, stated that any officer who gave orders which those who received them found "offensive" was a criminal.

Amongst its activities in its earlier years, the Council indulged in extraordinary suggestions for a "fundamental restructuring of the world economy" apparently by means of the deliberate transfer of capital and non-technical intensive industries to "countries with insufficient capital but abundant manpower". At a conference in Geneva in 1966 the "dislocation and possible suffering" the carrying out of this plan would admittedly cause large numbers of people was apparently considered a necessary preliminary to creating a "wider world order". However, despite such aberrations, up to the end of the 1960s most observers would seem to have considered that the WCC had been successful in accomplishing a considerable amount of humanitarian work and in creating a needed link between a large number of different Churches. The section of its activities which has attracted the largest volume of criticism has been the Programme to Combat Racism. This was established at a meeting of the World Council of Churches' Central Committee in August 1969. It was to operate a special fund with an ultimate target of half a million US dollars.

The following year, in September 1970, the WCC's Executive Committee unanimously adopted a set of recommendations proposed by a panel of 26 international advisers that grants from the special fund should be distributed to a number of "liberation movements". It was also agreed that the situation in South Africa should be regarded as a priority matter. This decision was endorsed by the organisation's Central Committee meeting in Addis Ababa in January 1971.

An amount of 100 000 US dollars held in the Council's reserve funds were thereupon promptly utilised for grants to 19 "liberation movements", most of them already engaged in "armed struggle". They included the PAC, ANC, SWAPO, ZANU, ZAPU and the various groups opposed to Portuguese rule operating in Southern

Africa.

The decision at once came in for attack even from those often critical of the White governments of Southern Africa. *The Times,* for instance, commented that Christian bodies had no business to support movements which were openly engaged in the use of violence and terrorism. The *Daily Telegraph* said that while once it had been missionaries who had received Church-sponsored funds for genuine humanitarian work, now it was obscure many lettered organisations which "plant explosives by night and are enemies, conscious or unconscious, of all peace and prosperity". The West German *Die Welt* stated bluntly "Christian faith and terrorist power are incompatible".

Such criticism, however, had little effect on those in charge of the Programme to Combat Racism. At a meeting in East Berlin in February 1973 the WCC Executive Committee allocated a further amount of 450 000 dollars to the aid of a number of "racially oppressed" groups, including "liberation movements", operating in Southern Africa.

This was followed by a move to set up a new fund within the framework of the Special Fund to Combat Racialism, with an annual target of 100 000 dollars, for the purpose of assisting deserters from the Portuguese armed forces in the same way that US deserters had been aided during the Vietnam war. Later this plan was, however, watered down into an appeal to all governments to give refuge to Portuguese deserters as "political refugees".

Although the official justification for the committee's attitude towards the situation in Southern Africa was the "combating of racism", indications are not lacking of the presence of other and somewhat wider motives.

The indications were particularly clearly portrayed in a booklet produced by the Programme entitled *Cabora Bassa and the Struggle for Southern Africa.* After calling on member Churches to bring pressure to bear to dissuade governments and commercial concerns in their respective countries from lending any form of financial support to the construction of the Cabora Bassa Dam in Moçambique, which, it was held, would help entrench racialism in the area, it was stated:

Last, but not least, Cabora Bassa is providing the countries of Western Europe with a much needed outlet for their surplus capital for their heavy industries ... What happens at Cabora Bassa is central to the fight for Moçambique and to the future of the whole of Southern Africa, it is also important to the survival of Western capitalism. Action against the West's involvement at Cabora Bassa is not just a blow struck in solidarity with the people of Moçambique, it is part of a wider struggle against a world economic system which exploits the peoples of the colonising countries only to a lesser degree than those of the colonies.

The Programme to Combat Racism has also been responsible for a campaign aimed at securing the withdrawal of all investment from South Africa.

In the spring of 1974, following a WCC Executive Committee meeting in Berlin, the German Lutheran Church, one of the largest Churches affiliated to the World Council, announced that it would no longer support the Programme to Combat Racism while it continued to give grants to movements and groups involved in the use of violence. A number of churchmen in Southern Africa who, although themselves often critical of the White governments under whose rule they lived, have also spoken out clearly against the World Council's activities in this regard. Father Arthur Lewis, Chairman of the Rhodesian Christian Group who has often found himself in conflict with the Government of Mr Ian Smith, nevertheless in the winter of 1975 attacked statements by the Programme's representatives to the effect that "there must be a smashing down before there can be a building up". Describing some recent atrocities perpetrated by members of the "liberation movements" in Rhodesia, he called on all Christians everywhere to resist the "implications of the Programme". He said:

The time has come for Christians to rise in force against the false religious prophets of our time. Their place is in the Kremlin, not in the Christian Church.[22]

In the presence of the 40 British delegates who were amongst those who attended the WCC Fifth Assembly in Nairobi in December 1975, the General Secretary, Dr Philip Potter, a West Indian, attacked Britain as being "the most racist country in the world". This charge was promptly refuted by the Archbishop of Canterbury, who led the British delegation, as being "30 years out of date". However, Dr Potter continued his attack by proclaiming that the British had established a racist system "wherever they had gone in the world" and that the British colonial system had been one of the "most racist in history". Later the Archbishop of Canterbury, Dr Donald Coggan, issued a press release which, whilst admitting that the British had "much to repent of", emphasised the

> immense contributions which they, with many others from the West, have made and are still making in the realms of evangelism, medicine and education, to mention but three, to the less wealthy nations.[23]

During the course of the Assembly, efforts were made by some Western delegates to block the election of the Soviet-controlled Russian Orthodox Church Metropolitan, Nikodin of Leningrad, as one of the Council's six new Presidents, because of their belief that he was too much under the influence of the Soviet Government. These efforts failed owing to their being unable to find a suitable candidate to oppose him.

The Assembly was also told that during the year grants from the Programme to Combat Racism amounting to $128 000 had been given to four African "liberation movements". These being the ANC of South Africa ($22 500), the PAC ($22 500), SWAPO ($41 000) and ZANU and ZAPU (a joint grant of $41 000).

A senior member of the British delegation, the Right Rev Graham Leonard, Bishop of Truro, said in Nairobi that while the Church of England remained "totally committed to the Council", it was critical of some of its policies such as the support of "liberation movements" by the Programme to Combat Racism. However, he also said that he had detected a shift on the part of members of the Assembly away from the proposition that violence was necessary in order to bring about progress in Southern Africa.

Spokesmen of the Programme to Combat Racism and members of the WCC who support its efforts have always maintained that money raised for the "liberation movements" is not for the purchase of arms and military equipment but purely to meet medical and other welfare needs. Although the question of effective control of such money once it reaches its destination must raise questions of

309

obvious difficulty, in fact it would seem that the great majority of the "liberation movements" do not at present have any pressing need for money for the purchase of arms and military stores, the simple reason being that these are provided in great abundance free, or virtually so, by Communist countries as explained earlier in this study.

This is not to say, however, that the funds provided by the WCC and other similar-minded bodies do not play an important part in the "liberation campaign". On two particular counts, they are of very considerable assistance. Firstly, they can set free money raised by the "liberation movements" themselves for purposes more directly connected with their military effort, if need be, and the money may be used for the equally important task of propaganda. Secondly, and perhaps most importantly, their arrival undoubtedly acts as an important morale booster for those in the ranks of the "liberation movement", allowing their leaders to present their organisations as being part of an immensely powerful worldwide movement composed of active sympathisers dedicated to assuring the triumph of the "liberation movements".

There is no suggestion that the majority of the members of the radical protest movements mentioned or of those who support the World Council of Churches wish to see a Communist victory in Southern Africa. But there would also seem no doubt that as propaganda organisations fervently and often uncritically supporting the cause of the "liberation movements" they have had a very considerable effect on Western thinking.

REFERENCES

1. *The Guardian,* 21 June 1973.
2. *Portuguese Colonies: Victory or Death. op. cit.,* p. 127.
3. *The African Communist,* Vol. 2, No. 1.
4. *The African Communist,* No. 66.
5. *Moçambique: Sowing the Seeds of Revolution.* Committee for Freedom in Moçambique, Angola and Guinea, p. 1.
6. *Ibid.,* p. 13-14.
7. *The Morning Star,* 29 October 1975.
8. Social Democracy and the Colonial Question. *Revolution,* Vol 1, No. 16.

9. *World Marxist Review,* April 1964, p. 86.
10. *Sourenenni Vostok,* No. 4, 1960.
11. *The Morning Star,* 13 September 1976.
12. *Ibid.,* 15 September 1976.
13. *The Guardian,* 28 **February 1976. A left-wing U.S. publication, not to be confused with the British daily newspaper.**
14. *The African Communist,* No. 62, 1975.
15. *Ibid.*
16. *Africa in Struggle,* Vol. 1, No. 60.
17. *Ibid.*
18. *Principles of Liberation of Support Movements: Anti-Imperialist Work.* Liberation Support Movement Information Centre, Richmond, B.C., Canada, p. 1-5.
19. *Ibid.,* p. 111.
20. Anti-Apartheid Movement Annual Report on Activities and Developments, October 1974, September 1975.
21. *Reader's Digest,* November 1971.
22. *Rhodesia Herald,* 26 June 1975.
23. *The Times,* 12 December 1975.

Chapter 10

The Deepening Crisis and Conclusions

During the latter part of 1974 a conference took place in Baghdad. Although it attracted little, if any, interest in non-Communist circles in the West, it was to prove of considerable significance in view of later events. This conference was held under the auspices of the influential magazine *World Marxist Review*, based in Prague, and the National Patriotic Front of Iraq.

The theme of it was the "Alliance of the Socialist World System and the National Liberation Movements". To it came representatives of the Communist Party of the Soviet Union, all the countries of the Soviet bloc as well as those Communist and Workers' Parties from a large number of countries, including Algeria, Chile, the Lebanon, Iran, Morocco, Senegal and South Africa.

The conference was also attended by representatives of what were called "left progressive and patriotic parties and organisations" from a further range of countries, amongst which figured Egypt, Guinea, Madagascar and the Yemen. Representatives of "liberation movements" taking part included those of the Zimbabwe African People's Union, the People's Front for the Liberation of Oman and the Saudi Arabia National Liberation Front.

The proceedings, which were held in the presence of a number of "prominent Iraqi public figures" were opened by the circulation of a discussion paper specially prepared for the conference by the

Editor-in-Chief of *World Marxist Review,* Mr Konstantin Zaradov. This discussion paper began by stating that the problems the conference had to consider did not "arise in the seclusion of study rooms, but in the crucible of revolutionary battles against imperialism and for the progress of the new society". Developing his theme, Mr Zaradov went on to say:

> These battles are forging the alliance of the socialist community and the national liberation movements. And on its consolidity, as all active and con,istent fighters against imperialism know, depends the future of world development and likewise their own political success.
>
> To be sure, our enemies know this as well, the political servants of world capitalism spare no effort in their attempts to prevent the countries that have broken out of colonial servitude from continuing along the road of anti-imperialist struggle, which objectively evolves into struggle against all forms of exploitation. The ideologists and politicians of imperialism count on the developing countries as a source of "fresh blood" for the senile body of capitalism, hoping thereby to delay its inevitable end. They are making special efforts to disrupt the time-tested and growing alliance between the socialist countries and the forces of national liberation.
>
> Hence the heated polemics at international forums and in world literature over the question of the alliance of the socialist countries and the national liberation movements. Hence its immense theoretical and political relevance.[1]

Mr Zaradov then continued by defining how the phrase "alliance of the socialist countries and the national liberation movements" should be interpreted. It should, he said, be taken to mean:

> An objective and naturally shaping interaction of all three components of the single world revolutionary process.

The third element in this alliance is the Communist Parties and "progressive elements" in the West, particularly those of a highly militant type such as had brought about the Portuguese Revolution. Mr Zaradov reminded his audience that Lenin had always considered that the "national liberation movements" in the colonies had "tremendous revolutionary potential", and that, therefore, the theories behind the formation of such an alliance were most soundly based.

Having propounded these theories, Mr Zaradov then proceeded to suggest that the time was becoming increasingly ripe for putting them into practice. Amongst the reasons he advanced for this line of thinking were the fact, as he saw it, that the Communist countries had "registered tremendous economic gains over the last 10 to 15 years", whilst the "defence potential of socialism has increased". All this, he wrote, had greatly increased the prestige of the countries of the "socialist community" and given them "immensely enhanced" chances of exercising "international leverage and influence".

At the same time, he thought that it was important that an increasing number of revolutionary and national "liberation movements" in the Third World were developing a "more marked class character", or in other words showing marked leanings towards Marxism-Leninism, as against pure nationalism, as their main driving force. This meant that the bonds between the "liberation movements", "the socialist community" and "progressive forces" in the West were becoming cemented in an even firmer fashion. Only the consolidation of such an alliance, Mr Zaradov informed the delegates, would

> make it possible to consummate our world-historic cause: the ultimate defeat of imperialism and social liberation of all mankind.[2]

During the conference, a series of delegates rose to support this thesis. Mr Lansana Diane, Inspector-General of the Democratic Party of Guinea, for instance, said that the "democratic coup" in Portugal had demonstrated how the struggle of the "liberation movements" in Portuguese Africa had affected the situation in Portugal itself. Mr Richard Howe, a member of the Chimurenga General Council of the Zimbabwe African National Union (ZANU), claimed that his movement's "armed struggle" in Rhodesia was weakening "imperialism" and "undermining the very foundations of capitalism" and so "bringing mankind fresh victories

314

in the fight for social progress", whilst Mr Ali Yata, General Secretary of the Moroccan Party of Liberation and Socialism, stressed the need for even closer ties with the "socialist world" in order to "demolish the last bastions of colonialism".

Speakers also expressed their gratitude for the help extended, and still being extended, by the Soviet Union to "national liberation movements" and newly independent countries. The representative of the Algerian Socialist Vanguard Party, for instance, said that the members of his National Liberation Front had been keenly aware of the value of Soviet aid during the whole of the "war of liberation". Another representative of ZANU, Mr George Silundika, described the "socialist countries" as being the main base of material support for the "liberation movements" of Southern Africa, whilst according to the *World Marxist Review,* Mr Michael Harmel, a Central Committee member of the South African Communist Party, said that:

> The Soviet Union and other members of the socialist community have always been an inexhaustible source of inspiration for African people fighting racism and apartheid. From its very inception, the Soviet State has dealt one telling blow after another at the very foundations of racialist theory and practice.

In addition, he said:

> Distinguished anti-imperialist fighters such as Amilcar Cabral, Eduardo Mondlane and Aghostino Neto, publicly paid tribute to the way the socialist countries helped the fight against Portuguese colonialism and fascism. The joint offensive of the socialist and developing countries against imperialism and racism led to the collapse of the hated colonial system.[3]

Perhaps, however, one of the most interesting events of the conference was a remarkably frank statement by Mr Vitaly Korionov, political commentator of *Pravda,* who emphasised:

> The policy of peaceful co-existence of states with differing social systems is a special form of the class struggle.

315

Its aim is to curb the more aggressive imperialist elements and thereby create even more favourable conditions for the development of the liberation revolution. That finds its logical continuation in the détente policy of the socialist states, and it is gaining support in the developing countries too.[4]

Summing up the results of the conference, *World Marxist Review* reported that:

> The revolutionary democratic forces in the newly-free countries are now aware that it is inconceivable to achieve the lofty ideals of patriotism, democracy and progress without the support of the Socialist world. They have set their strategic sights on the closest possible co-operation. Co-ordination of action by all the detachments of the revolutionary movement against the designs of imperialism, reaction and opportunism, and for social progress, strengthens the alliance between the Socialist world and the national liberation movement.

This conference was to prove of estimably greater significance than the mere isolated gathering of theorists it might have seemed to be at the time. For it provided the platform for one of the first public presentations of what Soviet leaders have since frequently declared with increasing emphasis to be the main strategy upon which the Soviet Government at present relies for increasing its influence in the outside world, and bringing about the eventual destruction of its external opponents; the growing strength of the Soviet bloc, "the international working class movement" (i.e. Communist Parties and other extreme-left militants in non-Communist countries) and the "national liberation movement" in the Third World.

One Western expert, Mr Victor Zorza, has said that it is in those writings which are intended to explain the purpose of détente to "the party faithful" and not to Western readers that Soviet leaders make no secret of the fact that the purpose of Soviet foreign policy is to change what they describe as the "correlation of forces" throughout the world so as to channel the tide of events in favour of the Soviet Union and its global strategic designs. The means by which it is hoped to do so being the co-ordinated efforts of each segment of the alliance, including the political influence and growing economic and military power of the Soviet Union.[5]

It follows that aid to the "liberation movements" is, in fact, no longer to be just an adjunct of Soviet foreign policy but one of its *main planks*. Soviet support for such movements engaged in "armed struggle", even in areas of vital concern to the West, is (it is made plain by Soviet spokesmen), just part of the price the former will have to pay for "détente".

In the early part of 1977 the situations which appeared to present extremely tempting opportunities in Africa for the furtherance of such tactics were only too obvious. First and foremost, in the wake of the breakdown of the Geneva Conference and the failure of the talks between the British Government and Mr Smith, was the escalating guerrilla war in Rhodesia. The extent to which young Marxists, many of whom had been trained in the Soviet Union, had now almost totally taken control of the main Rhodesian guerrilla movements had become increasingly apparent during 1976, as had the extent to which the new revolutionary government of Moçambique was ready to provide backing for their campaign. A steady continuation of the increased flow of Soviet arms and equipment entering the area of operations through such Moçambique ports as Beira and Nacala, which had been one of the features of 1976, was also reported in the opening months of the New Year.

In early March Mr Joshua Nkomo, one of the leaders of the newly formed Patriotic Liberation Front, visited Moscow at the invitation of the Soviet Committee for Afro-Asian Solidarity at the head of a delegation from the Front. Speaking in an interview over Moscow Radio on 3 March, Mr Nkomo said that the results of his visit had been "wonderful" and that the discussions he had held had been "extremely constructive".

He added:

> We highly appreciate the principled position of the USSR and the socialist countries which gave selfless help to the African peoples in their struggle for liberation and independence. And in this year of the 60th anniversary of the Great October Socialist Revolution, we would like to convey the sincere gratitude of the repressed peoples of Africa to the Soviet people and the peoples of the socialist countries for the all-round support for our cause.

Meanwhile his co-leader of the Patriotic Liberation Front said, whilst passing through Moçambique a few days later, that the guerrillas in the shape of the Zimbabwe African People's Army (ZIPA) would shortly be holding talks with the Patriotic Liberation Front on the means of acquiring more sophisticated military equipment, including anti-aircraft weapons. Speaking over Maputo Radio on his return from participation in a meeting of the Organisation of African Unity ministers in Togo, **Mr Mugabe** said:

> We are thinking of intensifying our armed struggle. It is necessary that we transform the present stage into a more effective one, and to do that naturally we have to get more facilities for the training of our cadres and more equipment to arm them with.

Speaking in Lusaka near the end of the month and just before the visit of the Soviet Prime Minister, Mr Podgorny, Mr Nkomo was quoted as saying that the Patriotic Front had asked the Soviet Union and "other Socialist countries" for increased assistance in order that the guerrilla campaign might be stepped up.

In South West Africa, the extent to which the guerrillas of SWAPO would be able to continue their occasional raids across the Angolan border and into the Caprivi Strip (reputed to contain some of the roughest country in Southern Africa) remained uncertain. Much clearly turns upon whether the promising results of the Turnhalle Constitutional Conference are to be allowed to lead to a peaceful and stable transition of independence for the territory by the end of 1978. Another important factor is the extent to which the Cuban Government allows its forces stationed in Angola to give assistance to SWAPO.

An ominous note had, however, been struck by Mr Jannie de Wet, the senior South African administrator in the country, who said in a statement at the end of 1976 that SWAPO seemed to be planning a full-scale intensification of its activities aimed at raising their level to the same pitch of intensity as those of the guerrillas in Rhodesia. It seemed that the SWAPO plan was to strike deeper and deeper into the territory and it was known that a considerable number of new bases had been established just north of the Angolan border in order to enable them to do this. Mr de Wet said that in his judgement future SWAPO attacks would involve the use of advanced Soviet weapons and would be assisted by the same "foreign soldiers" who had helped the MPLA secure victory in Angola. Officials of the Wambo tribal homeland in the extreme north of the country had said that at least 5 000 tribesmen had gone abroad. Almost at the same time as this warning was issued came the news that six SWAPO guerrillas had been killed when a party of 30 had tried to infiltrate across the frontier.

In addition to the guerrilla threats in Rhodesia and South West Africa, the danger also clearly existed of the development of a third campaign along the frontier between South Africa and Moçambique.

Mr Podgorny's visit to Zambia at the end of March provided a striking testimony, if any were needed, as to the Soviet Union's determination to do all it could to take full advantage of the situations outlined above. He arrived in Lusaka on 25 March to be received by crowds chanting such slogans as (despite Zambia's evident alarm at the expansionist indications of Soviet policy only a year before, during the Angolan crisis), "We hail your anti-imperialist stand in Angola—keep it up" and "Proletarian dictatorship is our aim here". Foreign observers were surprised to note that the first figures to be presented to him at the official reception, even before all the members of the Zambian cabinet, were Mr Joshua Nkomo and the leader of SWAPO, Mr Sam Nujoma.

At the beginning of his talks with President Kaunda, Mr Podgorny stated that the Soviet Union "would not rest" until Africans living under "colonial rule" were free. Later during his visit, with General Sergei Sokolov, Soviet Deputy Defence Minister, standing beside him, President Podgorny stood on the Zambian side of the Zambesi River near the Victoria Falls and peered through binoculars at the opposite bank. Although his only recorded comment when told that the buildings he saw there stood in Rhodesian territory was a non-committal "Ah", the following day he described the Zambesi river as "the border between freedom and slavery in Africa", and said that it would "not be long" before "freedom and equality" crossed the Zambesi into Rhodesia, "Namibia" and South Africa.

Far more important than such rhetoric, however, was the meeting held by President Podgorny in conditions of tight security in the Soviet Embassy in Lusaka with the leaders of three major "liberation movements". These leaders were Mr Nkomo of the Rhodesian

Patriotic Front, Mr Nujoma of SWAPO and Mr Oliver Tambo of the South African African National Congress. At the conclusion of these talks, a communiqué was issued in which the Soviet President stated that in future the Soviet people would "permanently support the just struggle of the fighters for the liberation of Southern Africa".[6] Amongst the members of Mr Podgorny's delegation taking part in the talks, were General Sokolov, one of whose chief tasks is regarded as being the supervision of the supply of arms to Third World countries which the Soviet Government wants to provide with military backing, Major-General Viktor Samodurov, deputy head of the KGB, and Mr Vasil Solodovnikov, believed to be the principal KGB planner responsible for the Soviet Union's current policies in Africa.

On the same day (28 March) that President Podgorny was holding this meeting in Lusaka, Dr Fidel Castro was addressing a mass rally in the Angolan capital, Lusaka. Despite the fact that Dr Castro had been considerably more cautious during his African tour in making overt promises of new Cuban aid in the form of Cuban soldiers to African "liberation movements" (possibly because of the considerable casualties believed to have been suffered by the Cuban forces in Angola), there was no mistaking the forthrightness of his promises of further Cuban military assistance to Angola on this occasion.

The *Daily Telegraph* of 29 March reported him as saying:

> Our duty is to maintain military collaboration while the Angolan forces are organised, trained and equipped.
> The day will come when Angola has sufficient military units, tanks, cannon, aeroplanes and soldiers to confront all imperialist aggression.
> The imperialists ask that Cuba withdraws military aid to Angola. They have no right to say how the brother peoples of Angola and Cuba collaborate. How many years, how many (Cuban) soldiers will remain in Angola? We don't have to give an answer to that to the Yankee imperialists.

Whilst the spotlight of world attention tended to be focused on Soviet and Cuban activities concerned with providing aid to governments and movements in conflict with the White-ruled countries in the southernmost part of Africa, that was by no means the only area of that vast continent which provided increasingly tempting opportunities for intensifying the influence of the aforementioned countries by means of aiding insurrection or local conflict.

One such area yielding an increasingly complicated situation ripe for such exploitation is the strategically extremely important "Horn of Africa" abutting on the northernmost stretches of the Cape Route. Here Ethiopian forces remained as they had since the late 1960s locked in increasingly bitter conflict with the guerrilla forces of the Eritrean Liberation Front (ELF). This movement at one time received considerable support from Communist China but more recently relies on Soviet arms either smuggled across the Red Sea from the People's Republic of South Yemen or delivered through Libyan channels.

The coming to power of a revolutionary government in Ethiopia was hailed in Moscow as the appearance of a "truly revolutionary movement" in that country and was followed by a growing switch in Soviet policy away from support for ELF and its ally the AFAR Liberation Front towards the granting of military aid to the revolutionary soldiers now in power in Addis Ababa. The Ethiopian capital was one of the stopping places for Dr Castro on his early 1977 tour of Africa, and, whilst there, he was reported to have heard an appeal from the Chairman of the ruling Revolutionary Military Council for Cuban military support to enable it to defeat both its external and internal enemies. His reply was not known, but he did state that he had followed the course of the Ethiopian revolution closely and that it had won the respect of progressive revolutionary forces throughout the world. Previously the Cuban military commander in Angola had visited Ethiopia and it was thought that Cuba might well be willing to send advisers to train the new Ethiopian "People's Militia". The situation in the "Horn" has been particularly complicated by the fact that the two new fervently "revolutionary" states of Somalia and Ethiopia are engaged in increasingly bitter dispute over the future of the former French colony of Djibouti, with its important Red Sea port. Two guerrilla movements, the Somali Coast Liberation Movement based in Mogadishu, and the Djibouti Liberation Movement based in Addis Ababa, carried with them the threat of the outbreak of a new armed conflict in an area which the American State Department was said to have previously hoped might prove to be a reasonably reliable bastion against the expansion of Soviet influence.

At the southernmost edge of the base of the "Horn", the Government of the Sudan was said to be still nervous regarding the possibility of the outbreak of yet another revolt backed by Libya and, behind Libya, the Soviet Union. Along the Mediterranean coast the Egyptian Government also kept a wary eye on the growing Soviet influence in Libya. A number of terrorist outrages in Egypt had been officially blamed on the activities of terrorists trained in Libya and equipped with Soviet-made explosive devices whilst the serious riots in Cairo and elsewhere had been followed by the claimed destruction of a Communist cell system embracing not only members of the orthodox Communist Party but also three other extreme left-wing or revolutionary groups.

Thousands of kilometres away, not far from the shore of the western Atlantic, Moroccan and Mauritanian forces continued to fight a growing and increasingly bloody campaign against the Algerian backed guerrillas of the People's Front for the Liberation of Saguiat El Hamra and Rio de Oro (Polisario). Reports in 1976 had spoken of Cuban advisers having taken part in the training of this predominantly Marxist movement engaged in disputing the future of the former Spanish Sahara with Morocco and Mauritania. Moroccan officials were convinced that Algerian backing for the movement which was seeking to gain control of the phosphate-rich former Spanish possession had full Soviet approval.

In Morocco itself, charges laid against 178 extreme left wingers at the beginning of a mass trial alleged that they had plotted to overthrow the Government of King Hassan and to launch a civil war in the country. The plot was said to have been supported by "well-known foreign organisations".

In sub-Saharan Africa, the sudden news of the invasion of Zaire by a force of former Katangese gendarmes based in Angola and allegedly trained and advised by Cubans, added a new and unexpected feature to developments in an area already notorious for its political instability. It was also a development which carried with it the possibility of consequences far beyond those of a purely local nature, owing to the great importance to the United States steel industry of a regular supply of cobalt imported from Zaire. No less than 50% of the industry's supplies of that vital raw material come from that country. Fierce attacks by the African service of Radio

Moscow on the "reactionary" attitude of the Zaire Government and alleged American moves to provide it with assistance strongly indicated that the move (one of the aims it was thought might be to cut off sources of supply to the anti-Marxist guerrillas of UNITA still operating in Angola), had Soviet support.

Meanwhile, the consolidation of Soviet gains in the former Portuguese colonies of Angola, Moçambique and Guinea-Bissau proceeded at a rapid pace. There was a constant interchange of delegations at all levels and of considerable variety.

On 14 March the Presidium of the USSR Supreme Soviet meeting in the Kremlin ratified the Friendship Treaty between the Soviet Union and Angola signed in Moscow the previous October. A Tass report broadcast over Radio Moscow's Foreign Service on the same day quoted President Podgorny as saying that the treaty

mirrored in essence our country's policy in its relations with peoples struggling for national and social liberation and with developing countries in Africa and on other continents who have won independence.

The TASS report also described the Soviet President as saying that the Soviet Union and Angola solemnly undertook to continue the consistent struggle against the forces of imperialism and to uproot colonialism and neo-colonialism, racialism and apartheid. He further said that the USSR and Angola would naturally co-operate with all the progressive and peaceful forces in this noble task and that the member countries of the socialist community attached much importance to the solving of such pressing problems. The declaration adopted in November 1976 by the Warsaw Pact Treaty members reaffirmed their readiness to continue their aid and support to the people of Rhodesia, South West Africa and South Africa.

The Soviet Foreign Minister, Mr Andrei Gromyko, said that the Soviet Union would continue to give "diverse aid" to Angola and that the treaty laid a "firm political and legal basis" for the development of Soviet-Angolan relations.

One small indication of the growing links between the Soviet Union and Angola was the announcement by the Soviet airline Aeroflot about the same time that from April onwards one of the line's newest types of aircraft, the aircraft I-62, would be used on the route between Moscow and Luanda. These aircraft are much bigger than those presently being used and each is capable of carrying 140 people. From mid-summer there would be two such flights a week.

It had previously been announced that in the spring of 1977 a special congress was to be held for the purpose of bringing about the transformation of the MPLA into a political "vanguard" party, as had already been accomplished with Frelimo in Moçambique. In the meantime, the country was being governed under the direction of a "revolutionary action programme". Writing in the American extreme left-wing publication *The Guardian* on 17 November, the well-known Australian journalist, Mr Wilfred Burchett, quoted the MPLA Central Committee resolution which initiated this programme as stating:

> Faced with the threat of neocolonialist domination, the only possible road is that of scientific socialism. The MPLA socialism is not to be called "African socialism". For the MPLA there is only one socialism, that of Marx, Engels and Lenin, scientific socialism which explicitly provides for the end of man's exploitation of man.

In Moçambique, a growing number of East German and Bulgarian specialists were making their appearance. The East Germans were particularly active in assisting in the setting up of a security service.

Early in March it was announced that the scope of economic co-operation between the USSR and Moçambique was to be extended and that Soviet experts were to assist the Frelimo Government in developing a basic economic plan. The Soviet Union was to set up a specialist trades schools in the country the rôle of which would be to produce agricultural and industrial specialists and a cadre of school teachers. At the same time, Moscow Radio put the number of Soviet specialists working in "the various organisations of this friendly African country at about 60". Almost certainly a considerable under-estimate as Western sources had put the number of Soviet military advisers there alone at 20 by the middle of the previous year. Plans were also under way for the establishment of a joint Soviet-Moçambique fishing company, the plan encompassing arrangements for parties of Moçambique fishermen to go to the Soviet Union for special training. The modernisation of Moçambique's harbours, railways and power supplies were also said to be included in the subjects on which Soviet experts were giving advice.

Clearly the outlines of the "red belt across Africa", talk of the creation of which had been dismissed little more than 12 months before as wildly alarmist, was now rapidly taking shape for all to see.

The outlines of that "belt" became all the plainer when, at the end of March, President Podgorny arrived in Moçambique in the course of his African tour and a Friendship Treaty was signed between that country and the Soviet Union. Under its terms, this treaty bound the two countries not only to continue to develop co-operation in the military sphere on the basis of appropriate agreements and to consult with each other if any situations arose that "threatens or breaks peace" in order to eliminate "the arising threat" or to "restore peace" in addition to working with other "peaceful states" in the struggle for freedom, independence, sovereignty and social progress, but also to active co-operation in a large number of other fields.

Amongst the subjects mentioned in which such co-operation was to be engaged in were: industry, transport, communications, agriculture, fisheries, natural resources, energy production, trade and shipping. Mutual aid was also to be stepped up in the fields of science, culture, art, literature, education, health, the press, radio, tourism, and sports. In addition, the treaty also provided for co-operation in the "development of national cadres". A joint statement issued by Presidents Machel and Podgorny at the time of the signing of the treaty welcomed the strengthening of links between the Communist Party of the Soviet Union and Frelimo, and the joint adherence of the two parties to the principles of Marxism-Leninism and proletarian internationalism.

President Podgorny's visit to Zambia appeared to produce less tangible results as regards inter-governmental co-operation. However, it was announced that it had been agreed to broaden such co-operation between Zambia and the Soviet Union in the field of economic, technical and cultural affairs and to establish a direct air link between Moscow and Lusaka.

That President Podgorny's tour was a carefully planned operation intended to give major stimulus to the promotion of Soviet policy in Africa, is shown by the fact that Mr. Vasily Solodovnikov, the

Soviet Ambassador in Lusaka, previously mentioned as being responsible for much of the tour planning, was formerly Director of the Africa Institute in Moscow and his successor in that post, the able and energetic Mr. Anatoly Gromyko, son of the Soviet Foreign Minister, was also heavily engaged in the same task. The serious purpose of the tour was stressed by the number of senior Ministers and officials who formed part of the President's delegation. In addition to those already mentioned, these included Mr. Ilyichev, First Deputy Foreign Minister, Mr. Smelyakov, Deputy Foreign Trade Minister, Mr. Chemyschev, Deputy Chairman of the State Committee for Foreign Economic Relations, the Deputy Chairman of the Council of Ministers, Mr. Arckhipov, and the Minister of Merchant Marine, Mr. Gozhenko.

In the weeks that immediately followed the end of President Podgorny's tour and his return to Moscow (where he was immediately joined for consultation by Dr. Castro) reports spoke of a markedly increased flow of Soviet war materials intended for the "liberation movements" of Southern Africa and the arrival of heavy equipment, tanks and MIG fighter aircraft in Moçambique. According to Western intelligence sources, another 40 Soviet military advisers had arrived in that country by late May and the number of Cubans assisting in the training of guerrillas was said to have risen from an estimated 600 to 800.

The same period provided an adequate reminder that Moscow's attention was far from being entirely limited to Southern Africa. In early May, the leader of the new revolutionary Ethiopian Government, Colonel Mengistu Haile-Miriam, visited Moscow and whilst there signed a Declaration of Friendship with the Soviet Government. In this declaration, both sides declared themselves willing to "broaden mutually profitable" economic, scientific, and technical co-operation, and to exchange information regarding industry, agriculture and the development of natural resources. The Declaration in addition provided for the training of "national personnel" and measures to increase trade. Contacts were to be encouraged between "state bodies", political, professional and other public organisations and in the fields of science, the arts, literature, education, medicine, the news media, the film industry and tourism.

Both governments agreed to have regular exchanges of view on international questions and to do all they could to support the "liberation struggle". About the same time, reports appeared of the arrival of considerable quantities of Soviet arms in Ethiopia, including some T34 tanks. At the end of May, the American State Department stated that it had received information confirming the arrival of a number of Cuban military advisers in the country. Despite the possibility that Soviet moves in Ethiopia could seriously disrupt the former's now well established good relations with Somalia, a delegation from the Somali Revolutionary Party was in Moscow in May. That month also saw the appearance of news which could lead to some repairing of the up-to-then worsening relations between the Soviet Union and Egypt. This took the form of an announcement by the Egyptian Foreign Minister, Mr. Ismail Fahmi, that he had received an invitation to meet the Soviet Foreign Minister, Mr. Gromyko, "in an unnamed city in Europe" early in June. Mr. Fahmi described the invitation as a constructive Soviet gesture which Egypt welcomed.

President Podgorny's tour of African countries and the Soviet moves regarding Africa immediately preceding and following it, were accompanied by a Soviet propaganda barrage directed against the West's African policies. Its tenor had a bitterness and abusiveness that, whilst it would not have been surprising in the chilliest days of the Cold War, rang a discordant note indeed in these days of alleged "détente". Perhaps typical of the tone of this propaganda campaign was a broadcast over Radio Moscow in its English service beamed to Africa on 11 May, part of which read:

"The imperialist powers have exploited and continue to exploit the peoples of Africa. Scores of imperialist monopolies are pumping fabulous profits out of Africa. The imperialists are doing everything to prevent the Africans from freeing themselves from the economic, financial and other shackles, and also from using their own national resources to improve their life. The imperialists and their puppets from among the African reactionaries either use direct military force or resort to intrigues or plots to impose their will on the liberated peoples and block the road to economic and social liberation."

Specific attacks on aspects of Western policy made over Radio Moscow or its companion station, Radio Peace and Progress, included during May an attack upon the Central Intelligence Agency for conspiring together with the South African security service to carry out operations aimed at "debunking" SWAPO in South West Africa. The allegation was made that the Western powers were supporting the activities of the Cabinda Liberation Front which had threatened to blow up installations belonging to Gulf Oil. Further accusations were that South Africa was, with Western support, preparing an attack upon Angola and that "French militarists" were still planning to retain Djibouti as a major imperialist base in the Indian Ocean. Nor did some African countries escape; Senegal for instance was severely censored for allowing "monopoly capital" to retain control of the country's raw materials whilst continuing to act as an important supplier of such materials to the West. The Sudanese Government also came under the lash for permitting the carrying on of "anti-Soviet propaganda" within the country. The "pro-imperialist" and "reactionary" policies of the Government of Zaire also continued to be a focus of attack, whilst time was also found for an account of the stand of the Communist Party on the Island of Reunion. Moscow Radio explained on 13 May that Communist supporters there were then demanding the closing of the French naval base which "formed part of the military strategy of the imperialists in the Indian Ocean area".

The main brunt of the propaganda offensive was, however, clearly focused upon Western efforts to help find a peaceful solution to the situation in Southern Africa. The talks in Windhoek between the South African Prime Minister and the representatives of five Western Powers to discuss the future of South West Africa was stigmatised as being merely an attempt to secure the domination of this country "rich in diamonds, uranium and natural resources" by an imperialist puppet government. Mr. Andrew Young's African tour was interpreted as being intended merely to whitewash "the USA's expansionist and colonialist policy towards Africa". The newly formulated Anglo-American plan for a settlement in Rhodesia was described as another plot designed to keep this country "rich in copper, chrome, manganese and gold in the sphere of imperialist influence". America's "so-called new African policy" was attacked as being no more than a cover operation designed to preserve the status quo in South Africa for as long as possible, etc.

The obvious intense Soviet desire to disrupt any chance of a peaceful solution in Southern Africa was particularly clearly expressed in a statement by Mr. Vladimir Shubin, Secretary of the Soviet Afro-Asian Solidarity Committee, read over Radio Peace and Progress on 19 May at the time of the UN-sponsored Conference on Southern Africa in Maputo. After expounding the view that the "racialists" in the countries of Southern Africa only continued to hold sway because of the support of Western imperialists, the statement concluded with the words that the Soviet people considered that the exploration of means of rendering "political and practical support" to the "fighting peoples in the South of Africa" must become the main result of the work of the conference.

Sir Winston Churchill once described Soviet foreign policy as being "a riddle wrapped in a mystery, inside an enigma". Whilst the enigma and mystery still surround many aspects of such policy even to the present day, the events of the last three years have dispelled most of the uncertainty regarding Soviet intentions toward Africa. Today there would seem to be no logical reason to doubt that these are, in fact, what events plainly indicate them to be. These are first to establish the position of the Soviet Union and its allies as the dominant external influence over Africa. Secondly, to establish a network of economic, political and military agreements with as many African states as possible (particularly those occupying important strategic positions) so as to bring them to an ever closer degree within the direct influence of the Soviet bloc. Thirdly, to do all in its power to aid in the destruction of what it terms the "imperialist bastion" in the south of the continent and the establishment of Marxist rule throughout that vital area.

Such Soviet policies should not be viewed in isolation, but as forming part of a general pattern in which Soviet leaders increasingly confident as a result of their country's rapidly growing military strength and what they see as an increasing degree of economic and political disruption within the Western world, are basing their actions upon the belief that the march of events is now headed irreversibly in the direction of the total victory of the "socialist camp" over Capitalism and Western liberal democracy. The obvious difficulty which the Western powers have found in establishing an effective counter policy (as evidenced particularly by events in Angola) has probably suggested to Soviet planners that it is in this area of the world that they can for the time being most safely attempt to push forward the boundaries of Soviet influence

329

with the minimum of risk.

The immensely serious implications of such a strategy for the West have, it is hoped, already been indicated in the pages of this study. They are:

Firstly, the events of the last year have already added considerably to the potential threat to the security of the Cape Route. Long distance Soviet reconnaissance aircraft based in either Angola or Moçambique (as they quite possibly soon will be) would have a formidable radius of action over the Southern Indian Ocean and South Atlantic. Equipped with the latest long-range radar, they would have little difficulty in monitoring the whole of the vast flow of shipping passing between the Cape of Good Hope and the southern ice cap. These aircraft could also be used as target-spotters for directing attacks upon such shipping if the occasion arose. A number of factors, including the current absence of any sizeable Western naval forces in those areas and the long distance from any Western bases currently in use, makes it likely that it is on the southernmost leg of the Cape Route that any Soviet attempt to disrupt the vital stream of oil and raw materials in ships bound for Western countries would be made.

The deployment of Western warships from the South Atlantic to the Indian Ocean and, at a time of a closure of the Suez Canal, also to the Persian Gulf area could be seriously affected by the loss of ports in Angola and Moçambique, especially with a continuation of the ban on the use of South African ports which the governments of major Western countries at present enforce on their navies.

As an illustration of the above point, it is as well to remember that the distance of sea between Luanda and Maputo, through often stormy waters, is some 2 800 nautical miles. At the time of the last closure of the Suez Canal smaller warships of the US Navy were only able to move freely from the Atlantic to the Indian Ocean by making regular use of these two ports for refuelling.

Two American experts, Dr. Walter F. Hahn and Alvin J. Cottrell in a study produced by the University of Miami entitled *Soviet Shadow Over Africa*, have forecast that it may well become Soviet policy to use shore facilities at such ports in Moçambique as Maputo and Nacala to enable its fleet to dominate the Moçambique Channel through which most of the Cape Route shipping passes. They state that although France still possesses some naval facilities on Mayotte Island, the southern most of the Camores

330

group, an archipelago in the northern part of the channel, these and similar facilities on Reunion Island would probably become politically untenable should the whole African coast the from tip of Somalia down to the South of Moçambique fall under the control of anti-Western régimes. The last remaining such Western facilities in the whole of the South West Indian Ocean would then have been eliminated. Should Madagascar come under control of a pro-Soviet government, the potential threat to Western sea communications would be pushed noticeably further east into the Indian Ocean.

Off the west coast of Africa, the Soviet Union has been paying considerable attention recently to the potentialities of the Cape Verde Islands. Here a useful port and naval base was established by the Portuguese on the island of Mindalo and an international airport capable of handling large jets exists on the island of Sal. A similar Soviet interest has also been displayed during the last 12 months in the islands of São Tomé and Principe at the southern edge of the Gulf of Guinea. Their Prime Minister, Mr. Miguel Trouvada, signed an agreement with the Soviet Union in October 1976 providing for co-operation in economic, scientific and cultural matters and for Soviet assistance in the training of national cadres. Contacts between state political, professional and other public organisations were to be encouraged, as was the development of trade between the islands and the Soviet Union. An agreement for co-operation in various fields was also signed during 1976 between the Soviet Government and that of Guinea-Bissau which is currently engaged upon finalising plans for a unification of that country with the Cape Verde Islands.

Some strategic experts consider that the possibility of the Soviet Union eventually obtaining facilities equivalent to those of a major naval base in some African country have implications of an even wider nature than increasing still further the potential threat to the Cape Route, serious enough though this would be. The two American experts previously mentioned, for instance, Drs. Hahn and Cottrell point out that the Soviet Union has long been interested in establishing submarine bases beyond the comparatively narrow passages to the open Atlantic between Norway, Iceland and Greenland. One instance of this interest was the thwarted Soviet attempt to establish such a base at Ciefuegos in Cuba. They maintain that were it to become possible for the USSR to deploy a part of its missile-carrying submarine fleet and long range naval aircraft in African ports, not only would the whole problem of the surveillance of Soviet submarine movements be greatly increased but the "most significant strategic threat" would be posed to the United States itself.

The recent, and it would seem to some extent Cuban supported, invasion attempt against the South of Zaire turned the spotlight on the extent to which the United States as well as Western Europe is dependent upon raw materials imported from the southern half of the African continent. However, it is probably still not realised how extensive this present dependence is. South Africa is for example the major supplier of no less than seven of the 20 minerals of which the United States imports, more than 50% of its total requirements. The importance of Southern Africa to the West as a major supplier of raw materials is now quite frequently mentioned in Soviet writings, the train of thought behind such mention being strongly indicated by the theories presented in a study entitled *Strategy and Economics,* produced by the Soviet economic warfare expert, Major General A.N. Lagovisky, as long ago as 1957.

In this study, General Lagovisky pointed out that certain fairly scarce minerals were essential for the production of modern armaments, these minerals including chrome, platinum, nickel, cobalt and titanum. He continued by stating that major Western nations were almost entirely dependent upon imported supplies of such raw materials. In particular, he emphasised that, for instance, chrome was essential for the production of alloys used in the manufacture of guns, armour-piercing projectiles, gas turbines, jet engines, and a number of high technology weapons systems and explained that despite this fact, the United States had virtually no chrome deposits within its own territory at all. The General proceeded to produce a theory based upon this "discovery" which he called the "weak link" principle. In this theory, he held that the Soviet Union should do all it could to take advantage of and exploit the Western dependence upon critical raw materials.

The particular relevance of the General's theory to Southern Africa is seen from the fact that of the minerals mentioned above South Africa is estimated to possess 65% of the known non-Communist world's reserves of chrome ore (a further 33% lying in Rhodesia), 90% of its reserves of the platinum group of metals and is also a major producer of titanium, nickel, and many other strategic materials. The only major producer of chrome, other than South

332

Africa and Rhodesia, is the Soviet Union itself.

Should the whole of Southern Africa fall under the rule of Marxist pro-Soviet régimes such as now exist in what used to be known as Portuguese Africa, as is undoubtedly the aim of Soviet policy, the Western world would clearly face a two-edged threat to the safe supply of such materials. Firstly, the Soviet Government might use its influence over such régimes to bring about a total interdiction in the flow of vital raw materials to Western countries as a means of exercising political and economic pressure upon the West at some moment of crisis. As the strength of its fleet in African waters increases and the number of shore facilities it obtains on the continent grows, the possibility of the USSR one day using its naval strength to assist in the enforcing of such a ban becomes obviously greater. Secondly, the Soviet Government could attempt to encourage the governments under its influence, who would almost certainly have nationalised the exploitation of all natural resources at an early stage, to step-up very sharply the prices of the materials upon which Western countries were most dependent. The effect would be the creation of the same sort of economic catastrophe in the West that followed excessive price rises by the oil-producing states.

It is hoped, therefore, that enough has been said to indicate clearly the enormity of the disaster that would befall the whole Western military and economic position should present Soviet policies succeed. Not only would virtually all hope of protecting the Cape Route from menace have long since disappeared and sources of vital raw materials be under constant threat, but in time of war, the West's opponents would be able to cut the world in two. It is essential that the Western nations' justifiable anxiety to see an equable solution of the racial problems of Southern Africa does not lead them to forget these cardinal and undeniable facts.

Surely after the experience of the last decades, not only in Africa but also in South East Asia   it is high time for a concerted effort by Western leaders to bring home to the Soviet Government that the West cannot be expected to accept a one-sided "détente" which, in fact, applies to only one area of the world, while the rest is left wide open for any disruptive move the Soviet Union sees fit to make.

If it is hard to believe that a Western policy of offering the least resistance in the face of growing Soviet aggressiveness can long continue, it is equally hard to believe that the majority of the black inhabitants of the continent of Africa will accept the kind of régimes which have come to power in Angola, Moçambique and Guinea-Bissau. Many are aware that leaders of Southern African "liberation movements" have openly proclaimed their intention of imposing almost precisely similar régimes upon their home countries when their "day of victory" comes. The continuing struggle of UNITA and other anti-Marxist elements in Angola, in fact, provides convincing evidence that some black Africans fight even in the face of the heaviest odds against the new imperialism which so alarmed not a few of Africa's leaders in the wake of the MPLA's victory.

It cannot have escaped many in Africa that whilst continuing to pose energetically as the most forceful champion of freedom and democracy for all the African people, the Soviet Government has not hesitated to attempt to advance its interests through providing active support and lavish praise on the most tyrannical and bloodthirsty régimes on the continent; those of President Amin in Uganda and of the present revolutionary government of Ethiopia.

Africans cannot be expected to fight the West's battles; particularly when the West's reputation for giving effective aid to those in the Third World who align themselves with it is still at an all time low in the wake of Vietnam and Angola. Bearing the above points in mind, however, it would seem perhaps not too optimistic, given strengthened Western will and greater realism, to believe in the possibility of the birth of a new concert of mutual interest transcending racial issues which will at least point the way to the attaining of genuine freedoms, security, and prosperity for all the peoples of Africa, whilst holding at bay the efforts of alien Communism to use the "liberation" of Africa as but a stepping-stone in its own proclaimed goal of world domination.

REFERENCES

1. *World Marxist Review,* October 1974.
2. *Ibid.*
3. *Ibid.*
4. *Ibid.*
5. *The Guardian,* 26 January 1976.
6. *The Times,* 29 March 1977.

Bibliography

Addie, W.A.C. *The Communist Powers in Africa,* Institute for the Study of Conflict, London, 1971.
Africa and the Defence of the West. Le Monde Moderne, Paris, 1975.
Angola After Independence. Institute for the Study of Conflict, London, 1975.
Barron, John. *KGB,* Hodder & Stoughton, London, 1974.
Biggs-Davison, John, M.P. *Nailing a Lie,* Congo Africa Publications, London.
Bunting, Brian. *Moses Kotane,* Inuleko Publications, London, 1975.
Chailand, Gerard. *Armed Struggle in Africa,* Monthly Review Press, New York, 1969.
Crozier, Brian. *The Soviet Presence in Somalia,* Institute for the Study of Conflict, London, 1975.
Desseks, John. *Chinese and Soviet Aid to Africa,* Praeger Publishers, New York, 1975.
De Pinto, Rui. *The Making of a Middle Cadre,* Liberation Support Movement Information Centre, Richmond, B.C., Canada.
Eprile, Cecil. *Sudan: The Long War,* Institute for the Study of Conflict, London, 1972.
Eppstein, John. *Does God Say Kill?* Tom Stacey, London, 1972.
Frolik, Joseph. *The Frolik Defection,* Leo Cooper, London, 1975.
Fiennes, Randolph. *Where the Soldiers Fear to Tread,* Hodder & Stoughton, London, 1975.
Gilbert, Wynfred, Joshua and Stephen P. *Arms for the Third World,* John Hopkins Press, London, 1969.
Hahn, Walter F. and Cottrell, Alvin J. *Soviet Shadow Over Africa,* Centre for Advanced International Studies, University of Miami, 1976.
Hale, Julian. *Radio Power,* Paul Elek, London, 1975.
Hutchison, Alan. *China's African Revolution,* Hutchinson, London, 1975.

Janke, Peter. *Southern Africa: End of Empire,* Institute for the Study of Conflict, London, 1974.

— *Southern Africa: New Horizons,* Institute for the Study of Conflict, 1976.

Larkin, Bruce D. *China and Africa, 1949-70,* University of California Press, Berkeley and Los Angeles, 1971.

Leibzon, Boris. *The Communist Movement Today,* Novosti Press Agency Publishing House, Moscow, 1975.

Lessing, Pieter. *Africa's Red Harvest,* Michael Joseph, London, 1962.

Maxey, Kees. *The Fight for Zimbabwe,* Rex Collins, London, 1975.

Millar, T.B. *The Indian and Pacific Oceans: Some Strategic Considerations,* International Institute for Strategic Studies, London, 1970.

Moore, Captain John E. *The Soviet Navy Today,* MacDonald & Jane, London, 1975.

Morris, Michael. *Armed Conflict in Southern Africa,* Jeremy Spence, Cape Town, 1974.

Moyo, Temba. *The Organiser,* Liberation Support Movement Information Centre, Richmond, B.C., Canada.

Nikanarov, Anatoli. *Password "Anguimo",* Novosti Press Agency Publishing House, Moscow, 1974.

Pennar, Jaan. *The USSR and the Arabs,* C. Hurst & Co., 1973.

Rees, David, *Soviet Strategic Penetration of Africa,* Institute for the Study of Conflict, London, 1976.

Rubinstein, Alvin Z. *Soviet and Chinese Influence in the Third World,* Praeger, New York, 1975.

Schatten, Fritz. *Communism in Africa,* George, Allen & Unwin, London, 1966.

Spence, J.E. *The Strategic Significance of Southern Africa,* Royal United Services Institute, London, 1970.

Starushenko, Gleb. *Africa Makes a Choice,* Novosti Press Agency Publishing House, Moscow, 1975.

Turok, Ben. *Strategic Problems in South Africa's Liberation Struggle,* Liberation Support Movement Information Centre, Richmond, B.C., Canada, 1974.

Venter, Al J. *Africa at War,* Devon-Adair Co., Old Greenwich, Connecticut, 1974.

— *The Zambesi Salient,* Robert Hale, London, 1975.

Wall, Patrick, M.P., Harrigan, Anthony, Addie, W.A.C. *The Indian Ocean and the Threat to the West,* Tom Stacey International, London, 1975.

Weinstein, Warren. *Chinese and Soviet Aid to Africa*, Praeger, New York, 1975.

Wilkinson, R. *Insurgency in Rhodesia*, International Institute for Strategic Studies, London, 1975.

Index

Armed forces:
  American, 3
  East German, 4
  NATO, in Europe, 3,4
  Soviet 3, 19
  Soviet, in Europe, 4
  Soviet, on Chinese frontier, 4
  Warsaw Pact, in Europe, 3
Armed Struggle of the Peoples of Africa for Freedom and Independence, The,
64, 79 *n*
Arms:
  Chinese supplies for Africa, 81, 179-180, 243
  Soviet supplies for Africa, 1, 45, 81, 100*et seq*, 179, 180 *et seq*, 243,
250 *et seq*
Artillery:
  NATO, 4
  Soviet, 4
Asia, revolution in, 75
Asia-Africa Society, 72
Association of Scientific, Technical and Managerial Staffs
(ASTMS), 299
Atlantic Ocean:
  Exercise Okean in, 11
  Soviet convoy operations in, 20
  Soviet presence in, 11
  Soviet warships in, 20
L'Aurore, 270
Aventura, 165
Ayland, Tony, 299
Azores, 266
  Exercise Okean off, 11
  Soviet convoy operations off, 20

Babakr-Al-Nor, Colonel, 144
Babu, Sheik, 155, 195
Bahrain, 32
Baku Conference, 51, 284
Balante tribe, 202
Ballistic missiles, Soviet, 6

Dupont, Clifford, 221
Durban, 37, 39

ELF *see* Eritrean Liberation Front
East Africa, Exercise Okean off, 11
East Germany, 127, 324
    Angola, involvement in, 251, 258
    army units, 5
    parachute battalion, 5
    Portugal, involvement in, 17
    Soviet forces in, 4
    Yemen, involvement in, 25
East London, 39
Eastern Europe, air forces, 5
    see also Europe
Eastern Toilers, University of, 52
Economic aid:
    Chinese, to African countries, 81, 97 *et seq*
    Soviet, to African countries, 81, 89 *et seq*
Economist, 252
Egypt, 143, 312
    China, relations with, 67 *et seq,* 85, 112, 156
    Czech arms for, 100, 107
    guerrilla training in, 164, 170, 186
    KGB agents in, 137, 142, 147-149
    six-day war, 7
    Soviet aid to, 89 *et seq*
    Soviet arms supply, 82, 102, *et seq,* 180-181
    Soviet Union, relations with, 7-8, 24, 69, 82, 112, 327
Eliseev, Viktor, 24
Emilia Romagna, 280
End Loans to South Africa (ELTSA), 301
English Channel:
    Exercise Okean in, 11
    Soviet naval operations in, 20
Ennals, John, 297
Eppstein, John:
    Does God say Kill? 216
Equatorial Africa, 99

Jung-Chen, 69

National Union of Students, 300
Nationalist, The, 133
Nato Review, 14-15
Naval building, Soviet, 7
Nedosekin, Pavl, 148
Netherlands, Soviet occupation of, 19
Neto, President Aghostino, 88, 127, 193 *et seq,* 250, 253, 271, 272, 279, 303, 315
    *Portuguese Colonies: Victory or Death, 244*n
New Age, 158
New China News Agency, 79 *n,* 156, 157
New York, 11
New Zealand Air Force, 33
Newens, Stan, *M.P.,* 302
Niger Republic, relations with China, 155
Nigeria, 69, 141
    KGB agents in, 137
    Soviet aid to, 89 *et seq,* 104, 212
Nikanorov, Anatoli, 217
Nikodin, Metropolitan, 309
Nikolai, Metropolitan, 305
Nimrod matirime reconnaissance aircraft, 41
Nkomo, Joshua, 88, 220 *et seq,* 317, 318
Nkrumah, President, 101, 123, 156,186
Norfolk, Virginia, 29
North Atlantic Treaty Organisation, 264
    artillery strength, 4
    battle tanks in Europe, 4
    Cape shipping route, importance of, 37, 38
    forces in Europe, 4
    American reinforcements for, 4, 11
    Hillex 75, 13-14
    merchant shipping of NATO countries, 13-15
    Portugal assistance to, 48
    Southern Africa, in 276, 282-283
    Soviet amphibious capabilities, on 36
    Soviet ballistic missiles, on, 6
    Soviet concentration on, 12-13
    Soviet naval and military build-up, concern at, 12
North Sea, oil resources, 26

Oramas, Oscar, 128
Orestov, O., 89
Independent Africa in the Making, 133 *n*
Organisation of African Unity, 47, 86, 189, 232, 296, 318
Orgunsawo, Cornelius, 132
Oriov, Nikolai, 144
Osman, President, 87
Otlieno, Israel, 173
Ovamboland People's Organisation (OPO), 242

PAC *see* Pan-African Congress
PAIGC, 65, 193 *et seq,* 282
    arms supplies for, 177*et seq,* 181
    FARP, 202, 210
    guerrilla training, 184 *et seq*
    Young Pioneers, 213
PAIGC Actualities, 213
PFLOAG see Popular Front for the Liberation of Oman and the Persian Gulf
PO Tropan Voyny, 79 *n*
Paarl Commission, 238
Pacific Ocean, Soviet activities in, 10, 33
Padmore, George, 55
Pakistan, Chinese arms supply to, 111
Palestinian guerrilla groups, 150, 170, 182, 186 *et seq*
Pan-African Congress, 238, 306, 309
    Chinese arms for, 180
    guerrilla training, 190
Parachute divisions:
    East German, 5
    Polish, 5
    Soviet, 5
Paris Peace Agreement, 16
Parti Solidaire Africaine, 176
Partido Africano da Independencia da Guide e Cabo Verde *see* PAIGC
Party for the United Struggle of the Angolan Africans (PLUA), 194
Password "Anguimo", 47, 63, 79 *n,* 217, 244 *n,* 245 *n,*
Patrice Lumumba University, Moscow, 113, 114, 152, 170

Psychological warfare, 205 *et seq*, 235 *et seq*

Quatar, 32

Slyusarenko, Petr, 143
Smelyakov, Deputy Foreign Trade Minister, 326
Smith, Ian, 222, 288, 308, 317
Smolin, Nikolai, 143
Soavida, Dioganes, 259
Socialist Worker, 299
Socotra, 25
Sofinsky, Nikolai, 112, 113
Sofinsky, V.N., 124
Sokolov, S.L. 124, 319, 320
Sollum, 8, 96
Solod, Danil Senyonovitch, 82-83, 100, 139, 140, 142
Solodvnikov, V.G., 320, 325
  Africa Vysirayetput, 133 *n*
Somali Coast Liberation Movement, 274
Somalia, 67, 74, 327, 331
  China, relations with, 85, 86, 87, 99
  missiles, stockpiling of, 30
  National Security Service, 126
  Soviet activities in, 30 *et seq*, 46, 49, 124, *et seq*, 153
  Soviet aid to, 89, 94, 95, 102, 108, 111
Soumialot, Gaston, 154
Sourenenni, Vostok, 311 *n*
South Africa, 65, 69, 312, 328
  Angola, involvement in, 256 *et seq,* 282-283
  arms supplies for guerrillas, 176
  Communist Party, 55, 58, 190, 237 *et seq,* 278 *et seq,,* 315
  economic importance of, 37-38, 48-49
  espionage against, 138
  guerrilla activities, 159 *et seq,* 183
  liberation movements, 237 *et seq*
  military power, 40-41
  ports, 38, 39
  raw materials, 42-43, 48-49, 332-333
  shipping surveillance, 40
  Soviet Union and, 2, 48, 84
  United Kingdom, trade with, 43
South African Congress of Trade Unions, 160
South African Non-Racial Open Committee, 299
South China Sea, 37

South Vietnam *see* Vietnam, South
South West Africa (Namibia):
  Cuba and, 243
  liberation movements, 237 *et seq*
  mineral resources, 42, 328
  refugees from Angola, 252
  Soviet Union and, 2, 48, 84, 328
  United Nations office, 282
South West African National Union, 242
South West African People's Organisation (SWAPO), 242 *et seq,* 278
et seq, 306, 309, 318, 319, 328
  arms supplies for, 178
  guerrilla training, 164, 186
Southern Africa:
  Anglo-American peace proposals, 2, 328
  anti-Western control of, 2
  Chinese arms for, 77
  liberation of, 276 *et seq*
  propaganda broadcasting to, 117
  Soviet involvement in, 16
  World Council of Churches and, 304 *et seq*
Soviet Aerospace Almanack, 21 *n*
Soviet Afro-Asian Solidarity Committee, 59, 62-63, 317, 329
Soviet Attack — NATO Defence Studies, 21 *n*
Soviet Military Review, 36, 112
  Navy of the Soviet Union, The, 43 *n*
Soviet National Asian Committee, 122
Soviet Peace Committee, 282
Soviet Society for the Furtherance of Friendship with the Peoples of
Africa, 59
Soweto, 242
Space satellites, Soviet developments, 6-7, 70
Spain, United States Polaris submarine base, 93
Spear of the Nation, 238
Special Committee on Relations with the Peoples of Africa, 72
Stalin Joseph, 50 *et seq,* 74, 84, 135
  Selected Works, 89 *n*
Stanis, Vladimir, 114
Star, The, 245 *n,* 258
Starushenko, Gleb:

armed forces, cuts in, 3
Indian Ocean activities in, 33 *et seq*
maritime support base at Diego Garcia, 34
Mediterranean, Sixth Fleet in, 8
military aircraft production, 5
NATO forces, reinforcements for, 4, 11
nuclear warheads, 4
oil imports, 25
Polaris submarine base at Rota, 93
Southern Africa, joint policy on, 2
Soviet action against, 6
Soviet submarine patrols off, 10
Suez Canal, use of 28
Tanzania, plot against, 151
wireless station in Ethiopia 93
Universities and colleges, AAM activities, 299-300
Ustinov, V.A. 124
Uvarev, Igor Ivanovitch, 261

Valentinin, L. 49
Valonia, 7
Van Den Boeynants, Paul, 94
Venter, Al J, 187
   The Zambesi Salient, 245 *n*
Viet Cong, 37, 282
Viet Cong Strategy of Terror, The, 214
Vietnam Heroica, 127, 255
Vietnam, North, 257-258
   supply of Soviet weapons to, 1, 16, 37
Vietnam, South, 16
Villa Salazar, 231
Vinogradov, Valter, 145
Vinogradov, Vladimir M, 142
Visakhapatnan, 29
Voight, Werner, 262
Vorobyev, Boris, 128
Voronezhsky Komsomlets, 8
Voronin, Aleksei, 142
Vorster, B.J. 230, 263, 288

KGB agents in, 147
Soviet involvement in, 25, 103
stockpiling of Soviet arms, 183
Yen Leng, Colonel 186
Yen, Ignat *and* P. Mikhalev:
  N H Zapade et Zambesi 79 *n*
Young, Andrew, 328
Yogoslavia, aid to India, 29
Yukalov, Yuri, 141
Yung-Lo, Emperor, 68

ZANLA *see* Zimbabwe African National Liberation Army
ZANU *see* Zimbabwe African National Union
ZAPU *see* Zimbabwe African People's Union
ZIPA *see* Zimbabwe People's Army
Za Rudezhon, 143
Zaire, 65, 72, 264, 322, 323, 328, 332
  arms for, 176, 179, 180, 181
  China, relations with, 86, 153 *et seq*
  FNLA relations with, 249
  guerrilla training, 185, 195
  KGB agents in, 137, 139, 140-141, 142
  Polish aid to, 89
  Simba rebels, 179
  Soviet military aid to, 101
Zakharov, Marshal, 107
Zambesi Salient, The, 245 *n*
Zambia, 264, 325
  China, relations with, 85, 86, 99, 156
  guerrilla training in, 163 *et seq,* 189-190, 195, 243
  KGB agents in, 137
  Soviet aid to, 113-114, 183
  Zambai-Tanzania railway, 97-98, 120
Zanzibar, 31, 68
  China, relations with, 85, 99, 103, 111, 155
  Chinese arms for, 176
  guerrilla activities, 195
  guerrilla training, 189